Merry Scilia,
Love

★

THE ART AND SCIENCE OF SAILS

★

Also by Tom Whidden (coauthor):

Championship Tactics:
How Anyone Can Sail Faster, Smarter, and Win Races

Also by Michael Levitt (coauthor):

Upset: Australia Wins the America's Cup

A Tissue of Lies: Nixon vs. Hiss

★

THE ART AND SCIENCE OF

SAILS

A GUIDE TO
MODERN MATERIALS,
CONSTRUCTION, AERODYNAMICS,
UPKEEP, AND USE

TOM WHIDDEN AND MICHAEL LEVITT

Illustrated by JAY GOEBEL

★

ST. MARTIN'S PRESS · NEW YORK

Grateful acknowledgment is made to North Sails, Inc. for permission to reprint materials from the ''North U.'' course books.

Library of Congress Cataloging-in-Publication Data

Whidden, Tom.
    The Art and science of sails : a guide to modern materials,
  construction, aerodynamics, upkeep, and use / Tom Whidden and
  Michael Levitt.
        p.   cm.
    ISBN 0-312-04417-8
    1. Sails.   I. Levitt, Michael.   II. Title.
  VM532.W48   1990
  623.8′62—dc20   89-77895
                                                                       CIP

10   9   8   7   6   5   4   3

★

CONTENTS

facturing • Resin Impregnation: Urethane for Racer; Melamine for Cruising Sailor • Heat-Setting and Calendering • Polyester/Mylar: Bidirectional Molecular Orientation for Stretch-Resistance • Growing Popularity with Cruising Sailors • Laminates, and Preventing Delamination • Types of Laminated Cloth • Kevlar/Mylar • Spectra/Mylar • Nylon

★

ACKNOWLEDGMENTS

★ Many people were instrumental in the writing and production of this book. Foremost among them is Arvel Gentry, of Boeing Commercial Airplane, who provided the aerodynamic basis for much of this book. What Gentry was doing seventeen years ago with the most primitive tools is just becoming understood and appreciated today. *Sail* magazine, too, should be acknowledged for having the foresight to publish Gentry's ideas back in 1973. The writings of C. A. Marchaj, in his books *Sailing Theory and Practice* and *Aero-Hydrodynamics of Sailing*, were invaluable. Also, Bill Bergantz, whose knowledge of sails and sailing is encyclopedic, as well as Brian Doyle, Jay Hansen, Burns Fallow, and John Gladstone, all of North Sails. Plus, Bill Whidden, of Freedom Sails, and Peter Wheeler, of Halsey Sails. Further, Jay Goebel, who created the computer illustrations as well as provided his considerable technical expertise. In addition, Michael Sagalyn, senior editor of St. Martin's Press, for his energy, enthusiasm, and tenacity.

The authors also wish to thank Lowell North, founder of North Sails, and Ted Hood, founder of Hood Sails. In addition, Peter Mahr, of North Sails Cloth, Mike Schreiber, Al Gooch, David Hirsch, and Blake Marriner, of North Sails; Phil Marriner, of Marriner Associates; Duncan Skinner and Richard Pierce, of Bainbridge/Aquabatten; and Jack Sutphen and John Sparkman, Jr. Also Dave Ezzy, of North Sails Windsurfing, for his tips on tuning the boardsail. Further, Jim Marshall for his writings on target boat speed as well as sail construction. The boardsail-tuning photography was done by Eric Aeder. And Milliken & Company provided the electron-microscope photographs of sailcloth. Also, Fanatic A.R.T. for the photograph of Pascal Maka. And *Sailing World* magazine for several drawings in Chapter 11.

Also, John Marshall and Robert Hopkins, who wrote the first *North U. Fast Course*, and David Dellenbaugh, who wrote the second version. Further,

Sohei Hohri, New York Yacht Club librarian, for information on the derivation of the word *spinnaker*, and Platt Johnson, owner of Island Windsurfing in Middletown, Rhode Island, for his comments on Chapter 13, "Boardsails."

And finally and especially, Linda M. Levitt and Molly Morgan Levitt, and Betsy Whidden, Avery Whidden, and Holly Whidden—our best supporters.

★

THE ART AND SCIENCE OF SAILS

★

Tom Whidden (Courtesy of North Sails, Inc.)

★

CHAPTER 1

THE VOYAGE

★ My business is sailmaking and my passion is sailing. I have spent a lifetime making sailboats go faster, first as president of Sobstad Sails International and now as president of North Sails —the largest sailmaker in the world. It has been a lifelong love affair, a lifelong fascination that has taken me farther and in some ways faster than I ever dreamed possible. It has taken me into the sail-trimmer's cockpit of Dennis Conner's *Freedom*, which won the America's Cup in 1980; into the tactician's spot on *Liberty*, which lost the America's Cup in 1983; into that same position on *Stars & Stripes '87*, which recaptured the Cup in the winds of war in Western Australia in 1987, and on *Stars & Stripes '88*, which defended it in San Diego in 1988. Through sailing, sailmaking, and the America's Cup, I have twice been President Reagan's guest at the White House, enjoyed a ticker-tape parade through the icy streets of Manhattan, received a key to New York City from then Mayor Ed Koch, appeared on the ''Today Show'' a half-dozen times, even shared a ''Today Show'' dressing room with the incomparable Dolly Parton, and had the opportunity to know and work closely with some of the prime players in the sport.

SOARING WITH THE EAGLES

Two of the most visible performers in sailing are Dennis Conner and Jim Kilroy. If a sailmaker wants to soar with the eagles, he must learn to make sails for, race with, and in some cases train for years with the likes of these two. In my opinion, they provide the toughest tests in the sport. It's not always easy, not always kind, but these guys play the yacht-racing version of hardball.

Stars & Stripes '87, *skippered by Dennis Conner, won the 1987 America's Cup in Western Australia. I sailed aboard as tactician and sailmaker. In addition to* Stars & Stripes '87, *I sailed with Conner on* Freedom, *which defended the Cup in 1980;* Liberty, *which lost the Cup in 1983 to* Australia II; *and the* Stars & Stripes '88, *the catamaran, which defended in 1988. (Courtesy of North Sails, Inc.)*

If you or your sails don't measure up, you'll be weeded out quicker than a spinnaker run aboard *Kialoa* in 30 knots.

Dennis Conner has rewritten the record books: He is a four-time winner of the America's Cup and the only skipper to lose the Cup and then win it back. On the strength of his talent and incredibly focused personality, Conner has almost single-handedly changed the face of the America's Cup from a clubby, cliquish, parochial contest—of interest to about two thousand members of the New York Yacht Club and a handful of others here and there—to a major TV sport that captures a worldwide audience. To the public, Conner is considered more a man of action than words. Yet through his actions, he has eloquently explained the beauty, majesty, and high physical and mental performance levels of this complex sport. Seeing Conner's *Stars & Stripes* battling *Kiwi Magic* or *Kookaburra* on the television screen in 1987 brought yacht racing into the modern age.

Jim Kilroy is America's Maxi Man. Beyond his "rich-and-famous" lifestyle and his leading-man looks, there is a technologist of the first order. He has long campaigned a series of eighty-foot ocean-racing Maxis called *Kialoa*. He presently owns two of these behemoths, *Kialoa V*, which he uses for racing, and *Kialoa III*, which he and his wife, Chantel, use for cruising. Kilroy has won the Maxi World Championship four of the six times this competition has been held and has changed Maxi racing from something of a sideshow—where size and expense were its most notable attributes—to a center-stage event where the high technology, beauty, and awesome power of these outsized machines positively glimmer in the sun.

USER-FRIENDLY SAILS

Sailmaking and, by extension, sailing have benefited immeasurably from those who play on this level. Conner and Kilroy and a few others like them have made a commitment to research and development that has helped hurry sails and sailing into the future. What works for Dennis Conner on an America's Cup yacht or for Jim Kilroy on a Maxi often finds its way, in one form or another, to your 40-foot One Tonner or 28-foot cruising boat. For example, because the middle of a Maxi sail is so far from its corners, sailors can do little to affect its overall shape. This has resulted in what we call user-friendly sails. The mains and headsails are a little straighter in back, they can be sheeted a little harder without the leeches coming around, and the spinnakers are easier to fly. Obviously such things are as desirable on a 28-foot cruising boat or a 40-foot One Tonner, so these sails, too, have become better mannered.

SAILMAKING AND THE SCIENTIFIC APPROACH

But product is only a part of it. No matter what one thinks of the America's Cup and Maxi racing, the high stakes of the games and the commitment of the players to winning and to an edge have brought about a fundamental change

After regaining the America's Cup in 1987 in Perth, Western Australia, the crew of Stars & Stripes *'87 is given a ticker-tape parade in New York City. Conner and I are waving. New York's mayor at the time, Ed Koch, and Donald Trump, who hosted the event, are in the front row. (Courtesy of North Sails, Inc.)*

in attitude, or approach, that permeates the sport on all levels. Things aren't better, faster, or easier because I say they are or because I want them to be; they are better, faster, or easier because someone can prove it. Proving it to inherently skeptical, hypercritical people, such as Conner and Kilroy, has brought sailmaking and sailing into a scientific high-tech age. Because of this, I have been part of a revolution that has forever changed sailmaking.

Some may lament that change, but they must be considered sentimentalists, because sails today have never been better, faster, easier to handle, and more durable, and if you care to factor in inflation, cheaper. This is true not because I say so, but because someone can prove it.

NEW MATERIALS, NEW TOOLS, BETTER SAILS

Much of the change has to do with new materials. Prior to laminated sailcloths, which burst on the scene in the late 1970s, the most desirable qualities for sails—light weight, low stretch, high strength, and durability—could not be combined in one package. Low stretch meant heavy; light weight meant delicate. Laminated sailcloth—in particular, polyester/Mylar, known to the sailing world as Mylar—was a liberating recipe. It gave rise to an amazing cloth, which is light, low stretch, strong, smooth, and durable. The cloth has been as important to the cruising sailor as to the racer. Further, facility with Mylar film opened the door to Kevlar/Mylar, known as Kevlar, and Spectra/Mylar, known as Spectra. These cloths have vastly changed the racing game.

The new tools of design and manufacturing—in particular, the computer—have also improved sailmaking and sailing. The computer's gift to sailmaking is considerable. Most notably, the computer allows good designs to be repeated. Prior to the computer, there was no guarantee that a good design could even be reproduced, since the design, or data base, resided in someone's head, and the myriad pieces were cut and assembled by people, some who were good and others who weren't, some who were having good days and others who were having awful ones. With repeatability, design progresses down a more logical, more direct path; without it, progress is hit or miss—too often miss.

The computer also allows much more complicated solutions to the geometry of sailmaking. To give a two-dimension piece of cloth a three-dimensional airfoil shape, sailmakers use a process called broadseaming. One edge of a panel of cloth is cut straight and sewn to another that is curved (see Figure 1.1). This process forces shape into the sail, so much so that the sail is unable to lie perfectly flat on the floor. Humans are limited by the number of seams they can effectively shape; the computer, however, is not so limited. It can shape all the seams and in any direction, vertically as well as horizontally. Whereas a person can give shape to four seams, or even eight, a computer can shape all ninety seams that might make up a Maxi main. Obviously, computer shaping makes for a smoother sail—without hard edges—and one need not be an aerodynamicist to realize that an airfoil with smooth curves is faster than an airfoil with hard edges.

For sail designers, computer-aided design (CAD) and computer-aided manufacturing (CAM) have been extremely helpful. Prior to the computer, designers worried how to build a sail before designing it. Now they design it on the computer and tell the computer to build it. The computer eliminates

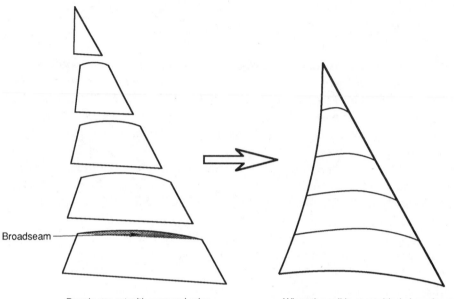

Broadseam

Panels are cut with a curved edge, or broadseam.

When the sail is assembled, broadseaming gives the sail a "built-in" shape.

Figure 1.1 Shaping a sail with broadseaming

many of the unknowns and much of the drudgery. It has, in fact, made sail design more, rather than less, creative.

That said, the best hammer doesn't guarantee that one will build a great house. Nor does the best CAD-CAM program guarantee that one will build a great sail. Many great sails have been designed without the computer—such sails were used to win the 1987 America's Cup—and many great sails will be designed without it. So despite this dazzling technology, sailmaking remains an art as well as a science. That, too, is one of its fascinations for me.

A NEW THEORY OF SAILING

The Art and Science of Sails is the name and focus of this book. By the time you've finished it, you will understand the forces that move you. You don't need to understand the internal-combustion engine to drive an automobile, but you can't really be a sailor without understanding completely the incredible physical reaction of wind passing over cloth bent in the shape of an airfoil. It is this action that has fascinated humans for eons.

It is also this action and the resulting reaction that has confused us for about the same amount of time. Most sailors know that the air travels faster on the leeward side of a sail than on the windward, that this difference in speed causes a difference in pressure, and that the result is a force, often termed lift. This relationship between speed and pressure was first noted by Daniel Bernoulli in 1738. However, more than two hundred and fifty years later, very few sailors know—including those at the very top of the sport—what causes that difference in speeds. It is not, as you have probably heard, because "a sail is like an airplane wing, and air traveling over the curved upper surface has to travel faster to reach the trailing edge at the same time as air traveling on the flat lower surface." That facile and most common explanation, as will become apparent in Chapter 5, simply does not "fly" anymore, whether you are discussing a sail or an airplane wing.

Without a fundamental knowledge of why a sailboat sails closer to the wind than a broad reach, little in sailing makes sense. Sail trim without a sound theoretical basis becomes only a practiced response to conditions. Think of that next time you feel the urge to shout at a crew member standing up in the slot. You've heard it, perhaps even said it: "You're disturbing the air in the slot." The truth is that the old slot-effect theory (which says the air is speeded up in the slot, and this acceleration helps the efficiency of the main) is wrong, utterly wrong. Actually, the air is slowed in the slot, and a crew member standing up there is likely to have no more effect than a crew member standing anywhere. More important is the fact that this slowing down, rather than speeding up, of the slot air actually helps the efficiency of the main. Although that may appear to be a small correction, that fundamental shift requires a completely new explanation of the relationship between the headsail and mainsail. This, too, is discussed in Chapter 5 and is developed throughout the book.

Treating the main and headsail as a unit is another theme of this book. The wind "sees" a sail plan as one long foil, not two separate ones. Good sailors trim the front of the headsail and the back of the main. The best, as will be discussed, then trim the back of the headsail and the front of the main: the slot.

USEFUL INFORMATION

This is a book about what is true and why it is so. Another focus, as the Table of Contents indicates, is useful information for both the cruising sailor and racer; such subjects as sail care, inventory, preventing a broach, minimizing the effects of a broach, winter storage, sail repair, and the pros and cons of various products are explored.

A PERSONAL HISTORY AND TECHNOLOGY

The story of sails is also a story about people—some artists, like Ted Hood, and some scientists, like Lowell North—who have made great strides in thinking and in technology. In this book you will meet these and also some of sailing's other prime movers. The vast philosophical and personal differences between Hood and North—both of whom once led the sailmaking organizations that still bear their names—and the ferocious competition between them and others like them carved out a broad technical territory that has benefited the sport of sailing and cloth technology as a whole. No other industry uses Dacron, polyester/Mylar, and Kevlar/Mylar with more facility than sailmaking. This is all the more surprising when one recalls that sailing is a sport, a pastime, and sailmaking is not a big business. In its small way, sailmaking is a noteworthy example of the free-enterprise system.

Through sailing and sailmaking, I have learned a few things about life: about winning and losing in the sport's ultimate races, about sailing with and against the greats in the sport, and about the freedom and serenity of sharing a summer's cruise with my family. As a result, this is an eclectic book meant to share my love of the sport as well as to inform.

CRUISING SAILOR AND RACER: SIMILARITIES AND DIFFERENCES

Although my reputation was made on the race course, this is not just a book for the go-fast fraternity. Cruising sailors have as great a need—perhaps even a greater one—to understand the forces that move them. Whereas the racer's driving principle is speed, the cruising sailor's first consideration should be efficiency. These are flip sides of the same coin, and the cruising sailor and racing sailor have more in common than they might think.

The efficient use of time—even leisure time—is important. It was not supposed to be this way, however. In 1959, *Life* magazine predicted a brave, new world of vastly increased leisure time. It saw an America that would be "freer and bolder than the Greek, more just and powerful than the Roman . . . saner than the French, more responsible than the Victorian and happier than all of them together." Thirty years later one might ask: What happened? We're working harder and we're working longer—and we're proud of it—so an efficient use of leisure time is important to most of us.

Cruising sailors should be able to get from here to there as efficaciously as possible. Their sails should take full advantage of the new labor-saving devices on the market, thereby requiring the minimum crew. Cruising sailors should demand sails that are light in weight because their boats have more accommodations and less stability than racing sailboats. Sails should be strong and durable, as cruising sailors don't typically have the crew or inclination to respond to failures. Cruising sailors should be able to go fast when desired, have sails that hold their shape to give them enough weatherliness to claw off a lee shore, and go in safety whatever the weather. The sails should be the best looking and last for the longest possible time. A sailboat with poor sails is like an eight-cylinder car running on seven cylinders—and it can be more dangerous.

Although the underlying aerodynamic theory is the same for both the cruising and the racing sailor, the practice is often different. Thus we linger in these pages on such subjects as the design and use of full-battened mainsails for the cruiser, and the design and use of mains cut for the cruising sailor's Stoway Mast. These are contrasted to the shape, construction, and use of the International Offshore Rule (IOR)–style mainsail, with its short battens. Also explored is why stretch resistance is sometimes sacrificed to achieve greater flexibility and ease of handling in cruising sails; why, in racing sails, flexibility is often sacrificed to achieve lower stretch; how varying the weight and materials used in genoa construction has allowed the cruising sailor to have one reefable genoa that is light enough to fly in 5 knots, yet strong enough so that the sail will not self-destruct when reefed in 30 knots. This same technique, called step-up construction, has allowed the racer to have a lightweight, yet low-stretch sail—as noted, something that was impossible until most recently.

Discussed, too, is why a luff treatment, foam or AeroLuff, is so important to the shape of that reefed headsail; why a draft-forward headsail provides a larger sweet spot, placing fewer demands on steerers, be they people or machines, and why a draft-aft sail can be devastatingly fast for the racer, given certain conditions. We discuss the effectiveness of various mainsail-reefing systems and headsail-furling and -reefing devices, and we point out why some of these units are better for the cruiser who races on occasion; and we address what the trade-off is in the cruiser's high-clewed short-luff headsail, and how aspect ratio of the rig and, for that matter, the keel is dependent on sailing angles. (Or, to put this another way: If you do not go upwind very often, you don't need high-aspect-ratio foils; indeed they are less efficient in reaching and running situations.)

The design of cruising spinnakers and how to set, trim, jibe, and douse them is also explored, as is the design and use of the racer's reacher, runner, and all-purpose spinnaker and why many cruising sailors opt for the racer's all-purpose spinnaker, which while requiring somewhat more work is a better compromise between reaching and running. We discuss trim angles for cruising headsails and compare them to trim angles for headsails used by the racer. And we discuss why for both the cruiser and the racer, the headsail is usually reefed before the main, and why the cutter rig, so popular with cruising sailors, makes the boat easier to steer upwind in a blow. An annotated Table of Contents and an Index are provided to help the cruising sailor or racer wend his or her way through this broadly focused book.

COMPLEXITY IS A VIRTUE

As I said earlier, sailing has taken me farther and faster than I ever thought possible. There is an irony here—in fact, an underlying irony in the entire sport—that sailing has taken me at such speed and to those distant places at a pace many distance runners can muster for hours on end. I have spent a large portion of my life trying to make a 12-Meter go a half knot faster, but it's not the magnitude of the number that counts but the compelling challenge of the problem. For me, getting that half knot has been a sublime search, a lasting fascination.

Sailing means different things to different people—that, too, is one of its great attractions for me. People sail because the principles of moving on the water without the thump and stink of an internal-combustion engine are so magical, so sublime. They sail because they like being connected to something that has fascinated humans for almost six thousand years. They sail because they love a technology that is simultaneously very old and, as you will see on these pages, brand-new. They sail because they love the feelings of power, glory, and serenity they get aboard a sailboat. They sail because they love the sense of speed, be it the 82-foot *Kialoa* dropping down the face of a Gulf Stream wave or a sailboard, the "fastest gun" on the water, which has crossed the 40-knot barrier and is now managing freeway-legal speeds. They sail because they learn something new each time they tug on a sheet or wiggle a tiller. They sail because they love coexisting so perfectly with a natural force that can't be seen, only sensed. Sailing engages one completely.

My coauthor, Michael Levitt, and I wrote this book to share some of these pleasures with you. Welcome aboard; I hope you'll find it as fascinating a voyage as it has been for us.

★

CHAPTER 2

AN ARTIST AND A SCIENTIST—THE HISTORY OF MODERN SAILMAKING

★ Two men who for many years were fierce business competitors, as well as fierce competitors on the race course, are most responsible for modern, or high-tech, sail design. They are Ted Hood and Lowell North, who are as different from each other as is Marblehead, Massachusetts, from San Diego, California.

Ted Hood, who started in sailmaking in 1952, is bulky in appearance and unpretentious in style. Hood, whose sails powered America's Cup defenders from 1958 to 1977, and who was a winning America's Cup skipper in 1974, has a Yankee's measured way with words. His lack of verbal excess is balanced by what must be the best eye in sailmaking, perhaps the best one there ever will be. If sailmaking can be considered an art, Ted Hood is its Michelangelo.

North, who began making sails in 1959, is a man of the future. He is long and lean and bubbles with creative fire—some of it right on the mark, some of it off by a country mile. An engineer by training, he fervently believes in the credo of progress. His unflagging belief in better ideas is strengthened by a typical Californian's love of what's new, what's now, and what will be. North, who has won Olympic gold and bronze medals and four Star World Championships, has a fundamental mistrust of art, or intuitive sail design. In sailmaking, he was never interested in what looked better, only in what could be proven to be faster. So he turned to numbers—sailmaking quantified by measurements, sailmaking backed up by a rigorous scientific methodology— to make sails. He recognized early in his career that if a sail design can't be repeated, it can't be improved or shared with anyone else in the company to allow for a creative synergy. With this emphasis on numbers and sharing, he embraced the computer, then a relatively obscure and expensive device, to

11

make sails. If sailmaking can be considered a high-tech science, Lowell North is its Steve Jobs.

We live in a computer age, in which the validity of science and its technically sophisticated machinery, like the computer, is only questioned after a terrible disaster such as the *Challenger* spacecraft explosion or the nuclear accident at Chernobyl. From our present perspective, this war of the worlds, the battle between the scientist and the artist, seems an unfair fight, but the truth is, it would take North and his disciples—the scientific sailmakers from any number of other sailmaking organizations who chose to head down the same path—some twenty-one years to prevail over Ted Hood. Their foe was that formidable.

Theirs was the battle royal in sailmaking. The competition between these two very different men, from either end of the country and from either side of the sailmaking spectrum, hurried sailmaking into a brave new world it might not have reached as soon, if at all, had there not been such ferocious competition. The sailmaking field has never been of a sufficient size to be an innovator in the use of materials; rather, it has been a borrower of existing material technology. Yet in the application of Dacron, Mylar, and Kevlar, the fierce competition between these two sailmakers and others caused these materials to become the most sophisticated products of their type.

As a boy, I read about the battles between Hood and North; as a young man, I had brief contact with both of them, which in many ways explains why I became a sailmaker. As someone whose livelihood is based on making better sails, I have long thought about this battle between art and science and how it applies to modern sailmaking. Perhaps I've thought more about this than others have because my career, though it has only had two stops in sixteen years, has taken me from pole to pole: from Sobstad, which employed more of an intuitive, or artistic, approach to sailmaking, to North, one of the leaders in the high-tech movement. I was not alone in this philosophical and, indeed, economic struggle. From 1956 to 1980—when the machine, the computer, finally prevailed—it was the pivotal battle in the business, whether you worked at Sobstad, Ulmer, Ratsey, Hood, North, or any other large sailmaking concern.

How I came to know Hood and North reveals something of the distance that separated them. My life in sailing began when I was ten with an invitation from a friend whose parents owned a cottage on Long Island Sound, near Westport, Connecticut. After that first afternoon, I sailed regularly with Lenny Raymond, and we competed in a few Cedar Point Yacht Club races. We did fairly well, as I remember, although my greatest source of enjoyment was the freedom and independence I felt as a kid out on the water, doing something on my own, something grown-up.

When I was thirteen, my father, an advertising executive and an accomplished sailor in his own right, presented me with an old, rather tired Blue Jay, which I named *Rebound* for obvious reasons. Although it had been around a bit and wasn't as fast as some of the fancier Blue Jays my friends had, it taught me that when you aren't fast, you'd better be smart or lucky, or both. The people I was involved with then were fascinated by sailing, and we all started taking a more in-depth look at how to make boats go faster. By 1961, when I was fourteen, I knew three things: I wanted to be a sailmaker, I wanted to sail in the Olympics, and I wanted to sail in the America's Cup.

In 1961, I bought a suit of North sails for my Blue Jay. In those days, North Sails was a west coast company, although its principal, Lowell North, was famous throughout the sailing world. As far as I know, I was the first sailor on Long Island Sound to purchase a suit of North sails. I called San Diego and asked to speak to Lowell North. For a fourteen-year-old who was completely wrapped up in sailing, the coast-to-coast telephone call was a little like placing a call to the president or to Mickey Mantle. The secretary put me through. In a voice barely under control, I asked Lowell North if he'd ever made Blue Jay sails. "Not many," he replied. I said that I'd heard good things about his sails, particularly in light air, and that's something we have a lot of here on the Sound. He said he appreciated my kind words and would be happy to make some sails for me. They arrived; they weren't perfect in every way but they were darn good, and I had a very creditable record in the Blue Jay after purchasing them.

When I was seventeen, I taught sailing at the Wianno Yacht Club in Osterville, Massachusetts, on Cape Cod. The people there were even more consumed by sailing than my boyhood friends. I got to know Jack Fallon, a real-estate developer, fairly well. Fallon sailed a Wianno Senior, a gaff-rigged 25 footer, which was also sailed by the Kennedy brothers Jack, Bobby, and Ted. I mentioned to Fallon my dream of sailing in the America's Cup. It so happened that he knew Ted Hood, who at the time was preparing the 12-Meter *Nefertiti*, a boat of his design, for the 1964 America's Cup.

Fallon got me aboard that boat, which had been unsuccessful in its first America's Cup bid in 1962. I was put on a coffee-grinder winch. I can remember just barely hanging on to the madly spinning handles while facing off against an overstuffed guy who looked like a football lineman. He was grinding away with what seemed sufficient force to move mountains, let alone the genoa clew. To an awestruck adolescent on the biggest day of his life, the 12-Meter seemed as if it was going a million miles an hour. Whenever I could, I would sneak a look back into the cockpit at Hood. I was amazed at how quiet he was. Hood barely said five words the entire day. He spent all his time looking at the sails. He made a lot of notes; he even drew notes on the sails.

Although I wasn't sure exactly what he was doing then, I understand it now. Hood had an extraordinary eye for what a sail should look like, and his idea of the sailmaking exercise was to cut the sail on the floor as best he could and then go out on the boat and see what was right or wrong. Then he would recut it. His pencil drawings were to show him where to relieve areas that were too tight and where to take up areas that were too loose. It was a very practical approach to shaping sails, based on experience.

That sail with Hood left an indelible impression on me. Being young and a complete stranger to this level of the game, I was taken by it all. Even then I realized that Hood was the greatest of the great. That day had as much to do with molding my future as anything or anyone ever has.

Several years later, I had the opportunity to sail with Lowell North on the 12-Meter *Enterprise*, while helping Dennis Conner train for the 1980 America's Cup. This was a very different experience. North looked at the sails—much as Hood did—and he obviously had ideas about making changes to them, but he didn't do a thing until he consulted the computer cut-sheet. If he couldn't relate what he saw in a particular sail to the computer numbers that built it, the process didn't help him. It might have made that particular sail better, but it wouldn't help the other sails he would make for this or other boats, and it wouldn't advance his data bank or that of his company.

During that same week, Ted Hood also sailed with us aboard *Enterprise*. He sailed the boat upwind beautifully, as well as anyone I'd ever seen. He was right on; he always made the boat go a little bit higher than I thought possible. He offered about four comments during the entire day—comments about the sails. I'd been looking at the sails all summer, and Hood's observations were things that had never occurred to me. I realized then that he had much more than just a lot of experience, but also a lot of ideas. He just knew them; they probably came to him through osmosis. Maybe that's a reasonable definition of genius.

North, on the other hand, was aflame with ideas. He was a rocket scientist on a sailboat. Some of his ideas were brilliant, but many more of them were so off the wall that they astounded me. Yet I realized that North and Hood were probably both right in their own ways, true to themselves and true to their time. The sport of sailing has benefited inordinately from their differences and their journeys down such divergent roads. It is likely this distance between them that is responsible for the far-ranging technology that characterizes the business and sport of sailing.

Hood and North put their stamps not just on the companies that bear their names but also on the entire industry. How these two men came to dominate sailmaking tells much about sails and about the recent history of the sport. Their personal histories also allow us to make a less-daunting start to the journey into the high-tech world of sails. The story of sails is as much a story about the people who shaped the technology as it is about that technology.

THE ARTIST

Ted Hood, now retired from sailmaking, is still deeply involved in the marine business in Portsmouth, Rhode Island, where he works with his three sons.

Before Hood moved to Rhode Island, eleven generations of Hoods lived and worked on the north shore of Massachusetts. By any measure, they were

Ted Hood
(Peter Barlow photo)

an innovative lot. Three generations of Hoods lived in the home in Danvers, Massachusetts, where Ted Hood and his younger brother, Bruce, spent their formative years. Hood's father, Ralph Stedman Hood, nicknamed "the Professor"—mostly because he was absentminded, although he did teach in a midwestern college for a few years—worked for Monsanto Chemical Corporation in nearby Everett and had numerous patents in electronics to his name.

Hood's grandfather, Ralph O. Hood, invented the electric starter, which he sold to General Electric for $75,000—a veritable fortune at the turn of the century. He used the money to start building the Hoodmobile, a four-seater sedan. He built six of them, and then like so many others who chased the dream of motorizing the American public, he went broke. Ted Hood remembers coming home from school and working with his grandfather in the cellar workshop: "My grandfather was home all the time. After school we'd go down to the cellar and work with him on whatever he was doing, and he'd teach us. I think that's something a lot of people miss today because families don't live together anymore."

Although there was never a surfeit of money when Hood was growing up, the family always had boats. Hood remembers his father driving an old R-boat in races in Marblehead, his grandfather trimming the spinnaker, and

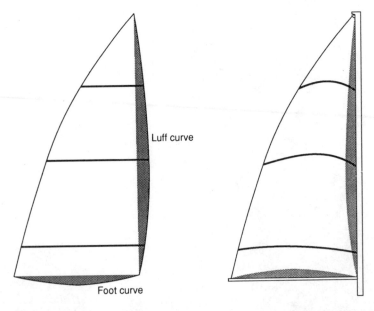

Luff curve

Foot curve

Extra material is added to luff and foot to shape the sail.

When flown, extra material sags into sail, creating shape.

Figure 2.1 Shaping a sail with luff and foot curve

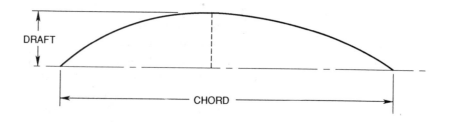

DEPTH = DRAFT / CHORD (%)

Figure 2.2 How sail depth is computed

seven-year-old Ted trying desperately to make himself inconspicuous as they argued about sail trim. They didn't do particularly well, Hood recalls, because they had poor sails.

Hood rebuilt and then made the sails for his first boat when he was nine. He read a small library book on sailmaking. From it, he learned that there are fundamentally two ways to give a two-dimensional piece of cloth a three-dimensional airfoil shape. He also learned how shape translates into power. The simplest way to put shape in a sail is to cut a curve into one or all of the sides of a triangular sail. A sailmaker might start, for example, by cutting a curve into the luff of a sail (see Figure 2.1). Then, when the curved luff of the sail is affixed to a straight mast, the extra material pushes shape into the sail.[1] This is called luff curve.

As noted, the other way to create an airfoil is to cut shape into the individual panels of a sail (see Figure 1.1, page 6). Then, if the straight edge of one panel is sewn to a curved edge of another, shape is again forced into the sail. This is called broadseaming. Hood, recalling his earliest experiment in sail shaping, said, "I didn't put curved seams in my sails, but I curved the luff and foot. I also puckered the rope around the edges with the idea of building in some shape."

The degree of shaping in a sail is determined by its depth or draft. Up to a point, more shape or depth means more power; less shape, less power. The draft of a sail is determined by drawing an imaginary horizontal line from luff to leech. Until most recently, sails had horizontal (rather than vertical) panels, so this could easily be done by imagining the line along a seam. This line is called the chord (see Figure 2.2). Then the deepest part of the sail is determined along the line. This is draft. Sail depth is then simply draft/chord,

---

[1]If, however, the mast is bent aft, the curve of the mast better matches the curve of the sail's luff, and shape is removed. This explains why when a flat sail is desirable—when sailing upwind in moderate or heavy air—the mast is bent aft. When, however, more shape is needed—when beating in light air or when reaching or sailing off the wind—the mast is straightened (see Figure 10.2, page 208).

expressed as a percentage. (Vertical sails have horizontal speed stripes as a visual aid to help compute depth.) Thus, a 1-foot draft in a 10-foot span is described as a 10 percent depth. This number tells how deep the sail is relative to its width at that particular (horizontal) section of the sail. A 10 percent depth is fairly flat and could be, as we will see, an effective sail when the wind blows. An 18 percent sail (1.8 feet of depth in 10 feet of span) is full and could be an effective sail in light winds when more power is desirable. It was simple lessons like these, gleaned from a tired library book, that the boy Ted Hood began to build on.

When Hood was an adolescent, sailing came to dominate his life. There was nothing in life that he did better, nothing in life he ever wanted to do more than to sail boats. But after serving an unhappy tour of duty in the U.S. Navy at the end of World War II, he turned away from the sea for a career. He attended Wentworth Institute, an engineering school in Boston, to study architecture and home building. While in school, he helped support his family by fixing sails. He used the opportunity well. Rather than just repair sails, he often improved them, when asked by locals. Sometimes he would add length to the bolt rope of a main, giving the sail a fuller shape; other times he would take length away. If a sail required major surgery, he would take the seams apart and sew them back together, changing the broadseaming and the shaping. He learned by trial and error—a method that would serve him well for nearly thirty years.

Completing his college course work, Hood started in the construction business. He began building his first house, a three-bedroom Cape, on the waterfront in Marblehead. Hood recalled: ''I started building it, had the foundation in, and as soon as the framing started going up, the next-door neighbor started complaining to the owner that this house would spoil his view. He offered the guy everything he had in it plus $5,000. Back in 1950, that was a lot of money. That was the end of my building business. I enjoyed it, however. I often think I would have done pretty well at it. But I started into sailmaking.''

Hood began his career as a sailmaker at a propitious time. Sailmaking was going through vast changes in the early 1950s as a result of new cloths perfected during the war years. Cotton sailcloth, the industry standard for a century, was replaced by nylon, then Orlon and, by 1953, Dacron.

Prior to Hood's emergence, the dominant sailmaker in the Northeast—and probably in the nation—was Ernest A. Ratsey, a descendant of the famous George Ratsey, who started a sailmaking business in 1790 on the Isle of Wight in England. A George Ratsey foretop sail was used by Lord Nelson in his victory in 1805 at the Battle of Trafalgar.

Ernest A. Ratsey came to the United States in 1902 with his father,

George Ernest Ratsey. The fifth and sixth generations of this distinguished sailmaking family established Ratsey & Lapthorn on City Island in the Bronx section of New York City. Ratsey & Lapthorn would become best known for its America's Cup sailmaking. Most of the American J-boats, which sailed for the America's Cup in the 1930s, used Ratsey sails. Better sailcloth allowed the American Ratseys to flourish in the first half of this century, just as better sailcloth would allow Ted Hood to flourish in the second half. The Ratseys brought with them long-staple Egyptian cotton, which stretched less than American cotton, canvas, or flax. Although sails made from Egyptian cotton were a vast improvement, they were, like all cotton sails, extremely sensitive to moisture, were prone to rot and mildew, and had to be broken in. These problems remained the Achilles' heel of this material.[2]

Ernest Ratsey was famous for his handwritten "Gore" books, which detailed nearly all the sails made by the firm. These days such Gore Books would be called a data bank. There was progress to be sure, but the art of sailmaking moved ahead slowly. As Ratsey would write in *Yacht Sails, Their Care & Handling*, the book he coauthored with W. H. de Fontaine, "Sailmaking remains an art which is handed down from generation to generation."

After the war, Egyptian cotton was no longer available, but synthetics such as nylon, Orlon, and Dacron began to appear. Nylon, named for New York and London where research on the fiber was conducted, was the first, but the early nylon used in sailmaking had problems with ripping, elongation, and water absorption. In time these problems would be solved, and today nylon is the material of choice for off-the-wind sails like spinnakers and the cruising equivalents. Orlon was tried next, but since it could only be woven into lightweight (3.8- and 5-ounce) cloth, its application was limited to small One Design sails. Dacron, invented in 1941 in England by H. R. Whinfield and J. T. Dickson, was a by-product of oil refining. In 1945, Du Pont purchased from ICI Fibres in England the rights to what was then called Terylene, but it would be eight years before sailcloth was made from it. Du Pont called it Dacron; polyester was the generic name.

From the beginning, Hood and his father realized that sailcloth would be the key to making better sails. "We concluded," Hood said, "that the big variable in making sails was cloth. It would stretch differently, which changed everything. So I figured that having a good sailcloth was the key to making a consistently good sail, because if the cloth can come out the way you want it, you can control the sailmaking."

---

[2]The Dacron revolution in sailmaking had nothing to do with the material's greater strength, smoother finish, and greater resistance to stretch; rather it came about because of Dacron's resistance to rot. The other features were discovered later.

Rather than buying cloth from the major sailcloth manufacturers, such as Howe & Bainbridge or Lamport, Hood and his father decided to manufacture it on their own. In 1952, they purchased two pillowcase looms from Pequot Mills, in Salem, and set them up in a sail loft in Marblehead. The Professor, who through his work on fiber at Monsanto was well acquainted with the process of weaving and finishing cloth, experimented with weaving Orlon and, then in 1953, Dacron. Not only was Hood the first to make sails from Dacron, but it is fair to say that over the next twenty-five years, no one did it better.[3]

Hood and his father wove Dacron tighter than any sailcloth manufacturer ever had or could. On their pillowcase looms, they wove the cloth in 20-inch sections (commercial cloth most commonly came in 36- or 28½-inch sections), and then Hood's father worked on heat-finishing and pressure-treating the cloth with hot calenders. The heat would shrink the material to 18 inches, and the calender, which resembles an old-fashioned clothes wringer, would crush the threads together, tightening them further. Finally, after washing, the cloth would be treated with a silicate (sand) bath that increased the friction between the filaments and fibers. This gave the material what Ted Hood describes as a "nonskid effect."

Sails made from Hood cloth looked different. Since they were made from 18-inch panels of cloth, they had twice the number of seams as, for example, sails made from the more common 36-inch panels. And since a big part of sail shape is determined by how the seams on a sail meet—broadseaming—Hood had more places, or more structural opportunities, to shape a sail. This resulted in a smoother shape.[4]

The Hood sails were a different color. They had a slight yellow-brown cast, caused by the yellowing of the Dacron as it passed over the hot calender, by the silicate bath, and by the use of a signature brown thread at the seams. Hood sails also felt different—softer, like the familiar cotton material they replaced. Most important was that sails made from Hood Dacron and shaped by the keen eye of Ted Hood won races, first for the sailmaker himself and then for an ever-expanding roster of customers in Marblehead, then the Northeast, elsewhere in the country, and ultimately the world.

---

[3]Another early pioneer with Dacron sailcloth was Sol Lamport, an American sailcloth manufacturer, who in 1955 introduced a product called Plysail. This involved the gluing together of two lightweight Dacron materials and was a very early example of the lamination of sailcloth, which is so popular today. Gluing was the problem, however, and after Plysail failed, Lamport introduced Drysail. This Drysail cloth was used successfully in sails on an ocean racer named *Hootman* and on the 12-Meter *Columbia*, which sailed in the 1958 America's Cup. *Vim* was *Columbia*'s major competitor in this, the first postwar America's Cup, and *Vim* had Dacron sails designed by Hood.

[4]Although commercial cloth finishers manufactured some Dacron in 20-inch panels, this was typically heavyweight cloth.

The Hood legend would actually be written in stone in the America's Cup. Following the war years, the America's Cup was renewed in 1958. For that competition, the famous Emil "Bus" Mosbacher, who would later work for President Richard Nixon, invited the thirty-four-year-old Ted Hood to join the crew of the twelve-year-old *Vim* and to bring along some of his sails. There were three new American twelves that year, but the stars of the summer were the aged *Vim* and the brand-new *Columbia*. So close was the racing between these two boats, both designed by Olin Stephens, that the New York Yacht Club's America's Cup Committee seemed unable to choose a defender. Finally, in a winner-take-all race, *Columbia* beat *Vim* by a slim boat length. In the America's Cup series, *Columbia* made good use of Hood-designed and -patented cross-cut spinnakers, loaned by the *Vim* crew. The American 12-Meter won four straight races over the British 12-Meter *Sceptre* by an average margin of eight minutes.

It was a good showing for Hood. *Vim*'s near success couldn't be attributed to yacht design as the boat was twelve years old. Rather, it was attributed to Mosbacher's organizational skills and Hood's brilliance with sails. After that summer, Hood became known as "the Sailmaker to the Twelves"—even in

Ted Hood talks to Bus Mosbacher, in sunglasses, during the 1958 America's Cup.
(*Courtesy of Ted Hood*)

Life magazine—and he would not relinquish that title for twenty-two years, despite some formidable challenges.

Hood's sails were on *Weatherly*, which defended the America's Cup in 1962; on *Constellation*, which defended in 1964; and on *Intrepid* in 1967 and again in 1970. In 1970, *Gretel II*, the Australian challenger to *Intrepid*, won a race using sails made from Hood cloth. The rules of the competition were then changed to forbid foreign challengers to use American-manufactured cloth.[5] Hood sails were also on *Courageous*, which defended the Cup in 1974 and again in 1977.

THE SCIENTIST

Lowell North was born in 1929 in Springfield, Missouri, two years after Ted Hood was born. North's father was a geophysicist who searched for oil, and often found it, in practically every dusty little California town from Bakersfield to Stockton. When Lowell was ten, the family moved to Los Angeles, and his father bought a 36-foot powerboat, which he and his son used for fishing. The powerboat had an 8-foot dinghy as a tender, which North appropriated for his own use. Like Hood, the young North went through a similar process of rebuilding the boat and making a sail for it. "I built a mast for the boat and put a keel on it that weighed about a hundred pounds . . . ," recalls North. "Sort of an iron keel. I made a sail for it. I'm sure it was the world's worst sail. The boat would barely sail to windward. It was a real struggle."

Part of the problem was design; another was the boy's lack of sailing technique. At Newport Beach, 30 miles below Los Angeles, North honed his skills on rented boats. Eventually his father gave him a 12-foot Penn-Yan dinghy. North wasn't able to race the boat, as there were no other birds of this particular feather in Newport Beach. A family friend suggested that he get a Falcon, a 17-foot One Design, which was popular in Newport Beach where the family had moved in 1944 when North was fifteen. He raced the boat with varying success until his father, who was now working in electronics, took a job in San Diego.

There was little enthusiasm for the move, as the family enjoyed Newport Beach. To mollify his adolescent son, the senior North bought a Star, a boat he learned was popular in San Diego. He crewed for his son on the 23-foot keelboat, which, almost since its inception in 1911, attracted the sport's best and brightest. In such airy company, they were off to an inauspicious start, recalled North. "We got last place for the entire summer. I think maybe we

---

[5]This was changed again in 1983, when the rule-makers from the New York Yacht Club recognized that sailmaking had become an international business.

Lowell North
(Courtesy of North Sails, Inc.)

beat a couple of boats at the tail end of the fleet toward the end of that first year. . . . I learned that the Star was really too much boat for my level of experience, but it was a good teacher. In those days we had cotton sails, and you had to learn how to break them in. The boat we bought had awful old sails, so I started learning about what makes sails fast.''

North attended college at San Diego State and then the Berkeley campus of the University of California. He majored in civil engineering and minored in structural engineering. In 1951, he found work at Ryan Aircraft, doing stress analysis. In 1953, he went to work for Narmco, a small manufacturing concern that made fiberglass parts for the aircraft industry. North worked in research and development as chief engineer. The position was far grander in title than in reality, said North. He designed, among other equipment, a center section for a U.S. Air Force missile.

Instruments of war were not the only things on his mind, however. With the help of a friend, North designed an innovative pair of metal snow skis. Skiing was a passion of his, particularly after he married his wife, Kay, who loved skiing. This was around the time when Head Skis was beginning to sell metal skis to recreational skiers but, North recalls, ''they were having trouble with the metal edges of the skis coming off.'' In North's design, the bottom skin worked as an edge as well as being part of the structure, and his skis were designed for the racer rather than the more casual recreational skier.

"They seemed to be fairly decent. I decided we should manufacture them, but I couldn't convince Narmco. Then I said that I'll do it on my own, except that being chief engineer at Narmco, any idea I had was *their* property. They wouldn't give me a release to do that, even though they weren't interested in it. That made me a bit unhappy, and about the same time my wife, Kay, announced she was pregnant for the first time."

North decided it was time to strike out on his own: "It was now or never." Just as Ted Hood surveyed his future from the reflection of a never-to-be-finished house, North quit his job building missiles and impetuously decided he would become a sailmaker.

Unlike Hood, whose timing was impeccable, North did not have a cloth revolution to herald his coming. So his primary focus was on sail design—the shape of the airfoil—rather than on cloth. North started in the business by building an odd mainsail for his Star, which he used in the Mid-Winter Championship in Los Angeles in 1959. The main employed stretchy welding hose in both the luff and the foot. The thinking was that this elastic material—a rubber band, in essence—would stretch, allowing more shape in the sail when sailing off the wind. There was a lot of reaching and running in that regatta, and North won the series. The fledgling sailmaker thought it a breakthrough design, but thirty years later he recalls it differently. "I thought it was a hell of a good idea because I thought of it. It was a different thing, and people like to buy different things, but, in truth, it was a gimmick. The reason it seemed fast was because sails were terrible in those days. These were the very early days of Dacron, and the cloth was just awful."

With that win, people began to pay some attention to Lowell North the sailmaker, but it wasn't sufficient to feed and shelter his growing family. Thus, North started an engineering-consulting business, and his wife kept her job working for an attorney. He hired an experienced sailmaker to work days, and during the few hours in the evening he could devote to it, North tried to learn what makes one sail fast, another slow. "Actually I had learned to win races in the Star early on by taking a sail apart and putting it back together until it was a little faster, and this is really the way we won races. Sails were so poorly designed and made in those days that practically anything you did to them made them better. I really thought I knew what a fast sail should look like; I had preconceived notions of which shape was fast, but, in truth, this thinking was really a detriment to progress. It took me about five years to learn that I hadn't the foggiest notion of what a sail should look like. What I thought looked good often wasn't, and what I thought looked awful often was fast."

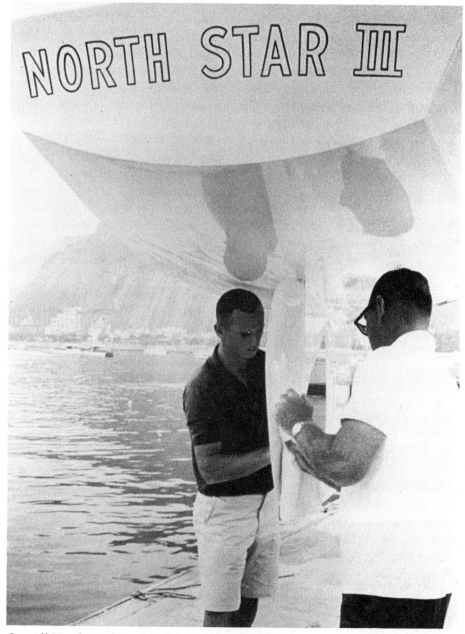

Lowell North readying his Star for the 1960 Worlds in Rio de Janeiro. North, a four-time world champion in this most competitive class, won an Olympic gold medal in the Star at the Acapulco Games in 1968. (Courtesy of North Sails, Inc.)

North took a radical step. He closed his eyes. He turned away from what sailmakers had been doing for centuries, and what Ted Hood had been doing better than any of them since 1952: designing sails based on what *looks* right or what *appears* to be the perfect airfoil shape. "This realization came about from some sail testing we did," North said. "The shapes I thought would be faster weren't. The realization that I didn't know anything about sail shape was really a big help. I was then willing to test a great variety of shapes, some of which tested faster. This objectivity helped us to make a lot of progress in sail shape for the next several years."

One other thing strengthened North's lack of faith in intuitive sailmaking. An early 12-Meter campaign allowed him to use a small research grant to do some wind-tunnel testing of sails at MIT. "One of the most interesting results came when we turned one of the mainsail shapes backwards and attached the leech to the mast. We found the draft-aft shape in the mainsail gave us the best force forward. We tried this full scale, and it actually worked—gave us more power: more lift and less drag. It led us into a lot of shapes that we might not have thought of or tested otherwise."

When North decided to challenge Hood directly, he looked long and hard at Hood's cloth. He concluded that Hood's advantage in the weaving of cloth could be overcome. With effort, North could learn to duplicate the process. Nevertheless, North concluded that rather than chasing Hood, who had a five-year head start, he would travel a different path. North decided that the area of greatest gain would be in the finishing of cloth. He concluded that his company's emphasis would be on low-stretch finishes, in what is collectively called resin finishes.

So rather than weaving Dacron tighter, as Hood did, North would have plastics applied at the end of the process to better control stretch.[6] This was similar to Hood's silicate bath, but in this case, the plastic, applied in an aqueous bath, would become rigid through curing. The plastic, most typically melamine, would fill the interstices between the yarns and filaments to help resist stretch. When the sail was new, the plastic seemed to give the sail a more rigid—more three-dimensional—shape.

Controlling stretch in the weaving or in the finishing was another fundamental difference between Hood and North and most of the other sailmakers of that day. Although sailcloth wasn't North's primary focus, he realized he had to gain control of the stretch characteristics of Dacron. Dacron sailcloth may have been less stretchy than the cotton cloth it replaced, but it still stretched. Furthermore, practically every bolt of Dacron cloth had different

---

[6]The work was done for North by Howe & Bainbridge, a well-known Boston fabric supplier.

stretch characteristics. Up to a certain limit, cloth stretch can be corrected in the design by constructing the sail flatter. Then after the sail is "broken in," it will assume its proper shape.

However, rather than relying on "educated" guesses, North needed to know precisely the stretch of a fabric so that he could compensate for it. One of the first steps he took was to devise a simple testing device that would pull the cloth in three directions, along the bias, fill, and warp, to measure stretch (see Figure 3.2, page 36).[7] Sailcloth is best able to resist a pull in the two thread directions, along the fill and warp, but shows less resistance to stretch off the thread line, on a diagonal, for example. This is because the threads resist pulls that run parallel to them, but pulls on an angle, on the bias, are only resisted by the interlocking of the threads. There is more room for movement, and this increases the propensity for stretch.

Stretch wasn't all North tested for, however; he was also concerned about cloth longevity. Thus, in the early days of North Sails, he drove between his original loft in San Diego and a new one in Seal Beach, about a two-hour drive, with strips of sailcloth attached to the radio antenna of his car. After this drive, North stretched these fatigued strips on the same graph as unfatigued samples from the same bolt of cloth. The difference in stretch predicted the relative breakdown to be expected in a season of use. As ad hoc as it was, the test became the industry standard. In the interest of energy conservation as well as to cut down on his driving, North developed a sailcloth longevity machine, which spins the samples on a windmill-like device.

A few years later, North was testing Soling sails. One of the people recruited for the on-the-water test was a professor, Heiner Meldner, from Germany, who was teaching at the University of California at San Diego. Meldner's specialties were fluid dynamics and laser fusion. Although new to sailing, Meldner was an expert glider pilot, and he positively bubbled with creative fire. In the course of the day, he offered North a lot of ideas on how to make boats go faster. North, a man cut from the same bolt of cloth, loves such discussions. At the end of the day, Meldner told him he thought sail testing could be done better and faster on a computer. North told him, "If that's so, you might make both of us fairly rich."

North didn't see Meldner for a year. Then Meldner reappeared and said, "Well, now I think I can do sail testing analytically. Let's give it a try." It was good timing. When Meldner made this offer, North had just completed

---

[7]The textile industry had cloth testers, such as the Scott tester, but North couldn't afford to purchase one. So he devised a rather crude tester, using a hundred-pound weight and vise grips. North says he was likely the first sailmaker to use a cloth-testing device. "I used to drive Bainbridge crazy," he said, "trying to get them to test cloth."

ten days of testing sails for a 470, for an upcoming Olympic campaign. Five jibs were tested in front of one mainsail, and after hours and hours on the water, North felt confident that he could rank the speed of these five jibs. "To be honest," said North, "there was no way that I could have told you beforehand or even by looking at the shape of these sails which ones were faster. So I thought this would be a good chance to see how Meldner's computer program would do the work analytically. We gave these shapes to Heiner and said, 'Okay, you try to get the jibs in the right order of speed.' To my amazement, he got the five jibs in exactly the same order we did. I thought he had to be awfully smart or awfully lucky. To confirm this, we gave him a few additional tests, and again he got the right answers."

For the next five years, Meldner did practically all of North's testing in the computer, from sails for Blue Jays to sails for 12-Meters. Meldner's computer tests would be confirmed on the water in full-scale testing, and on occasion, said North, he would come up with shapes that couldn't be built. "But we made more progress in sail shape during the five years of this work than ever before or ever since."

Shortly after Meldner started his work, North learned about Tom Schnackenberg, from New Zealand, who was working in the company's Canadian loft. Before becoming a sailmaker, Schnackenberg was only a dissertation away from a PhD in nuclear physics from the University of British Columbia. North met Schnackenberg. "I learned that he was on a level with Heiner Meldner, maybe better, because he had a lot of practical sailing experience as well as theoretical experience." He lured Schnackenberg to San Diego, where he worked with Meldner.

Schnackenberg's first program for building sails in the computer worked this way. He developed about two hundred sets of curves, called strip patterns. The various curves, which ranged from 20 to 50 feet, were cut into Mylar. Some were simple arcs of various radii; others were very straight in back and very curved in front; still others were somewhere in between. Then he developed a computer program that would pick out which of these two hundred curves should be used for a particular seam and how it should be used. The program worked, said North, "amazingly well." Schnackenberg continued with this work, and within ten years or so, the company would be designing sails in the computer, testing them in a computer-simulated wind tunnel, running them through a computer-simulated structural analysis, and cutting them out with a computer-controlled X/Y plotter/cutter.

It would be wrong to conclude that the computer launched North down an unwavering path of progress. There were many, many times that the company seemed to take one step forward and three back. North was undeterred, however. He saw computer-aided design and manufacturing as an investment in the future. He wasn't interested in being a follower, and if going his own way took extra time—if there were numerous false steps along the way—so be it. He was committed to the synergy made possible by computer design.

These were good times for North, and for Hood, but Hood's dominance of the America's Cup, sailing's most visible spectacle, was the proverbial thorn in North's side. The America's Cup of 1974 proved to be the most interesting showdown between the philosophies of Hood Sails and North Sails. North's John Marshall, who had opened a loft in Stratford, Connecticut, to challenge Hood, sailed aboard *Intrepid*, the two-time defender of the America's Cup; and by summer's end, Hood would be sailing aboard *Courageous*, skippering the boat.

Hood had had no intention of sailing in the America's Cup that year. He had been asked by Bob McCullough, head of the *Courageous* syndicate, to skipper the new boat, but turned it down, not liking the boat enough to spend a year with it. He handed the sailmaking chores on *Courageous* over to his able lieutenant, Robbie Doyle (later the head of Doyle Sails), and Hood loaded his One Tonner, *Robin*, on a freighter for a trip to England where he expected to sail her in a competition. The freighter broke down and had to return to port. At loose ends that summer, Hood did the New York Yacht Club Cruise, which ended in Newport. That summer the seven-year-old wooden *Intrepid* was dominating the new 12-Meters, *Courageous* and *Mariner*, which were the first generation of 12-Meters built in aluminum.

When Hood pulled into Newport in August of 1974, he was met by McCullough. McCullough asked Hood if he would join *Courageous* "to help out." Hood agreed; he joined Bob Bavier, *Yachting* magazine's publisher, who was skippering the boat, in the afterguard. Asked if he had seen *Intrepid*, equipped with North sails, as a threat to his commercial empire, Hood answered, "Maybe some, I don't remember feeling that strongly about it. While I was interested in seeing our sails do well, more interesting was the excitement of sailing the boat."

Courageous had started life with Hood sails, as practically all America's Cup yachts had since 1962, but *Intrepid*, with North sails and John Marshall of North Sails aboard, won both the June and July trials. In August, the *Courageous* syndicate was floundering. They purchased North sails and seemed to be doing a bit better with them, and Hood trimmed the North sails as best he could; winning seemed more important to him than the plastic finish on the sail or the logo at the tack. Then Bavier departed, leaving Hood as skipper. Shortly thereafter, Dennis Conner, who had been sailing with Ted Turner on the vainglorious *Mariner*, joined *Courageous* as starting helmsman.

The 1974 America's Cup was a showdown between the sailmaking philosophies of Ted Hood and Lowell North in the forms of Courageous, *to leeward, and* Intrepid. *Note the 18-inch panels on the Hood sails on* Courageous *versus the wider North panels on* Intrepid. *Narrow panels were a Hood signature. (Michael Levitt photo)*

The score was tied at four when *Intrepid* engaged *Courageous* in what was obviously the final race among defenders. The last time the racing had been this close was back in 1958 when *Vim*, with Hood aboard, battled *Columbia* to the bitter end. On this September day in 1974, the wind was gusting to 30 knots—unknown territory for 12-Meters in the pre-Perth days of the America's Cup—but time had run out. A defender had to be named this day to face the Australians on *Southern Cross*, the first of the challenges led by Alan Bond.

The summer had dwindled down to one precious race. But as exciting as the outcome of this race was, equally interesting to the sport's insiders was the outcome of the commercial battle between Hood and North. The order of the sailmaking world might very well change this windswept September day.

At the starting line, Hood took the wheel of *Courageous* from Conner, who was aboard primarily for his genius at the starting line. Leaving no doubt who was in charge, Hood also decided to use his sails, not those made by North. Furthermore, it was a seven-year-old main he had built for *Intrepid*, and it was a light-air sail at that. When the Hood mainsail, with the distinctive brown thread and the slight yellow cast, was hoisted in 30 knots of wind, McCullough grabbed the radio microphone on the tender. A large, blustery man, he ordered Hood to change back to the North heavy-air main. Hood responded quietly, as is his way, but adamantly, "As long as I'm skipper of the boat, I'll decide what sails to use." It was the boldest possible move, and had Hood been wrong, he would have been vilified. Hood and *Courageous* beat *Intrepid* that day.

The taciturn Hood was asked if that was the best day of his life. "Probably," he said, "but not to a great extent." Hood and Conner went on to defend the America's Cup 4–0 over *Southern Cross*. They used mostly Hood sails. It would take North another six years to secure a proper invitation to the America's Cup ball, when in 1980 Dennis Conner used North mains and headsails and Sobstad spinnakers on *Freedom*.

Hood's interest in sailmaking waned with the passing of that decade. After a quarter century at the top of the game, he began to see sailmaking as a young man's game, and his marine empire had expanded well beyond sailmaking. His loss of enthusiasm for sailmaking was perhaps deepened by another revolution in sailcloth: Mylar. Mylar is a laminated material in which the Mylar film is laminated (glued) to Dacron. The result is a lightweight, low-stretch material. It is not a coincidence that North was the first sailor and sailmaker to use this material successfully, on *Enterprise*, the boat he skippered for a time in the 1977 America's Cup trials.

Hood had little patience with computers, which were beginning to appear in most sail lofts. He once spent $100,000 in an attempt to computerize his sailmaking operation but lost patience with the error-prone machine. "I threw it out the door." That would prove a rash decision.

Hood had another liability: Ted Hood, himself. No one in the organization—and it is fair to say the world—had a better eye for sails than Hood. A more verbal man or a man more comfortable with the language of computers might have found it easier to share his thinking with others in the company, but with the "data bank" in one man's head, the company was vulnerable. Into this breach, at long last, rushed North. Hood would sell his interest in the sailmaking business and eventually move to Rhode Island to concentrate on yacht design, a lasting fascination; boat building and importing; rigging, including his famous Stoway Mast; and building and running his huge boatyard

Ted Hood winning the SORC's Ocean Triangle Race in 1975 on Robin II, Too, *a Two Tonner of his design. This was a year after Hood defended the* America's Cup with Courageous *and was named Yachtsman of the Year. (Michael Levitt photo)*

and marina complex on Narragansett Bay. He has also maintained a lifelong love for ocean racing.

As we move into the last decade of this century, the computer now dominates the design and manufacturing side of sailmaking, as it does so many other high-tech businesses. Today, computers are used to design sails and even test the shapes by flying them in the computer. Computers driving lasers or knives also cut the cloth into as many as ninety shaped panels that, when sewn together, turn a two-dimensional piece of cloth into a sophisticated airfoil, a form that has more in common with a computer-designed and -tested fighter wing than a shape created by an artist, even a Michelangelo.

CHAPTER 3

CHARACTERISTICS OF SAILCLOTH

★ In the late 1820s, Mahlon Dickerson, secretary of the U.S. Navy, was concerned about the supply of sailcloth for his warships. Up to that time, most of the sailcloth used in the United States was flax imported from Europe. In the event of war, this supply would certainly be cut off. A small domestic sailcloth industry had been growing for the previous thirty years, but it was based on cotton fiber rather than flax.[1] Cotton fiber was fairly new to sailcloth, and its technology was unproven. Secretary Dickerson surveyed the captains of his warships for their opinions of cotton sailcloth. He heard conflicting reports: some said that cotton absorbed more water and was more difficult to handle; others opined that flax was stronger and easier to use; still others claimed that cotton stretched less and would hold more wind. Whether to embrace the new technology or the old was a most difficult choice. There were many variables and conflicting opinions. Guess wrong and the sovereignty of the country could change, and the loss of life be considerable. In the end, the Navy chose cotton sailcloth, but for reasons that had less to do with naval strategy than with the results of a yacht race.

In 1851, the yacht *America* raced around the Isle of Wight in England against a fleet of crack English cutters and schooners. *America* easily beat the others and won the Hundred Guineas Cup, which came to be known in her honor as the America's Cup. Britannia, which thought of itself as "ruling the waves," was shaken by the victory of this upstart schooner from the New World. The English public saw it as a disquieting—indeed threatening— change in the world's order.

Knowledgeable observers, however, saw the outcome in less consequential terms. They were impressed by the radical design of the schooner *America*,

---

[1]Flax, like cotton, is a plant fiber. Flax fiber is extracted from the stems of the plant; cotton fiber comes from the seed case.

but they were even more impressed by the cut of her sails, made of American cotton rather than flax. The "Special Correspondent" of the London *Times* wrote: "*America*'s canvas was as flat as a sheet of paper. While the cutters were thrashing through the water, sending spray over their bows, and the schooners were wet up to the foot of the foremast, the *America* was as dry as a bone."

Not only was *America* drier due to her flatter cotton sails, but for the same reason, she was more close-winded. The yachts of this day could only sail at about 55 to 60 degrees to the wind. It was said that *America* could sail about 6 degrees closer. This windward ability produced a lasting impression on the nautical community. In the nineteenth century, the ability to sail upwind was recognized as a tactical advantage on the race course or in the course of war. The use of flax sails, on yachts, naval warships, or commercial vessels, steadily declined, replaced by cotton sails.

What made cotton sailcloth so much more desirable than flax? Weight for weight, flax is actually stronger than equivalent cotton, but cotton stretches less. Sailing to windward requires relatively flat well-shaped sails to form an effective airfoil, and although strength is still an important consideration, maintaining this airfoil shape without stretching is more critical. Therefore, American cotton and eventually Egyptian cotton with lower stretch became the material of choice for triangular sails.

Cotton was used almost exclusively in sailcloth design until after World War II, when synthetic fibers, with their wide array of desirable properties, including lower stretch and lighter weight, gradually became available. These synthetics, most notably Dacron, quickly replaced cotton just as cotton had replaced flax.

Sailmaking today, with its great variety of synthetic-polymer fibers and films, is a much more complicated technology than it was in the nineteenth century. We now have a complex choice of materials all known as sailcloth. These include woven fabrics, woven fabrics with resins, nonwoven fabrics, and laminates with fibers and films. Of these, the most important are 1) woven polyester, more commonly known as Dacron; 2) woven nylon; 3) laminates made of polyester and Mylar film, more commonly known as Mylar; 4) laminates of Kevlar fiber and Mylar film, commonly known as Kevlar; and 5) laminates of Spectra fiber and Mylar film, known as Spectra.

To avoid confusion, the laminates will generally be referred to in this book by their more correct designations; Mylar will be denoted as polyester/Mylar, Kevlar, as Kevlar/Mylar, and Spectra, as Spectra/Mylar. The confusion comes from the fact that when used in sailcloth all three fibers, polyester, Kevlar, and Spectra, are bonded to Mylar film. This also will allow us to

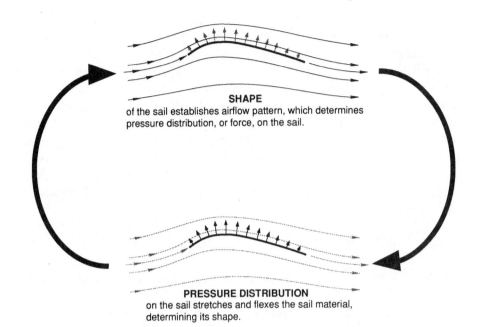

SHAPE
of the sail establishes airflow pattern, which determines
pressure distribution, or force, on the sail.

PRESSURE DISTRIBUTION
on the sail stretches and flexes the sail material,
determining its shape.

Figure 3.1 Relationship of sail shape and pressure distribution

distinguish between the fibers of polyester, Kevlar, and Spectra and the laminated fabrics that bear the same names.

Sailmakers have an interesting problem. Rather than relying on rigid frames and solid materials for positive shape control, sailmakers must shape their foils by balancing the forces of the wind with the tensions in the sail. This is a difficult and ever-changing problem. The force or pressure distribution of the wind changes constantly and is affected by the shape of the sail, while the shape of the sail, through cloth stretch and flexing, is affected by the pressure distribution of the wind (see Figure 3.1). It is easy to see that the properties of the cloth—stretch resistance, strength, flex, and weight—play an important role in balancing these forces and shaping the sail.

Below is a list of the properties that must be addressed or controlled in the design and manufacturing of most sailcloth:

Cloth Geometry: Warp, Fill, and Bias   Tear Strength
Stretch resistance   Porosity
Strength   Water absorption
Cloth weight   Ultraviolet stability
Flexibility

The old question of the relative importance of stretch resistance and strength is the same today as it was in the nineteenth century. And the answer is the same: In general, stretch resistance is more important than strength for mainsails and headsails. Just as the lower-stretch cotton sails of the yacht *America* allowed her to sail closer to the wind and defeat the English fleet, modern sail materials, such as laminates and in particular Kevlar-reinforced laminates, emphasize stretch resistance for sailing upwind. On the other hand, for downwind sails, such as spinnakers, cruising spinnakers, bloopers, and the like, strength is the more important requirement. For this reason, lightweight nylon fabrics are generally used in such sails because they provide higher strength in a shock-loading situation, the typical lot of off-the-wind sails.

CLOTH GEOMETRY: WARP, FILL, AND BIAS

Directions in woven fabrics for sails are usually defined using traditional textile terms related to the weaving process (see Figure 3.2). The warp is the longest direction in a roll of fabric because the warp yarns are the long yarns that unroll from a spool and pass through the loom during the weaving process. The fill direction is parallel to the filling yarns (known as weft yarns in England). During weaving, the fill yarns are passed back and forth through the warp yarns and are perpendicular to them. The bias direction bisects the other two at a 45-degree angle to each. The important aspect of the bias direction

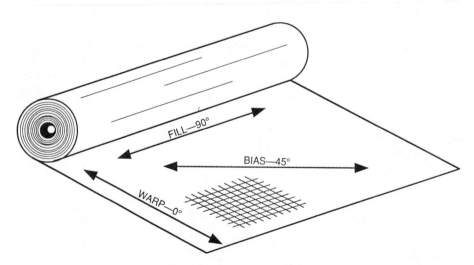

Figure 3.2 Cloth directions

is that in almost all applications yarn never runs parallel to it, and without this direct support, the cloth is much more likely to stretch when pulled in the bias orientation.

In sailmaking, the textile terms of *warp*, *fill*, and *bias* are gradually being replaced by the more modern angular conventions used in the fiber-composite industry. In this system, the 0-degree direction is parallel to the warp, the 90-degree direction is parallel to the fill, and the 45-degree direction is the same as the bias.

STRETCH RESISTANCE

Stretch resistance and strength are not simple properties to consider. They can be measured and defined in many ways. (A typical graph of stretch versus load for sailcloth is shown in Figure 3.3.) Let's first look at stretch resistance. The primary aspect to note about stretch resistance is that it can have different values in different directions in the fabric. For instance, a woven fabric may

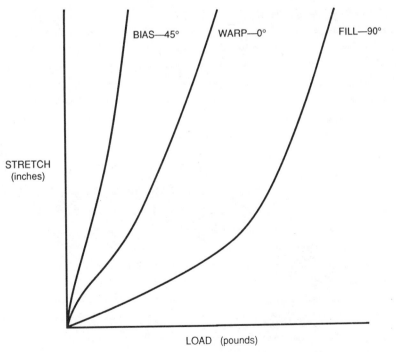

Figure 3.3 Comparison of stretch under load for different cloth directions. This is fill-oriented cloth.

have much lower stretch along one thread line than the other and, as shown in Figure 3.3, will probably have much higher stretch still when measured off the thread lines, on the bias, for example. It is easy to see that a detailed knowledge of the stretch resistance in the warp, fill, and bias directions of a fabric is very important to a sailmaker when planning the panel layout and fabric orientation of a sail. This must complement a sailmaker's knowledge of the load distribution—that is, where, how much, and in what direction the wind pressure impacts the sails. Complicating this further is that the pressure distribution is different in each of the three groups of sails: headsails, mainsails, and off-the-wind sails.

Stretch resistance can also be dependent on time. Some materials, when initially loaded, will stretch little, but if the load is maintained over a long period of time, they will gradually elongate. When the load is removed, some of these materials will—again over time—recover, or return to their original dimensions. In fact, this tendency in sailcloth is known as recovery. On the other hand, some materials when loaded will gradually elongate over time and will never recover their initial dimensions. Creep is the engineering term that describes this nonrecoverable stretch.

Stretch is caused by many things. Some sources of stretch are geometric, inherent in the geometry of the weave or in the construction of the sailcloth. Other sources are simply due to the elongation of the fibers, films, or other components used in manufacturing sailcloth. One of the most important sources of geometric stretch is crimp. Crimp refers simply to the serpentine path that yarns must take in crossing over and under other yarns in a weave or a knitted construction (see Figure 3.4). From the standpoint of stretch, crimp is a nec-

BALANCED-PLAIN WEAVE

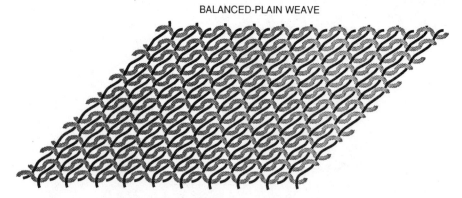

Figure 3.4 In this balanced-plain weave, both directions have an equal amount of crimp.

HIGHLY ORIENTED PLAIN WEAVE

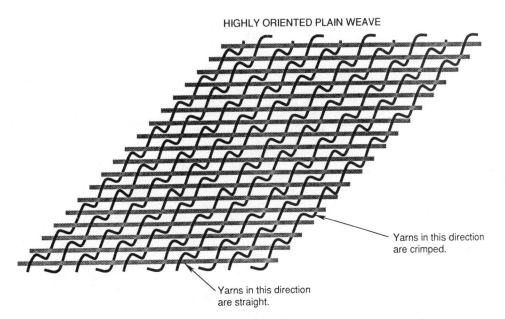

Yarns in this direction
are crimped.

Yarns in this direction
are straight.

Figure 3.5 In this highly oriented plain weave, crimp is limited to one direction.

essary evil in forming fabrics for sailcloth, but it can be controlled. For example, manufacturers can put most of the crimp in a given weave in either the warp or the fill, leaving the other direction nearly crimp-free and therefore much less susceptible to stretch (see Figure 3.5). This will be discussed in more detail later.

Another type of geometric stretch is bias stretch. In woven fabrics, this is simply the deformation of the weave that causes the warp and filling to cross at other than right angles (see Figure 3.6). Once again, bias stretch is a necessary evil in woven fabrics, but as we will see, it, too, can be controlled. One of the primary advantages of laminated sailcloth is the elimination or reduction of the two geometric stretch problems: crimp and bias stretch.

Stretch due to elongation of the very materials forming sailcloth is determined primarily by the choice of materials. Elongation takes place on a molecular level. This explains why cotton replaced flax as the material of choice for yacht sails. Polyester, which stretches less than nylon, is used in triangular sails (mains and jibs); nylon, which absorbs shock loads through high stretch, is used in spinnakers; Mylar film, which stretches less than most other films, is used for laminates; and Kevlar, the ultimate in low-stretch fibers, is important in modern racing sails.

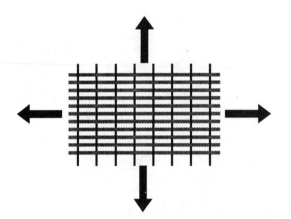

Loads in the 0° and 90° directions pull directly on the yarns. Fabric is better able to resist loads in these two directions.

Loads in the 45° or bias direction cause the yarns to "squish," or parallelogram— that is, cross at other than a right angle. Fabric is less able to resist loads off the thread line, or in the bias direction.

Figure 3.6 Loads on the thread lines and in the bias direction

Stretch characteristics are very important in determining where a cloth can best be used. They determine how the designed shape of a sail will change with the wind, sheet, and halyard loadings, and whether it will change permanently with use. Until the 1960s, the standard testing method for ascertaining the degree of stretch was simply to feel the material. The stiffness, or "hand," told experienced sailmakers what to expect in terms of stretch. Soft meant stretchy; stiff meant low stretch. This method works adequately within a small range of different materials. For example, it gives a generally correct answer when comparing a number of productions of a certain weave. However, feel isn't very precise, and it doesn't allow for numerical comparison for record keeping or for two sailmakers to compare results. More scientifically sophisticated methods were needed.

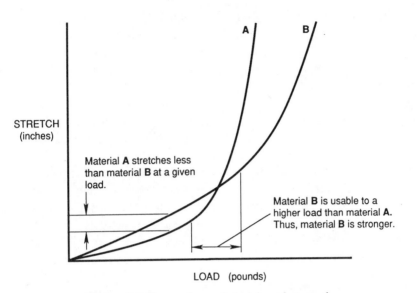

Figure 3.7 Comparison of stretch and strength
in polyester, or Dacron (A), and nylon (B)

Once the importance of quantifying stretch was recognized, cloth manufacturers and sailmakers began testing stretch on standard industrial stretch testers. As noted earlier, Lowell North was the first sailmaker to test sailcloth. This he did on a homemade device. The first machines used by the industry at large were Scott testers. A strip of cloth is mounted in the machine, and the stretch-versus-load behavior of the cloth is measured. To get reasonably accurate results, it became standard practice to use 2-inch-wide samples that are clamped between jaws set 16 inches apart. Tests of the cloth in the three principal directions, warp, fill, and bias, show the basic performance of the cloth. More modern stretch-testing machines have been developed since the Scott tester, but they generally work in the same manner.

STRENGTH

Strength, like stretch, is a complicated property. It, too, varies with direction in the fabric. There are two kinds of strength with which we are concerned. One is simply the breaking strength. In off-the-wind sails, breaking strength is the primary consideration. Just as flax was chosen over cotton for square-rigged sails because weight for weight it did not break as easily as cotton, today nylon rather than Dacron is used for downwind sails (see Figure 3.7).

The second type of strength is yield strength. Yield strength is the dividing line between recoverable, or elastic, elongation and nonrecoverable, or permanent, elongation. As experience was gained with the use of cloth testers, it became obvious that there is a load above which the material will no longer return to its original length after the load is removed. This load number is important since it establishes the maximum load capacity of the cloth. This is called yield strength. Combining the yield-strength number with the predicted sail-load number allows the sailmaker to determine the ''maximum wind-speed capability'' of a given sail (see Figure 3.8).

Obviously, this is an important number to know, and sailmakers should provide it to customers. If a sail is flown in winds beyond which it was designed, it will change shape dramatically and, worse yet, will continue to change shape each time it is used thereafter. These days, few sails actually fail by breaking, but many are flown in more wind than they are designed for and fail by becoming permanently distorted or ''blown-out,'' according to the descriptive expression.

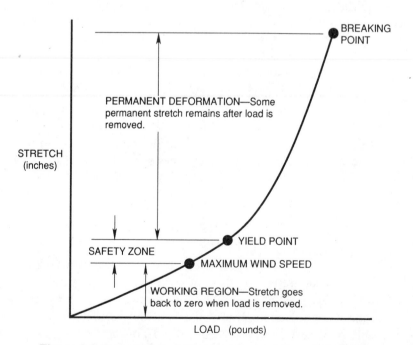

Figure 3.8 Typical plot of stretch under load for sailcloth

CLOTH WEIGHT

It would be easy to make sailcloth with very high strength and very low stretch if weight were not a consideration. But weight can be a very important factor. One reason is sail-handling. It is obviously easier to set, stow, and handle a lighter sail than a heavier one. Another consideration is weight aloft. It is always desirable on a sailboat to minimize weight aloft. The deleterious effects of weight aloft become clear when one recalls the expression "If I had a lever long enough, I could move the world" or, even more simply, when watching a large man climb to the top of the mast of a small boat. Minimizing weight aloft decreases the heeling moment and alleviates the pitching of the boat.[2] From the standpoint of safety as well as comfort, limiting weight aloft is as important to the cruiser as the racer.

By far the most important consideration of weight is, once again, shape. In light air, the shape of a sail can suffer simply because the sail is sagging under its own weight. Probably the most useful way to think about weight is to consider it as a ratio of weight to yield strength. From this ratio, the effective wind range of a sail can be computed. The lower limit of a sail's wind range is determined by the minimum wind required to fill a sail of a certain weight to its optimum shape; the upper limit is determined by the yield strength of the sail or the load at which the sail must be taken down to avoid permanent distortion.

The remaining properties of sailcloth are usually of secondary importance because they are, for the most part, achieved in the course of addressing stretch resistance, strength, and weight.

FLEXIBILITY

Cloth flexibility is determined by a combination of factors, including the stretch of the fibers used and the thickness and weight of the material. This property differs in racing and cruising sails. In racing sails, flexibility is often sacrificed to achieve lower stretch; in cruising sails, stretch resistance is often sacrificed to achieve greater flexibility and ease of handling. One way to improve flexibility is to place the load-carrying elements of a sailcloth in the center of the

---

[2]The concept of weight and distance from a balance point is expressed in moments, defined as weight × distance. Thus a 60-pound child, six feet from the balance point (fulcrum) of a seesaw, can balance his or her 180-pound father two feet from the balance point (60 × 6 = 360 foot-pounds and 180 × 2 = 360 foot-pounds).

material and to make this load-carrying material as thin as possible. This is the opposite of what is done in many composite hull lay-ups where rigidity, rather than flexibility, is important. Here, the load-carrying members are separated by a center core that is made as thick as possible to make the laminate as rigid as possible. Then should the hull strike some flotsam, it is less likely to be damaged or punctured.

Some high-performance laminated sailcloths, such as Kevlar/Mylar, polyester/Mylar, and Spectra/Mylar, are known to shrink with use. This is related to their lack of flexibility. The material does not literally shrink, but appears to because thousands of small wrinkles and buckles in the Mylar film cause it to contract. These creases form when the material is sharply bent or folded. Some call this the dollar-bill effect. If you measure the length and width of a new dollar bill, then crumple it, you can never quite spread it out to its original dimensions. Avoiding the dollar-bill effect is why high-tech sails are typically rolled rather than folded. (Sail care is discussed in Chapter 14.)

TEAR STRENGTH

Tear strength is, of course, important in saving a sail from an untimely death, or at least disfigurement, at the hands of foredeckmen and other sail-handlers. Tear strength is sometimes a limit to the minimum weight of lightweight woven materials, such as lightweight Dacron and nylon, and is certainly a serious consideration in the lightest-weight spinnaker fabrics. Tear strength is adversely affected by resin finishes, such as melamine or urethane, which are applied to the fabric. The more the resin or finish immobilizes the yarns and filaments within the fabric, the lower the tear strength. The threads of such heavily resined fabrics tend to break one at a time, and the tear strength goes down accordingly. On the other hand, when a fabric has little or no resin, the filaments and fibers are free to move and tend to bunch at the leading edge of a tear, effectively stopping its progress.

Tear strength is often closely associated with seam strength. This is because many factors, including the size of yarns, their placement, and the level of the finish, contribute to higher tear strength as well as higher seam strength.

In practice, Dacron sails are the most resistant to tearing. As cruisers more often opt for Dacron sails, tear strength is less of a problem. Polyester/Mylar sails also show good resistance to tearing, until such time as ultraviolet degradation—exposure to the sun—causes them to rip. Kevlar/Mylar sails, however, are the most susceptible to tearing. According to anecdotal information, Kevlar/Mylar sails have an effective life of about two seasons. Recently, an attempt was made to quantify the useful life of Kevlar/Mylar sails. *Merit*, the Swiss Whitbread Maxi, flew one Kevlar/Mylar main back and forth across the Atlantic Ocean while training for the 1989 Whitbread Round the World Race. After two thousand hours, the crew concluded that the sail's effective life was finished. In truth, the experiment was never completed— the Kevlar/Mylar sail never ripped or broke—but the crew had little faith in the sail.

POROSITY

Porosity is only seldom a consideration in sailcloth. The processes of tight weaving, resin impregnation, and lamination (used to control strength and stretch) almost always produce zero porosity as a side effect. Zero porosity makes it impossible for air to leak through the fabric as if blowing through a screen. The exception to this is very lightweight nylon spinnaker cloths.

Before addressing the exception, however, we should explain how sailcloth is weighed. Sailcloth weights are expressed in units of ounces per sailmaker's yard (SMY). This is the weight of a piece of cloth 28½ inches wide by 36 inches long. The reason for the odd-sized width is obscure. One author claims it is the length of Henry VIII's arm; another says that the standard was set by the U.S. National Bureau of Standards.[3]

Nylon spinnaker cloths, weighing less than one ounce per sailmaker's yard, are so light and thin that it is difficult to achieve zero porosity. Some spinnaker cloth has a resin coating smeared over the surface to achieve this, but most is designed with zero porosity as the lower limit of its yarn count.

During the 1980 America's Cup, Dennis Conner and I became quite concerned about spinnaker porosity. It seemed to us that a zero-porosity spinnaker should be faster. Hours and hours were spent testing this theory at Kenyon Piece & Dye Works, in Kenyon, Rhode Island, and on the water. We could never prove it; in fact, there were times when a more porous spinnaker tested faster. In light winds and lumpy seas, the more porous spinnaker seemed to hold its shape better, but whether or not this had to do with relative porosity couldn't be determined. So when in doubt, we opted for the low-porosity sail. This gave us a psychological edge, if nothing else.

---

[3]Metric weights are expressed in grams/meters^2. Dividing this by 42.9 will convert it to oz/SMY^2. For example, 230g/m^2 cloth is 5.4oz/SMY^2.

WATER ABSORPTION

Water pickup is certainly a problem for some sailcloth. An obvious example is cloth used in sailboard sails, which are repeatedly immersed in the water when the sailor falls. If the sail absorbs water, it becomes harder to uphaul, waterstart, and, indeed, hold up. Less obvious is the effect of water on the strength and stretch of nylon sails. Few know that nylon loses about 15 percent of its strength when damp and becomes three times stretchier. This explains why a wet spinnaker or blooper is more likely to blow out. Interestingly enough, the material regains its strength when dry. Occasionally resins and fillers are applied to the cloth to fill in the voids between the filaments and the fibers in order to diminish water absorption, but more often small amounts of hydrophobic (water) repellents, similar to Scotchgard, are applied to the cloth. If concerned about water absorption, which you should be, ask your sailmaker how this problem is addressed in the cloth.

ULTRAVIOLET STABILITY

Ultraviolet (UV) radiation from the sun can break the molecular chains and weaken the materials in sailcloth. Nevertheless, the ultraviolet stability of sailcloth is only sometimes a consideration. Recreational sails used in northern or far-southern latitudes are exposed to sunlight only intermittently and for relatively short periods of time when compared with other textile products, such as awnings and tents. Then, too, Dacron, the most common material used in sailcloth, has a self-screening property. The sun causes some initial degradation to the surface of Dacron, but this weakened material remains on the surface and forms a skin that protects the body of the fiber from further damage.

On the other hand, cruising sails used near the equator are likely to suffer from severe ultraviolet degradation. To counteract this, very effective coatings have been developed to screen the underlying sailcloth from ultraviolet light. An effective way to do this is to use this specially coated cloth in the leech and foot of roller-furling sails. The coated cloth then protects the rest of the sail when it is rolled up. No matter where you sail, it is important to cover sails when not in use. Acrylic fabrics, which have very good UV stability, are generally used for such items as mainsail covers.

★

C H A P T E R 4

THE MAKING AND APPLICATION OF MODERN SAILCLOTH

★ Now that we know the desirable and undesirable characteristics of sailcloth, let's examine the most commonly used materials to see how they measure up and how they came to be that way.

DACRON

Dacron, or polyester as it is more properly called, is the most common type of sailcloth. Most cruising sails are made of Dacron. Dacron is Du Pont's name for its polyester fiber, and since so much polyester sailcloth is woven from Du Pont Dacron, this has become the popular name of the cloth. We use the names Dacron and polyester interchangeably in this book. Du Pont has had good luck—if *luck* is the correct word—with the naming of sailcloths. Mylar and Kevlar are names of other Du Pont products. Mylar is the Du Pont name for oriented-polyester film, which is manufactured by several other manufacturers around the world, and Kevlar is the Du Pont name for aramid fiber, which is also manufactured in the Netherlands and Japan under different names.

Early synthetic sailcloths were woven with Orlon and nylon. When polyester was first available, it became the clear choice for sailcloth. Its popularity can be accounted for by its low stretch, high strength, and low affinity for water. Polyester, or Dacron, is more durable than nylon in resisting ultraviolet degradation.

The early polyester fabrics looked very much like their cotton predecessors. The weight of the yarns, in both the warp and the filling, and the spacing of the yarns were very similar to cotton, and so the strength of the material and its resistance to stretch were not the major advantages. These pluses were only realized later. The impetus for the change from cotton to polyester was, as noted, simply that polyester did not mildew and would last longer than cotton.

In time, the change to polyester created new opportunities and technologies for improving it. For example, polyester allowed the use of new resins and new textile-finishing techniques. From these techniques, firm finishes were developed. These firm and very firm finishes created very low-stretch cloth and, better still, low stretch in almost all directions. As the loads and distribution of the forces in sails were very poorly understood at this time, this resistance to stretch in all directions was very important. It also made for fine-looking sails.

Later, as the loads and angular distribution of the loads became better understood through a complex computer process called stress mapping, it was possible to design weaves that, when appropriate, relied more on weave geometry for precisely oriented strength and less on resin for overall stretch resistance.

Since this concept is the absolute theme of modern sailmaking, a brief analogy is helpful. Imagine shaking hands with someone. Now suppose, for whatever reason, this person decides to pull you over. It is easiest to resist that pull if the force is in line with your arm. You have to be much stronger to resist the pull if it is at some other angle, and stronger still if you have no idea from which direction the pull is coming. Lack of knowledge about the direction of the pull—before the development of accurate stress maps—is why the early Dacron sails were strong in all directions.

The emphasis in modern sailmaking is to determine the direction(s) of the forces in a sail through stress maps, and then correctly orient the strong fibers to resist the forces—thereby aligning the arm to the pull. This may mean making the threads in one direction much stronger, for example, warp-oriented cloth, which is often used in vertically cut high-aspect-ratio mainsails, and high-aspect-ratio Number 3 jibs, used in heavy air. Another solution is to make the cloth strong in all directions, for example, balanced cloth, used in low-aspect-ratio Number 1 genoas, used in light winds.

The relative aspect ratio of sails—are they short on the foot and tall on the luff (high aspect ratio), or long on the foot and short on the luff (low aspect ratio)?—figures prominently, so this is a good time to define and characterize the term. The aspect ratio of a sail is computed by dividing the luff by the foot. Modern offshore racers carry Number 3 jibs with an aspect ratio up to 3.5:1, and some go as high as 3.75:1; the mains are up to 3.5:1. The mains of cruising boats show an aspect ratio from 2.7 up to 3.5.

The stress mapping of sails shows that in a high-aspect-ratio mainsail, the loads tend to line up clew to head. In a low-aspect Number 1 genoa, the loads spread radially from the clew and swing through gradual arcs toward the head (Figure 4.1 shows simplified stress maps for these two working sails). In a spinnaker, the loads tend to follow the classic radial route from each corner with surprisingly strong loads up the leeches. Unfortunately, it isn't quite so simple as the figure shows, as the precise directions of such loadings change through the wind range and during the useful life of the sail. The knowledge of the location, extent, and direction of the loads resulted in specially tailored weaves in which cloth strength is matched to load.

This is done through the careful selection of different-weight yarns for the warp (the warp runs the length of the roll of cloth) and the use of calculated yarn spacings in the warp and fill (the fill runs across the roll). It is also important to control the distribution of crimp. (Remember that when yarns cross other yarns in a weave or knit, one or both of them will be crimped, or bent, and will be more likely to stretch in that direction.) The weaves gradually became more sophisticated, and different weaves are used for low-aspect Number 1 genoas and high-aspect-ratio (Number 3) blade jibs and mainsails.

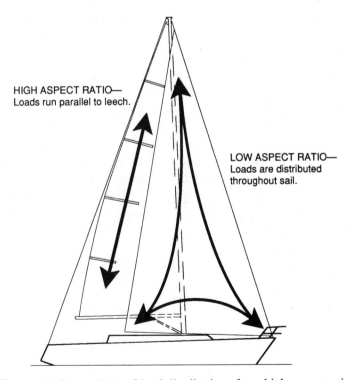

HIGH ASPECT RATIO—
Loads run parallel to leech.

LOW ASPECT RATIO—
Loads are distributed
throughout sail.

Figure 4.1 Comparison of load distributions for a high-aspect-ratio
mainsail and a low-aspect-ratio Number 1 genoa

Let's look for a moment at the way a weave can be tailored to give specific stretch properties. Two concerns when designing a weave are the distribution of crimp between warp and filling of the fabric and the ability of the geometry of the weave to resist bias stretch.

Yarn weight and distribution of crimp determine the stretch resistance in each direction. Addressing yarn weight first, high-aspect sails, such as mainsails, have much of their thread concentration lined up the leech—the direction of the load (see Figure 4.1)—and very little across the sails; whereas low-aspect sails, like Number 1 genoas, have similar-weight threads in both directions. This provides good bias support, which is appropriate as the loads in this low-aspect-ratio sail are more diffuse or spread out.

Turning to crimp, it is, as noted, possible to control the distribution of the crimp in different cloths by varying the weight of the yarns in the warp and fill and by manipulating the yarn spacing. For instance, the opposite photograph shows a weave with very little fill crimp at the expense of extensive warp crimp. This is achieved by selecting warp yarns that are a factor of three to three-and-a-half times smaller than the filling yarns and spacing the warp yarns very close together. During the weaving, the warp yarns tend to form a tube through which run the filling yarns—which are much heavier and less likely to bend. This type of construction, be it fill- or warp-oriented, is commonly used today in mainsail cloth. When bias loading tries to stretch such weaves from their normal perpendicular orientation, resistance comes primarily through mechanical interference of the adjacent warp yarns pressing against one another. This is, as will be apparent, not the most effective mechanism, or geometry, to resist bias stretch.

There is, or should be, a direct relationship between the aspect ratio of a sail and the weight ratio (warp to fill) of the yarns used in the sail's cloth. For example, weaves for a moderate-aspect-ratio Number 2 headsail and a low-aspect-ratio Number 1 are derived by adjusting the warp and the fill yarn weights and their spacing.[1] For instance, the ratio of yarn weights for a moderate-aspect-ratio Number 2 is approximately 2:1, with the warp yarn being half the weight of the filling yarn. For these fabrics, the warp yarns are not spaced quite so closely together as in mainsail fabric, and the filling yarn tends to crimp to a certain extent when woven through the warp. Due to crimp, some of the stretch resistance of the fill direction is compromised, but this

---

[1]The size of a headsail is most precisely described as a percentage of the foretriangle. First overlap is computed by comparing the LP (which stands for Luff Perpendicular and is a line drawn perpendicular to the luff through the clew) with the J measurement (the length base of the foretriangle). If, for example, the J is 15 feet and the LP is 22½ feet, then the headsail is described as a 150 percent genoa (see Figure 7.4, page 137). A Number 1 is typically 150 to 160 percent; a Number 2, 125 to 140 percent; and a Number 3, sometimes termed a blade jib, 95 to 105 percent.

The 8.8-ounce polyester (Dacron) mainsail cloth at 30× magnification. Note low-crimp fill yarns running from lower left to upper right encased by highly crimped warp yarns. This is fill-oriented cloth, suitable for cross-cut mains for about a 40-foot cruising boat. Also note the density of the weave as seen along the cut edges. (Courtesy of Milliken & Company)

gives a warp direction that is somewhat less stretchy than an equivalent-weight mainsail cloth and a lower-stretch bias, which is desirable in moderate- and low-aspect-ratio sails, where the loads are spread out.

The better bias stretch resistance of Dacron comes from the interlocking of the crimped warp and filling yarns. As can be seen in Figure 3.4, page 38, balanced cloth is supported equally in the warp and fill, so when pulled on the bias, the yarn crossings show more resistance to "parallelogramming." They are more likely to remain rectangular or square. Compare this with the highly oriented weave in Figure 3.5, page 39, where there is one strong (thick and uncrimped) yarn and one weak (small and crimped) yarn. This is unbalanced cloth, which shows good stretch resistance to pulls in the direction of the thick threads, but poor resistance to pulls in the direction of the small and crimped yarns as well as to pulls along the bias. The linkage between the warp and fill yarn systems pivots more easily in the case of the highly oriented fabrics. It parallelograms more.

With Number 1 genoa fabrics, we reach the logical conclusion of this trend. Fabrics for such sails are generally woven with the same-weight yarn in both warp and filling and with approximately the same crimp in both directions. The yarns interlock completely, giving the minimum bias stretch for a woven construction, but the filling and warp can be quite stretchy. In these low-aspect headsails, controlling bias stretch is more important as the loads are more diffuse.

While much of this may seem to be the sailmaker's concern, customers should ask their sailmakers how the recommended fabric is going to address the aspect ratio of a particular sail. If, for example, the sailmaker recommends a balanced construction for a high-aspect-ratio Number 3 jib or mainsail, find another sailmaker.

Obviously, weaving technology plays an important role in all of this. Sailcloth is the most tightly woven textile in the world. Polyester sailcloth weaving is a specialized business requiring extensively modified heavy looms to generate the forces necessary to "beat up" the fabric into such a dense construction. Manufacturer's technical data, such as loom motions, timing, and tensions, are closely guarded industrial secrets. Although there are many sailcloth weavers throughout the world, the highest grade, densest, and most desirable polyester fabric is woven by Warwick Mills, a small mill in the southern hills of New Hampshire, which in addition to sailcloth has produced the fabric that covers the Goodyear blimps and the fabric that made up the flotation ring used in the ocean landing of the *Apollo 11* spaceship after its historic visit to the moon. No other weaver in the world has been able to duplicate Warwick's ability to weave dense fabrics with controlled crimp.

Dacron sailcloth is only woven in what is known as a plain weave. This is the type of weave used in bed sheeting, for instance, as opposed to the twill weave used in blue jeans or the satin weave used in fashion scarves. In plain weave, which is the most simple weave, every yarn passes over and under every other yarn (see Figure 3.4).[2] When the plain weave is balanced, you obtain the highest number of yarn crossings per square inch and, as discussed, the best possible bias control.

When polyester sailcloth is removed from the loom, it is not recognizable as sailcloth. In this state it is known as greige cloth, which is derived from the old French term for raw silk. In the United States this is more commonly called gray cloth. A complicated multistep process known as finishing turns greige fabric into sailcloth as we know it. In finishing, the cloth is cleaned to prepare the fiber surfaces to accept resin. Next, it is impregnated with resin, usually melamine, which bonds the fibers together to resist stretch, and it is

---

[2]In a twill weave, the yarns do not pass over and under every other yarn, but pass over and under more than one. This makes for a stretchy bias and thus comfortable pants. More yarns are skipped in a satin weave, which gives it a shiny appearance.

treated with heat and pressure to further increase the fabric density and to interlock the fibers to decrease stretch.

Some of this warrants further discussion. In scouring, or cleaning, the fabric is simply dragged through a bath of hot water with detergent. This removes sizing and oils, which are applied to prevent the threads from breaking during the weaving process. The fabric is then dipped into an aqueous bath of melamine resin, which serves to lock in the woven geometry and to decrease stretch. Melamine, a very common plastic resin, shows up in our homes as Formica and in the plastic plates found in TV dinners. Melamine is chosen for sailcloth because of its toughness, clarity, and durability.

Resins used to treat polyester, or Dacron, sailcloth have evolved over the years. You might recall from Chapter 2, "An Artist and a Scientist—The History of Modern Sailmaking," that the earliest finishing chemicals applied to polyester consisted of dispersed silicates, similar to sand. Microscopic grains of silicate were applied to the sailcloth in a slurry. The grains of silicate remaining in the weave were simply intended to roughen the surface and therefore increase the friction between filaments and fibers. This rudimentary attempt by Ted Hood to decrease bias stretch was not wholly successful because the sharp sand crystals tended to cut the filaments, sooner or later weakening the fabric.

Soon after this, the melamine-based process, which is most commonly used today, was developed. Some polyester sailcloth, in addition to or in lieu of being treated with melamine, is coated with a very firm urethane coating. This coating spreads over the surface of the fabric and cures on it to form a very low-stretch material. This cloth, sometimes called Yarn-Tempered, Duroperm, or HTP, is used primarily in sails for racing dinghies. Other manufacturers, particularly those making higher quality cloth, apply other additives, silicone or wax, to the melamine in order to repel water, improve durability, and give the cloth a more kindly hand, or feel. If Dacron is the material of choice, the dinghy racer—for whom holding shape is more important than handling—would likely opt for fabric made with a urethane coating. The cruising sailor—for whom the feel of the cloth is important—would generally choose cloth made with the softer, more pliable melamine-impregnation process.

There has been an evolution from nonreactive silicates, which simply increased internal friction in the weave, to plastics, applied in an aqueous bath, that impregnate the weave and fill the interstices between yarns and filaments, to a hard urethane coating that cures on the surface of the cloth and further resists stretch. The next step, as we will see shortly, was laminated sailcloth, or polyester/Mylar, which precipitated a revolution in sailmaking that has affected both cruiser and racer alike.

Whether coated or impregnated, the polyester fabric is dried and then heat-set. In heat setting, the fabric is passed through an oven at temperatures approaching 400° F. Polyester yarn shrinks at these high temperatures, causing the fabric to contract 20 to 25 percent. This makes what is already a densely woven fabric denser still, further decreasing bias stretch. Finally, in calendering, the cloth is passed between two rollers under very high pressure. Typically one is a heated steel roll, the other very hard fiber. These rollers can be several feet in diameter and are pressed together at forces exceeding 50 tons. Calendering serves to press the warp and filling yarns into one another, causing them to form about each other and further locking the geometry of the weave.

POLYESTER/MYLAR

Mylar is a film formed by melting polyester resin, which is then extruded. When the polymer is melted and extruded, the long molecules of the polymer are oriented randomly, both in the plane of the film and perpendicular to the plane of the film (see Figure 4.2). Next the material is mechanically drawn, or stretched, in both the warp and fill directions. This has the effect of stretching the molecules and changing them from a random orientation to a bidirectional orientation. The molecules line up primarily in the two directions in which they were pulled. In these two directions, the molecules are more solidly linked and have more resistance to stretch; furthermore, a greater number of all the molecules in the film are ready to resist stretch. The result is a very low-stretch polymer film.

Simply applying resins to sailcloth, as occurs with impregnated Dacron, could not achieve the same low-stretch characteristic because the molecular orientation in these simple resins is random. (In fact, it is impossible to apply oriented polymers to fabrics because the orientation must be done in a separate process.) The next step in sailcloth evolution was to form the fabric, called the substrate, and oriented resin in separate processes and then bond them together. Thus began the revolution in laminated sailcloth, or polyester/Mylar, in the 1970s and 1980s.

When laminated sailcloth first appeared, there was controversy over its performance, utility, cost, and even safety. There was also confusion over the properties of the new laminated cloth. However, sails made from even the earliest polyester/Mylars were almost always faster than the Dacron sails they replaced. The reason for this was at first a matter of great debate. Some claimed it was simply because the polyester/Mylar surface was smoother and caused less aerodynamic drag. Others claimed that it was because the material was

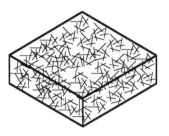

After extrusion, polyester molecules have a random orientation.

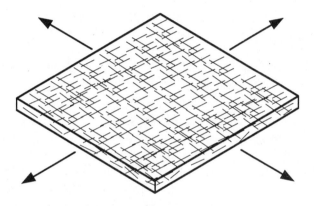

Mechanically drawing in both directions produces a thinner film with the molecules oriented bidirectionally—parallel to the drawing directions.

Figure 4.2 Molecular orientation of Mylar film

lighter and would stretch less, thus better holding its designed shape, even in gusts. This latter thesis proved correct because, as we now know, stretch resistance and then light weight are the most important characteristics of a triangular sail.

Confusion about the properties of polyester/Mylar created hostility, even burning controversy. Many class associations outlawed it, saying it was too expensive and delicate, and lacked durability. In the case of the early laminated materials, these charges were certainly true, but development continued in the face of the storm. Durability and utility were improved, and ultimately laminated sailcloth was accepted. This was primarily because sails made of these materials are nearly always faster than polyester sails. Today sails, including cruising sails, made from laminated sailcloth typically last as long, if not longer, and hold their shape better than sails made from resinated or coated Dacron sailcloth. Given the recent advances in the durability of light, low-stretch Mylar laminates, choosing between polyester/Mylar and Dacron for a cruising sail will be chiefly a matter of price. Even then, it is a close call since a polyester/Mylar sail is only about 10 percent more expensive than an equivalent Dacron sail.

The earliest attempt to build Mylar sails was in 1964 when pure (unlaminated) Mylar spinnakers were made for America's Cup yachts *Constellation* and *American Eagle*. These sails were unsuccessful because the material was too delicate. The next serious attempt at using Mylar film was in headsails built for the 12-Meter *Enterprise*, skippered primarily by Lowell North in the 1977 America's Cup trials. Noah Lamport, the brother of Sol Lamport, an early pioneer in polyester sailcloth, laminated Mylar to both sides of some lightweight Dacron material to provide it with tear strength. This was known as garbage-bag material because the Mylar used was the familiar dark green garbage-bag color. The adhesive used in the laminating process in the early polyester/Mylar was the fatal flaw, and therefore, delamination plagued these early sails.

By 1980, several polyester/Mylar sailcloths, consisting of lightweight woven substrates laminated to one side of Mylar, were on the market. In these laminates, the Mylar film itself was the primary load-carrying element in the material, and the woven substrates, almost always made of polyester yarn, served mainly to protect the Mylar from tearing and to provide some seam strength in the stitching. Laminated sailcloth designs proliferated rapidly in the first half of the 1980s, and today we have a broad range of products from which to choose. Most of the modern products might be better called fiber-reinforced Mylar films, because in a major shift, the polyester fiber component of the laminate (the woven substrate) is now the primary load-carrying element, and the Mylar serves to prevent stretch in directions off the thread lines. Laminating techniques and adhesives have been perfected so that delamination is now uncommon. When it does occur, the cause may be faulty manufacturing or the use of the sail above its designated wind range.

The load-carrying polyester filament is melted and then extruded. However, whereas Mylar film is pulled in two directions, polyester filament is only pulled in one (see Figure 4.3). Although the unidirectional polyester filament is lower in stretch than the bidirectionally oriented Mylar film, after the polyester yarn is woven, it is susceptible to bias stretch due to crimp. Therefore, it tends to be higher stretch in almost all directions when compared with pure Mylar film. The best of both worlds can be achieved by marrying the unidirectional polyester fiber and the bidirectional Mylar film in such a way as to

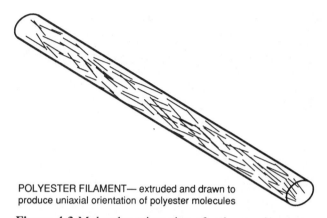

POLYESTER FILAMENT— extruded and drawn to
produce uniaxial orientation of polyester molecules

Figure 4.3 Molecular orientation of polyester filament

realize the most desirable properties of each. The polyester fiber shows good resistance to stretch on the thread line; the more balanced Mylar film shows good resistance to stretch off the thread line. This is what is done in the finest Mylar-laminated materials today. Through weaving, knitting, or simply bonding, a suitable form of polyester fiber is added to Mylar film, thereby reinforcing the most highly loaded direction of the material.

The lamination process itself is quite simple—though there can be many variations—and there is quite a bit of technique involved in making it work. As shown in Figure 4.4, a carefully measured film of solvent-based adhesive is first applied to the Mylar. This then enters an oven where the solvent is evaporated. The Mylar film leaving the oven has a coating of uncured adhesive with little or no solvent remaining. It is then mated to the polyester and passed between heated rollers. The pressure of the rollers causes the adhesive to flow around the substrate fibers, and the heat of the rollers activates the adhesive. Laminates involving more than two plies, for instance, Mylar film with polyester fabric on both sides, require multiple passes through the manufacturing process to bond all the layers. The variables in laminating are in choice of adhesive, quantity of adhesive, and speeds, pressures, and temperatures of the process.

Laminated sailcloth comes in many forms. The primary categories are

Laid-up yarns
Woven scrims
Knits
Fabrics

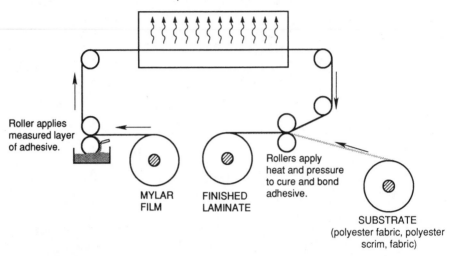

Figure 4.4 Schematic of the lamination of Mylar and polyester

Laid-up Yarns The lightest-weight polyester/Mylar materials (.5 ounce and lower) are made by a patented process owned by Orcon, a company in Union City, California. In this process .25-mil (.00025-inch) and .5-mil (.0005-inch) Mylar films are reinforced with fibers, or yarns, that are individually glued to the film. Imagine a machine that takes one thread, puts glue on it, and then pastes the individual thread to the Mylar. (Another company does a similar process by hand.) Reduced to its essentials, this is the laid-up yarn process. Obviously, it has to be done more than a few times to make sailcloth. These very delicate laid-up yarn materials are suitable only for the lightest-weight spinnakers and staysails.

Laid-up yarns are used in fabrics where light weight is most important. An advantage of this construction is the straight and uncrimped yarns in the two directions. Disadvantages are that tear strength is less than woven scrims (see next page) and yarn spacing is sometimes uneven.

One new example of the laid-up yarn process is multidirectional fabric. In the process, a third yarn is used in the fabric substrate. Thus, the yarns no longer cross at 90-degree angles, and the fabric, as one might guess, shows good bias control. In this instance, the fiber, rather than the film, is relied on more to control bias stretch. The fabric is still very experimental.

Woven Scrims Scrims, with Mylar laminated on both sides, are also generally reserved for lighter-weight laminates of 3 ounces per sailmaker's yard and lower. The term *scrim* applies to any lightweight, open-weave fabric. Open weave means that scrims have measurable space between adjacent yarns. The advantage of a scrim is that it permits the manufacture of lightweight fabric—always desirable—while using heavy yarns. Heavy yarns provide good tear strength and good stitch-holding ability. Another advantage of scrims is that two Mylar films encase the scrim yarns and actually touch in the holes between the weave, bonding it very securely. When compared with laid-up yarns, a woven scrim has better tear strength, but due to the crimp imparted by the weaving process, it is slightly more susceptible to stretch. That said, since the weave is so open, there isn't much crimp (the yarns cross at such gentle angles), so the difference in stretch when compared with laid-up yarns is slight.

Knits Scrims aren't the only choice for lightweight laminated sailcloth; it is also common to see "knits" with Mylar on both sides. These knitted constructions are often called weft-, or fill-, insertion knits. In this process, warp yarns and filling yarns are laid on top of one another, but do not interweave. A third, very light yarn is then knitted around both warp and weft to hold all the yarns in place. This system has the advantage of very low crimp in both directions as the warp and fill yarns do not intertwine, although some crimp is imparted by the light knitting yarn. Knits are generally very uniform with even yarn spacing (unlike scrims, whose weave is slightly less uniform), because they are positively held in place by the light knitting yarn (see Figure 13.7, page 321). Similar to scrims, knits have the advantage of light weight while allowing the use of heavier yarns, which, as described, provide good tear strength and seam holding. They are also very durable due to the spaces in the fabric where the two Mylar films meet.

One disadvantage of both scrims and knits is low flexibility. Because it is necessary to laminate Mylar to both sides of the construction to protect the rough surface of the scrim or the knit, the total laminate tends to get fairly thick and therefore loses flexibility. An advantage, however, of both scrims and knits is that they are relatively cheap to produce.

Fabrics Another common form of laminated sailcloth has fabric laminated to film, either one sided (see photograph on page 60) or with fabric on both sides of the film (see photograph on page 61). Unlike the early fabric-film laminates, the fabrics in these modern laminates have an important structural function. They are specially designed to be laminated to Mylar and generally have no crimp in one direction. These are usually lightweight taffetas (plain weaves), although some use twill weaves to decrease crimp in some directions. They are most commonly warp oriented, which means that the lowest stretch direction is in the warp orientation. These laminates tend to be very flexible, with high performance and very low stretch.

Because flexibility is good, these fabric laminates are used for heavier-weight cloth, above 3 ounces. They are durable and stand up well to surface abrasion and tearing, and they hold seams well. This is particularly true in the case of two-sided laminates. Because less adhesive is used in the laminating, they also tend to be lighter in weight than scrims and knit laminates. In the case of scrims and knits, adhesive is sometimes trapped between the films.

Ratio of Fiber to Film   The ratio of fiber to film—polyester to Mylar—in a laminate is an important consideration to the sailmaker in determining the stretch ratio of the material. In high-aspect-ratio sails, like Number

The 3.2-ounce Norlam (polyester/Mylar) cloth at 30× magnification. Mylar is on bottom; polyester (taffeta) is on top. Note the low-crimp warp yarns running from upper left to lower right in this warp-oriented fabric. (Courtesy of Milliken & Company)

Norlam (soft polyester/Mylar) at 30× magnification. This is a two-sided laminate; the Mylar is in the middle, and the polyester (taffeta) is on both the top and bottom. Again, note the low-crimp warp yarns running from upper left to lower right in this warp-oriented fabric. (Courtesy of Milliken & Company)

3s or mainsails, where through computer-generated stress maps the loading is well documented, it is possible to use less film and simply orient the fibers in the load direction. In lower-aspect-ratio sails, however, where the load is diffuse, or in mainsails, which can be drastically reshaped by mast bend, Cunningham, outhaul, and so on, it is important to use more film to spread out the stretch resistance and strength of the material.

Laminated sailcloth gives the sailcloth manufacturer more freedom in working with various fibers, fiber orientations, and fabric-forming techniques. This is because it is no longer necessary to worry as much about the fabric density and the bias stretch as in the old days when Dacron sailcloth was the only choice. This has opened the door to the use of exotic fibers such as Kevlar, which is Du Pont's aramid fiber (shortened from aromatic polyamid), and Spectra, which is a very high-strength and low-stretch fiber made by Allied Signal Corporation.

KEVLAR/MYLAR

Kevlar fiber is about eight times less stretchy than polyester yarn (see Figure 4.5). Such miracles, however, come at a price; it is also ten times as expensive as polyester yarn. Kevlar is expensive for a very good reason. The filaments are formed in a very complicated process, wherein the polymer is liquefied in sulfuric acid (it cannot be melted) and extruded into filaments. The solvent must then be removed from the polymer, purified, and recycled. All of the machinery must handle extremely corrosive low-pH sulfuric acid solutions. Kevlar is a difficult fiber to apply in sailcloth, but its ultimate resistance to stretch makes the effort worthwhile.

Kevlar is naturally gold in color. It cannot be dyed or colored using customary textile techniques. Upon exposure to light, this color rapidly changes to brown or golden brown. The change happens so quickly that, for example, a pair of scissors left on a new roll of Kevlar/Mylar over a lunch break leaves an outline on the fabric.

Ted Hood was the first to use Kevlar in sailcloth when it was known in the early 1970s during initial commercial development as Fiber B. Kevlar was used in both the warp and the fill of these experimental fabrics. This application of Kevlar in both directions turned out to be a mistake—indeed the fatal flaw—because crimp diminished the low-stretch properties of the yarn, and the crossed yarns tended to abrade each other, causing the fabric to break. These early failures and the extremely high price of the fiber led manufacturers

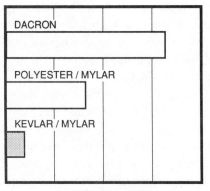

Figure 4.5 Stretch vs. weight of sailcloth

to doubt that Kevlar would ever be used successfully in sailcloth. As with polyester/Mylar, there were attempts to ban its use.

In the early 1980s, the yacht *Merrythought* had a dramatic-looking mainsail, made with experimental Kevlar cloth. It was, oddly enough, black. In those days, ultraviolet degradation was considered the major problem of Kevlar, so the fabric was treated with carbon black to protect it from the sun. It turned out that ultraviolet light was much less of a problem than flexing, and UV-protective coatings have now been eliminated.

Running Kevlar in one direction—either the warp or the fill—and polyester in the other and then marrying the resultant fabric to Mylar opened the door to the use of Kevlar/Mylar in sailmaking (see the below photograph). It

Weaving the Kevlar material. For reasons of cost and in order to minimize abrasion, Kevlar is typically run in one direction, usually the warp (long direction), as it is being done here. Polyester is in the fill direction. (Courtesy of North Sails, Inc.)

has been, like cotton, then Egyptian cotton, Dacron, and polyester/Mylar, a miracle material.

In addition to being low stretch, Kevlar/Mylar is also about five times stronger than Dacron of equivalent weight (see Figure 4.6) and essentially has no yield point. The elongation of the yarn itself is perfectly elastic and recoverable up to the breaking point. The breaking point occurs at a very low (3 percent) elongation. For this reason, Kevlar/Mylar is susceptible to breaking in shock-loading situations.

The primary problem with Kevlar/Mylar sailcloth is the degradation of the yarn through sharp flexing and creasing. Notice racing boats luffing their sails when they arrive early at a starting line, and you'll see flexing in action. Creasing is less dramatic. As sails are handled, they tend to crease at certain points, which get creased again and again. The yarn can degrade in compression, and after thousands of cycles, its strength is lost.

When Kevlar was first used for sailcloth, it was fairly common to see sails break due to these problems, but in modern Kevlar/Mylar sailcloth, it is extremely unusual to see this happen—simply because in selecting a fabric with sufficient weight and yarn to control the stretch and shape of a sail, sailmakers automatically choose fabrics that are many times stronger than otherwise might be necessary. As the strength of the fabric degrades, this fail-safe margin ensures that the fabric is still much stronger than it needs to be.

There are two forms of Kevlar, Kevlar 29 and Kevlar 49, each coming in a variety of yarn weights. Although the technical differences between them

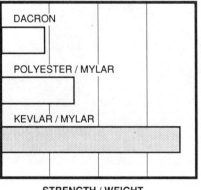

Figure 4.6 Strength vs. weight of sailcloth

are kept a trade secret by Du Pont, Kevlar 49 is twice as resistant to stretch as Kevlar 29. Nevertheless, Kevlar 29 is used in sailcloth, because Kevlar 49 is much more sensitive to flexing and thus less durable.

Kevlar is only used in laminated sailcloth. It does not shrink when heated and is too delicate to be woven with the "high beat-up" technique used to make Dacron sails. Therefore, it is impossible to control bias stretch without some sort of film lamination. Kevlar fiber is distributed in laminates in many of the same ways as polyester fiber. Woven scrims, knits, and woven fabrics are formed from Kevlar and laminated to Mylar, which is used either one or two sided. Kevlar, as discussed, is generally used in only one direction in the fabric (see the following two photographs). This is for a variety of reasons, some financial, some technical. First, Kevlar is very expensive. Furthermore, reinforcing more than one major direction in a laminated fabric is generally unnecessary. Then, as noted, when used in more than one direction, Kevlar tends to abrade the fiber. Finally, when Kevlar is used in both directions, both

In this Norlam 180T2 Kevlar at 30× magnification, note the nearly zero-crimp warp (Kevlar) yarns running from lower left to upper right and the highly crimped polyester fill yarns. Running Kevlar in the warp and the lack of crimp in this orientation indicate that this is a warp-oriented Kevlar/Mylar. See the following photo for detail. (Courtesy of Milliken & Company)

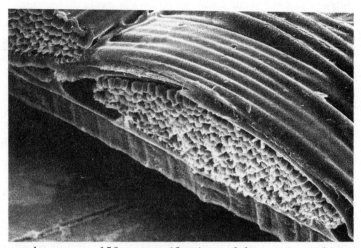

This is an enlargement, 150 × magnification, of the previous photo. Note the small filament diameter of Kevlar yarns compared with the polyester. Also note 2-mil Mylar laminated to bottom of cloth. (Courtesy of Milliken & Company)

yarns crimp, which increases stretch. The sailmaker thus plans the panel orientation of sails to orient the Kevlar in the direction of the primary loads.

Early Kevlar/Mylar sailcloth was manufactured so that the Kevlar yarns made up the fill direction, in what is called fill-oriented cloth. At that time, the best polyester sailcloth and the early laminates were all fill oriented, and sailmakers were accustomed to shaping their sails with horizontal panels. This aligned the strong fill fibers along the leech, the direction of the load. A problem arose, however, because with this cross-cut panel orientation, the major loads in the sails cross many seams. The Kevlar/Mylar fabric was so low in stretch that the small amount of slippage in the seams became a larger problem than the stretch of the cloth itself. Today, most Kevlar-based sailcloth has the Kevlar oriented in the warp direction. With this type of orientation, sails are made with vertical panels with fewer seams crossing the Kevlar, and once again cloth stretch, rather than seam slippage, becomes the determining factor in the control of sail shape.

Kevlar/Mylar sailcloth was such a large step forward in controlling sail shape and stretch that today it is virtually impossible to win a major ocean race without using sails made of the best Kevlar/Mylar sailcloth. In 1980, *Australia I*, the Australian challenger for the America's Cup, had a very radical

KEVLAR CONTENT (DENIER PER INCH)
REQUIRED FOR RACING SAILS

Boat Size, LOA	20'	25'	30'	35'
Masthead Main	5,000	7,000	10,000	
Fractional Main	5,000	7,000	7,000	10,000
Light #1	—	—	—	—
Medium #1	2,500	5,000	6,000	7,000
Heavy #1	4,000	7,000	8,000	11,000
#2	—	—	—	—
#3	12,500	18,000	21,000	27,500

Boat Size, LOA	40'	50'	70'	80'
Masthead Main	20,000	30,000	50,000	55,000
Fractional Main	15,000	25,000	40,000	50,000
Light #1	5,000	7,000	9,000	10,000
Medium #1	9,000	11,000	14,000	16,000
Heavy #1	12,500	16,000	20,000	23,000
#2	17,500	22,000	28,000	32,000
#3	32,000	40,000	55,000	62,000

bendy mast. This was patterned after the bendy rig of Britain's *Lionheart* and was done for two reasons: one, to maximize sail area, and unmeasured sail area at that; and, two, to make the main more elliptical in shape in order to minimize induced drag (discussed in Chapter 6). The Australians needed the best Kevlar/Mylar sailcloth to make sails for this rig. For these sails, the Kevlar cloth was woven in Germany and then laminated to the Mylar in the United States. A protest was filed, and the New York Yacht Club disallowed the use of this material. In those days, there was a rule that the cloth used by foreign challengers could not be American-made. The Australians were forced to use an inferior Kevlar/Mylar cloth.

Ironically, in that same America's Cup, *Freedom* used a Kevlar/Mylar main that was not well bonded. So bad was it that the Mylar film moved due to the soft nature of the glue. We had many concerns in the summer of 1980 that the sail would deteriorate, dramatically change shape, or even break. As unbelievable as it sounds, that sail turned out to be our favorite racing main.

This shows that no matter how carefully sails are designed and manufactured, some aspects of sailmaking have more to do with art than science.

In 1983, when warp-oriented Kevlar-reinforced laminates had just been developed in the United States, the New York Yacht Club waived its rule forbidding challengers to use American-manufactured cloth for that year's America's Cup. *Australia II* made excellent use of American-manufactured warp-oriented Kevlar/Mylar sailcloth. The boat, skippered by John Bertrand, beat us and won the best of seven races and took the Cup, which had resided in America since 1851 when the yacht *America* won the race around the Isle of Wight. *Australia II* was unquestionably a breakthrough boat with a radical keel, but her excellent vertical-cut sails, made of warp-oriented Kevlar/Mylar fabric, were a consequential part of the entire effort.

Kevlar/Mylar cloth comes in a wide variety of designs. Cloth weight is important but designs from various manufacturers differ, so it is generally better to consider the Kevlar content measured in denier per inch rather than in weight. (Denier is the weight of the fiber in grams per 9,000 meters.) The table on page 67 shows a fairly typical measurement of the yarn weight of Kevlar used in sails for boats ranging from 20 to 80 feet.

Many sailors, however, may be more familiar with cloth weight than with denier. Figure 4.7 is a graph relating denier to cloth weight in ounces per sailmaker's yard.

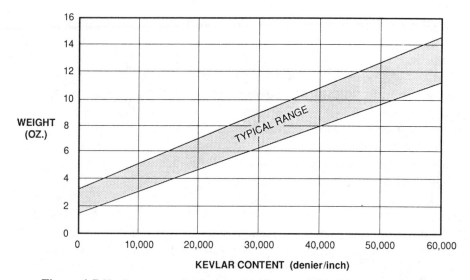

Figure 4.7 Kevlar content in denier related to more familiar cloth weight

SPECTRA/MYLAR

There are other high-performance, ultra-low-stretch fibers on the market such as carbon, ceramic, and even glass. None of these are appropriate for sailcloth because they are too brittle and break easily in response to flexing. But one new fiber, which has only been available for a few years, shows some promise for use in sailcloth. This is Spectra.

Spectra was developed in state laboratories in Holland many years ago. Allied Signal Corporation acquired the technology and perfected the industrial process for producing this type of yarn. It is an unusual yarn, to be sure: a most highly oriented polyethylene polymer, characterized by very low stretch, similar to Kevlar, but much lighter. Kevlar is 1.41 times as dense as water (specific gravity of 1.41), whereas Spectra is .98 the density of water. In fact, Spectra will actually float. The stretch-to-weight ratio of Spectra is therefore much better than that of Kevlar. Spectra/Mylar also has the advantage of not degrading when flexed sharply, like Kevlar.

However, Spectra/Mylar has its Achilles' heel. When Spectra/Mylar is loaded to 30 percent or more of its breaking strength, it will creep—stretch permanently—over time. Thus, if Spectra/Mylar sailcloth is very highly loaded (30 percent of the breaking strength is a very high load) for a long time, it will stretch permanently, and the sail will lose its shape. Some early Spectra-reinforced sailcloth is on the market at this time. To prevent creep, it must be designed and used carefully to avoid loading it too highly. The manufacturer is working on this problem, and Spectra/Mylar sailcloth will have a place in the sport.

NYLON

Recently nylon celebrated its fiftieth anniversary, and it still reigns supreme in off-the-wind sails. Developed by Du Pont in 1938, nylon is a plastic that can be extruded, injection-molded, or formed into fiber. Nylon fiber is very strong, but typically has somewhat higher stretch than polyester fiber. Like flax, nylon is strong, but somewhat stretchy, and is best used in off-the-wind sails, such as spinnakers, the cruising equivalents, and bloopers.

In these sails, which are cut very full, light weight and strength are more important than stretch resistance. When sailing with the wind, the wind pressure in the sail is relatively low; thus in light winds, the sail can droop under its own weight, creating less than optimum aerodynamics.

When manufacturing cloth at such extremely low weights as is typical with nylon, strength and porosity become limiting factors. Nylon has high strength to weight and fortunately shows fairly high elastic (recoverable) elongation. This makes it less susceptible to breaking under shock loading, which occurs, for example, when the sail fills suddenly. Porosity is limited by using yarns with a high number of fine filaments, which spread out when finished (see the below photograph). Some nylon sailcloth is coated to control porosity. As resin is less expensive than nylon fabric, this coating is a less costly option, but a fabric with less fiber and more resin will not be as strong as an equivalent-weight fabric formed entirely from fiber.

Nylon is easily dyed in bright colors; in fact, it is more easily dyed than polyester yarn. Sailcloth manufacturers use this desirable characteristic to supply nylon in an array of rainbow hues.

Nylon fabrics are not tightly woven, nor are they heat-set to the same degree as polyester to consolidate them into a very dense weave. Therefore, nylon fabric is often subject to very high stretch on the bias. Sailmakers must take this bias stretch into account when designing sails made from nylon.

Bainbridge/Aquabatten 30/20 nylon at 90× magnification. Note how yarn filaments spread to form a single layer to minimize porosity. Porosity, which allows air to leak through the cloth, is a consideration in light nylon spinnaker cloth. (Courtesy of Milliken & Company)

Modern spinnaker cloth is warp oriented, and large spinnakers are made from a large number of narrow pie-shaped panels with the strong warp threads aligned to the loads radiating from the corners of the sail. The result is the familiar tri-radial sail (see Figure 11.1, page 248). With this type of construction, there is almost no bias load on the cloth.

Nylon is finished using some of the same techniques as polyester. For example, it is first scoured to remove weave sizing and oils. After scouring, nylon sailcloth is frequently dyed and then impregnated with the same melamine resin used on polyester. Some nylon products are coated with urethane or silicon, either in lieu of or in addition to the melamine resins. In some cases, the coating is used to achieve low porosity in very lightweight fabrics where the fiber density alone is not sufficient to completely cover the surface.

After application, the coatings and resins are cured using high temperatures. This heat-sets the fabric, but nylon is not allowed to shrink nearly as much as polyester. Finally, nylon is calendered to spread out the filaments in the yarns to decrease the porosity of these lightweight fabrics. Calendering also locks the fibers together to minimize bias stretch as much as possible.

It is amazing how little a well-designed and well-constructed spinnaker stretches in view of the actual stretch characteristics of the fabric. This is because modern spinnaker fabrics are stronger by design (i.e., warp oriented and tri-radial in construction) and lower in stretch by the nature of the weaving and finishing.

CHAPTER 5

A NEW VIEW OF SAILBOAT AERODYNAMICS

★   For sailors, it is as close to a universal lesson as there is. It begins: "A sail is like an airplane wing. . . ." If you missed that lesson early in your sailing career, you likely heard its antecedent in sixth-grade science: "An airplane flies because air passing over the curved upper surface of its wings has to travel a longer distance than the air passing under the flat lower surface. And since it has to go farther, it has to go faster to reach the trailing edge at the same time as its 'brother' particle. This difference in distance causes a difference in speed that causes a difference in pressure—low pressure on the upper side and high pressure on the lower —and there is lift or suction."

This has everything a good explanation requires: it is neat and simple, and it makes sense—more or less. In fact, the phenomenon it describes, high-speed flow and low pressure on one side of a foil and low-speed flow and high pressure on the other, does create suction or lift. Sailors often label this phenomenon Bernoulli's principle, after Daniel Bernoulli, the Swiss-born mathematician, who lived from 1700 to 1782. In 1738, Bernoulli declared that when airflow accelerates, the pressure goes down, and conversely, when the airflow slows, the pressure rises. More than 250 years later, Bernoulli is still right. However, what causes the speed to increase on the top, or leeward, side and decrease on the bottom, or weather, side remains a source of considerable confusion.

A closer look at the popular explanation of why sailboats sail to weather and airplanes fly raises as many questions as it answers. For example: Why does the air on the upper surface have to travel faster to get to the trailing edge at the same time as its brother particle? In fact, computer studies reveal that an air particle on the upper surface actually arrives at the trailing edge *ahead* of its brother particle on the lower side. Also, what is a "brother" particle anyway, and why this overpowering need for a family reunion? Further, if the upper surface has to be curved and the lower surface flat, why can an airplane fly upside down? And then you turn to a sail and realize it is not really like an airplane wing at all. Rather, it is a very thin membrane, and there is hardly any measurable difference in distance across the leeward and windward surfaces. So for a sail, the difference in distance can't be the cause of lift. In fact, if you put a perfectly flat board at an angle to wind, there will be lift—indeed, sufficient lift for a sailboat to sail to windward and sufficient lift even to fly.

Then there is the so-called slot effect—the second universal "truth" in sailing. The slot, the area between the overlapping headsail and the front of the main, is said in traditional sailing literature to do three things: One, the jib causes the air over the lee side of the main to have a much higher velocity, increasing the partial vacuum and hence the efficiency of the mainsail. Two, the higher-velocity air in the slot "revitalizes" the air over the main, which would otherwise be in a separated or stalled condition. Three, the increased velocity in the slot is a result of the fact that the distance between the jib's leech and the main is much less than the distance between the headstay and the mast, but it must accommodate the same flow per unit of time. This phenomenon creates a squeezing—often described as the venturi effect—that speeds the flow on the lee side of the main, increasing its efficiency. Despite the popularity and extremely long life of this explanation, the truth is that none of it is as described. In fact, if the wind is speeded up in the slot, the likelihood of the main stalling, ceasing to produce lift, is greater.

A fresh look is obviously called for, not simply because understanding why a sailboat sails to weather is important to those who think of themselves as sailors, but because without this understanding there is little or no basis for sail trim. Lacking a solid technical foundation, sail trim becomes merely a practiced response to conditions. It takes forever to assimilate—there are that many variables—and the lore that has been so painstakingly memorized is worthless when faced with changes in the wind, so to speak.

The discussion is far-reaching. Have you, for example, ever really questioned why a mainsail has battens and why longer battens are better than shorter ones; why a headsail is more efficient than a mainsail; why, when overpowered, headsail area is reduced before the main is reefed; why the safe-leeward position is advantageous; why the keels of modern racing boats and most cruising boats show a high aspect ratio and why, of late, race boat keels show a curved trailing edge; why a mast is bent and straightened as a function of wind direction and speed; why a yacht designer positions the mast and keel so there is some degree of weather helm; why draft-forward sails make a sailboat easier to steer upwind; why draft-aft sails can make a sailboat faster upwind but harder to steer; why dinghies and small boats are more lively than larger boats; why cruising boats are easier to steer than racing boats; why sails are progressively twisted (the trailing edge allowed to sag to leeward) from bottom to top; why sails get deeper (show increased camber) from bottom to top; why deeper sails are faster in some conditions and at some wind angles and slower in others; why, when sailing upwind, the main is trimmed more than the genoa; why a reach is the fastest point of sail; why racing boats carry so many headsails and spinnakers; and why the position of the headsail's lead is different for different points of sail?

The experienced sailor is likely familiar with most or all of these situations. Few, however, could explain why this is so or why that is done. The technical groundwork to answer such diverse questions will be established in this and the next chapters.

FLYING A FLAT PLATE

Earlier we said that a flat board, or plate, can provide sufficient lift for an airplane to fly and a sailboat to sail upwind. Let's fly that flat board, which can be thought of as an airfoil with no difference in distance over the top and bottom surfaces. We choose to fly a flat plate, rather than a curved sail or airplane wing, because if we can get that shape—or that explanation—to fly, so to speak, we can certainly get a wing to fly an airplane or a sail to drive a sailboat to windward. Also, using a flat plate avoids the added complication, at this early stage, of discussing three-dimensional shapes (camber, twist, etc.), which are not easy to visualize.[1]

Wind possesses energy, and it is wind, of course, or moving air, that fuels the process that is typically called lift. To an aerodynamicist, air is considered a fluid like water. Thus the laws of fluid dynamics apply to both elements. Considering air and water as fluids, we can make the following general remark: fluids have a small amount of viscosity. Viscosity can be thought of simply as stickiness. If, for example, you aim a hose at a sail, some of the water will stick to the surface of the sail. Air behaves the same way when it passes over the surface of a sail. Some of it sticks to the surface and is, in fact, carried along for the ride. This very thin but very important region where the air sticks to the sail is termed the boundary layer.

---

[1]The authors are most indebted to Arvel E. Gentry, of Boeing Commercial Airplane, for the explanation of circulation and the most important explanation of the relationship between jib and mainsail. Gentry first presented his findings on the multiple-airfoil theory as it applies to sails at an AIAA Ancient Interface Symposium in 1971. In 1973 he published a series of articles on the subject in *Sail* magazine. These articles were included in the book *The Best of Sail Trim*, published by Sail Publications, Inc.

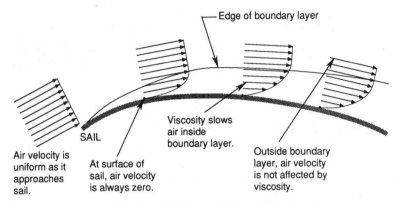

Edge of boundary layer

SAIL

Air velocity is uniform as it approaches sail.

At surface of sail, air velocity is always zero.

Viscosity slows air inside boundary layer.

Outside boundary layer, air velocity is not affected by viscosity.

Figure 5.1 Boundary-layer flow

Because of viscosity, or stickiness, the air that touches a sail stops (see Figure 5.1) and is carried along by it. Over this layer of air passes a second layer, which moves slightly faster than the first, and over this passes a third layer that moves slightly faster than the second, and so on. Beyond the boundary layer is the external flow, where the air velocity is not affected by viscosity. (The length of the arrows in the diagram is indicative of speed.)

Now that we have a cursory understanding of viscosity, let's pretend for a moment that it does not exist. There are computer programs that accomplish this bit of magic quite nicely. If there were no such thing as viscosity, or stickiness, there would be no frictional drag on sails and wings; nor, however, would there be lift. Boats would be unable to sail to windward, birds and airplanes to fly.

Let's look at what happens when we place our flat plate at an angle (called angle of attack) to the flow. In a computer-simulated nonviscous world, it turns out that the resultant flow, over and under the board, will be symmetrical, meaning all forces of lift and drag would cancel themselves (see Figure 5.2).

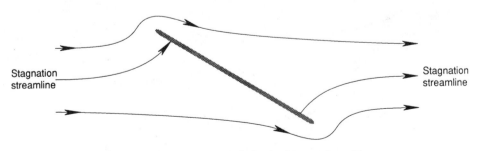

Stagnation streamline

Stagnation streamline

Figure 5.2 Symmetrical airflow without viscosity

The symmetry of the flow can be seen by turning this illustration upside down. In either orientation, it is the same. Note also that after the flow leaves the foil, it is going in the same direction as it was when it approached the plate. This is a further indication that the flow did not exert any net force on the plate.

According to fluid dynamics, a fluid, whether air or water, covers the entire region at all times. There aren't holes or voids in the flow. Turning to Figure 5.3, note that the flow leaves the top surface at a place denoted as the stagnation streamline, which will be defined momentarily. So to fill the void behind the stagnation streamline with fluid, the airflow from the bottom is able to turn the corner and even flow ''upstream.''

Enough of this computer magic. Viscosity very much exists in the real world, and so let's turn it back on. Then, as described earlier, the air begins to stick to the foil, and a boundary layer starts to form. An important feature to know about a boundary layer is that it is good at speeding up, but it is very bad at slowing down. It isn't particularly good at making sharp turns, either. In this regard, a boundary layer is like a turbo automobile with poor brakes and bad steering. Acceleration it handles easily; ask it to slow down too suddenly or to make too sharp a turn, however, and you may be asking for trouble.

A more formal way to put this is if the pressure rises too quickly in a boundary layer (the result of the flow slowing too abruptly), it will separate from the airfoil. *Separation* is a good word for the process. Rather than the airflow following the board, sail, or wing from front to back, it separates or

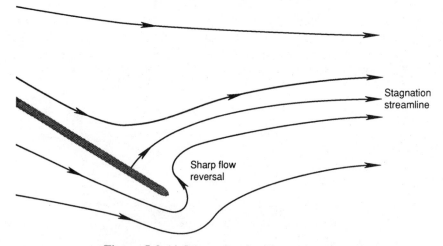

Figure 5.3 Airflow reversal without viscosity

This photograph of a foil in a water channel shows separated flow (the swirls on the leeward side). (Arvel Gentry photo)

departs from it prematurely. This separation, as we will see, decreases lift and increases drag (see above photograph). The theme of sail trim is to avoid separation.

Before viscosity was turned on, the flow was able to make the sharp turn at the trailing edge and even flow "upstream." Figure 5.4 shows what happens with viscosity. The boundary layer forms, accelerates as it makes the sharp turn around the trailing edge—to fill the void with fluid—and then runs smack into the flow on the upper surface. It slows, even stops, and then, because the

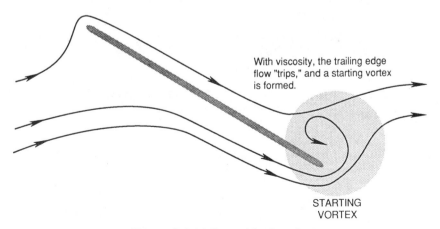

With viscosity, the trailing edge flow "trips," and a starting vortex is formed.

STARTING
VORTEX

Figure 5.4 Airflow with viscosity

boundary layer doesn't slow or stop well, it separates. This causes a swirl of air to form, called a starting vortex. This starting vortex (after doing a couple of very important jobs that will be addressed later) is swept downstream with the flow. Because the flow off the bottom side is unable to fill the void, fluid to do this has to come from somewhere. The need for fluid is so great that air that would have gone down the bottom side is actually diverted to the top to fill the void with fluid.

This phenomenon—air diverting from the bottom to flow over the top —can be depicted by a graphic device called streamlines. Streamlines show the direction and relative speed of airflow at different points in flow fields. A weather map, which uses isobar lines, or lines of constant pressure, is a familiar example of a similar graphic device. A weatherman, or a sailor for that matter, knows that when the isobars get close together, wind speed is up. This pattern holds true for streamlines, too: if the streamlines get close together or close to the foil, it is an indication that the velocity has increased and, per Bernoulli, the pressure has decreased. This is analogous to putting your finger over the opening of a garden hose; the water flows faster to get past the narrower outlet. On the other hand, when the streamlines get farther apart or farther from the foil, it is an indication that the velocity has decreased and pressure has increased. It is also important to note that, by definition, the airflow between two particular streamlines will always stay between them.

Additionally, two streamlines, denoted as·stagnation streamlines, are particularly important. An airfoil has two stagnation streamlines: one at or near the leading edge and another, as we have already noted, at or near the trailing edge (see Figure 5.5). Stagnation streamlines can be thought of as an aerodynamic "continental divide." The Continental Divide is a line, or point, of

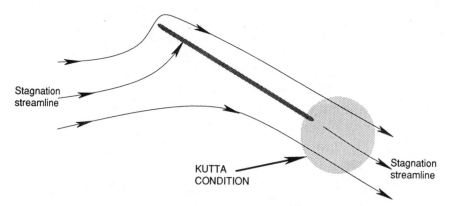

Stagnation streamline

KUTTA CONDITION

Stagnation streamline

Figure 5.5 Stagnation streamlines and the Kutta condition

demarcation separating streams, or rivers, that flow to opposite sides of the continent. In the case of an airfoil, the stagnation streamlines divide the airstream that flows on the upper surface from the one that flows on the lower. In Figure 5.5, all the air to the left of the forward stagnation streamline—rather than flowing down the bottom side—is diverted to the top.

Let's continue flying the flat board. To reprise where we are, in the absence of viscosity, the flow was able to make the sharp turn at the trailing edge and even flow "upstream." With viscosity, a boundary layer forms. The flow of the boundary layer tries to make the turn around the trailing edge, but because a boundary layer doesn't "like," to be anthropomorphic about it, sharp turns and likes even less being asked to slow suddenly, it trips. This causes more air (air that would have traveled down the bottom side of the board) to be diverted to the top. This can be shown graphically by the rearward shift in the forward stagnation streamline. Compare Figure 5.2 with Figure 5.5, and note how the forward stagnation streamline has shifted aft in Figure 5.5. In fact, the entire flow about the airfoil adjusts itself so that much more air is flowing on the upper (or lee side) of the airfoil.

One other thing must be mentioned about the viscous flow. Turning to the trailing edge in Figure 5.5, note that the airflow quickly adjusts itself so that both upper and lower surface flows stream smoothly off the trailing edge. Now the streamlines are parallel to each other and of equal distance from the airfoil. To an aerodynamicist, this pattern of streamlines means that the flows off the leeward and windward sides of the foil are traveling at the same speed. In aerodynamic jargon, this trailing-edge phenomenon is called the Kutta condition, after the scientist who discovered it in 1902. If the Kutta condition didn't exist—if, as so much of the literature states, the pressures on the two sides of the sail are unequal at the trailing edge—then once the sail is no longer separating them, the high- and low-pressure areas would mix.

ACTION-REACTION

As can be seen in Figure 5.6, with more of the air from the bottom being diverted to the top, the flow around the board is no longer symmetrical as it was in Figure 5.2. The flow leaving the board has been turned in a direction that is roughly parallel to the board. This change in the flow direction indicates that a force has been exerted on the flow to deflect its course. Sir Isaac Newton's familiar third law of motion says for every action there is an equal and opposite reaction, and this means that the action of turning the flow causes a reaction: a force on the plate.

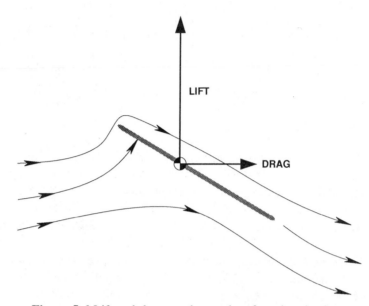

Figure 5.6 Lift and drag are the results of turning the flow.

In fact, the summation of the pressure forces around the airfoil will give a resultant force that has a component perpendicular to the flow direction (see Figure 5.6). This force is often termed lift. However, the scrubbing action, or friction, of the boundary layer also causes drag, a force in the same direction as the wind. Now, however, lift is quite substantial, and a flat plate can fly. The familiar paper airplane is an example of a flat plate flying.

CIRCULATION

Years ago, mathematicians found that the Kutta condition could be satisfied by adding another type of flow, called circulation, to the normal wind velocity. Circulation is a special mathematical solution where a second flow rotates around the airfoil. The circulation flow is greatest near the foil and progressively less moving away from it. In the mathematical solution, circulation air speeds are adjusted so that the Kutta condition at the trailing edge, or leech, is satisfied; that is, the calculated airflow speeds and pressures are the same off both sides of the trailing edge.

Figure 5.7 shows that on the top of the airfoil, the circulation flow is in the same direction as the normal, or noncirculating, flow. This means that the two flows are added together—resulting in a higher-speed flow. On the bottom

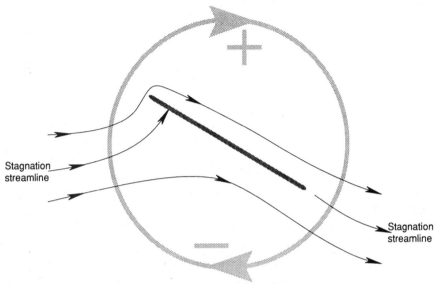

Figure 5.7 Circulation flow around a flat plate

side, however, the circulation direction is against the noncirculating flow, so the two flows cancel each other somewhat—resulting in a slower-speed flow. On the top (leeward) side, this complementary action gives high speed and low pressure; on the bottom (windward) side, this opposing action gives low speed and high pressure. This is the recipe for lift.

Circulation alone *can't* cause lift, exactly in the same manner as the linear, or noncirculating, flow can't cause lift. Trying to prove that linear flow alone produces lift has confused sailors for decades. It has given rise to such impenetrable statements as ''air passing over the curved upper surface has to travel a longer distance than the air passing under the flat lower surface, and since it has to go farther, it has to go faster to reach the trailing edge at the same time as its 'brother' particle.'' The recipe for lift requires that the two flows be added together on the top, or lee side, of the foil, and the two flows somewhat cancel each other out on the bottom, or weather, side. This gives the speed differential, top to bottom, the pressure differential, and then the lifting force.

With the combined efforts of the two flows, airplanes can fly upside down. An upside-down wing isn't an optimum shape—from the perspective of preventing separation—but it will work. Similarly, even though a sail is a thin membrane with almost no measurable difference in distance from one side to the other, the combination of the circulating flow and noncirculating flow allows a sailboat to sail to weather.

STARTING VORTEX

Circulation, however, is only a mathematical model. The need for such a solution doesn't necessarily prove its existence. Does this second flow, circulation, exist in the real world? The answer is yes. The circulation flow begins with the starting vortex. Without viscosity, you will recall, the air on the windward side is able to turn the trailing edge (see Figure 5.3). With viscosity, however, the air on the windward side attempts to turn the trailing edge but doesn't make it (see Figure 5.4). It separates, causing a swirl of air to form, and then this swirl, or starting vortex, gives rise to the circulation flow (see Figure 5.8).

This is illustrated quite clearly with a mechanical analogy. The starting vortex can be thought of as a cog or wheel, which turns a larger wheel, the circulation flow (see Figure 5.9). Returning to Figure 5.8, the starting vortex is shed once circulation is established. This happens when the rear stagnation streamline has been brought close to the trailing edge to fulfill the Kutta condition. Aerodynamacist and author C. A. Marchaj notes that since there is no longer a velocity difference on either side of the foil, there is no physical stimulus to maintain or support the starting vortex. However, any change causes the process to start anew.

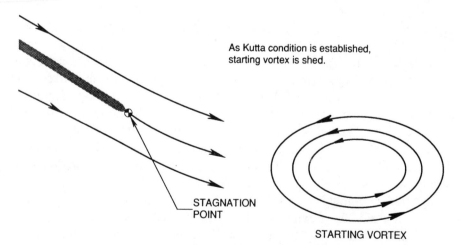

As Kutta condition is established, starting vortex is shed.

STAGNATION POINT

STARTING VORTEX

Figure 5.8 Formation of starting vortex

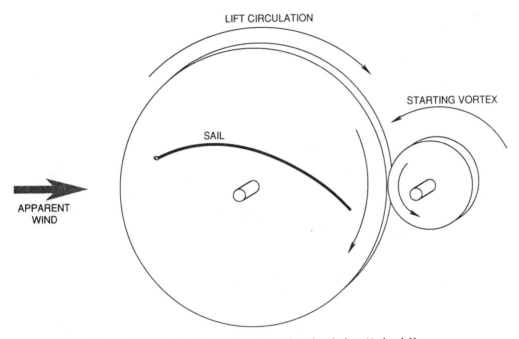

Figure 5.9 The starting vortex turns the circulation "wheel."

VISUAL EVIDENCE OF CIRCULATION

Seeing, as you've no doubt heard, is believing, and Arvel Gentry offers an ingenious way to see the effects of both the circulation flow and the starting vortex in a bathtub. First the bathtub is filled with a few inches of water, which is allowed to settle. Then fine sawdust, talcum powder, or even pepper is sprinkled over the water surface in order to better observe the flow around the foil. A 4- by 6-inch piece of stiff waxed paper cut from a milk carton serves as a foil. It must be bent so it has camber, or depth, similar to a sail. Then the airfoil is very carefully placed on the centerline of the bathtub as shown in Figure 5.10. The leading edge—pointing toward the left—is kept about an inch higher than the trailing edge to give the airfoil an angle of attack. The camber and angle of attack must be small to avoid excessive flow separation. Allow the water to settle again.

Handling the airfoil carefully to avoid disturbing the water, begin to move it down the centerline of the tub. Observe what happens near the trailing edge

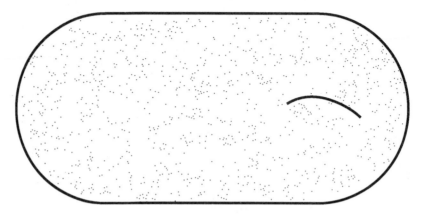

Figure 5.10 Airfoil stationary in bathtub

of the foil as it starts in motion. The flow at first tries to make the turn around the trailing edge, then it separates to form the starting vortex (see Figure 5.11). Having been shed, the starting vortex remains spinning at its initial position as the airfoil continues toward the left of the tub.

As the airfoil nears the center of the tub, shift your attention to the flow in front of and around the airfoil. In Figure 5.12, note that the flow in front of the airfoil seems to "know" that the airfoil is coming and starts changing its direction to flow over the top even before the airfoil arrives. If the airfoil is being pulled precisely down the centerline of the tub, some of the water in front of and even below the airfoil will actually end up flowing over the top of the foil. The upward flow in front of the foil is termed upwash by aero-

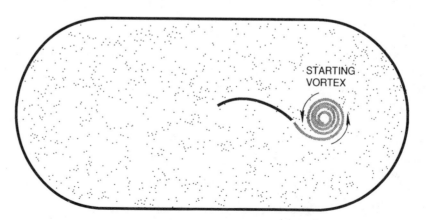

Figure 5.11 Starting vortex forms in water

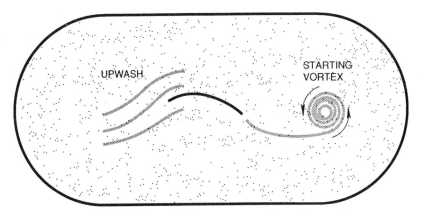

Figure 5.12 Upward flow in front of foil

dynamicists and is, you might have guessed, a result of the powerful need to fill the region behind the rear stagnation streamline with fluid (see Figure 5.5). Because of viscosity, the flow on the bottom can't do it, so water that would have gone down the bottom side is actually diverted to the top to fill the void with fluid.

Now comes the key part of this experiment. When the foil gets within about a foot of the left end of the tub, lift it completely out of the water (see Figure 5.13). When it is removed, all that remains are the rotational flows that were caused by the movement of the airfoil across the tub. At the right end of the tub, the starting vortex is still rotating in a counterclockwise direction (from this orientation). This is the small wheel (see Figure 5.9), or starting

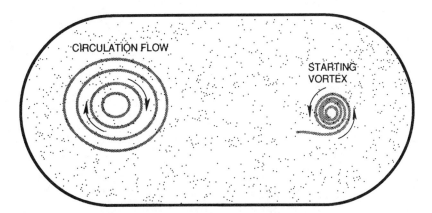

Figure 5.13 Airfoil is removed from water.

vortex, which turns the larger, clockwise circulation flow at the left end of the tub. All of the phenomena observed in the water experiment also happen in the air.

If you are still skeptical, circulation also accounts for the curveball in baseball, considered by sportswriters to be one of the great mysteries of life, and for the slice in golf. When a pitcher wants to throw a fastball, he throws the ball with very little spin. With little spin and little or no circulation flow, the ball sails straight and fast. When the pitcher wants to throw a curve, however, the ball is thrown with considerable spin. The spinning creates circulation, and when this is combined with the normal flow, it makes for high speed and low pressure on one side of the ball and low speed and high pressure on the other. The result is that the ball curves toward the low-pressure side.

Similarly, a golf ball slices because it is hit in such a way that it has excessive spin. A theme of golf is to avoid circulation, whereas a theme of sailing is to maximize it. Perhaps the fundamental differences and yet fundamental similarities of the two pastimes account for the fact that many sailors are golfers, too.

TIME

A good curve doesn't break 15 feet before the batter; it breaks near home plate. Implicit in this is time. It also takes time for circulation to form around an airfoil, and it takes considerably more time for the resulting lift to reach its optimum. For the pitcher, if maximum lift is reached too early, the ball is likely to be in the dirt well before it reaches home plate; if maximum lift is reached too late, the ball might end up in the cheap seats.

For sailors, the sooner circulation and, thus, lift build, the faster they go. Imagine a sail luffing in the wind. Without an angle of attack, the sail is flat, and there is no lift, only drag, and, of course, no starting vortex. Then the sail is suddenly pulled in 20 degrees, giving it an angle of attack, which, to define it formally, is the angle between the apparent-wind direction and the sail's chord line.

The flow tries to make the turn around the trailing edge, but because of viscosity, it trips, and the starting vortex forms. This takes a measurable amount of time. Next the starting vortex—the small wheel—has to start turning the bigger wheel, or the circulation flow (see Figure 5.9). To get that big wheel up to full speed also takes time. The larger the sail plan, as measured by its average chord length, the larger the circulation wheel is and, hence, the longer it will take for the lift to build. On the other hand, the more wind available to turn the crank, or starting vortex, the faster the circulation flow gets up to speed, and the faster the lift on the sail builds. Eventually, if the flow is constant, the lift will plateau at some constant value, known as steady-state lift.

So how long is eventually? Figure 5.14 shows the time it takes the sails on a 40-foot sailboat to approach steady-state lift for three wind speeds. To achieve 85 percent of steady-state lift at 20 knots of wind takes about 6 seconds; at 10 knots, 12 seconds; at 5 knots, 24 seconds. Although the numbers aren't absolute and are only indicative of trends, the third number is a good indication of why skilled sailors move delicately and cautiously in light air. Any change in sail trim or boat trim requires considerable time for the circulation to adjust and for the sailboat to reach steady state. It is also a good indication of why the differences between skilled and average sailors are most apparent in light winds and least apparent in stronger winds.

This time lag does not merely apply to filling the sails, but exists for

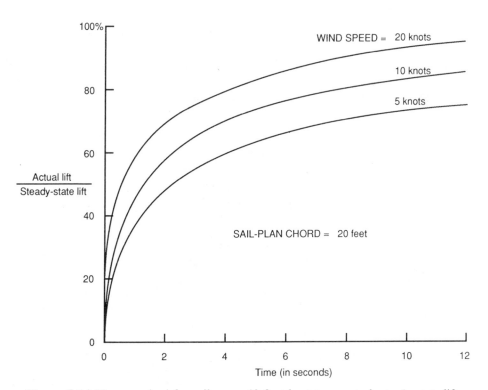

Figure 5.14 Time required for sails on a 40-foot boat to approach steady-state lift

every adjustment in trim that either increases or decreases lift. How often does everything on a sailboat stay constant for 10, 20, or 30 seconds? Almost never. If the wind keeps shifting or if the helmsman's steering is erratic, then things never quite settle down. Under those conditions, the data in Figure 5.14 suggest that one is not just a little bit off but can be 10, 20, or 30 percent off. In trimming sails and steering, sailors are always chasing the best performance from their sails. How close one can stay to the desired settings without making unnecessary changes is the mark of a skilled sailor.

The times noted above will vary in proportion to the average chord length of the sails. For example, sails with a 10-foot chord would achieve the same percentage of lift in half the time. This is a clear indication of why dinghies are more responsive than big boats. It is also an indication of why sail plans on modern racing and cruising boats have evolved to show a high aspect ratio. They get up to speed, or steady-state lift, sooner. (Other reasons for high-aspect-ratio sail plans will be discussed in the next chapter.)

The time it takes for lift to build is an important concept below the water, too. As Marchaj notes, keels with different chord lengths have different steering characteristics. He states that foils with shorter chord lengths—like the fin keel and separate spade rudder of an International Offshore Rule (IOR) boat—develop lift sooner than boats with long keels and contiguous rudders.[2] The relative speed in which lift develops on these IOR foils is, he says, why these boats are so difficult to keep in the groove. They heel this way, circulation forms, and lift develops in a relatively short amount of time; they pitch that way, and circulation and lift develop quickly. The speed at which lift develops around these short keels also accounts, in part, for their more ''spirited'' ride, in a seaway. On the other hand, boats with more traditional underbodies (long keels and contiguous rudders) are less responsive to the helm, as circulation takes longer to form around these long foils.

SLOT EFFECT

As described in the bathtub experiment, the water seems to ''know'' the foil is coming and starts changing its direction even before the foil arrives. In actuality, water in front of and even below the airfoil is diverted over the top of the foil. In sailing, this happens both above and below the surface of the

---

[2]A short, but deep, keel and a separate spade rudder hung well aft are fairly recent trends in yacht design. The first significant yacht to show this configuration was the Cal-40, an ocean racer from 1964, designed to the Cruising Club of America Rule by Bill Lapworth. The 12-Meter *Intrepid*, a two-time America's Cup defender (1967 and 1970), also showed this configuration. Prior to these two boats, all 12-Meters and most racing and cruising yachts had the rudder affixed to the trailing edge of a long keel. This underbody shape is still found on some cruising vessels.

water. The air "senses" that the sail is coming and bends to leeward in anticipation of it; the water senses that the keel is coming and bends in anticipation of it. This phenomenon, discussed earlier, is called upwash. Upwash is a good place to begin talking about the so-called slot effect and the important, if misunderstood, relationship between the main and the jib. As will become apparent, this discussion has far-reaching implications for sail trim.

The slot-effect theory says that since there is less area between the leech of the jib and the front of the main than between the headstay and the mast, the flow through the slot is speeded up. This is the garden-hose analogy again. Since there is less of an opening for the water to escape, it comes out at high speed. This squeezing accounts, says the old theory, for the high-speed flow over the mainsail.

Let's view the slot-effect theory in terms of circulation. Both the jib and the main have their own circulation fields, as shown in Figure 5.15. As is apparent, the two circulation fields oppose and tend to cancel each other in the slot. Thus, there is not the accelerated, or "revitalized," air speed that the old theory promises. Much of the air that one might think goes in the slot is actually diverted by the combined circulation fields so that it goes on the lee side of the jib. This, again, is upwash.

The clearest way to see what is truly happening to the two sails is through the use of streamlines. Figure 5.16 shows Gentry's calculated streamlines for a main alone. With the main only, note the stagnation streamline, designated as S_m, comes into the lower, or windward, side of the sail. Elsewhere we have described a stagnation streamline as an aerodynamic "continental divide," and thus all the air ahead (to the left in this orientation) of the stagnation

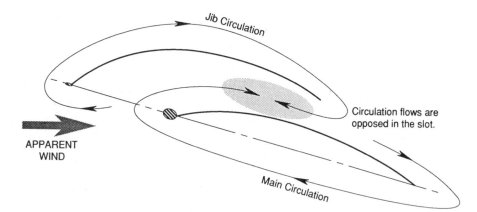

Figure 5.15 Circulation fields of jib and main

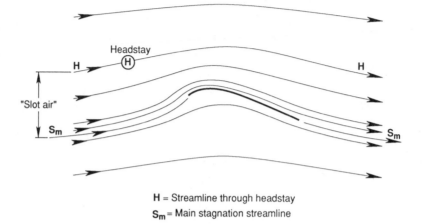

H = Streamline through headstay
S_m = Main stagnation streamline

Figure 5.16 Streamlines for mainsail without jib

streamline will make the turn around the leading edge of the mainsail and pass down the leeward side, and all the air behind (to the right of) the stagnation streamline will travel down the windward side.

Note how close the lee (or top) side of the sail is to the first leeward streamline. This pattern of streamlines indicates that this is an area of very high speed and, per Bernoulli, very low pressure. Then, after this rapid acceleration around the mast and onto the forward lee side of the sail, the "brakes" have to be applied immediately to satisfy the Kutta condition. The turbo-charged acceleration around the hairpin curve and then immediate slamming on of the brakes are as "uncomfortable" to a boundary layer as they are to passengers in an automobile. The boundary layer, you may recall, has trouble with sudden increases in pressure—the slamming on the brakes, so to speak —and sharp turns, and stall is the likely result.

For the sake of the exercise, let's ignore stall and keep the main at the same angle it would have if the jib was there. Turn your attention to streamline H in this figure. This line is selected because it passes through point H, which would be the leading edge of the jib—that is, the headstay—if the sail was there. The distance between the stagnation streamline of the main (S_m) and the headstay streamline (H) at the left side of the figure is a measure of the amount of air that passes between the slot without the jib being present and without any separation on the mainsail.

The headsail is introduced in Figure 5.17. The dotted streamlines represent the flow when sailing with the main alone; the solid ones represent the flow when sailing with both sails. Note that the stagnation streamline for the main (S_m) no longer comes in on the windward side; rather, it shifts to the leading edge of the mainsail, or in essence to the mast. This heading shift, called downwash, is important; it shows that the jib causes the main to sail in a header. Now that the flow comes smoothly into the leading edge of the main, it doesn't have to speed up nearly so much to get around to the lee side. And since it doesn't speed up so much, it doesn't have to slow down nearly so much to satisfy the Kutta condition at the trailing edge. This means that with the headsail present, the flow on the main is less likely to separate. This is the antithesis of the old slot-effect theory, which says that the flow speeds up in the slot, due to the venturi effect, and the increase in speed helps to prevent separation.

In this illustration, the stagnation streamline of the jib (S_j) comes in around on the weather side. This is upwash, a lift, and it means that the boat can be pointed closer to the wind without the jib luffing. Further, note that the stagnation streamline of the jib is now much lower than the old headstay streamline (H). As before, the distance between the stagnation streamlines of the two sails (S_m and S_j at the left side) is a measure of the amount of air that now goes through the slot when both sails are present. By comparing this distance with that in the previous illustration (with the main only), it is easy to see that much less air goes through the slot when both sails are present than when only the main is present.

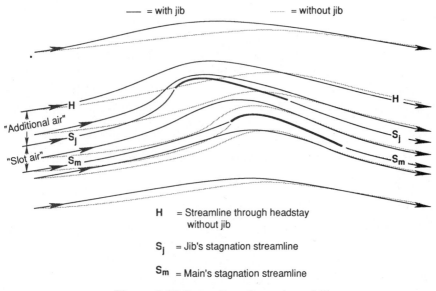

Figure 5.17 Streamlines for main and jib

Where is the air going? The fact that the stagnation streamline of the jib is now much farther to windward (much lower) shows that much more of it is being deflected around the lee side of the headstay—and therefore the lee side of the jib. The distance between the new and old stagnation streamlines of the jib reflects the amount of extra air that is diverted to the lee side. Without the two sails flying, this measure of air would pass through the slot. So in addition to a lift, the mainsail gives the jib more wind on its lee side, or to put it another way: increased velocities.

The main—already so generous with its gifts—has one final contribution to give to the headsail, that is, increased velocities at the trailing edge. We know that to satisfy the Kutta condition, the velocity at the leech of the mainsail must be equal on both sides and near to the speed of the normal, or free-stream, wind. This is true for the mainsail, typically the last sail in the sail plan, but it is not true for the jib. The leech of the jib ends in a relatively high-speed area: on the lee side of the mainsail. Detailed calculations show that the air flowing around the jib adjusts itself so that the Kutta condition is satisfied not at or near free-stream conditions, but at a higher speed that blends with the high-speed flow created by the mainsail in the region of the leech of the jib. In fact, the velocity at the jib's leech is about 30 percent higher than the free-stream speed. This further explains why the jib is such an efficient sail when compared with the main. The higher velocities on the lee side of the jib show the sail has greater lift.

This also means that the flow on the lee-side trailing edge of the jib is less apt to separate since it does not have to slow down the additional 30 percent to near free-stream conditions. As stated, the more precipitant that slowing, the more the flow is likely to separate. If it seems confusing that the jib helps the main from stalling by slowing the speed at the main's forward-lee side, and the main helps the jib from stalling by speeding up the flow at the jib's aft-lee side, it is the abruptness and the degree of the slowing that are important. The harder the brakes have to be stepped on, so to speak, to satisfy the Kutta condition, the greater the likelihood of stall.

If you are having trouble envisioning upwash and downwash, consider this: The jib's upwash—increased winds at a more favorable angle (a lift)—is the same phenomenon that makes the safe-leeward position desirable (see Figure 5.18). Not only does boat A in the safe-leeward position reap the benefits of upwash, but the mainsail of that boat ends in a high-speed flow region created by the weather boat (B) so that the Kutta condition is satisfied not at or near free-stream conditions, but at a higher speed. In every way, the boat in the safe-leeward position is analogous to the headsail in a sail plan.

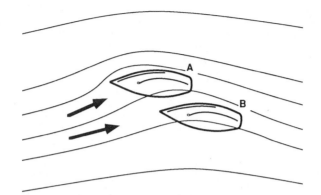

Figure 5.18 Why the safe-leeward position is advantageous

Because this aerodynamic theory has such far-reaching implications for sail trim—discussed in later chapters—it is worth summarizing.

How the Mainsail Affects the Jib

1. The flow ahead of the mainsail causes the stagnation point on the jib to be shifted around toward the windward side of the sail (a lift), and the boat can be pointed closer to the wind without the jib luffing. This lifting shift is upwash.
2. The leech of the jib is in a high-speed flow region created by the mainsail. The leech velocity on the jib is, therefore, higher than if the jib alone was used.
3. Because of the higher leech velocity, velocities along the entire lee surface of the jib are greatly increased when both the jib and the main are used, and this contributes to the high efficiency of the headsail.
4. The higher lee-surface velocities on the jib mean that the jib can be operated at higher angles of attack (more trim) before the jib lee-side flow will separate and stall.
5. Because of the aforementioned, proper trim and shape of the mainsail significantly affect the efficiency of the overlapping jib. Anything that causes a velocity reduction in the region of the jib's leech, such as some separation on the aft part of the main, results in the jib contributing a lower driving force.
6. The trim of the main significantly affects the pointing ability of the boat, for it directly influences the upwash that approaches the luff of the jib.

7. The drag from the mast—in front of the mainsail—has always been blamed for making the main less efficient than a jib. Another, probably equally important factor is the increased velocity on the jib, and the fact that the Kutta-condition requirement of the jib is satisfied in a local high-speed flow region that is created by the mainsail.

How the Jib Affects the Mainsail

1. The jib causes the stagnation point of the mainsail to shift around toward the leading edge of the mast, placing the mainsail in a header. This is downwash.
2. As a result, the peak suction velocities on the forward-lee side of the main are greatly reduced. Since the peak suction velocities are reduced, the rise in pressure is less abrupt.
3. Because the speed of the flow is reduced on the mainsail, the possibility of the boundary layer separating and the airfoil stalling is reduced.
4. With the jib up, a mainsail can be operated efficiently at higher angles of attack (more trim or higher traveler angle) without flow separation and stalling than would be the case with just a mainsail alone. This, too, is caused by a reduction in velocities over the forward-lee part of the mainsail. Since the air is moving fairly slowly at the front, further slowing at the back to satisfy the Kutta condition is not a dramatic event. This disproves the slot-effect theory. If the air were speeded up in the slot as the old theory promises, the air on the main would be more likely to separate.
5. Much less air goes between the headstay and the mast when the jib is placed in the flow with the main. The circulations of the main and jib tend to oppose and cancel each other in the area between the two sails, and therefore more air is forced over the lee side of the jib.

CHAPTER 6

FROM AERODYNAMIC THEORY TO PRACTICE

★ For the sail-trimmer, the practical implications of the previous chapter are that the mainsail and headsail must be considered as a unit, as one large foil, not as two separate and distinct ones. That is how the wind "sees" a sail plan. The best sail-trimmers know that the trim of one sail can profoundly affect the other, and when one sail is changed, they look for secondary effects in the other.

Arvel Gentry has an interesting drawing. It shows what happens to wind in the slot, as well as the shifts in the stagnation streamlines when the relative settings of the two sails are changed. Figure 6.1A shows the two sails properly trimmed for upwind sailing. Figure 6.1B shows the jib in 5 degrees while the main is unchanged. Note that flow through the slot is decreased 60 percent. This huge reduction means that very little air is filling up the slot, and what little air there is has to spread out to fill the region. Thus, the air is moving very slowly through the slot, and the pressures are high on the leeward side of the main—likely higher even than the pressures on the weather side. This means there is low speed and high pressure on the leeward side and higher speed and lower pressure on the windward—the complete opposite of what is normal.

Thus the sail, rather than being sucked—which is the actual process— to leeward, actually is sucked to windward. This is what sailors refer to as backwind.[1] It can be seen in the shift of the stagnation streamline of the main well to the leeward side. Even then, the mainsail contributes upwash to the jib, but it is less than if the two sails were properly trimmed.

---

[1]Backwind is something of a misnomer. It implies that the headsail is throwing air against the lee side of the main—the old slot-effect theory—when in actuality, the mainsail is just reacting to an increase in lee-side pressure caused by the genoa's slowing down of the air in the slot. Nevertheless, as most people are familiar with the visual evidence if not the cause and effect, the term *backwind* is used in the book.

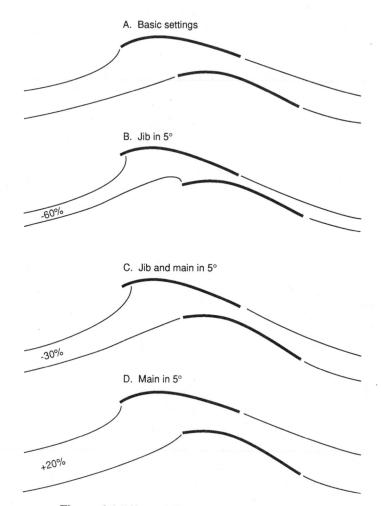

Figure 6.1 Effect of jib and main sheeting angles
on slot flow and stagnation streamlines

Figure 6.1C shows both sails trimmed in 5 degrees. This setting causes a dramatic shift in the stagnation streamline of the headsail. The wind to its left has to speed up and make the sharp turn around the headsail to get to the lee side. As a result, the flow on this sail is likely to stall unless the boat is pointed closer to the wind or the headsail is let out—either of which will move the stagnation streamline to the leading edge of the sail. Figure 6.1D shows the main trimmed in 5 degrees. There is a 20 percent increase of flow in the slot, and the stagnation streamline for the main has shifted slightly to weather. Thus the air in the slot is speeded up and more likely to separate. To prevent this, we could trim the jib, which would slow the velocities in the lee side of the mainsail, or turn the boat closer to the wind.

This discussion does not pretend to teach sail trim—whether to sail low and fast with full sails or high and slow with flat sails is among the most complicated decisions in sailing. Sail trim involves several factors, including the shape of the hull and keel as well as the shape of the sails. This section shows the connection between the sails. Addressing the big picture, a correctly trimmed headsail slows the wind in the slot just the proper amount, so the air on the lee side of the main does not separate when it is trimmed at a tight angle. A correctly trimmed main places the jib in a lift, meaning the boat can be pointed closer to the wind without the jib luffing. A correctly trimmed main also speeds up the leech velocities of the jib, making it a much more effective sail. This speeding up of the flow and the fact that the Kutta requirements of the jib are satisfied in a high-speed flow region mean that the flow around the jib is less likely to separate. Again, the theme of sail trim is to avoid separation.

FORCES ABOVE AND BELOW THE WATER

As we saw earlier when flying our flat plate, when a sail deflects the airflow, forces are produced. This is Sir Isaac Newton's action and reaction. On a sail, the pressure forces include the relatively strong pulls (negative pressure or suction) on the leeward side and weak pushes (positive pressure) on the wind-ward (see Figure 6.2). If we add the magnitude and direction of the strong

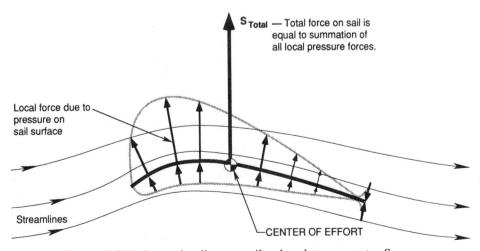

Figure 6.2 Pushes and pulls on a sail reduced to one vector S_{Total}

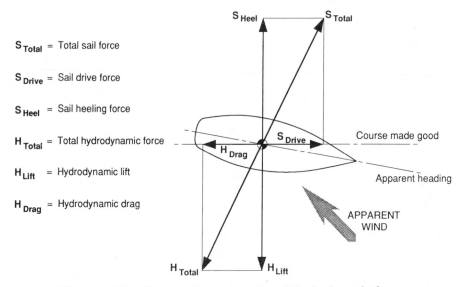

S_{Total} = Total sail force

S_{Drive} = Sail drive force

S_{Heel} = Sail heeling force

H_{Total} = Total hydrodynamic force

H_{Lift} = Hydrodynamic lift

H_{Drag} = Hydrodynamic drag

Figure 6.3 Equilibrium of aerodynamic and hydrodynamic forces

pulls and weak pushes, the forces can be reduced to one force vector (S_{Total}) which emanates from the sail's center of effort. If there were no drag, S_{Total} would be perpendicular to the apparent wind, but because of drag, it is always aft of perpendicular.

Another way to view the force on a sail is to break it into two equivalent forces that, when added together, are equal to the sail force (S_{Total}) (see Figure 6.3). One such pair of forces is shown in the figure and labeled S_{Drive} and S_{Heel}. S_{Drive} is the part of the sail force that is pushing the boat forward. S_{Heel} pushes perpendicular to the direction of the boat's travel and causes it to heel. An interesting aspect to note about vectors S_{Heel} and S_{Drive} is that on a weather leg, heel is about four times longer than drive. This is one reason why dinghy racers hike and keelboat racers congregate on the weather rail.

The keel keeps the boat from simply going in the direction of the sail force (S_{Total}). Without a keel, or centerboard, sailboats would be unable to sail above a broad reach. The keel is a foil, and the way it interacts with the water is analogous to the way the sail interacts with the wind. In turning the water, the keel produces a force (H_{Lift}) that opposes and balances the sideways, or heeling, force of the sail. H_{Lift} emanates from the keel's center of lateral resistance (CLR).

The keel (centerboard), rudder, and especially the hull produce a significant amount of drag when driven through the water by the sails. This drag force (labeled H_{Drag}) is the force that opposes the forward motion (S_{Drive}) of the boat. When the boat is moving at a steady speed, the aerodynamic (sail) forces and the hydrodynamic (keel) forces balance. For example, hydrodynamic drag (H_{Drag}) and sail drive force (S_{Drive}) are equal and opposite. If the sail drive is suddenly increased, as in a gust of wind, the drive force will temporarily exceed the hydrodynamic drag, and the boat will accelerate. If the force from the sails drops, the boat will slow until the forces once again balance.

LEEWAY

Sailboats don't sail in the direction they are pointed; rather, they crab and slide to leeward. To use the jargon of sailing, the course made good is lower than the course actually steered (see Figure 6.3). The difference between the apparent heading and the actual course made good is called leeway. In 10 to 15 knots of breeze, a typical boat of recent design will average about 3 or 4 degrees of leeway. Since the keel is aligned with the centerline of the boat, this angle is also the keel's angle of attack. This narrow angle of attack is sufficient for the keel to deflect the water flow and create the sideways force H_{Lift}, discussed above. Without leeway, or an angle of attack, there could be no deflecting of the water and no lift from the keel.

OPTIMUM RUDDER ANGLE

If the wind were perfectly steady and the water smooth, we could set up a boat so that the keel and sail forces balanced perfectly, and the boat would sail in a straight line. However, normal sailing conditions are typically anything but steady, so the rudder is used to trim the balance between the keel and the sails. To sail a straight course, a modern displacement yacht will have its rig tuned so that the rudder must be angled slightly (3 to 5 degrees) to weather. In other words, the boat will have some degree of weather helm and will need to be steered down, or away, from the wind.

Should steering the boat down seem a strange way to improve upwind performance, this becomes clearer by highlighting the relationship between the center of effort (CE) of the sail and the center of lateral resistance (CLR) of the keel, as seen in Figure 6.4. If the center of effort of the sail plan is directly over the center of lateral resistance of the keel, the boat will have a neutral helm or will steer straight without rudder movement. If, however, the CE is behind the CLR, as in the illustration, the boat will have weather helm. If CE is ahead of CLR, the boat will have lee helm.

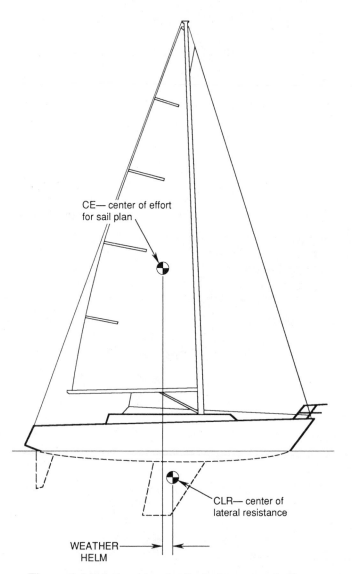

CE— center of effort
for sail plan

CLR— center of
lateral resistance

WEATHER
HELM

Figure 6.4 Relationship of sail plan's center of effort
and keel's center of lateral resistance

In Figure 6.5, the forces on the keel and rudder are shown when sailing with weather helm. As stated, it is normal, indeed desirable, for a boat to have about 3 to 5 degrees of weather helm. The weather helm requires the rudder to be angled so as to drive the boat down or away from the wind, and as a result, the rudder has an angle of attack and creates lift in its own right, instead

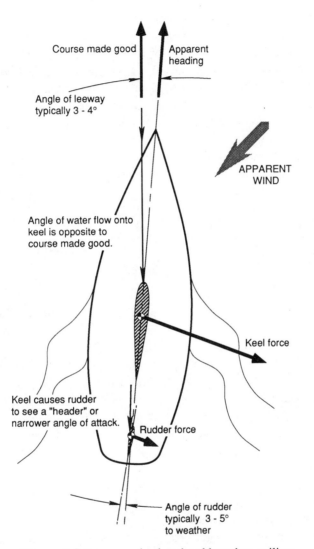

Figure 6.5 Forces on keel and rudder when sailing
with weather helm are in the same direction.

of simply streaming behind the keel and only creating drag. This added lift
from the rudder moves the CLR of the hull slightly aft (see Figure 6.4) until
it ends up directly under the center of effort of the sail, and the boat steers
straight.

Note in Figure 6.5 that the force produced by the rudder is in the same
direction as the keel force. With weather helm, the rudder works with the keel

to counteract the heeling force of the sail. If we were steering the other way (lee helm), the rudder would be working against the keel, and the keel would be called upon to balance the force of the rudder as well as the sails. Since increasing the rudder or keel force always increases drag, it is better to have them work together (weather helm) than against each other (lee helm). By balancing the boat with 3 to 5 degrees of weather helm, you leave yourself room to steer the boat while always maintaining some weather helm. This improves speed to windward.

Weather helm has an additional benefit because the relationship of the keel to the rudder is similar to the relationship between the headsail and the mainsail. Thus by angling the rudder to weather—in essence trimming it— the upwash of the keel is increased, which is the underwater equivalent of more wind on the lee side of the headsail.

LIFT AND DRAG

There are, as should be apparent by now, many ways to describe the forces around sails—in fact, around any lifting surface. One of the most straight- forward ways is to split the forces into lift and drag (see Figure 6.6). The lift force is, by definition, perpendicular to the apparent-wind direction; drag is parallel to it. The primary way to get more lift, or power, from a sail is to increase its angle of attack.

The angle of attack of a sail, you will recall, is the angle between the apparent-wind direction and the chord line of the sail. There are two ways to increase a sail's angle of attack: trim it (see Figure 6.7) or turn the bow off the wind (fall off) without easing the sails. The most important thing to know about angle of attack is the greater it is—or to put this another way, the more the sail deflects, or turns, the airflow—the greater will be the lift, up to a point. Obviously, if the sails turn the flow so much and generate so much lift and corresponding heeling force that the spreaders are nearly dragging in the water, you will not go very fast.

A secondary way to get more lift, or power, from a sail is to increase its camber, or depth. Increasing camber, which can be done in any number of ways (trimming the sail, easing halyard tension, easing the outhaul, straight- ening the mast, increasing headstay sag, moving the lead forward, or changing to a fuller sail), is a more subtle way to increase lift. Camber provides a smoother introduction of the foil to the flow.

This becomes clearer by turning to Figure 5.5, page 78. The leading edge of the flat plate requires the wind to make an abrupt turn around it. This abrupt

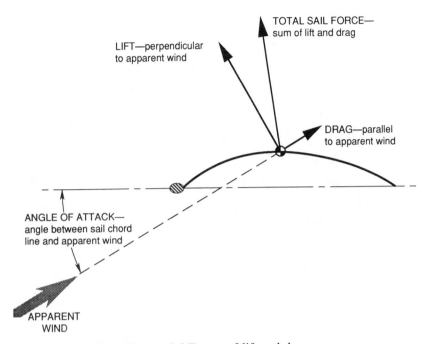

Figure 6.6 Forces of lift and drag

turn causes the wind to accelerate around the leading edge, and because of this acceleration, the air is likely to separate from the foil. Imagine, however, curving the leading edge down so it cleanly meets the flow. With this smooth introduction, the air is more likely to stay attached. The car-driving comparison works well here, too. Without camber, the flow is asked to make a sharp turn around the leading edge. Try doing that at speed, and you will likely drive off the road. With camber, it is as if you are driving around a well-designed curve. Speed is less dangerous on such a course of travel. For a sail, correct camber provides a more gentle turn. This, incidentally, is a primary benefit of the curved airplane wing—to provide a more gentle introduction of the wing to the flow, which helps to keep the flow attached to the foil. It is not curved to provide a ''longer distance'' for air molecules on the upper surface to travel.

Sail trim is a balancing act, however, and too much camber also can present problems, as the flow has trouble staying attached to a deeply curved section. With too much camber, the likelihood is that it will separate—the nice even curve above becomes an abrupt hairpin—and the flow will depart prematurely from the sail. Too much camber can decrease lift and increase drag. This is why, interestingly enough, steeply pitched roofs are less likely to blow off in high winds. With a steep roof (deep camber) the air is less likely

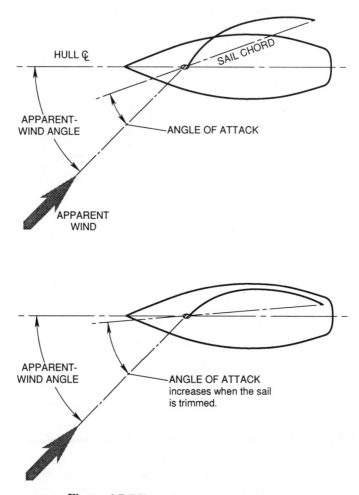

HULL ₵

SAIL CHORD

APPARENT-
WIND ANGLE

ANGLE OF ATTACK

APPARENT
WIND

APPARENT-
WIND ANGLE

ANGLE OF ATTACK
increases when the sail
is trimmed.

Figure 6.7 Effect of trim on angle of attack

to make the sharp turn at the peak of the roof, and separates. So attached flow is only working on, at the most, half the roof. With a low-pitched roof, the flow may be attached to the entire roof. The latter can be considered a significantly larger sail, and more likely to lift off.

In summary, the most direct way to get more power from a sail is to increase its angle of attack, by trimming it or turning from the wind without easing it. Then, given a certain angle of attack, increased camber—since it cleans up the flow around the leading edge—can further increase lift, at least up to a point. In the case of a main, increased camber has an additional benefit. It helps to get the sail away from the separated flow around the mast.

For sailors, the practical reality of this discussion is that creating lift is a cinch. All it requires is oversheeting the sails or sailing a course too low for the sail settings (both of which increase angle of attack), or sailing with sails that are too full (show too much camber) for the conditions. Unfortunately, sail trim is not so easy because lift is offset by its undesirable cohort, drag. Reducing drag, primarily because it is so difficult to see, is the tough part.

Drag varies with angle of attack, in exactly the same manner as lift is dependent on it. First note in the bottom curve of Figure 6.8 that there is some drag at 0 degrees—that is, when the sail is flapping in the wind—because of form and frictional drag (to be defined and discussed momentarily). Initially,

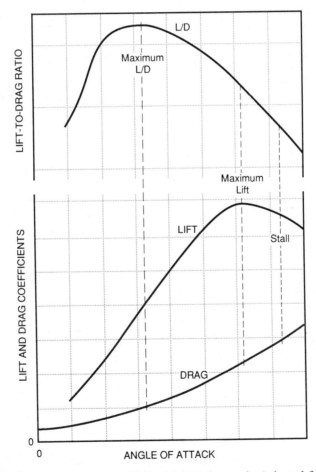

Figure 6.8 Plots of drag, lift, and lift-to-drag ratio (adapted from drawings that appear in Marchaj's *Aero-Hydrodynamics of Sailing*)

as the angle of attack of the sail plan increases (the sail is trimmed), drag increases very little. At greater angles of attack, the increase in drag becomes much more pronounced.

The plot of the lift-to-drag ratio, the top curve in Figure 6.8, shows how both of these component forces are changing together. Note that the best ratio of lift to drag (which means that the highest proportion of the force of the sail is going to drive the boat) is at a point only halfway up the lift curve. At the point at which the lift is at its maximum (middle curve), the lift-to-drag ratio is well on its way downhill. Sails tend not to stall abruptly as high-performance airplane wings do, so a distinct stall point is difficult to detect.

The genoa telltales are a good indicator of where you are in terms of lift and drag, at least from the perspective of angle of attack, which is, as we now know, most important in terms of sail trim. When the windward telltale is just lifting (Figure 6.9), the lift-to-drag ratio reaches its highest point. As the angle of attack of the sails increases, both the windward and the leeward telltales start streaming. Here lift is near its maximum, but now it is at the expense of drag. The result is that the lift-to-drag ratio is lower. Keep increasing the angle

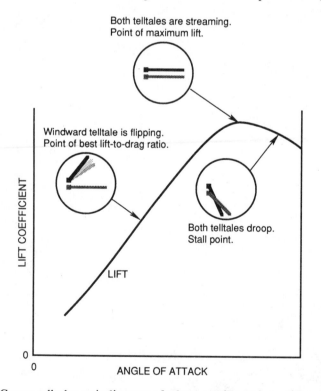

Figure 6.9 Genoa telltales as indicators of where a sailboat is on lift curve

of attack (trim the sails more or fall off the wind without easing them), and the flow stalls. This can be seen in the figure, or on a boat, with both telltales drooping.

From the preceding, it might seem that the first angle of attack—with the windward telltale lifting—is optimum for sailing to weather, but one additional point must be made: That particular angle of attack does not always generate the fastest velocity made good (VMG).[2] More lift is often needed— despite the problem of even more drag—to accelerate the boat to its hull speed or to power through chop. For example, in smooth water and medium air, if the main is trimmed more such that its lift-to-drag ratio decreases, that loss could be more than offset by a better angle of attack from the rudder (as just discussed), or from the fact that more of the total force created is turned into drive force.

There are, unfortunately, no easy-to-use telltalelike devices to indicate the proper amount of camber. Instead, guidelines are provided.[3] For example, the proper amount of camber for the middle section of a genoa when sailing upwind is approximately 15 to 16 percent in very light winds (0 to 2 knots), 18 to 19 percent in moderate air (3 to 12 knots), and then the sail should grow progressively flatter as the wind builds above that. Camber is increased when reaching. (Camber will be discussed in more detail later in this chapter as well as in Chapters 9 and 10.)

As mentioned, creating lift is the easy part; the difficult part is minimizing drag and preventing the separation of the airflow.[4] Obviously, drag reduces the driving force. It increases the amount of side force (heel) for a given

---

[2]If you experiment with your boat, you will find that there is one boat speed and wind angle where the VMG is better than all others. This is maximum VMG for a given wind angle. Upwind VMG can be calculated from the formula: boat speed × cosine of the true-wind angle. As a short-term indicator, VMG is not particularly useful. For example, you can turn your boat into the wind, which will maximize VMG for a few moments. This certainly would not pay off in the long run, however.

One could test to find the best boat speed, i.e., target boat speed, for a true-wind speed and true-wind angle, or purchase what are termed polar diagrams from private sources or from the United States Yacht Racing Union (PO Box 209, Newport, RI 02840), which has polar diagrams for about six hundred standard racing and cruising hulls. According to the polar diagrams, when your upwind speed is too fast for the wind speed, you would head the boat up until the speed bleeds off to the target boat speed, and then fall off again. If too slow for the wind speed, head off until your speed rises above the target speed, and then head up again. The polar diagram packages cover reaching and running as well as beating. The racer's need for this information is obvious. USYRU is selling more of these packages to cruising sailors since the answer to the question low and fast or high and slow? can get one to Nantucket, for example, an hour or so earlier.

[3]Camber, you will recall from Figure 2.2, page 17, is draft divided by chord length expressed as a percentage.

[4]Bear in mind that this discussion focuses on sailing upwind. When sailing downwind, the name of the game is to increase drag or to stop the flow of wind. Reaching is a combination of the two, and the fact

amount of lift, and this increased side, or heeling, component can overwhelm those things that work to counterbalance it: the keel, rudder, underbody, and ballast.

FRICTIONAL DRAG

Aerodynamic literature identifies three types of drag: frictional, form, and induced. For proper sail trim, it is important to be familiar with each of them.

You will recall that because of viscosity, the air that directly touches the sail stops, or has zero velocity with respect to the surface of the airfoil. It is carried along for the ride. A small distance from the sail, the airflow moves with some finite speed relative to the airfoil. At the edge of the boundary layer, the flow moves with the same speed as the external air, or at the normal wind speed (see Figure 5.1, page 75).

The three states that characterize the fluid flow in a boundary layer are laminar, transitional, and turbulent (see Figure 6.10). In all three states, the flow is along the surface. As mentioned, an important thing to remember about

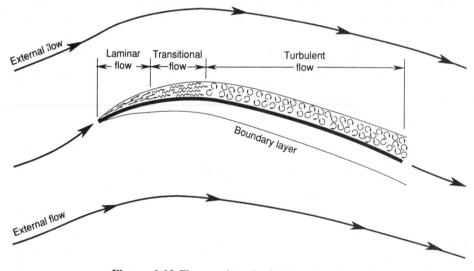

Figure 6.10 Flow regions in the boundary layer

that drag becomes a benefit rather than a liability, as it is when beating, is one of the reasons why a beam reach is the fastest point of sail. Another reason is that on a beam reach the sail forces (S_{Total} in Figure 6.3) point much closer to the direction (S_{Drive}) the boat travels, increasing the drive force and reducing the heel force (S_{Heel}).

a boundary layer is that it cannot easily tolerate a rapid increase in surface pressure (i.e., slowing down). Aerodynamicists term this abrupt slowing down and accompanying rapid increase in pressure as an adverse-pressure gradient. This situation can be further aggravated by a simultaneous change in direction. The boundary layer is likely to separate, and when this happens, a bubble forms, and this bubble is characterized by rapid changes in flow direction and a dynamic mixing with the external flow. It takes considerable energy to fuel this mixing, and the loss of energy obviously decreases lift and increases drag. This is frictional drag.

As can be discerned from the illustration, laminar flow is the smoothest, and the ability to maintain smooth laminar flow—without the shift to the more agitated transitional and turbulent flows—is the oft-given explanation of why porpoises are such extraordinary swimmers. According to some theories, these marine mammals, which can show bursts of speed of up to 40 knots and sustained speeds of 18 knots while being fueled by a few pounds of fish, can sense the change on their skin from laminar to turbulent flow and reshape their bodies to prevent it. The ability of the porpoise to swim so fast on so little fuel is, in fact, why the shape of the modern submarine is similar to that of the bottle-nosed dolphin.

When it comes to maintaining smooth laminar flow, sails and keels are not so well endowed. As can be seen in Figure 6.10, the smooth laminar flow, be it on sails or keels, is a brief, or transitory, state in the real world of sailing. Further, sails aren't like airplane wings. They bend, contort, flap, wave, and crease. Similarly, a hull and its underwater appendages move this way and that, even in the smoothest seas. Thus, it is very difficult for laminar flow to form on these foils.[5] A sail presents a second obstacle to the formation of laminar flow: no sail, with the possible exception of a new, pristine, and completely unwrinkled one, has sufficient smoothness to allow laminar flow to exist beyond its forward section. Even then laminar flow exists only part of the time.

Assuming that laminar flow seldom exists in sailing, the flow over most of a sail is turbulent. This occurs when the airflow disrupted by surface friction, for example, forms a more turbulent layer. Although this relative lack of smoothness and the corresponding increase in frictional drag may be disconcerting to sailors, some very bright people interested in making things like golf balls or airplanes move faster go to considerable lengths to change laminar flow into turbulent flow. Changing laminar flow into turbulent flow is why

---

[5]This suggests that if keels and rudders likewise sail in turbulent flow, it might well be a waste of time to sand the bottom of a sailboat to glossy perfection with fine-grit sandpaper.

golf balls have dimples on them and why some wings, both those in nature and those made by humans, have turbulators, small projections on the leading edge designed to break up the laminar flow.

The reason why nature and humans are so interested in changing laminar flow to turbulent flow is that with laminar flow, separation occurs in a severe and drastic manner, thereby greatly increasing the chances of stall. (Stall is the point where most of the flow over the leeward or suction side of the foil is separated. When this happens in aviation, for example, airplanes drop from the sky.) Turbulent flow, on the other hand, allows for a smoother transition to the separated state, thus minimizing the propensity for the flow to stall. To put this another way, laminar flow has lower drag, but turbulent flow is more forgiving. The practical reality of this is that turbulent boundary-layer flow is better able to withstand a sudden increase in pressure.

FORM DRAG

Since the days that OPEC had us lining up at the gas pumps, automobile manufacturers have been talking about "low coefficients of drag." One need not be an aerodynamicist to recognize that something low, sleek, and round, a Honda CRX sports car, for example, has a lower coefficient of drag than a bus. All one needs to do is listen to the difference in wind noises when driving down the road to know that a sports car has less form drag than a bus. Or, for that matter, compare gas mileage between a vehicle that is low, sleek, and round and one that is boxy. There are, indeed, shapes that trouble the air less than others. Less energy is wasted on cheating the wind, to use another popular post–gas shortage expression.

In sailing, the form drag of the mast adversely affects the mainsail. A loss of kinetic energy occurs as the wind encounters the mast. What happens is that the air attempts to follow the contours of the mast but ultimately lifts away from it, creating a pocket, or bubble, of disturbed air. The front of the main coincides with this area of disturbed air, and a major reason that the main is less efficient than the headsail can be traced directly to this fact. Not surprisingly, much work in sailing has concentrated on reducing the form drag of the mast. The focus of this work is to minimize the area of disturbed flow behind the mast so that the airflow reattaches itself as close to the front of the mainsail as possible.[6]

[6]The boardsailor's RAF sails (rotating-asymmetrical foil; see Figure 13.1, page 312) were designed to reduce turbulence, or separation, between the mast and the sail on the leeward side. The boardsailor's camber-induced sail (see Figure 13.2, page 313) was designed to reduce turbulence on both windward and leeward sides.

A sail, too, has form drag—drag due to its form or shape. As we know, once bent, the airflow accelerates around the leeward side of the sail. In the process, it does not perfectly adhere to the sail surface but lifts slightly away to form a separation bubble over which subsequent air passes. The flow also lifts, or separates, on the lee-side trailing edge in an effort to join up with the free stream. On the windward side, the flow doesn't precisely follow the curve of the sail but is slightly straighter (but windward separation is less of a problem since relatively little force is produced on that side). The air between these lines and the sail is very slow-moving turbulent flow that that must be dragged along for the ride. These sections of dead air underneath the flow are like bubbles. Aerodynamic engineers describe this condition of excess baggage as parasitic, or form, drag.

For sailmakers and sailors alike, it is important to reduce the size of this band of slow-moving air. For example, in the early 1970s North Sails asked Heiner Meldner, a specialist in fluid dynamics who is discussed in Chapter 2, to do computer-flow studies of this phenomenon. Meldner discovered that by slightly flattening the middle sections of the mainsail in the horizontal direction—in essence, decreasing its camber and producing a slight Frisbee shape—that pocket of dead air would be less, form drag reduced, and drive force increased. It seemed to work.

Sailors, too, can help to reduce the size of the band of dead air. If, for example, the shape of the mainsail is highly curved near the leech, then separation will be more likely to occur there. In effect, those aforementioned bubbles burst. Not only does that affect the main, but as we now know, separation on the main also affects the upwash on the genoa, which is such an important sail. However, make the leech of the mainsail straighter (by reducing camber, i.e., easing the mainsheet and/or bending the mast), and the size of the band of slow-moving air will be reduced, meaning the bubbles are less likely to burst.

Angle of attack also determines the size of the band of slow-moving air. With a sail just on the verge of luffing, the stagnation streamline comes in at the luff, and the flow on the leeward side remains attached, unseparated. As a sail is sheeted inboard, the angle of attack increases, and the stagnation streamline moves around to the weather side. Then the flow has to make the sharp turn around the sail to the lee side. It accelerates in the process, and a bubble forms at the luff where the flow separates. Often, it reattaches itself to the sail. Then, of course, the flow has to slow down to satisfy the Kutta condition, and if the now accelerated flow is going too fast to slow easily, a bubble can form near the trailing edge, too. Those bubbles can grow, front to back for leading-edge stall or back to front for trailing-edge stall. Telltales mounted luff to leech on the leeward side of the sail would indicate this.

INDUCED DRAG

Form and frictional drag are certainly important, but when compared with induced drag, are small players. As we know, the air on the windward side is generally at a higher pressure than the air on the leeward side, and in an attempt to reduce the pressure differential, the high-pressure air "leaks" over the top and under the bottom of the sail (see Figure 6.11). This is induced drag.

Another way to think about induced drag is that while a sail or an airplane wing ends abruptly, the circulation flow does not. The circulation flow spins off the ends of airfoils in a dramatic fashion (this, too, is shown in Figure 6.11). In the case of a Boeing 747, the spinning, sometimes described as "tip tornadoes," can continue for miles. It is, not surprisingly, a hazard for smaller aircraft. The energy required to produce these tornadoes takes a considerable toll on the lift or the drive force of the wing.

Because a wing, sail, or keel has to end, there is induced drag around any lifting surface. Thus, to minimize induced drag, airplanes sometimes have

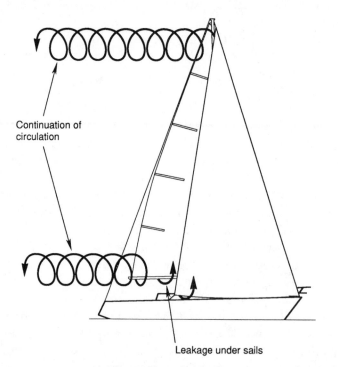

Continuation of circulation

Leakage under sails

Figure 6.11 Induced drag

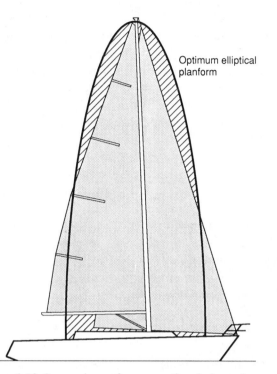

Optimum elliptical
planform

Figure 6.12 Comparison of a conventional sloop rig to
the optimum elliptical shape of the RAF Spitfire wing

fences on their wing tips, and keelboats—in particular, 12-Meters since the
era of *Australia II*—have wings on the bottom of their keels.

A high-aspect-ratio shape also has a significant effect on minimizing
induced drag. In the case of a sail, for example, a high aspect ratio means
there is less foot and less head area relative to the rest of the sail for the flow
to escape. Obviously, the lift-to-drag ratio is higher in the high-aspect-ratio
foil.

By World War II the designers of the famous RAF Spitfire airplane
determined that the optimum profile, or planform, for a wing of uniform cross-
sectional shape is an ellipse—U-shaped (see Figure 6.12).[7] It is optimum
because every section of the wing has the highest lift-to-induced-drag ratio for
a given aspect ratio and area. From the perspective of induced drag, the worst
shape for an airfoil is a triangle, the shape of a headsail and, to a lesser extent,
the main. If the ellipse is a U, the triangle can be thought of as a V, and the

---

[7]A wing of constant cross-sectional shape is the same as a sail with constant camber.

main and jib as upside-down Vs. An upside-down V obviously has higher lift at the bottom and lower lift at the top when compared to the optimum ellipse.

From this discussion, it becomes apparent that the optimum planform for a sail is as close to an ellipse as possible. Practically speaking, this means a mainsail with battens—ideally full battens—supporting a good-size roach (*roach* is the extra area outside the straight line from clew to head) set on a mast with considerable aft bend.[8] This is the sailmaker's art imitating the airplane-wing designer and both of them imitating nature, as this foil shape is similar to that of a hawk's wing. This elliptical shape works for a hawk, a mainsail, or an airplane wing because it has the highest lift-to-induced-drag ratio or, more simply, the best lift-to-drag ratio.

One interesting conclusion here is that based on the planform shape, a genoa is less efficient than a main. This is because when compared with a main, the genoa is more triangular in shape. Although true in terms of sail shape, the headsail is more efficient because it receives so much help from the main and is typically much larger.

Following this to its logical conclusion: Why not make the headsail more like a main? Shouldn't that provide the best of all worlds? For racing boats, at least, sail profiles, or planforms, are limited by racing rules but, more importantly, by practical considerations. For example, using battens to support an increased roach in a Number 1 genoa doesn't sound like a bad idea until you have to tack it. Thus, sailmakers, yacht designers, and, yes, sailors have found other ways to maximize lift and minimize drag in both overlapping headsails and mains. This will be addressed at the end of this chapter. (Boats that race under the International Offshore Rule [IOR] or International Measurement System [IMS] are now allowed to put as many as four battens of unlimited length in Number 3 genoas. Since such sails do not overlap the mast, the battens cannot foul it when tacking.)

---

[8]It is interesting to note that minimizing induced drag through an elliptical mainsail shape was the primary reason for the bendy topmast on the British 12-Meter *Lionheart*, which sailed in the 1980 America's Cup. The rig was designed by the aerodynamicist and author C. A. Marchaj, who is referenced throughout this chapter. Many observers concluded that the primary reason for the success of the rig was the increase in *unrated* sail area. While the influence of more sail area is almost always paramount, the reduction in induced drag was, Marchaj thinks, also significant. He claims that because of the decrease in induced drag, the drive force of the bendy rig was increased 30 percent in wind-tunnel tests. Sailing upwind in 12 knots, this would allow a speed increase of .25 knot or an improvement of 4 percent in the upwind speed of a 12-Meter. *Australia I*, the boat that sailed in the actual Cup races that year against U.S. *Freedom*, also used a bendy mast. The boat won one race in the series. In those days of America's near-total dominance of this contest, that was a considerable feat.

TWIST AND VERTICAL CHARACTERISTICS OF WIND

It should be clear by now that there is friction when wind passes over a sail; similarly, there is friction when the wind passes over land or water. As the speed of the airflow increases as it rises through the boundary layer of a sail, so, too, does the velocity of the wind increase with height above the water (see Figure 6.13). Marchaj suggests that in the open ocean if the wind speed at 5 feet is 5.4 knots, then the wind speed at 50 feet will likely be 8.7 knots, or fully 60 percent greater.[9]

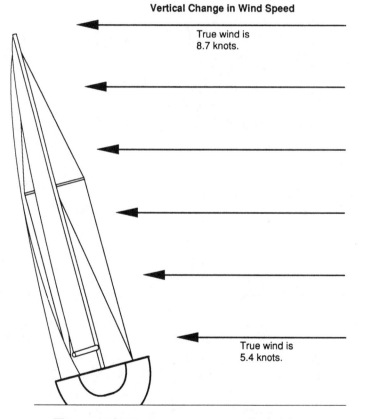

Vertical Change in Wind Speed

True wind is
8.7 knots.

True wind is
5.4 knots.

Figure 6.13 Wind speed increases with height.

[9]There are exceptions to this, however. Because of wind shear, there are times when the flow at the top of the mast is less than at the bottom and at a very different angle. Wind shear is caused by the influence of micro–weather systems or wind thermals. Although not common, wind shear is not an unknown occurrence either. Because of its unpredictability, wind shear is a very dangerous condition in aviation.

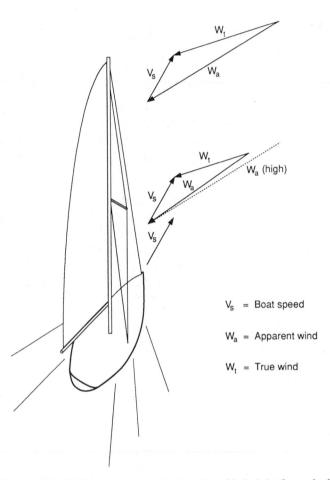

Figure 6.14 Shift in apparent-wind angle with height from deck

As velocity increases with height, or gradient, there are corresponding changes in apparent-wind direction, as seen in the vector diagram (see Figure 6.14). A vector represents speed (by the arrow's length) and direction (by its compass orientation). Combining vectors for both boat and wind speed shows that with constant boat speed, a velocity increase in the true wind (W_t) causes the apparent wind (W_a) to shift aft in direction.[10] In other words, from bottom to top, the wind has a natural vertical twist. Typically that twist is about 3 to

___
[10]The true wind is the wind you feel when the boat is stationary; the apparent wind is the wind you feel in a moving boat. The speed and angle of apparent wind are the vector sum of the true wind plus the boat speed and heading.

5 degrees on an average 40 footer (see Figure 6.15). The natural twist in the wind has far-reaching implications for sailmakers and sail-trimmers alike.

Sails are twisted, in part, to account for this vertical shift in the wind. Twist can be defined as the change in the angle of the chord lines of a sail to the centerline of the boat at various heights up the sail (see photograph on page 118). Due to the vertical shift in the wind, the bottom of the sail is beating (when sailing upwind), while the top is close reaching. The top of the sail is further twisted to account for induced drag. Marchaj notes that induced drag causes the head of a sail to stall prematurely, so the sail is twisted at the top even more.

The wing tips of many airplanes are likewise twisted. Thus, if the wing stalls from a loss of speed or from too great an angle of attack, separation is less likely to occur over the entire wing. The twisted tip, sometimes described as washout, is more likely to stay unstalled, meaning that at least part of the wing continues to work, and, it is hoped, the airplane remains in the sky.

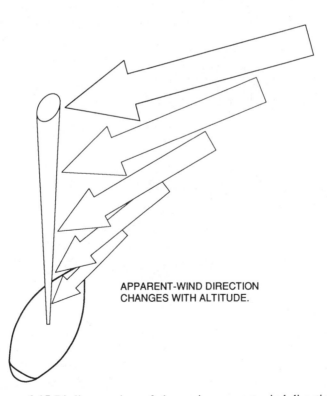

APPARENT-WIND DIRECTION
CHANGES WITH ALTITUDE.

Figure 6.15 Bird's-eye view of change in apparent-wind direction

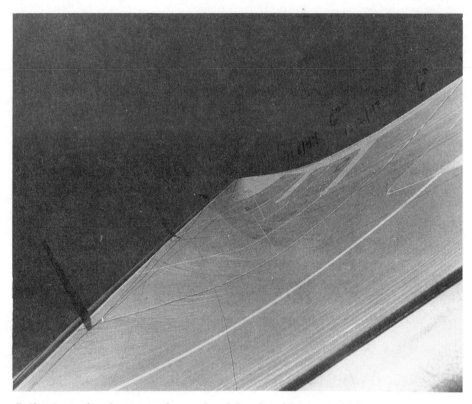

Sail twist is the change in the angle of the chord lines of a sail to the centerline of the boat at various heights up the sail. (Courtesy of North Sails, Inc.)

CAMBER AND TWIST

Sailmakers have found ways in the design of mainsails and headsails to maximize the lift-to-drag ratio. This is done through variations of camber and twist up and down the sails. As we know, camber increases maximum lift attainable, given a certain angle of attack. Twist, on the other hand, reduces angle of attack and therefore lift.

Suppose, for example, that the bottom section of a main was kept deep —high camber—then high lift is possible. This is an intriguing idea since the bottom of the main is a high-lift area because the sail chords are longest at the bottom of the triangle. Just under the boom, however, there is a gapping hole, a perfect breeding ground for induced drag. So by reducing camber in the bottom quarter of a main, we sacrifice some lift but greatly reduce induced drag and actually improve the lift-to-drag ratio, or net drive force of the sail as a whole.

In the middle sections of a main (half to three-quarters up), sailmakers want the highest angles of attack and good camber to generate the most total force. Too much induced drag will result if this is done too near the bottom of the sail. As we move to the very top of the sail, it is also important that the sail shows maximum camber. As there is very little sail area at the top of a triangle, this part of the sail has very little lift, but camber can help to maximize lift. Camber at the top also helps to get the main away from the form drag of the mast. This is particularly needed at the top of the triangle, where sail chords are so short.

What we are doing to the main with camber is making it more elliptical, pushing in its bottom via the mechanism of decreased camber and pulling out its top via increased camber. Returning to our letters, by pushing in the wide part of the V and pulling out the narrow part, the V becomes more like a U, the shape of the ellipse. This gives a more elliptical lift distribution and a better lift-to-drag ratio (see Figure 6.16).

Turning to sail twist, the total twist of a flying shape measured from the centerline to the head is surprisingly large, about 25 degrees for a genoa and 20 degrees for a main. Let's examine a genoa first to determine why.

First, the natural twist in the apparent wind for a 40 footer is, as described previously, 3 to 5 degrees. Second, in order to smooth the transition from high-lift areas in the midsections to the zero-lift area at the very head, a sail designer attempts to twist the sections to reduce gradually the angle of attack. Then, as discussed, induced drag at the top of a sail causes this section to stall prematurely, so it is twisted to prevent this. This man-made aerodynamic twist accounts for about 7 degrees on a genoa. (The need for twist is less for the main, since the presence of roach reduces drag by making the sail more elliptical in shape.)

The third and the most significant reason for increased genoa twist involves the interaction of the genoa and main. As we know, the main provides upwash to a headsail—increased winds at a more favorable angle (i.e., a lift). To match this lift in the wind, the sail designer twists the sections of the genoa out to leeward. This is the equivalent in sail design of moving the sheets outboard when reaching (see Chapter 9). This accounts for about 15 degrees of the total twist.

Twist is different for the main. Total twist is less since the main sails in the downwash of the headsail (less wind and a header). Downwash is why before hull speed is reached, the boom is sheeted on the centerline while sailing upwind. (As will be discussed in Chapter 10, the direct effect of increased

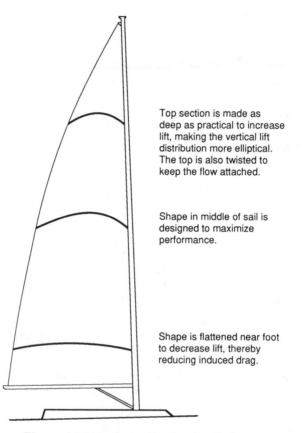

Top section is made as deep as practical to increase lift, making the vertical lift distribution more elliptical. The top is also twisted to keep the flow attached.

Shape in middle of sail is designed to maximize performance.

Shape is flattened near foot to decrease lift, thereby reducing induced drag.

Figure 6.16 Vertical tour of mainsail shape

sheet tension is to remove twist.) Second, less aerodynamic twist is needed in the main since, as described earlier, the main is more elliptical in shape, therefore less affected by induced drag. The twist to account for induced drag is about 5 degrees for a main versus 7 degrees for a genoa. Third, with less induced drag, there is less of a transitional problem between high lift in the middle and low lift at the head, and thus less twist is needed. These factors account for approximately 5 degrees of difference between mainsail and genoa twist.

In summary, total jib twist is increased from the lifting effect (upwash) of the main, whereas total main twist is decreased from the heading effect (downwash) of the jib. Also note that the interaction is different for a fractional rig as compared with a masthead rig. Since the part of the fractional main above the hounds is not affected by the downwash of the genoa, its angle of attack should be less. Thus more total twist for the fractional main is necessary.

In minimizing induced drag, twist serves an important function for the sail-trimmer as well. By matching the angle of attack to the ever-changing direction of airflow, twist is the sail-trimmer's tool for preventing induced drag. However, it is not always easy or obvious to maintain optimum twist angles because the airflow at varying heights is affected by so many factors. Therefore, it is helpful to place several telltales across the top of a mainsail and try not to have too many of them stalling. If too many are, the sail needs more twist. This will be addressed more fully in Chapter 10.

Other things—indeed, things less subtle than camber and twist—are done to both headsails and mains to minimize induced drag and maximize lift-to-drag ratio. One way induced drag is minimized in a headsail is to extend its foot down to the deck. Called a deck-sweeper jib and sometimes described as foot roach, this treatment effectively prevents the air from leaking from the high-pressure windward side to the low-pressure lee side. This solution is more common for the racer than the cruiser, because as we will see, foot roach dramatically reduces visibility to leeward; also, most headsail reefing and furling devices, so popular on cruising boats, make it difficult to extend the headsail tack and, thus, foot to the deck. For cruising and racing boats alike, the aspect ratio of headsails has also grown dramatically higher along with higher-aspect-ratio rigs, because as we now know, high-aspect-ratio sails have less top and less bottom, in proportion to the rest of the sail, for the flow to escape. Therefore, induced drag is less, and the lift-to-drag ratio of the headsail is higher.

Turning to the main, it is best—from the perspective of minimizing induced drag—if the boom is close to, even touching, the deck. Like a deck-sweeper jib, the deck and boom form an effective seal, making it harder for the air to leak under the boom.[11] In the interest of crew safety, however, racing rules usually prohibit this. In contests where rules are few and far between, as in the unique 1988 America's Cup, this low boom was clearly seen on the huge monohull *New Zealand*. This treatment, called the end-plate effect, makes it harder for vortices to leak from the high-pressure weather side to the low-pressure leeward side. It is analogous to the aforementioned fences on wings or wings on keels. Many racing boats carry wide booms for the same reason. This trend dates back to the J-boat *Enterprise*, which defended the America's Cup in 1930. The boat used a 4-foot-wide boom, labeled "the Park Avenue boom" after that wide avenue in midtown Manhattan, to minimize induced drag.

---

[11]For the same reason, sailboard sails, in particular those designed for speed, show exaggerated foots. This treatment (see Figure 13.5, page 318) keeps the foot of the sail on the deck of the board, minimizing induced drag.

Full-length battens—which Chinese junks have used for hundreds of years—became popular on recreational sailboats in the 1980s because of their positive effect on the lift-to-drag ratio. High-speed catamaran sailors were likely the first to employ them; this was followed by boardsailors and, most recently, by cruising and racing sailors, except for those who race under the International Offshore Rule, which at this writing doesn't permit them.[12] Full-length battens allow even greater roach, making a mainsail more like an ellipse—the V more like a U—decreasing induced drag and improving the lift-to-drag ratio.

KEEL SHAPE AND INDUCED DRAG

From the preceding discussion, it becomes clear that minimizing induced drag has had a profound influence on the planform of the keel of modern racing boats and most cruising boats. For example, the modern keel for both cruiser and racer has a high aspect ratio because there is less tip area, in proportion to the rest of the keel, for the flow to escape. On the other hand, when draft is severely limited by racing rules, such as the 12-Meter rule, or when shoal draft is desirable for cruising boats, wings are often used to minimize induced drag.

Most recently, designers of racing boats have begun to curve the trailing edge of the keel—making it more elliptical in shape, more like the trailing edge of the Spitfire wing, the wing of a hawk, or the shape of a mainsail. Indeed, the planform of the modern racing keel is close to the profile of the full-battened main.

---

[12]If all full-length battens did was to improve the lift-to-drag ratio, they would not likely be so popular with the cruising fraternity. They also improve sail durability because of reduced flogging, hold shape better, and are quieter. This is discussed in Chapter 10, ''Mainsails.''

CHAPTER 7

THE SHAPES OF CRUISING AND RACING SAILS

★ Sails are designed to be folded in bags and stowed when not in use. In some fundamental ways, this has made the life of a sail designer even more complicated than that of an aeronautical engineer. Imagine the complexity of designing an airplane wing if it had to be folded away in a bag at the end of a flight. Or imagine the work of a sail designer if the airfoil could be made of rigid materials with a solid framework supporting it. The latter idea requires no great leap of imagination; the solid wing we used in the 1988 America's Cup on our multihull *Stars & Stripes '88*, combined with her light and slippery catamaran hulls, showed the world the efficacy of a winged sail.[1] The major problem with this rig was not aerodynamic efficiency or speed, but what to do with the wing when not sailing, and what would have happened if it got too windy and we had to reduce sail (see photograph on page 124).

Sailmakers are dealing with what is, in essence, a living, breathing, ever-changing membrane. They must shape their foils by balancing the forces of the wind with the tensions in the sail. This can be difficult. In a genoa, for example, the controlling mechanisms are basically cloth, line, and wire. These devices may seem perfectly adequate if your frame of reference is a 197-square-foot J-24 headsail; however, if your frame of reference is a 2,300-square-foot Maxi headsail, that is asking a great deal of cloth, line, and wire. This helps to explain why sailmakers have so readily embraced high-tech materials, particularly as the boats and their sails get bigger. Anything that gives something soft many of the properties of something solid—while permitting it to be folded away in a bag—is most desirable.

---

[1]*Stars & Stripes* was not the first sailboat to use a solid-wing sail. The wing was based on C-Class catamaran technology; indeed, two class stalwarts, designers Duncan MacLane and Dave Hubbard, who worked on the *Patient Lady* series of catamarans, were instrumental in the design of the Cup boat's wing.

The multihull Stars & Stripes '88, *which sailed against the huge monohull* New Zealand *in the 1988 America's Cup, showed the world the value of a winged sail.* (*Courtesy of North Sails, Inc.*)

Described this way, sail design—indeed sailing—is a complex phenomenon, but complexity shouldn't necessarily be viewed as a negative quality. Although the problem is complex, the solution is elegant enough to have fascinated humans for centuries. If simplicity was all one cared about, we would all play old maid rather than contract bridge and drive powerboats rather than sailboats.

HISTORY OF SAIL DESIGN

The earliest evidence of sailing dates back almost six thousand years. A 133-foot sailing ship was found near the tomb of the pharaoh Cheops, who lived from 3960 to 3908 BC. Although the boat was apparently built for his funeral and likely never touched the waters of the Nile, rock carvings from this period show that the Egyptians used similar oar- and sail-powered vessels for trading on the Mediterranean. In the ensuing years, the "art" of sail design progressed slowly—until most recently. It was less a case of brilliant thinking or inspired problem solving than a case of what worked in the past is good enough. Developments and advances were often mistakes that worked.

Times have changed, particularly in the last decade, and even a cursory look at some recent advances reveals how far sail design has progressed. For example, there are the new cloths, polyester/Mylar, Kevlar/Mylar, and Spectra/Mylar, which give something soft many of the desirable properties of something hard. Further, high-tech racing and cruising sails are now divided into a plethora of panels in order to align precisely the strongest threads in the cloth with the greatest stresses in the sail. Then there are roller-reefing and -furling cruising sails, which stay up through thick and thin, show good shape even when reefed, and require a minimal crew to attend to them.

The year 1983 was a turning point in the America's Cup, as well as in yacht design and sail design. It was the year when Australian designer Ben Lexcen used a computer-driven velocity-prediction program (VPP) in the design of *Australia II*. Since then, such programs, or codes, have become a fundamental tool in yacht-design studios. It works this way: A VPP is fed numerical details of the hull, displacement, rig, wind angle, and wind speed as input, and gives as output the speed, heel angle, and leeway angle (leeway angle [see Figure 6.3, page 98] is the difference between the compass course and the actual course made good). More recently, sail designers have begun to avail themselves of this VPP technology. In special projects—such as sails to be used in the America's Cup or Olympic Games or for a new class or type of racing or cruising boat—output of the velocity-prediction program is sometimes used as a first step in the process of sail design. Such programs can give the sail designer at least a rough idea of what the sail forces and hence sail shape will have to be.

Of late, programs more specific to sail design have been developed. Designers are now able to predict the sail forces, heeling moments, and centers of effort for any sail configuration in any given wind condition and on any given heading. These data are, in turn, related to such yacht-design concerns as the location of the hull's center of lateral resistance and the lifting forces from the keel or centerboard and from the rudder (see previous chapter). Then by adjusting the position and sheeting angles of sails and their planforms in the computer, the sail designer may be able to suggest alterations to the sail plan that will increase its driving force, hence boat speed.

Although this computer modeling may be done on the most sophisticated racing boat or the most efficient and comfortable cruising boat, not every project warrants this degree of computer work—the wheel isn't reinvented every time a sail is designed. However, computer modeling is most helpful for new projects, or when a rig shows an unusual aspect ratio or a boat is of an unconventional design. It is, of course, most helpful when new cloths become available or when design philosophies change.

INVENTORY

Sail design starts with inventory. Due to One Design class rules and, in some cases, limits set by rule-makers, as well as space aboard a boat and space in one's bank account, hard choices typically have to be made about the boat's inventory. To the sail designer, such compromises mean it is important to know if the boat in question is going to spend most of its time racing in Cowes, England, or in San Francisco Bay. A One Tonner sailing in the Admiral's Cup in the typically light winds of Cowes might carry three Number 1 genoas (light, medium, and heavy), whereas the same yacht sailing in windy San Francisco Bay might have a light-medium Number 1, a medium-heavy Number 1, and a slightly smaller Number 2. The reason for this is that much stronger winds are typically encountered in San Francisco Bay, and the latter inventory gives the crew a better match to the conditions. (Inventory is discussed in Chapter 12.)

MOLDED SHAPE

Once the inventory has been determined, the sail designer turns to the design of the sails: the shape, size, configuration, and construction. At North this design, or blueprint, is called mold, or molded shape. The molded shape is the unstretched, or unloaded, form that a sail assumes before being subjected to sheet and halyard tensions and wind pressure. Imagine a genoa being held aloft by three people. The three corners are held up but not stretched, and the weight of the cloth lets the sail relax and assume its predetermined profile, or molded shape. To a sail designer, the mold of a sail consists of such factors as the position and length of the edges of the sail (luff, leech, and foot) and the offsets. Offsets are a two-dimensional way to describe a three-dimensional curve. The familiar sail-draft measurement, as shown in Figure 2.2, page 17, is an offset. Draft shows how far the curve varies from the straight line, or sail chord. Several offsets on the horizontal line give a good indication of the curve in that particular horizontal section. Do this in several horizontal sections and then describe the lengths and positions of the edges, and you have a good indication of the shape of a sail.

There are, as discussed, two techniques used to shape sails. The simplest method is to put extra material in the luff of a sail and, in the case of a mainsail, in the foot. These are called luff and foot curve, respectively. When the sail is flown, the extra material sags into the sail, creating shape (see Figure 2.1, page 16).

Broadseaming is the second technique used to shape sails. In broadseaming, one edge of a panel is straight, while the adjacent edge of the next panel is curved—usually a convex curve (see Figure 1.1, page 6). (In highly curved sails, like spinnakers, both edges may be curved.) When the two edges are joined, it is impossible for the cloth to lie perfectly flat on the loft floor.

As in the days of Hood and North, the shape of the foil can come from trial and error or from scientific testing. Although my bias is toward the scientific method, used by North and others, this is not the only way to design sails. As we will see in the next chapter, many eminently successful sails have been, and will continue to be, designed through the instincts and experience of a sailmaker and then fine-tuned by trial and error. All good sailmakers have to address the same problems, and this design work can be done in the mind's eye, on the back of an envelope, on the loft floor, or with the rapid-fire on-off switches of a computer. In the same way as a writer is judged by the words on the page and not by the word processor or computer that put them there, the tools of the sail-design trade are secondary to the practical result: the sails.

Once the sail is designed, it is lofted, or laid out. This can be done on the floor with a designer using long sticks, or battens, to draw curves, or on a computer using eminently sophisticated software. If done in the computer, the machine determines a surface that fits the shape and works out the appropriate curvature at any point on the sail. The next step is to divide the sail into its panels and evaluate the change of curvature across the panel, hence the broadseaming. This, too, can be done by designers on the floor making educated guesses or by machine. Here the computer is vastly superior in that a person can shape only a limited number of seams, typically in a horizontal orientation, whereas a machine can effectively and efficiently shape all of them in any direction. The result is that the former may have hard edges, or bumps, where the seams are shaped, particularly in its vertical profile; the latter is relatively smooth. To complete the process, each panel is cut into its appropriate shape. This, likewise, can be done by a man or woman using scissors or by feeding the instructions into a computer-controlled X/Y plotter/cutter, which cuts the sailcloth precisely to the correct size and shape (see photograph on page 128).

If all of the above is done in the computer, computer-aided design (CAD) and computer-aided manufacturing (CAM) are linked. This linkage—impos-

The panels that make up a sail are cut by the X/Y plotter/cutter, the link between computer-aided design (CAD) and computer-aided manufacturing (CAM). The sophistication of this approach and the need for it become apparent when you consider that a Maxi main can consist of ninety panels, each of which is shaped. (Michael Levitt photo)

sible until most recently—means that if a sail designer can dream it, the machine can usually figure out how to build it. This development has changed design from being a manufacturing-constrained process to a design-oriented one. In the former case, ease of assembly (cutting, sewing, and finishing a sail) is a major—typically *the* major—consideration; in the latter, the best possible aerodynamic shape is the major consideration. Today, design no longer need be limited by the fundamental question, Can we build it?

MAINSAIL DESIGN

Sailors have more control over the shape of the mainsail than the shape of any other sail. This is because only one of the three sides (the leech) is unsupported, and many devices allow the sail to be dramatically reshaped: outhaul, downhaul, Cunningham, halyard, mainsheet, and traveler. However, it is important that the correct three-dimensional shape be present when the sail leaves the loft. A poorly shaped main will be a failure no matter what the crew does to it. (This, indeed, holds true for any sail.) It is also important to fit or precisely tailor the main to the rig and not rely on exaggerated rig and sail adjustments to disguise design flaws. Using unusual adjustments, such as excessive mast bend, halyard tension, or Cunningham, to compensate for a poorly designed mainsail usually means that both the shape of the main and the tune of the rig are compromised. This is a perfect example of two wrongs not making a right. It is, in fact, worse than that. Since we now know that the mainsail has such a profound impact on the headsail, the efficiency of that most important sail is compromised, too.

Luff Curve Luff curve is an important element in mainsail design. When designing a sail, it is important to know the bend characteristics of the mast. For instance, the luff curve on a mainsail for a lightly rigged Farr One Tonner will be much greater than the luff curve for a sail for a robust Swan 40. Also, the distribution, or rate, of curve along a spar will vary from boat to boat, even among so-called sister ships. Thus, the distribution of luff curve must similarly be tailored to the rig. When luff curve is properly matched to mast bend, the mainsail gets fuller when the mast is straightened and flatter when it is bent. Sail shape as a function of mast bend works this way: When a mast is bent, its middle moves forward relative to the top and bottom. This moves the luff of the main forward, too, removing overall shape.

Where the draft falls is also important. First, the position of maximum draft is determined (see Figure 7.1). Then its location or distance from the leading edge is compared with the overall chord of the sail. Draft position is thus location/chord, expressed as a percentage. If the draft is 4½ feet back and the chord is 10 feet, draft is 45 percent. This is an important measurement

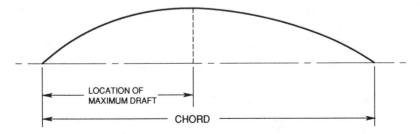

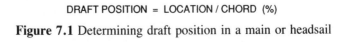

DRAFT POSITION = LOCATION / CHORD (%)

Figure 7.1 Determining draft position in a main or headsail

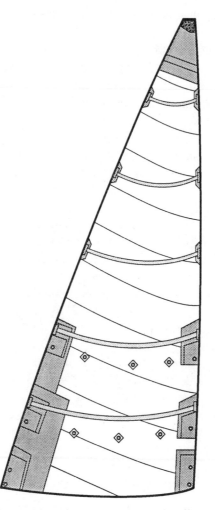

Figure 7.2 Full-battened mainsail

for headsails, too. (Many sailmakers sell an inexpensive optical card—such as a Sailscope—that makes it easy to determine draft and draft position.)

The sectional shapes of mains have become fairly standard over the years, with the position of maximum camber being located somewhere between 38 and 48 percent back from the leading edge. Turning to the trailing edge, aerodynamic theory, as discussed in the previous chapter, tells us that these sections should be quite straight to prevent the air on the leeward side of the sail from separating. However, as the trailing-edge sections become flatter, the leech becomes structurally unstable and flutters. In a mainsail, this problem can be alleviated by the use of long or full battens, which are becoming quite popular on cruising boats (see Figure 7.2); however, their use is sometimes restricted by class or rating rules, in particular the IOR. They conform to the rules of the International Measurement System (IMS), Performance Handicap Racing Fleet (PHRF), and Midget Ocean Racing Club (MORC).

So direct is the connection of batten length to leech support that a full-battened polyester/Mylar mainsail may well be faster than a considerably lighter and lower-stretch Kevlar mainsail (with short ''IOR-style'' battens). Full-battened Dacron cruising mainsails are faster than Dacron racing mainsails before the days of Kevlar; compare a good full-battened Dacron mainsail to a poorly designed or manufactured or tired Kevlar racing main, and the Dacron sail will likely be faster. Full-battened mainsails will be discussed in more detail later in this chapter.

The other major element of mainsail shape is twist (see photograph on page 118). The reasons why sails are designed with twist was discussed in the previous chapter, but to summarize them here: The wind has a natural vertical twist, and this twist in the wind must be matched to the twist in the sail. Also, twist helps to keep flow attached to the top of the sail, thus minimizing induced drag and maximizing the all-important lift-to-drag ratio.

THE RACING MAINSAIL

The most dramatic change in the design of the racing mainsail is the structure and panel layout of the sail. As recently as 1983, cross-cut Kevlar/Mylar mains were most common. The Kevlar substrate used then was strongest in the fill direction (across the roll of cloth), and in order to match the strengths of the cloth to the loads on the sail, mains were cross-cut. Or to put it another way, the seams roughly paralleled the boom. This was consonant with early stress maps. These stress maps, which show the direction and magnitude of the forces in a sail, revealed that the stresses in a main run in a straight line from head to clew.

During the 1983 America's Cup, however, *Australia II* carried the first vertically cut and radially clewed mainsails. These sails utilized warp-oriented Kevlar cloth. Since the primary strength of the cloth ran the length of the roll of cloth, vertical panels were required. As for the radial clew, advances in computerization led to better stress maps, which showed that the loads did not, as was thought, only run up and down the leech of the mainsail in parallel lines. There is a second important force component that radiates from the clew. Thus was born the radial clew. By matching the cloth's greatest strength to maximum loads, the sail stretches less and holds its designed shape for a much longer time.

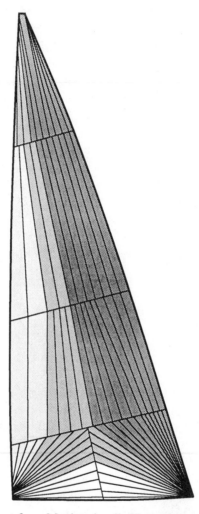

Figure 7.3 Panel layout for a Maxi mainsail. The white areas are polyester/Mylar and the shaded areas are Kevlar/Mylar. Each shade of Kevlar/Mylar denotes a different material, with the darker shades representing the heavier materials.

As should be apparent, none of this precise matching of cloth strength and sail load would be possible without accurate computer-generated stress maps. Accurate stress maps mean that sails can be reinforced precisely where extra strength is needed. This is analogous to building a high-tech fiberglass boat, in which carbon fiber or Kevlar is blended in the glass laminate where extra strength is needed, such as where winches and turning blocks are mounted.

Since 1983, the structure of the racing mainsail has developed further, with the sail being broken into more sections and smaller panels. This is an even more precise way of matching strength to load. It is now common for a North Sails One Ton main to have nearly fifty panels, and a Maxi main might have ninety panels. Figure 7.3 shows a typical Maxi mainsail (mainsails are the focus of Chapter 10). One ancillary benefit of the multipaneled mainsail is that more panels obviously require more seams, and seams, when aligned to the load, add strength to a sail.

THE CRUISING MAINSAIL

When it comes to the cruising mainsail, the first question the sailor must ask is, Do I want it to be easy or fast? The answer to that question sorely affects the design of the cruising main. Ted Hood, featured in Chapter 2 and no stranger to either world, decided on easy for the cruising main. In the mid-1970s, he brought to the market his inspired Stoway Mast. Here the mainsail winds up neatly on a roller-furling rod inside a specially designed mast. It is not an all-or-nothing solution as the mainsail can be partially furled, or reefed. Further, there was no need for a sail cover, as the sail was protected from sunlight and the elements inside the mast. Fifteen years later, it remains both an easy and an elegant solution to mainsail handling and is found on many cruising boats, particularly in the larger sizes and/or for those who often sail shorthanded. Dodge Morgan, for example, used a Hood Stoway Mast on his Hood-designed sloop, *American Promise*, in his record-setting solo circumnavigation.

Like practically everything in sailing, the Stoway Mast has trade-offs. It is expensive; since it can't be retrofitted, it requires a dedicated mast and a specially designed sail. Also, the mast must be oversized to accommodate the furled sail. The mainsail, which is in an unenviable position to begin with due to the form drag around the mast, suffers even more behind an oversized mast. Further, the mast weighs more than an ordinary mast, which can affect the sailing motion of a boat. Most important, however, is the fact that the mast requires significant compromises when it comes to sail shape. With the Stoway Mast, sail shape, or form, definitely follows function.

A major reason is that since the sail furls in a horizontal direction, regular (horizontal) battens can't be used. Without horizontal battens, however, little or no roach (the area beyond the straight line running from clew to head) is possible; in fact, most sails for this rig are built with hollow leeches. Battens that run up or down the leech are sometimes substituted, but this is nowhere as effective as horizontal battens. Also, to facilitate reefing and furling, the mainsail must be built with a short luff and foot. Depending on one's priorities, these criticisms may sound gratuitous; it is analogous to saying a great car isn't great because it's expensive and not the fastest car on the block. The Hood Stoway Mast and others like it went a long way toward taming that difficult customer, the mainsail. If one wanted a simple answer to the explosive growth of cruising in the last decade, devices like this, as well as devices that facilitate headsail reefing and furling, can take considerable credit. They have removed much of the drudgery and heavy work from sailing.

For cruising sailors who are willing to trade at least somewhat more work for more speed and for some other factors that affect the quality of life afloat, there is the relatively new full-battened mainsail. This design first became popular on small racing multihulls, then large ocean-girdling racing multihulls and sailboards. In such company, it is obvious that speed was the distinguishing feature of the full-battened main. The battens could support an oversized roach, and as you will recall from Chapter 6, this makes the sail more elliptical in shape, reducing drag and improving the all-important lift-to-drag ratio. This is another way to say such sails are faster.

Then someone noticed other benefits to be garnered from full-battened mainsails. For example, with such good luff support, these sails are less affected by what sailors term backwind. This means that they are easier to trim when going upwind, as well as faster. Such sails are also quieter, even when motoring with the main up into a breeze. They are far less likely to slat back and forth in very light winds, which is tough on a sail and eminently tough on the nerves of the crew. The rigidity makes dropping the sail easier. In summary, these factors make sailing less frantic and more tranquil. Full battens also make the sail more durable because it is no longer hinging where the batten pockets end.

There are trade-offs here, too. Battens weigh more than sailcloth, and the longer the battens, the more the sail weighs. Thus, some sailors who go this route opt for full-battened mains made from soft polyester/Mylar, which brings the weight back down to that of the conventional Dacron sail. This cloth is an exciting option for the cruising sailor. First of all, it shows a sandwich construction, which is very flexible for its weight because the stiff Mylar is concentrated in the middle of the structure where it can bend easily. Second, the double-cloth arrangement adds strength in both warp and fill directions, giving the material very high tear strength and good puncture resistance. Third, the seam-holding ability of the two Dacron layers is equivalent to that of traditional woven sailcloth—an important feature for a material intended to last many seasons. An added benefit is that having cloth on both sides gives the material the look and feel of Dacron.

Another trade-off is that the full-battened mainsail is likely to cost about 25 percent more than a conventional mainsail, although this is still nowhere near the cost of the new mast and specially designed sail that the Stoway

With the patented Dutchman system, vertical control lines, which weave through the mainsail and run to the topping lift of the main, keep the sail under control when it is dropped. The sail stacks neatly on the boom. (Courtesy of Dutchman)

requires. Part of the added cost of a full-battened sail is materials and labor —battens are expensive and batten pockets are difficult to make—but such sails also require solid engineering to ensure that the sail goes up and down without jamming. By any measure, a full-battened sail that jams is a failure —indeed, dangerous.

Most notably, such sails require somewhat more work on the part of the crew and somewhat more technique to set, stow, and reef. Differing from the Hood system, such sails have to be hauled aloft and lowered again so often. Although the difference between up and down and in and out may not seem that substantial, in practice it is. Also, at the end of the day, they have to be furled and covered with a sailcover.

The time-honored method of slab-reefing is typically used when shortening full-battened sails, and when compared with reefing with the Stoway, it is somewhat more difficult, too. However, new and old techniques and products, such as lazy jacks, Dutchman (see photograph on page 135), and LazyMate—devices that catch, hold, and sometimes control the sail when it goes up and down—make furling and reefing such sails easier.

A third mainsail choice for the cruiser is the conventional—or classic— mainsail. This is popular for cruisers for whom low price is most important or for those who like to race, now and then, under a rule that prohibits full battens. Such sails can be reinforced with heavier patching and stitching and use longer battens.

GENOA DESIGN

When sailing upwind, the genoa is typically the most efficient sail on a boat. As addressed in the previous chapter, this sail does not have to contend with the form drag of the mast, as does the main, and the mainsail directs more wind onto the lee side of the genoa and at a more favorable angle of attack, at that. Additionally, the mainsail ensures that the leech velocities of the genoa are higher, and due to the higher velocities, the flow on the lee-side trailing edge of the jib is less likely to separate.

Headsails are characterized in many ways. One method is overlap (see Figure 7.4). Overlap is computed by dividing LP (which stands for luff perpendicular and is a line drawn perpendicular to the luff through the clew) by the J measurement (the length base of the foretriangle). If, for example, LP is 22½ feet and J is 15 feet, then the headsail is described as a 150 percent genoa. Headsails are also described by numbers, with the Number 1 being the

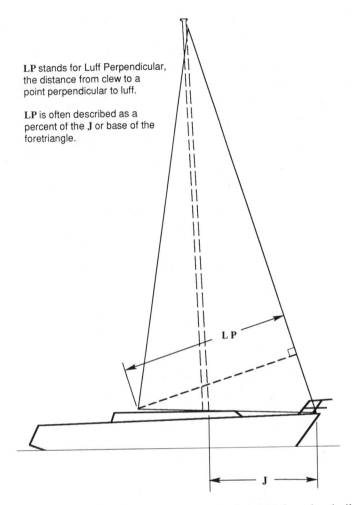

LP stands for Luff Perpendicular, the distance from clew to a point perpendicular to luff.

LP is often described as a percent of the J or base of the foretriangle.

Figure 7.4 Determining luff perpendicular (LP) for a headsail

largest sail. A Number 1 genoa for an IOR boat typically shows a 150 percent overlap. Such a boat might sail with three Number 1s, light, medium, and heavy, which are distinguished by progressively heavier cloth and progressively flatter shapes. (PHRF boats can usually sail with a 155 percent genoa, without penalty.) A Number 2 varies from about 130 to 135 or even 140 percent; a Number 3 has an overlap of about 98 percent. Incidentally, a 98 percent sail, like a Number 3, does not quite fill the foretriangle and, as such, does not overlap the main. Such a sail is a violation of the old slot-effect theory.

A third way a headsail is described is in terms of aspect ratio. A simple way to think about aspect ratio is to divide the headsail's luff length by overlap. These days Number 1s, 2s, and 3s are full on the hoist, or show a maximum-sized luff. So a Number 3, with its short overlap, shows the highest aspect ratio; a Number 1, with the largest overlap, shows the lowest aspect ratio.

As a main is designed to match mast bend, a genoa is designed to match headstay sag. Therefore, rather than the luff of the genoa being a straight line, it is designed with varying degrees of luff curve, depending on anticipated headstay sag, which is a function of wind speed and the power of the backstay adjuster. That said, even with the most sophisticated hydraulic backstay adjuster, headstay sag is unavoidable to some degree on all sailboats, so this must be addressed in the design of the sail (see Figure 7.5).

A light Number 1 generally has much more luff curve than a (heavy-air)

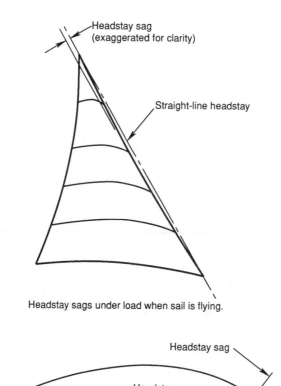

Figure 7.5 A headsail should be designed to match headstay sag.

Number 3. Obviously, the headstay sags more in the increased winds where the Number 3 works, and the direct effect of this increased sag is to make the sail fuller. What happens is that the three corners of the sail are fixed relative to each other, so when the headstay sags, it pushes extra material into the front of the sail. This makes a sail fuller, which is exactly the opposite of what is desired in heavy winds. So to keep the Number 3 flat, luff curve is removed.

If headstay sag varies from the design of the sail, the sail becomes either flatter or fuller than its designed shape. If headstay sag is less than what was designed for, the sail, particularly the front, is flatter; if the headstay sags more than the design, the leading edge is fuller (see Figure 7.6). As will be discussed in Chapter 9, there are times when increased headstay sag is beneficial, such as when trying to make a flat sail work in winds below its range or when extra power is needed to punch through leftover seas.

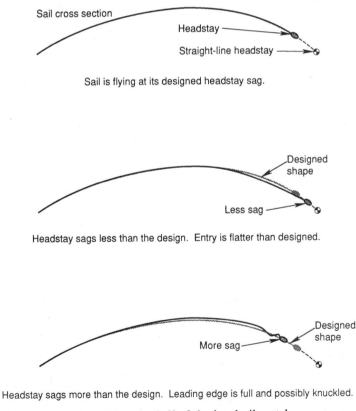

Sail cross section

Headstay

Straight-line headstay

Sail is flying at its designed headstay sag.

Designed shape

Less sag

Headstay sags less than the design. Entry is flatter than designed.

Designed shape

More sag

Headstay sags more than the design. Leading edge is full and possibly knuckled.

Figure 7.6 When the luff of the headsail matches headstay sag and when it does not

THE RACING HEADSAIL

For racing yachts in particular, the position of the clew of the headsail should be as close to the deck as possible—1 to 2 feet—to ensure an end-plate effect between the foot of the sail and the deck to minimize induced drag. Also, if the end-plate effect is achieved, the effective aspect ratio of the genoa is increased. This, too, minimizes induced drag (see Figure 7.7). The recognition of the benefits of high-aspect-ratio sails is why Number 3 genoas are now full-hoist and nonoverlapping, whereas a few years ago they would have been 80 percent on the hoist and overlapping the main. When speed is the first consideration, as it almost always is for the racer, high-clewed genoas are verboten.

The molded shape for a typical Number 1 has the maximum camber, or draft, at around 40 to 45 percent back from the leading edge, with the maximum depth varying between 15 and 18 percent depending on the application, weight of the boat, and sheeting angle. As a flatter sail is more desirable when the

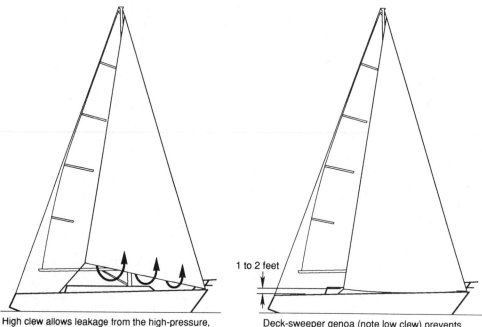

High clew allows leakage from the high-pressure, windward side of sail to the low-pressure leeward side—decreasing lift of sail.

1 to 2 feet

Deck-sweeper genoa (note low clew) prevents air from leaking and maximizes end-plate effect of deck.

Figure 7.7 Effect of genoa clew height

wind blows, a Number 3 has less depth than a Number 1, and the position of maximum draft in the Number 3 is about 40 percent, perhaps even farther forward. Draft positions vary because in the increased winds in which the Number 3 works, the headstay sags more, the cloth stretches more, and the draft shows more of a tendency to migrate aft than does the draft of a light-air Number 1. Thus, by putting the draft forward in the Number 3, it remains within effective limits, despite the shift.

The panel layout of a genoa is similar to that of the present-day main: vertically cut with a radial head and clew. This, too, could be seen on the genoas of *Australia II*. The keel of the boat deservedly received most of the attention for the victory, but the headsails and mainsails, designed by Tom Schnackenberg of North Sails, were also revolutionary (see below photograph).

Nearly as revolutionary as the famed winged keel of Australia II *were her vertical sails. Here* Australia II *(KA-6) practices with* Challenge 12 *before the start of the 1983 America's Cup races. The heavy-weather genoa of* Australia II *is made of warp-oriented Kevlar/Mylar. Also note the radials at the clew, head, and tack. The sophistication of the vertical sails becomes apparent when comparing them with the fill-oriented horizontal sails on* Liberty *in the next photograph.* (Courtesy of North Sails, Inc.)

Most of the headsails we used on *Liberty* were fill-oriented—thus cross-cut—sails (see below photograph).

A primary benefit of vertical panels is that they allow "step-up" construction, where the heaviest and strongest cloth is used in high-load areas, such as the leech. With the major load in a headsail running up and down the leech, it is an easy matter to make the long vertical panel out of heavy warp-oriented Kevlar/Mylar cloth. One panel can do this easily. With horizontally cut sails, made with fill-oriented cloth, step-up construction is a much more difficult proposition. It requires several horizontal panels and several seams.

This is why most racing sails since 1983 are vertically cut and made primarily of warp-oriented Kevlar. The heavily loaded leech area is made of the heaviest Kevlar cloth, as are such other highly loaded areas as the head and clew. These sails also have a lighter Kevlar in the middle of the sail. Areas where the wind loading is less, such as the front of the sail, are usually built out of polyester/Mylar. The polyester/Mylar is not as strong as the Kevlar/

The cross-cut main and jib on Liberty. *(Courtesy of North Sails, Inc.)*

Mylar (for the same weight of cloth), but this does not matter as the polyester/Mylar is only used in low-stressed areas of the sail. From the perspectives of strength and weight, this method of building a high-tech sail is structurally superior and much more efficient.

With the high loads felt at the head and clew, a genoa is heavily reinforced in these areas with large patches. The loading at the tack of the genoa, while less than the head or clew, is also counterbalanced by patches.

The effects of radial clews are more pronounced on a low-aspect-ratio sail, such as a Number 1 genoa, because the angle at which the sheet leaves the clew is pointed more into the center of the sail. Therefore high levels of stress will also radiate into other areas of the sail apart from the leech. Obviously, this sail benefits the most from radial construction. On the other hand, as the loads in a high-aspect Number 3 genoa run more parallel to the leech, the panels on this sail are aligned more vertically. Figure 7.8 shows how the panel layouts in racing genoas have changed over the years.

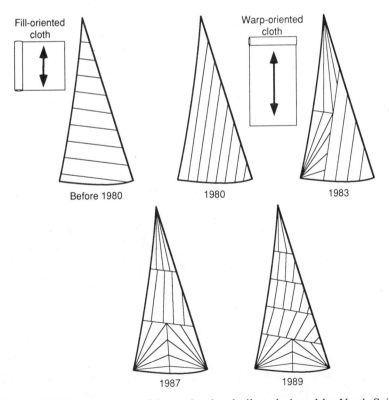

Figure 7.8 The evolution of the racing headsail as designed by North Sails

THE CRUISING HEADSAIL

Although developed for racing, the vertical sail with a radial clew proved to be most appropriate for cruising. The step-up construction allows the heavily loaded leech and the foot panel—the latter being vulnerable to waves breaking over the bow—to be made of heavier cloth. The panels get lighter and, at the same time, show less strength moving toward the luff (see Figure 7.9). This is acceptable because according to the stress maps, this part of the sail is less highly loaded. The result is a sail that is stronger for its weight. This is so important because the cruising sailor is now demanding a headsail that has the

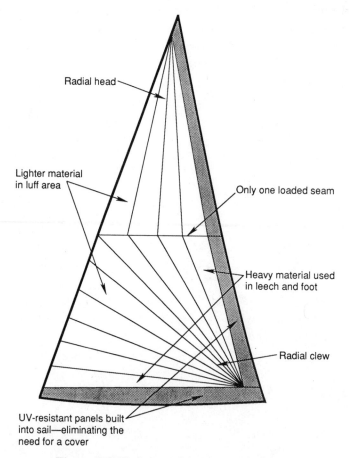

Radial head

Lighter material
in luff area

Only one loaded seam

Heavy material used
in leech and foot

Radial clew

UV-resistant panels built
into sail—eliminating the
need for a cover

Figure 7.9 Modern cruising genoa design

same range as a main, that is, not so heavy that it fails to work in 5 knots or so light that it stretches dramatically or even self-destructs in 30 knots. Such a hybrid headsail is impossible without step-up construction.

When roller furling, one other benefit of the vertical sail with the radial clew is that the leech and foot panels can be made out of special UV-resistant fabric. With cross-cut lay-ups, a separate UV-resistant vertical panel must be sewn to the leech. This vertical panel sewn across the horizontal panels that make up the leech adds unnecessary weight, compromising the performance of the sail in light air. If you sail with a roller-reefing unit, it is also desirable that the leech and foot of the sail be patched, or beefed up, at reef points, as they are under considerable loads at such times.

Such high-tech cruising sails can be made out of warp-oriented Dacron or the new soft polyester/Mylar. A problem with warp-oriented Dacron, however, is that it must be woven, and this process, as you may recall from Chapter 3, imparts crimp in the warp direction, making the fabric more stretchy in all directions. That said, holding shape is most important when sailing upwind, and not all cruising sailors think an extra 5 degrees of windward performance is worth going for lighter and less stretchy but more expensive polyester/Mylar cloth. A polyester/Mylar sail costs about 10 percent more than a comparable Dacron sail. From the perspective of performance, the soft polyester/Mylar is half as stretchy as traditional woven Dacron and about a quarter as stretchy as warp-oriented Dacron. It weighs 20 percent less.

Like the cruising mainsail, sail-handling gear has a profound effect on the design of the cruising headsail. While mainsail reefing and furling are relatively new concepts, headsail-furling devices have been around since the 1930s. Successful reefing, however, had to wait until the mid-1970s. It is the shape, particularly in the middle of the sail, that makes it hard to reef the headsail effectively. The reefed sail tends to be baggy—the exact opposite of what is desired in increased winds. The first attempt to improve the shape of the reefed sail was to make the sail flatter overall. Although the shape of the reefed sail may have been improved slightly, the shape of the unreefed sail was not. As most sailors in most places spend most of their time with the headsail unreefed, this was an unacceptable trade-off.

The next step was to marry the headstay unit to a specially designed headsail. The salient feature was a crescent-shaped piece of foam affixed to the luff. It is thicker in the middle of the sail and thinner at the top and bottom. Thus, when rolled, it takes more sail area from the middle—where the shape is—and less from the top and bottom. The result is a flatter reefed sail.

Reefing units require compromises of the unreefed headsail, too. The sail must be short on the luff, since the furling unit and the halyard swivel at the top take up space. This can amount to 18 inches or more of important luff length in a 35 footer. Since the tack fitting cannot be on the deck (it must be above the furling unit), a deck-sweeper jib is not possible. This increases induced drag, as does the fact that such sails typically are high-clewed. High-clewed headsails have advantages, however, particularly for the cruising sailor. They dramatically improve visibility to leeward. Also, such sails are less likely to catch waves that break over the foredeck and thus are less likely to direct the water onto the crew in the cockpit. Moreover, although high-clewed sails are not particularly good when beating, they are more effective when reaching. For the cruiser who likes to race on occasion, some headsail-furling and -reefing devices, like that made by Harken, are designed to be easily removed. This allows a racing headsail with a full luff and deck-sweeper configuration.

Not all cruisers, however, opt for such high-tech solutions. Most are quite happy with horizontally paneled Dacron headsails and mains. Dacron, as has been discussed, is quite stretchy, which compromises the ability of the sail to hold its shape. The stretchiness should be addressed in the design. Dacron sails are designed for the middle of their intended range, which means that they are a shade too full in the upper wind ranges and a shade too flat in the lower. This compromise is perfectly acceptable to many cruising sailors.

Some argue that the stretchiness of Dacron is a proverbial silver lining. A blown-out Dacron sail will still work—maybe not well, particularly when sailing upwind—but it will work. A blown-out polyester/Mylar sail is more likely to break. In the worst-case scenario, maybe a Dacron sail has better longevity than a soft polyester/Mylar, but there is no hard evidence to suggest that given reasonable and appropriate care, one is any more durable than the other.

SPINNAKER DESIGN

Spinnaker design is vastly different from triangular, or working-sail, design. The obvious difference is that these off-the-wind sails are free-flying. A traditional spinnaker is a symmetrical sail with the designed-miter curve running down its center, although today many asymmetrical designs as well are used in cruising and even in some racing applications. The luff and the leech of the traditional chute are geometrically the same—mirror images. When describing or designing this type of sail, the position of one luff and the miter must be specified, as well as the sectional data for half of the sail. Since the two halves of a symmetrical spinnaker are, by definition, mirror images, most sailmakers are concerned only with the design of half the chute.

There are three types of symmetrical spinnakers: runners, reachers, and all-purpose, and the way each sail is designed is also different. The differences may appear trifling or pedantic to the casual observer, but subtle alterations of the geometry of the sail can dramatically alter its stability and performance.

First consider the runner. Aerodynamically, the running spinnaker must act as a pure-drag device, which implies that projected area is the key. Or to put it another way, the more wind it stops, or blocks, the more effective the sail. The shape with maximum projected area is the rectangle, and interestingly enough, there is nothing in the racing rules that precludes the use of rectangular spinnakers. There is, however, something in the rules of nature because such a sail cannot be flown—at least without a square-rigger's yardarm, a boom at the top, which is illegal under all modern racing rules. This means that the spinnaker is essentially a triangle, but to maximize the projected area of the runner—to make it more rectangular—its maximum width is above the mid-point in the sail. The runner is, in essence, a compromise between projected area and stability, or between the rectangle and the triangle.

A reaching spinnaker acts more like a normal airfoil, with aerodynamic lift—rather than just drag—providing the driving force. Airflow, you may recall, has trouble staying attached to deeply curved sections, so the sail is flatter overall—something that encourages attached flow. This shape is achieved in the most common reduced-girth reaching spinnaker by putting its maximum width below the midpoint of the sail.

The all-purpose spinnaker lies somewhere between the previous two examples, and as the name implies, it is a compromise. There is a trade-off between maximum projected area for running and flatter sectional shapes for attached flow and stability when reaching. Predictably, the sail has its maximum width at or near the midpoint. (The three types of racing spinnakers are shown in Figure 7.10.)

The loads on spinnakers are much less than the loads on genoas. This is because when sailing upwind under a genoa, a sailboat builds apparent wind —to put this most simply, 6 knots of boat speed are added to the 14 knots of wind speed, so the wind seems to be blowing 20 knots and pulls on the sheet and sail with that force. This is one important reason why the polyester/Mylar cloth for a heavy Number 1 genoa might typically weigh 4½ ounces per sailmaker's yard, and Dacron cloth, 7 ounces.

On the other hand, when sailing off the wind (except perhaps at the very tightest reaching angles that a spinnaker might be carried), boats lose apparent wind. Thus, a spinnaker has less wind loading, and as a result, spinnakers are generally constructed out of very light fabrics, usually nylon, that vary in weight from .5 to 2.2 ounces. Because of the light weight of the sail as well

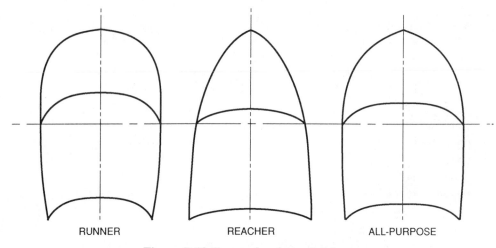

RUNNER   REACHER   ALL-PURPOSE

Figure 7.10 Types of racing spinnakers

as the fact that the luff is not typically restrained, the spinnaker is a particularly active sail.

In the early 1970s, it was discovered that the stress lines on spinnakers radiate from the corners. Thus, these sails were the first to benefit from radial construction. In hindsight one wonders why it took so long for sail designers to realize that the loads on genoas and mainsails also radiate from the corners, and these sails, too, would benefit from radial construction. On spinnakers, the two major stress areas are near the luff and the leech. When reaching, the loads near the luff are caused by the differences in aerodynamic pressure across the sail—similar to those that affect a headsail—whereas the stresses near the leech are primarily a function of sheet tension. The three corners of the spinnaker are typically reinforced with patches.

THE CRUISING SPINNAKER

The cruising spinnaker is very similar to the three types of spinnakers previously described, except that there is no longer an axis of symmetry down the middle. To put it another way, such sails are asymmetrical, as is a mainsail or jib. The sections are therefore defined in the same manner as these two working sails, with the maximum molded camber being located about 40 percent back from the luff. Because these sails are asymmetrical, they can only be flown with the designed luff serving as the leading edge.

There are two styles of cruising spinnakers: the "genoalike" sails and the "spinnakerlike" sails. The genoalike sails usually feed into the headstay, which obviates many of the handling difficulties associated with spinnakers. As is probably apparent in the descriptive appellation, such sails are better reachers than runners. The spinnakerlike sails are typically free-flying at the luff and are much larger and fuller in the head. Again as the name has it, such sails are more versatile, being relatively good runners and reachers. These sails are flown more like ordinary spinnakers—save for the absence of a spinnaker pole (neither type of cruising spinnaker requires one, though a whisker pole can help downwind performance)—but handling is typically abetted with spinnaker socks. (The genoalike and spinnakerlike cruising spinnakers are shown left and right, respectively, in Figure 7.11.)

Cruisers who don't mind the added work, added gear, and occasional aggravation of using a spinnaker pole sometimes opt for the all-purpose symmetrical spinnaker, described on page 147. Although the asymmetrical cruising spinnaker is likely to be a better reacher—all things being equal, a better reacher even than a traditional symmetrical spinnaker—it is not a great runner. This presents an interesting choice for the cruiser. On one hand, the asymmetrical chute is easier to fly, since it does not require a pole and is more efficient than its symmetrical cousin in most reaching conditions, but it is not

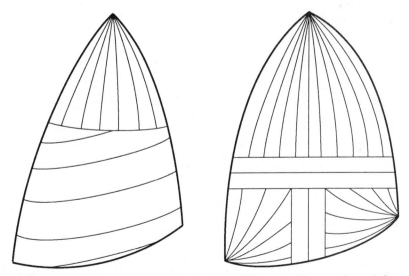

Figure 7.11 Types of cruising spinnakers: The genoalike one is on left; the spinnakerlike sail is free-flying, like a normal spinnaker.

particularly effective when running. On the other hand, the symmetrical spinnaker requires quite a bit of gear to fly. It is more efficient in running conditions and less so in reaching conditions. So a tough choice for the cruiser is between the cruising and the all-purpose spinnakers.

Although cruising spinnakers were specifically designed for this use, interestingly enough, they have played an important role in the last two America's Cups, which were characterized by either high winds or high boat speeds. In 1987, Tom Schnackenberg of North Sails pioneered the use of Gennakers on *Australia IV* during the America's Cup defense trials in windy Perth (discussed in Chapter 11). In the 1988 America's Cup, the huge *New Zealand* only used asymmetrical cruising spinnakers because the long, light, well-powered boat did not sail deep-enough angles to make ordinary spinnakers work.

Racing boats almost never sail directly downwind. When heading to the downwind mark, they reach up for speed, cover more ground, have to jibe, but typically get where they are going faster. The oversized and overcanvased *New Zealand* was so fast when reaching that her optimum course to get downwind was quite high. At such high speeds, the apparent wind moves even farther forward, making running, even beam-reaching, an uncommon event.

This was even truer for our *Stars & Stripes '88* catamaran, which only used asymmetrical cruising spinnakers and reachers, for closer wind angles. A reacher is typically fuller than a genoa and higher clewed but not as full as an asymmetrical spinnaker. This makes it an effective shape for very close reaching angles.

C H A P T E R   8

TURNING THEORY AND CLOTH INTO SAILS

★   Now that we have some familiarity with the theory of sail design, it is useful to see how it works in the real world in what is commonly referred to as a sail loft, but might be better called a sail factory and, in some places, a high-tech factory at that.

The North way of designing and manufacturing sails is described here for purposes of illustration, because it is among the most advanced approaches to designing sails, and thus, to my way of thinking, the most interesting, and because it is the method I know best. Also, this technology is becoming more common elsewhere. What should be stated again is that all sailmakers have to address the same problems, and this work can be done on the loft floor, on the back of an envelope, or in a computer.

For North, sail design and manufacturing became aligned with the computer in the early 1970s, through the work of Heiner Meldner and then Tom Schnackenberg (see Chapter 2, ''An Artist and a Scientist—The History of Modern Sailmaking''). In 1974, Schnackenberg, a former PhD candidate in nuclear physics turned sailmaker, wrote the company's first computer program to evaluate the broadseams for a given molded sail shape. This was called the Tin Sail program, and it allowed the designer to drape any number of panels in any direction over the desired molded shape.

Freedom and control were the gifts of Tin Sail to sail design. The program gave the sail designer great freedom to experiment with shape, and at the same time it allowed increased control of the manufacturing process, permitting a successful sail design to be repeated. Prior to the computer there was no guarantee that a successful design could be duplicated. Thus every sail was, to varying degrees, a one-off—a shot in the dark.

Repetition gave the sail designer a quantitative way of comparing one sail with another. It works this way: Suppose that by inspiration or perspiration,

Tom Schnackenberg wrote the Tin Sail program, which hurried sailmaking into the computer age. A gifted sailmaker as well as a computer programmer, Schnackenberg also designed the revolutionary sails for Australia II *(see photograph on page 141).*
(Courtesy of North Sails, Inc.)

a sail designer arrives at a great sail. By having a much better understanding of how it was designed and, as important, how it was built, he or she could repeat the design. Then elements like luff curve or broadseaming could be changed. This could be compared with the original sail, or a carbon copy of the original sail. If the new luff curve tested faster, this sail, too, could be repeated and improved. And so on. More than anything else, this process launched sailmaking down an analytical path.

The first programs ran on mainframe computers (at $1,000 per hour). The revolution in personal computers has meant that the new programs can run on smaller, more powerful machines, and the design software is more flexible than before.

The weekend sailor might well ask at this point, What does this computer design have to do with me? For starters, computers have helped to make sails more efficient, lighter, stronger, easier to use, and more durable. Few would argue with these qualities as they have dramatically improved life afloat. If this is not sufficient reason, computer-aided design and manufacturing have helped to make sails considerably cheaper. Factoring in inflation, sails today are quite a bit less expensive than they were ten or twenty years ago, much of which can be traced to the economies in the design and manufacturing process made possible by the computer.

The most recent North Sails CAD-CAM process, developed by Michael Richelsen, starts with a design program called Mold. Mold consists of the description of various sail shapes that have been tested on the water and optimized in the computer. It can be thought of as part of a design library, or data bank, where the measurements of the best sails are stored. First the designer selects a mold, based on the hard dimensions of the boat—for example, the P measurement, the distance from the boom to the black band at the top of the mast; and the E, the distance from the tack of the mainsail to the black band on the end of the boom (the inputs, or measurements, used by sailmaker and computer are described more fully later in this chapter). The numbers can then be run through another program, called Flow. Flow, in essence a computer-simulated wind tunnel, allows the sail design to be customized to a particular boat. If the computer says that this specific Number 3 will heel a boat too much, maybe the lead position is changed, the design is made flatter, or another standard shape—a flatter one, for example—is chosen (see photograph on page 154). Flow, however, treats the sail as a solid shape, a mold; it does not take into account the natural deformation, or stretch, that occurs from aerodynamic loading.

Michael Richelsen is responsible for the new generation of computer programs, such as Mold, Flow, and Membrane.
(Michael Levitt photo)

Flow is a computer program that simulates a wind tunnel by calculating pressure distribution on a sail. It allows the designer to customize a particular sail to a specific boat. (Courtesy of North Sails, Inc.)

Membrane, the third program, determines how the pressurized mold distorts from this aerodynamic loading. This computer-simulated structural analysis first divides a sail into thousands of tiny triangles. The aerodynamic loading subjects the sail to stretches and strains, and the sail and thus the triangles change shape—their sides start to bow—and become, in essence, diamonds. Then the computer computes the sum of the changes and determines the new shape of the sail. This can be shown graphically on a computer screen, or numerically. For example, the computer might say "the new leech is now 2 inches longer; the new luff, 1 inch longer; the depth is now 2 percent deeper." Membrane generates stress maps, from which the designer is able to match the layout of the panels to the loads in the sail.

As noted, the now distorted sail has a different shape, so the new shape, or geometry, is described again in Mold and then run back through Flow and Membrane, and then back to Mold in a process, or computer loop, called iteration. This might take an hour, a night, or a week until the designer is satisfied.

Through Mold, the designer can call up a visual representation of the molded shape of the sail on the computer screen and view it from any orientation. Because of the program's mapping, or descriptive, capabilities, Mold is also the link to the manufacturing process.

After the sail is designed and its geometry described in Mold, it is ready to be broken into its respective panels via a computer program called Meshgen. The designer can break the sail up into several sections (each section is separated by a joining seam), and the sections are paneled sequentially. The designer has total flexibility over the orientation of each panel. The theme of this work, as has been stated so often, is to align the strong threads of the panel with the major loads in the sail. The width of each panel is only limited by the width of the bolt of cloth. Meshgen also evaluates the degree of broadseaming at the edge of each panel.

The sail has now been reduced to a number of flat panels within the computer. The next task is to arrange these panels on a roll of cloth in order to minimize cloth wastage, but at the same time being sure that the thread orientation is correct. This is done using the Prepare program. After Prepare, the design of the sail is complete. The output from Prepare is used to drive an X/Y plotter/cutter that draws the shaped panels on the sailcloth and/or cuts the edges with either a rotating knife or a laser beam. The design and manufacturing loops are shown in Figures 8.1 and 8.2, respectively.

Thus is designed *one* sail, and the manufacturing information alone would fill three and a half yards of paper. The computer delivers this amount of hard copy, so the sail can be checked as it wends its way through the manufacturing process.

Before the laser or knife touches the panel of cloth, however, the material is rolled out, and the cutting-machine operator inspects the cloth for defects. Such factors as inconsistent color, extra threads, tight edges, or panel bow (in essence, fabric warp) can disqualify a section of cloth. Frequently the cutter will remove or bypass entire sections or may even reject the material completely if it does not conform to specifications. The material has already been tested for stretch characteristics but flaws cannot always be seen before this step. Then the cutting machine, controlled by the computer, goes to work. The fully cut sail may consist of ten different weights and styles of fabric and be made of as many as ninety pieces. All of these pieces need to be precisely stitched together.

Prior to being sewn, the triangular panels that make up a radial clew, head, and tack, called radial gores, are glued together to a 1-millimeter tol-

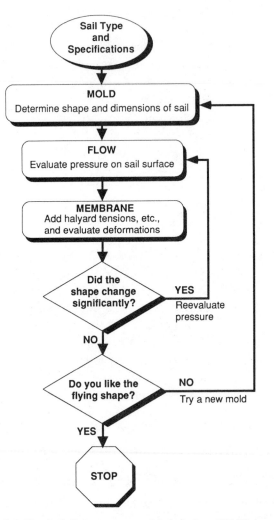

Figure 8.1 North Sails' computer-aided-design (CAD) process

erance. The new glues are very resistant to sheering forces, but like Velcro can easily be peeled apart. Thus if the designer is not happy with a seam after it is glued, it can readily be separated, repositioned, and reglued. Gluing also helps the stitcher.

The sewing machines used in this work are not household issue; rather, they can be as expensive as an automobile and have almost as many features. For example, a home machine has an 850 to 1,200 stitch per minute (SPM)

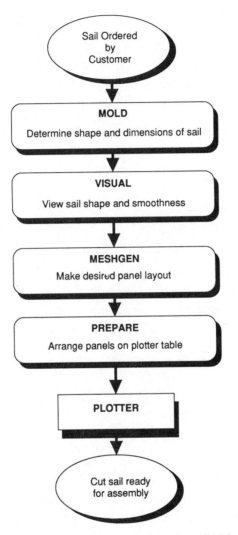

Figure 8.2 Computer-aided-manufacturing (CAM) method

capacity, whereas a dedicated seaming machine might do 7,500 SPM. The sail is pulled through the machine as needed; the thread is lubricated and the needle air-cooled. Making the job of the needle as easy as possible is important because the force needed to penetrate a half inch of multilayered Kevlar, which makes up a radial clew, is of the magnitude of a 22-caliber bullet. Kevlar, in fact, is used in bulletproof vests. All of this helps to provide a stitch without skips and thread burns, and whose lock—the vulnerable intersection between upper and lower threads—is buried in the fabric to better withstand chafe.

Radial-sail construction aligns the strongest fibers to the loads in a sail, but somewhere in the sail there are a series of horizontal load-bearing alignment points, or seams, where the radials come together. These seams aren't necessarily used for shaping; rather, they are used as places to turn the cloth in order to align it to the loads. The strength of these joining seams is critical—they can make or literally break a sail—and they require all of the CAD-CAM muscle of the computer to keep the complex geometry together. Once the geometry is determined, the seams are glued and then stitched with as many as five rows of heavy zigzag stitch.

The above is what a sailmaker refers to as layout, and when layout is finished, the sail has its windows, draft stripes, batten pockets, and custom features, but it still needs its patches. Today's radial patches—which, like the radial gores, must also match the load paths—are glued to the sail as smoothly as possible to achieve a light and strong foundation that will diffuse the loads from the sheet and halyard attachments. A patch is judged by its lightness, pliability, flexibility, smoothness, resistance to abrasion, and ability to diffuse loads. A perfect sail can be ruined by a bad patch, which might be too heavy or fail to fan the loads smoothly into the sail. A more subtle problem is that the stretch characteristics of a patch should match those of the sail. Many sailmakers use cloth seconds to make patches. Thus, if the sailmaker makes a patch from low-stretch Dacron fabric, and then joins it to a fairly stretchy Dacron sail, the sail will be out of balance and more likely to fail.

Finishing is the last sewing operation, and it is the ultimate test of the stitcher's art because every stitch can be seen and examined for tension, alignment, lock bury, and neatness. The well-finished sail must have stitching that is perfect even though the sail may weigh 400 pounds and a corner alone may be a half-inch thick. The end result must be a construction of solid foundation for the stainless steel or titanium hardware, which can carry sheet loads from 1,000 to 25,000 pounds.

The last step in the sail construction process is called handwork. Handwork, the oldest of methods, has been passed down from the sailors of the Nile. The handwork of today still uses the traditional palm, needle, and waxed twine but has incorporated the hydraulic-pressed full-tooth flared ring and the Kevlar-cored polyester webbing strap. In handwork, the clew rings, headboard, leechline cleats, battens, telltales, and handling hardware are added to the sail. This is also the last check to see if the sail conforms to the computer printout. The molded sail is finished; its success or failure, however, will be determined by its flying shape aboard the boat.

CONNECTING MOLDED SHAPE AND FLYING SHAPE

What the designer sees on the floor or on the computer screen is not exactly what one sees on the boat. Even with the most sophisticated computer programs, it is still a large step from the design of a sail to its on-board reality, or from its molded shape to its flying shape.

One reason is that there are so many variables. For example, wind loadings and sheet and halyard tensions can vary. Further, genoa shape is governed by the sheet-lead position and forestay sag, while mainsail shape is also affected by mast bend, traveler position, outhaul, Cunningham tension, and boom vang—or kicker, as it is sometimes called. The flying shape of these working sails is also influenced by the orientation of the panels. Also, the interactive relationship of mainsail and headsail affects the flying shape of both sails. Then, too, no two boats—not even so-called One Design racers or sister ships—are exactly the same; nor are any two sail-trimmers. Lastly, sails are assembled by people, and people have good days and bad. (These things will be further discussed later in the chapter.)

So complicated are all these elements that in the past few years, specialized computer software has been developed to help understand the connection between the molded shape and the flying shape. When this relationship is fully understood—when there is no difference between what is seen on the computer screen and what you get in the wind—sail design will be a far more exact science. Computer people call this WYSIWYG (pronounced wiz-E-wig), which is the acronym for "what you see is what you get."

Tightening the loop from design to manufacturing to flying shape may well be the most fertile avenue for a sailmaker. As noted, this is continuing to be done through better design tools: new computer programs and on-board photography. The photography process, called photogrammetry, works this way: The sail is designed in the computer—the mold—and its myriad curves are cut by computer. The next step is to take the finished sail and fly it on a boat. It is then photographed extensively, using several cameras. These hundreds of photographs are then digitized and brought back into the computer, where they are averaged. This gives an average flying shape that is then compared with the molded shape whence it came.

We call the difference between the molded shape and the flying shape aimoff. The goal of this work is to understand and accurately quantify differences between the molded shape and the flying shape, or aimoff, and ultimately to reduce the difference to zero. Then what the designer sees on the computer screen and what you get on your boat will be the same.

For a sail designer, the most fertile avenue for progress may well lie in tightening the connection between the molded shape in the computer and the flying shape. (Courtesy of North Sails, Inc.)

Determining aimoff has required a new way of measuring—in fact, a new way of speaking about—sails. We are now beginning to be more concerned with the actual curvature of sails, instead of such large-scale, or two-dimensional, measurements as offsets.

A NEW LANGUAGE OF DESIGN

The traditional language of sailmaking is offsets, where a curve of a sail is described in terms of its depth off a straight line. The new language is the rate of curvature, where a sail designer tells the computer the amount of curvature desired in the various sections of a sail. This difference represents a revolutionary step, but it is really closer to the way the eye works. Good sailors and sailmakers are always looking at and discussing curves: "That is too full, too flat; that needs more shape in the front, less in the back." We're trying to get away from such words as *more* or *less* and quantify the curve of each section of the sail. If this proves as promising as it appears to be, someday all sailmakers may say "We should have curvature of .55 in the back instead of .6."

One problem is that sailmakers use a two-dimensional language to speak about three-dimensional shapes. The sailmaker of today is like the English-speaking person who knows a little French. He or she thinks in English and then translates it into French. Someday—soon perhaps—we may speak in curves, a three-dimensional language, to describe more accurately a three-dimensional phenomenon like a sail.

A STANDARD OF EXCELLENCE

In the days before computer-aided design, there was no substitute for studying thousands or even tens of thousands of sails. Even today, a sail designer's advanced degree comes from many hours on the water and much hands-on experience. It is an all-consuming search for the perfect airfoil shape, or the "perfect rose" that is talked about in philosophy. Although I've yet to create a perfect sail, I have been lucky enough to have worked on the design of some very good ones, perhaps great ones. One of the best was a spinnaker we built for Dennis Conner's *Freedom*. The sail was fast enough to help us successfully defend the America's Cup in 1980, and fast enough to help propel me and the company I then worked for into the big time of the America's Cup and the big time of sailmaking.

Yacht designers have their favorite boats, and sailmakers have their favorite sails. That sail was important to me; it is the spinnaker I think about when I design all others. It came about this way: My relationship with Dennis Conner, which has spanned four America's Cups, started with what a salesman calls a cold call. With no invitation, only nerve, I telephoned him in November 1978 and said, "You've got to have our sails aboard *Freedom* in the next America's Cup." He did not mince words. "No way!" he said, but he was friendly, and we chatted for a half hour about his plans for the 1980 Cup. Before I got off the phone, I told him I'd keep bugging him about buying sails. He was a salesman, himself, so perhaps he wasn't offended by my aggressiveness. About a month later, he called back and invited me to skipper his trial horse, *Enterprise*. While flattered, I wasn't interested because I didn't see how being on the second boat—the second team—would help me as a sailor or how it would help my company get sails aboard an America's Cup yacht—something that is so important and something so few sailmakers actually accomplish.

Conner and I met a couple of months later at the Southern Ocean Racing

Circuit, the winter racing series in Florida and, in those days, the Bahamas. He asked me where I was going, and I told him back home to Connecticut. He commented, "Good, I'll come along." I said, "What do you mean, you'll come? Where are you going to stay?" He said, "I'll go to your place." We flew together, and he tried to convince me to become skipper of his trial horse. Talk about being a good salesman; by the time the flight was over, he had won me over, and in the ensuing decade, together we have won and lost some very big races and have become best friends. Both personally and professionally, that proved to be the best flight of my life.

After driving *Enterprise*, his trial horse, through the summer of 1979, Dennis must have been reasonably satisfied with my performance, because he threw me the proverbial bone. He asked me to make him a sail, *one* sail. Sobstad had a very talented designer, Peter Wheeler, and he and I bet the company's future on this roll of the dice. It might have been our only invitation to play in the big time. I knew exactly what I wanted because most of the spinnakers I'd seen on *Freedom* were poor. We made a few scribbles on a legal pad, wrote down a few numbers for such measurements as miter curve, maximum girth, and head angle, and built the chute. The amazing thing was that this sail was clearly faster than any spinnaker Conner had. We'd switch it back and forth, and whether it was on the first-string yacht, *Freedom*, or the trial horse, *Enterprise*, it was faster.

I parlayed that sail into a reasonably substantial spinnaker order from Conner, and I parlayed that second-string role on *Enterprise* into being a sail-trimmer aboard *Freedom* in the 1980 America's Cup. The funny thing about that spinnaker is that we never could improve it. We probably never built one equal to it. The subsequent spinnakers we built were probably good—they were certainly good enough to help win the America's Cup 4–1 against the very game *Australia I* with her radical bendy mast—but they were never as fast as the first one.

The moral of this story is that this spinnaker was, and in many ways still is, the best, if not the perfect, downwind shape. For me, it is the one with which all other spinnakers are compared. Whenever I design a spinnaker, this is the flying shape I think of. But, as discussed, a fundamental question for a sail designer is—or should be—How do you get that flying shape from numbers or sketches on a scratch pad or, these days, numbers or graphics on a computer screen? The fact that we were unable to make another as good shows how difficult a task this is, particularly in the days before computers had a place in sail design.

The inability to duplicate the *Freedom* spinnaker is an excellent example of how difficult it is to get humans to duplicate a complex set of curves like those of a spinnaker. The hands-on method of sail design and sailmaking depends on long sticks to draw curves, and it is very, very difficult to lay that stick down in exactly the same place and with exactly the same curve as you did four months and forty-five spinnakers ago. The tolerances, as will become apparent in Chapter 11, are that close. Another problem is that people tend to editorialize—they aren't machines and don't wish to be machines, and they always think they can do something a little bit better. This is the great strength and, at the same time, great weakness of human beings. Repetition is a cake-walk for a computer.

THE SAIL DESIGNER AND THE MACHINE

Since 1983, the computer has been very helpful in meeting the challenge of sail design. In sailmaking, the computer does certain procedures better than any human could, but like satellite navigation versus the sextant, the ascendancy of one does not completely obsolete the other. A small- or medium-size company staffed by gifted sailmakers can do a good job, perhaps a better one, on sails for a limited number of boats or classes. Only the biggest companies, which are asked to build sails for everything from a 10-pound, 8-foot sailboard that travels at 42.9 knots to an 80,000-pound, 82-foot Maxi boat that sails at 18 knots, find sail design harder to do without the computer.

It is easy to be dazzled by the leading-edge technology, but in sailmaking, the forest is far more important than the trees. Again, it is the sails in the wind that are paramount, not the tools used to design and build them. Sailmaking without the computer is still alive and well, even at the front lines of the sport. If I've had doubts about this on occasion, it was again proven to me in Perth, when in 1987 Dennis Conner's *Stars & Stripes* won the America's Cup using some "WeBe" sails, hardly a household name. WeBe was a diminutive of WeBeGe, which stood for "we be guessing" and later, when some of the guesses proved very good indeed, WeBeGood. WeBe was the sailmaking organization staffed by me; a handful of talented technicians such as Bill Peterson, with technical feedback from John Marshall, my predecessor as president of North, who served as the design director for *Stars & Stripes*; and, of course, the sailors, Dennis Conner, Bill Trenkle, and Jon Wright, to name a few. It was certainly the most unique and creative organization that ever helped power an America's Cup yacht to glory.

WeBe came about this way: While preparing for the 1986–87 America's Cup with Dennis Conner, I received a letter from my partner at Sobstad Sails that suggested it was time we went our separate ways. He and I owned equal amounts of stock in the company, but he had a family member who owned a few shares of stock and would side with him.

This was to be my third America's Cup as a sailor and sailmaker. While undoubtedly the America's Cup was good for our business, it was very hard on my relationship with my business partner. I'm sure he looked at it as if I was getting all the attention, and he was staying at home doing all the work. This had to be hard on him. I think I was sensitive to it, but there weren't any easy ways to handle it. I always tried to include him, to get him to sail with us, but it never seemed to work out well.

Because the communication with Sobstad in Connecticut proved to be so difficult, Dennis began ordering more sails from North Sails, San Diego. Never one to put all his eggs in one basket, however, WeBe was started at his behest. The WeBe way of sail design was like drafting a house. We wrote down every number and description that was relevant: luff curve, foot curve, leech curve, stretch characteristics of fabric, panel layout, and seam shaping. In no way was this computer-aided design.

It was fun to get immersed in sail design again. Prior to this, I was always involved in the politics of the event—keeping Dennis happy, keeping my business partner happy—and it was never easy to be the real creator of the sails. This gave me a chance to stick it out on my own. WeBe ended up making a couple of mains and most of the genoas we used in winning the Cup.

As Dennis was kind enough to write: "So as it turned out, we snatched a huge victory from what at first looked to be the jaws of defeat. Tom's dismissal actually worked to our advantage. No matter what we touched, it all turned to gold, In fact, Tom Whidden not only restored our sail program but soon attracted an offer to join his former foes at North as their president. . . ."

Little did I know how well it would work out for me in the end.

The import of this story is that although the computer's gift to sailmaking is considerable, it isn't indispensable. Without a computer, WeBe could build perhaps the best 12-Meter sails in Perth. Numerous niche-oriented lofts can build extraordinarily good sails with nothing more high-tech than long sticks and good hands and eyes. Even in this computer age, sailmaking remains an art and a science.

RULES AND EXCEPTIONS

Lurking behind the title of sailmaker is a person who must be an expert in aerodynamics, cloth technology, mechanical and structural engineering, perhaps computer technology, and such hands-on activities as sewing seams and pressing in rings. This person also has to be an expert sailor—intimately familiar with any number of types of boats—and, as important, be flexible enough to avoid being thrown by changes in the wind. Several of these disciplines and techniques can be the subjects of lifelong study. This job description is further complicated by any number of exceptions and variables. For instance, no two boats—not even so-called sister ships or One Design racers—are created exactly equal, nor are any two sail-trimmers. Also, sailcloth is different. Then, too, sails are assembled by people, and people are different: they have good days and bad. So a sailmaker's workplace reality is analogous to playing bridge or chess while changing the rules to varying degrees each time the game is played.

A perfect example of this is the variance in sailcloth. It stretches as well as shrinks and shears. This doesn't just mean that Dacron stretches more than polyester/Mylar, but that the degree of stretch may vary from one bolt of Dacron to the next. To the sail designer, the importance of this characteristic is that each bolt of sailcloth should be tested, and the results addressed in the design. Without adequate testing, making a sail would be like building a house without knowing the breaking strength of a 2-by-10.

Then, consider the rig of a sailboat, which is so fundamental to sail shape. A sailmaker learns quickly that masts are different—even those for the same model boat from the same manufacturer. A good sail flown on a nonstandard mast is likely to be a very different animal. The variance in rigs poses other problems for the sail designer. Mast steps in sister ships and One Design boats are not always in the same place; mast partners (where the mast penetrates the deck) are not always in the same place; and the length of the rigging may vary, so the amount of bend in a rig from one boat to the next may be different. All of this affects sail design to greater and lesser degrees.

MEASURING YOUR BOAT

This has practical implications for the sailor as well as the sailmaker. The fact that no two boats are created equal, not even One Design or production boats, means that every sail is, or should be, a custom or semicustom item. Thus when ordering sails, your sailmaker needs to know more than just the fact that you own a Puddlejumper 35. This amount of information is analogous to ordering a custom suit by telephoning a tailor you've never dealt with before and telling him you need a 40-regular. The odds of getting a perfect fit are slim.

If your boat is measured to one of the popular racing rules, much of the information the sail designer needs can be gleaned from the rating certificate.

If not, it means your boat should be measured—*literally measured*—before going to your sailmaker. Unfortunately, you can't assume that the manufacturer's or yacht designer's drawings of the sail plan and the deck are accurate.

Before Ordering Sails

1. With a tape measure, determine the distance from the deck to the top of the mast, which is referred to as the I.
2. Measure the distance from the top of the boom at the gooseneck to the black band near the masthead, which is called the P, or mainsail luff.
3. Measure the distance from the aft edge of the mast at the mainsail tack to the black band on the boom, which is called the E, or mainsail foot.
4. Measure the distance from the forestay at the deck to the mast at the deck, which is called the J.
5. Note where the spreaders are and their length (so sail patches can be placed in the appropriate spots).
6. Determine the genoa-track angles (see the next chapter) and describe and measure the tack fitting of the jib. Also, tell your sailmaker whether a headstay device (twin-groove or otherwise) is used and what type, and whether you use a roller-reefing and -furling device.
7. Determine the amount of mast rake, or aft lean. To determine mast rake, attach a weight to the main halyard. Then measure how far back it intersects the boom.
8. In the case of the mainsail, tell the sailmaker if you use roller-reefing or mainsail furling or a Stoway Mast or something similar; where the gooseneck is; and how the luff of the mainsail feeds into the mast and how its foot feeds into the boom.
9. Articulate clearly how the sail(s) will be used: racing, racing/cruising, offshore cruising, day sailing, or a combination. Each requires a different sail.
10. And lastly, know your budget.

It is also helpful for the sailmaker to know the ability of your crew and whether you plan to sail shorthanded. If you sail shorthanded, you might want lazy jacks to help control the mainsail when it is reefed or lowered, or a headsail-luff treatment, like foam or the newer still AeroLuff, discussed in the next chapter, which helps with the shape of a reefed headsail. In some ways, buying sails is like buying a car; there are any number of options, like UV protection or extra chafe protection, that can make your sails more durable and your sailing safer, easier, and more fun. Many sailmakers have a form that is helpful when measuring a boat for sails. It is a good idea to keep a copy for future reference.

EXPERIENCE MAKES THE BEST SAILMAKER

Major assets the sailmaker brings to the transaction are experience and firsthand knowledge of how various sails work on a given type of boat. The sailmaker needs to know the stability of a Puddlejumper 35, for example. In the best case, this is not merely a stability number provided by a yacht designer, but empirical knowledge of how your boat heels to various winds and various sail sizes and shapes. Similarly, the sail designer needs direct knowledge of how much mast bend is possible and typical in this type of boat. You probably wouldn't want the transmission of your car fixed by a mechanic making his or her debut in this type of repair, and you probably wouldn't want a sail made by someone who has never made a sail, or very few of them, for the type of boat you own and has little or no firsthand experience of the boat.

USER-FRIENDLY SAILS

Another variable that complicates the work of a sail designer is that sail-trimmers are not created equal. A sailmaker can design and build a perfect sail, and then when the sail leaves the loft, it is trimmed in a wholly different fashion than anticipated. This is because every sail-trimmer has his or her own ideas on how the sail should look. This gives, in essence, an entirely different sail.

The fact that all sail-trimmers and crews are not created equal has, in part, given rise to ''user-friendly'' sails—sails that are better, faster, and easier to use right out of the bag. Modern materials have had much to do with this. By giving something soft many of the characteristics of something solid, the new cloths allow a more precise execution of shape. One need not pull the strings with the precision of the late guitarist Andrés Segovia to make such sails go fast. Indeed, stretchy Dacron sails demand more technique for optimum performance than do high-tech sails.

GOOD HANDS

Even in the most modern sail lofts, computerization only goes so far. It can help with the hardest jobs, such as the design and the cutting of complex curves, but in most places, people are still required to sew the curves together and do the extensive handwork. Ultimately, a sail designer is no better than the people stitching the sails, pressing in the rings, and adding patches to the

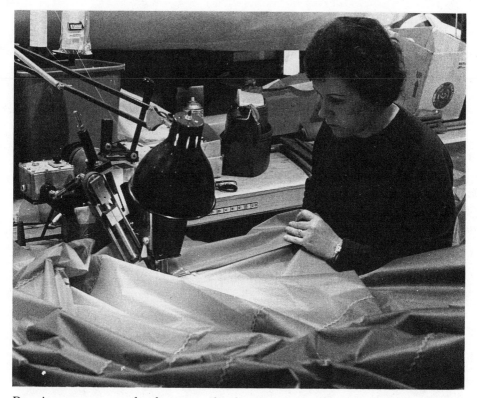

Despite space-age technology, a sailmaker is no better than the people stitching the sails and doing the other handwork. (Michael Levitt photo)

head, tack, clew, and reef cringles. Bad hands can break a sail—and even a company—as quickly as a plague of locusts in a computer program. Thus, it is important that a sailmaker have good systems and good checking to ensure that a sail doesn't fail because of how it is assembled. A way of saving money in sailmaking is to hire someone off the street, put him or her behind a sewing machine, and pay five bucks an hour to start. Then a year later, this person comes to you and asks for a raise. You eye the bottom line and say no, the person quits, and you hire the next person off the street for five bucks. For a sailmaker who wants to make quality sails, this philosophy leads to professional death, because it is going to take the next person at least a year before doing quality work. During that year, customers—likely to become former ones— are going to be saddled with those sails.

Obviously, employee satisfaction is a difficult, if not impossible, condition for a customer to gauge. Perhaps the best way to do this is to develop a relationship with your sailmaker. Get to know at least by sight the people who are designing the sails as well as the stitchers and the people pressing in the rings. If you see new faces every time you visit—or are kept far away from where the sails are assembled—you have reason to grow suspicious. Ask questions. The company may have found the best seamstress since Betsy Ross, or the continual employee turnover may be symptomatic of other, more serious problems that can have a direct bearing on the sails you carry out the door.

From the preceding, you can see that the playing field of the sail designer is complex, and the rules are changing all the time. The task is analogous to sailboat racing in a shifty wind. As in sailboat racing, the one who does the most right things along the way usually wins. The sailmaker who knows the most and does everything just a little bit better—from assembly to aerodynamics, to engineering, to design and manufacturing, with a total commitment to excellence—and yet remains flexible when the wind is truly shifting, will likely do the best job for you.

★

CHAPTER 9

HEADSAILS

★ Whether you race or cruise your sailboat, many of the fundamentals of headsail shape and headsail trim apply to both uses and a surprisingly broad range of boat sizes. There are exceptions—the most obvious being One Designs—but the fundamental principles nearly always remain the same.[1] To avoid unnecessary complications, we will focus on headsails for modern offshore yachts, both racers and cruisers.

DRAFT

The draft, or depth, is the single most important consideration when discussing a headsail, in fact, any sail. It is determined, you will recall, by focusing on a horizontal seam or line from luff to leech. Vertical sails have draft stripes for this purpose. This line is the chord (see Figure 2.2, page 17). Then the deepest part of the sail is located along the horizontal line, and its depth measured. This is draft. Sail depth is then draft/chord, expressed as a percentage. Thus, a 1-foot draft in a 10-foot span is described as a 10 percent depth.

There is no one depth that will be ideal in all conditions, but for any given wind velocity, wind direction, sea condition, and boat, there is a depth that will provide optimum performance. Given the number of variables, it is

---

[1]One Designs, which range from planing dinghies, like Lasers, to keelboats, like J-24s and larger, show a tremendous diversity. Their rigs may be unstayed, as in the former example, or stayed, as in the latter. Additionally, they typically conform to strict class rules. As the name implies, a major reason for One-Design racing is to keep the boats and sails as similar as possible so the contest is of the sailor's skill, not the sailmaker's, yacht designer's, or boatbuilder's. Not all classes, however, subscribe to a strict interpretation of this concept, and in such classes different sailmakers often have different ideas about sails.

misleading to be too specific, but fuller sails indisputably generate more power. This helps the boat to accelerate after a tack, assuming that the force is not simply converted to excess heel. The increase in power also makes a boat livelier—more responsive to the helm—and makes it less likely to be stopped by waves. These characteristics are particularly desirable in light winds of 3 to 12 knots.

As the wind increases to 10 to 18 knots, the desired headsail shape is flatter. This has been proven empirically time and time again. There are also sound theoretical reasons for it. Pointing is limited by the angle of attack of the sail, and the greater the angle of attack—or the more the sail is trimmed —the closer one can sail to the wind. (That is, of course, until the flow stalls.) Flatter sails can be thought of as trimmed sails; fuller sails can be thought of as eased sails. Furthermore, in increased winds, flatter is better because the airflow has difficulty following the large curves that characterize full sails. It is analogous to driving a car around a hairpin curve with too much speed. At such times, the problem is to avoid stalling, with its consequent decrease in lift, and increase in drag and heeling. In very light winds, below 3 knots or so, slightly flatter sails work better, too. If in moderate winds the flow separates from the sail, or skids off the road, because it is going too fast for the curve, in very light winds, the flow lacks enough speed to get around the hairpin turn.

The fact that fuller sails work better in light air and flatter sails work better in medium to heavy air and in very light winds confronts sailors and sailmakers with tough choices. The lack of an easy answer to this conundrum explains why a modern racing yacht carries so many headsails.

So how do you know what depth your sail should be at any given moment? What follows are some useful numbers. These numbers, which refer to the section of the sail (or draft stripe) in the middle, will be valid for most boats in anything other than extreme sea conditions.

Apparent Wind (Knots)	Sail Depth (Depth Divided by Chord Length)
0–2	15–16%
3–12	18–19%
10–18	16–17%
16–23	15–16%
20–26	14–15%
24 +	12–13%

These numbers aren't cast in stone, however, and in no way do they obviate the need to experiment with your boat to determine the optimum depth at various wind speeds and sea conditions.

VERTICAL DISTRIBUTION OF DEPTH

As explained in Chapter 6, good sails do not show uniform depth from top to bottom. Almost always, the depth percentage will be greatest at the head and flatten all the way down to the foot. Speaking again in very broad terms, the top quarter should be about 5 to 10 percent fuller than the midsection (as delineated in the table), and the lower part of the sail should be 10 to 15 percent flatter.

You will recall that velocity differences at varying heights cause corresponding changes in the wind direction. Thus the top, which is sailing in what amounts to a lift, should be fuller than the midsection or the bottom. Also, more shape, or depth, at the head gives the sail more power—something sorely needed at the top of the triangle where sail area is so limited.

FORE-AND-AFT DRAFT LOCATION

After draft, the next most important variable in headsail performance consists of where the maximum draft falls in a sail (see Figure 7.1, page 129). For headsails, this is typically about 45 percent back from the headstay. However, for fuller light-air sails (18 or 19 percent) and sails flown when the seas are flat, the draft can be as far aft as 48 percent. The draft-aft shape permits a slightly flatter entry and thus facilitates pointing. The trade-off is that this shape tends to round the back of the sail, which is undesirable, but this does not present the problem it might otherwise in a stronger breeze. In strong winds, a round-backed headsail may well cause the flow to separate from the leech of the jib. Since the leech velocities of the genoa, you will recall from Chapter 5, are so important to the overall driving force of the sail plan as well as key to allowing the headsail to operate at a higher angle of attack, this separation is undesirable. The round-backed leech can also cause the mainsail to flutter, or backwind, earlier than it otherwise might.

As the wind increases, the designed draft of the sail should be as far forward as 40 or even 38 percent, while the after section of the sail should be flatter. (As before, we are describing the section halfway up the sail.) The draft should be farther forward in lower sections, where the wind velocity is less and the angle of the apparent wind farther forward. Conversely, the draft should be farther aft in upper sections, where the wind is stronger and thus its angle farther aft.

Having the draft aft in the head can be risky, however. Although in full, light-air sails, the draft at 48 percent may be tolerable and even fast, performance will suffer as draft slides aft of 50 percent. The closeness of these two numbers means that this is not an easy situation to visualize. More obvious is when the draft in the head reaches 55 or 60 percent. At such times, the sail will not be at its optimum due to the possible onset of separation and stall and the increase in drag. As noted, this condition is even more critical in heavy-air sails, so draft cannot be aft of 45 percent in any part of such sails. This is particularly important because the first sign of deterioration of a headsail is usually the rearward migration of draft in the head, which only gets more pronounced with increased wind and age.

INFLUENCE OF DRAFT ON PERFORMANCE AND HANDLING

Varying the fore-and-aft location of maximum draft in a headsail can have significant effects on performance and handling. If draft is forward, the boat will likely show better acceleration, a broader steering groove—a margin of error of 10 degrees as opposed to 5 degrees—and make fewer demands on a helmsman's skill and concentration. This draft-forward shape can help inexperienced or unskilled steerers to do a more effective job. Also, if because of sea conditions, wind conditions, or an electrical or mechanical problem, the cruising sailor's self-steering device is unable to steer within 5 degrees of the course, this shape is desirable. If, on the other hand, the draft is aft, the boat will likely show greater top-end speed and higher pointing. This is particularly true in flat water.

Realistically, few boats are capable of tracking perfectly, and few helmsmen can steer perfectly either, even in flat water. Assuming that the boat can go straight, holes and shifts in the wind would demand constant small corrections by the helmsman. Although this may be the name of the game for the racer, it isn't for the cruiser. The cruising sailor knows that there is more to sailing than just wiggling the wheel or tiller. This means that to varying degrees, all sails, be they for the racer or the cruiser, have to have some forgiveness —a large sweet spot, if you will—built in.

Let's consider two headsail shapes, both with the same amount of draft, but one with the draft placed at the aft limit—say about 50 percent—and the other at the forward limit—35 percent (see Figure 9.1). For the sake of the discussion, we will further assume that the draft-aft shape has a relatively flat, fine entry and the draft-forward one has a much rounder front end.

First, How is the draft moved aft? This can be done by easing the halyard and/or moving the genoa lead forward. When the boat is going upwind and "in the groove," the draft-aft sail (50 percent in the example) is likely to be very fast and close-winded. However, as the bow strays a little too close to the wind, the sail will luff suddenly. This luffing will affect the sail a long way back from the headstay. When this happens, performance drops precipitately, and even an instantaneous correction by the helmsman and/or sail-trimmers will require painfully long seconds to get the sail drawing at maximum efficiency again, or to reach steady-state lift (see Chapter 5).

The draft-aft sail can be particularly effective if you sail in unusually flat water and if the helmsman can strongly resist the temptation to pinch the boat. It also helps if there are attentive sail-trimmers aboard who can quickly ease, trim, and reshape the sail when it is necessary to accelerate again. Some crews who have known how to use this draft-aft shape have done well with it, whereas the same sail in less experienced hands can spell disaster.

The draft-forward sail will respond to a little wandering or inattentiveness with a gradual and progressive loss of power. It will also respond to sudden power demands—as in bearing away to accelerate after a tack or after the boat is slowed by big waves—without major trim adjustments. This gives more latitude for sailing in waves and handling the disturbed flow off a competitor's sails, and is more forgiving of more casual or less skilled steering. What is lost is maximum pointing and the last tenth of a knot or two of top-end speed. The more pronounced the wave action, the more difficult and less desirable it

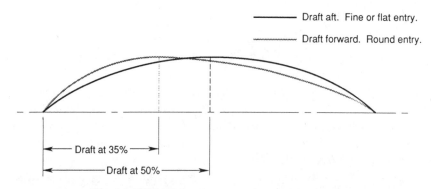

Figure 9.1 Effects of varying the draft position

is to steer a straight course, and the more the draft-forward shape comes into its own.

VERTICAL CURVATURE

It is most common to think of sails in terms of fore-and-aft (horizontal) curvature. This is the way the wind blows across them, and it is how we see them on the boat. If you get off the boat, though, you quickly see that there is a second curve from the head to the foot—or vertical curvature. According to computer-generated stress maps, the major loads in sails run from the head to clew, or vertically. In response to this load, the natural tendency of the sail is to sag to leeward, in the same manner gravity causes a rope to sag when tied between two trees. If you measure or plot the sag in the rope, you will find it is a classic catenary, that is, straighter near the trees, or supports, and more curved in the middle. To some degree, sails behave the same way; they are straighter at the top and bottom—where they are supported by the halyard, tack, and clew—and more curved in the middle.

Few sailors concern themselves with vertical curvature in a headsail because they can do very little to change it. This is true because vertical curvature is primarily a function of sail design and construction. Not being able to control something doesn't mean that it isn't important, and understanding it lies in what has already been discussed. First, all flow across a sail does not go in perfectly horizontal lines from front to back. A significant amount goes over the top, under the bottom, and even in reverse, from front to back. This, you may recall, is induced drag. It is a significant part of total drag, and careful design, manufacturing, and good low-stretch materials can reduce induced drag by limiting vertical curvature.

The relationship between vertical curvature and induced drag is as follows: If a sail has no vertical curvature—only horizontal curvature—it is relatively easy for the flow to go from the front of the sail to the back in more or less horizontal lines. If you introduce vertical curvature, or a second curve, the air is going to have to flow around the bulge. Some of it will be deflected up, some down. Obviously, this contributes to induced drag. During the America's Cup campaign of *Stars & Stripes '87*, we spent many hours testing the theory that less vertical curvature is better and conclusively proved it to ourselves.

Therefore, the ideal vertical shape of a sail is nearly straight, but achieving this is easier said than done. It takes good design, but even more important is the use of high-strength, low-elongation materials such as Kevlar/Mylar or polyester/Mylar. Good design and good materials make for a sail with a straight vertical profile—one that will keep the middle of the sail close to the rig. The undesirability of vertical curvature explains why many underbuilt sails are slow, and why it is physically impossible to achieve certain shapes in some materials and panel constructions.

The high-aspect-ratio Number 3 genoa is a case in point. Due to its aspect ratio, this sail is, at certain times, the most highly loaded sail on a boat. This loading manifests itself in vertical curvature. When high-strength, low-stretch Kevlar/Mylar was first introduced, the Number 3 was the first sail to be successfully made of this material, and the first in which the new material immediately established its superiority. It remains the one sail where a fair Kevlar/Mylar version will beat the best Dacron sail, even in smaller boats.

PERFORMANCE OVERLAP

It should be clear by now that broad-range sails are highly desirable, but that no one headsail can be optimized for all conditions. Therefore, a boat needs a sequence of sails, whether for maximum performance in racing situations or for safety and comfort when cruising. The exception to this statement is the cruising sailor's roller-reefing headsail. This will be discussed next.

Merely having the performance ranges of the sails adjacent to each other is not enough. There has to be an overlap in their ranges. For example, if the Number 1 genoa can be carried to 20 knots, the Number 2 should be able to move the boat without too much loss of performance in winds as low as 16 knots, or even lower if possible.

Think of driving a car with a manual transmission in stop-and-go traffic. You may be moving through a 10 mph range that is covered nicely by one gear, but you might as likely be traveling in a range that requires you to be constantly shifting up and down. At that moment, what would be desirable is the correct gear ratio, but even more desirable is a more flexible transmission that would give you, in effect, a broader range in each gear and more "performance overlap" between the gears.[2]

Where this problem surfaces on a sailboat is in rapidly changing and oscillating wind conditions. If the boat has one sail that works for one end of the range and another sail for the other end, but nothing that will provide satisfactory performance between them, you will be confronted with either

---

[2]The correct gear ratio, by the way, is the reason for the continuously variable transmission (CVT), found on the Subaru Justy ECVT. On this Japanese automobile, hydraulics change the size of the pulleys of the transmission to match automobile speed and engine rpm.

endless, frantic sail changes or with frustrating and even dangerous moments while you hope and pray for the wind to swing back to the range of the sail that is up.

It might be tempting to write this off as a problem for racers, since cruisers can safely put up their smallest sail and wait out the lulls, but cruising sailors are growing more sensitive to the feel and performance of their boats. So for them, the problem is even greater since they typically have neither the number of sails nor the crew to react quickly to changes in the wind. Also, more racing sailors have become cruisers and only occasionally race. Although they may have the variety of sails, they don't always have sufficient crew to change them easily. Thus, a good performance overlap between the sails in the cruising and racing inventory is essential.

PERFORMANCE OVERLAP AND ROLLER-REEFING HEADSAILS

Roller-reefing headstay devices and specially designed headsails have made performance overlap much less of a problem for the cruiser. A properly designed cruising headsail used on a modern headsail-furling and -reefing device is nearly as versatile as a main. Depending on luff treatment, some reefable headsails can now cover a range from a Number 1 to a Number 3. The technology that makes this possible is ubiquitous these days, but none of this would be feasible without a radical rethinking of the furling device and the design of the cruising headsail.

As noted in Chapter 7, roller furling—although not roller reefing—has been around since the 1930s. The principle is simple: the sail swivels around its luff and rolls itself up. If simple in theory, there were problems in execution, which account for the fact that the direct step from roller furling to roller reefing took nearly forty years. Most notably, because no one could figure out how to make a headstay swivel easily and without compromising its primary job of helping to hold the mast upright, the early furling devices were separate from the headstay. Thus, the headsail wasn't attached to a stay—it furled around its own luff. Without a headstay, it is difficult to tension the halyard, and halyard tension is very important to good headsail shape.

Ted Hood, whose contribution to the handling of the cruising mainsail was the Stoway Mast, came to the rescue of the cruising headsail and its furling devices with his invention of independent swivels for the halyard and the tack. This meant that the headstay and the furling unit could be integrated, allowing the sail to be attached to the headstay. Thus, the halyard could be tensioned and, due to the independent swivels, tensioned in such a way that it does not exert an upward force or torque on the roller-reefing device. Its genius, how-ever, was what with the pieces swiveling independently, the sail could be more easily reefed as well as furled.

Today, there are many other headsail furling and reefing devices on the market, made by such companies as Harken, Reckmann, Hood, Plastimo, and Goiot. Many of the companies that use double swivels pay a royalty to Ted Hood.

The reefing headsail had to be redesigned, too. First there was the issue of range. The problem was, How do you make one sail light enough so it will fly in 5 knots yet strong enough so it can withstand the terrific strains of reefing and at the same time will not blow apart in 30 knots, or more? As noted in Chapter 7, this is done via step-up construction, where the heavily loaded

Independent swivels, invented by Ted Hood, made headsail reefing a reality. This particular unit, manufactured by Harken, can be easily removed, per-mitting a full-luff genoa—particularly desirable for the cruising sailor who likes to race on occasion. The full-luff genoa allows a deck-sweeper jib, thereby reducing induced drag and helping windward speed. (Courtesy of North Sails, Inc.)

leech and the foot panels are made of heavier cloth. The panels get lighter and, at the same time, show less strength moving toward the luff (see Figure 7.9, page 144). The result is a sail that is stronger for its weight.

As far as the ability of the sail to handle reefing, it is beefed up, or patched, on the foot and leech at appropriate reef points. The sail, then, is reefed (or rolled) only to these spots.

There were other problems, too. A major consideration was, How do you protect a sail, which is up all the time, from degradation from the sun's ultraviolet rays? The best solution proved to be the use of specially coated UV-resistant cloth in the leech and foot of roller-furling sails.

More critical, however, was the shape of the reefed sail. A Number 3 should be smaller than a Number 1 or 2, but it should also grow flatter. This is why crescent-shaped pieces of foam came to be affixed to the luffs of such sails (see below photograph). The foam is thickest in the middle and tapered

A crescent-shaped piece of foam, affixed to the luff of a cruising head-sail, helps to shape the sail correctly when it is roller-reefed. (Courtesy of North Sails, Inc.)

the most at the top and bottom, so more area is removed from the middle, where the shape is, than from the ends. Without foam, a headsail can be reduced from a Number 1 to a Number 2. This might be sufficient for the day sailor, who never wanders far from home. With foam, the Number 1 can be reduced about as far as a small Number 2 or a large Number 3 jib.

Foam is a brilliant but imperfect solution. One disadvantage of foam is that when the sail rolls up completely, you are left with a large-diameter furl around the foam on the headstay. In extreme cases, this can cause some windage problems when sailing, as well as at the dock or at anchor. In the worst cases, it also can do damage to the forestay and furler itself.

Newer still is AeroLuff, which uses a sleeve sewn to the front of a genoa, which, in turn, zips around the headstay. Inside the sleeve is a bolt rope that fits in the headstay groove. The top and the bottom of this rope have been removed so that the bolt rope comprises about half the length of the headstay. When you haul on the reef line, the front of the genoa starts to roll where the bolt rope is—in the middle only. This removes depth from the center of the sail first; the top and bottom lag behind. The result is a much smaller and tighter-diameter furl. With AeroLuff, the sail can be effectively reefed to a normal-sized nonoverlapping Number 3.

There are times, however, when even a nonoverlapping Number 3 can be too large for the conditions. Also, no matter which system one uses, by the time you get to Number 3 size, the aspect ratio of the reefed sail may not be optimum, particularly if you have to slog to weather. As we now know, for optimum windward performance, the Number 3 should be a high-aspect-ratio sail, that is, be long on the luff and short on the foot. These problems speak for being able to change headsails in extreme conditions, which is not easy as all such sails have to be unfurled to drop them. Also, since nearly all of these sails use luff tapes, rather than hanks—which keep the dropped sail affixed to the headstay—the sail can be blown off the deck. The effects of this can range from inconvenient to dangerous.

For many, a better and safer solution is the use of a storm jib or heavy-weather staysail that is hoisted up a detachable inner staysail stay—assuming your boat is so equipped (many cruising boats are), and the mast and deck can handle the increased loads. Then, when the going gets rough, the headsail is rolled away, and the storm sail is flown on the staysail stay. Not the least of the advantages of repositioning the storm sail is that its center of effort moves back, too, causing the entire center of effort of the sail plan to move back. This can counteract the undesirable tendency in storm conditions for the bow to be blown away from the wind, the last problem one wants when battling off a lee shore in storm conditions.

SAIL AREA

Thus far we have been looking at the shape of headsails without regard to overall dimensions and configuration. Sail area in a headsail is customarily, if imprecisely, viewed in terms of overlap. Overlap (see Figure 9.2) is computed by comparing the LP (which stands for luff perpendicular and is a line drawn perpendicular to the luff through the clew) to the J measurement (the length base of the foretriangle). If, for example, the J is 15 feet and the LP is 22½

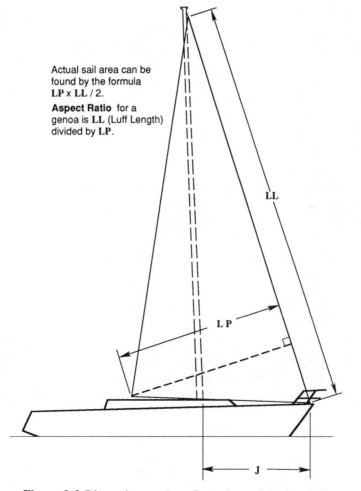

Actual sail area can be found by the formula **LP x LL / 2.**

Aspect Ratio for a genoa is **LL** (Luff Length) divided by **LP.**

LL

L P

J

Figure 9.2 Dimensions and configurations of the headsail

feet, then the headsail is described as a 150 percent genoa. Actual sail area can then be found by this formula:

$$\frac{LP \times LL \text{ (Luff Length)}}{2} = \text{Sail Area}$$

Common sense says that sail area has to be at least as important as shape to ultimate performance, and theory and practice have confirmed this repeatedly. In fact, everything else being equal, there is a fairly linear relationship between sail area and power.

But how much sail area is enough? For a start, we should accept the premise that more is better, that is, more sail area produces more power. In light air, this power translates to improved performance and a more purposeful and enjoyable feel to the boat. (Light air should not be confused with little or no air. In drifting conditions, a nonoverlapping headsail is more effective.)

Any boat, be it a racer or cruiser, should have sufficient sail area to provide steerageway in 2 to 3 knots of breeze. If sail area is insufficient, not only will the boat be slow and frustrating to sail in light air, but performance will continue to suffer in any sort of sea up to 10 or 12 knots. At the same time, the motion of the boat will be particularly sloppy and uncomfortable.

At some point, stability and control become concerns. When this occurs varies from boat to boat, but excessive heel and/or excessive weather helm are good indications that the point has been reached. Then, reducing sail area becomes first desirable and then essential if performance, enjoyment, and safety are to be maintained.

In racing situations—where there may be no limit on the number of headsails or on the ability to change them quickly—boats are set up to use maximum-sized headsails, principally distinguished by progressively flatter shapes and progressively stronger construction.[3] Then, somewhere between 16 and 24 knots apparent wind, sail area is reduced in 15 to 25 percent increments. This has proven to be the best solution for racers who face the compromises of sufficient area for light air, stability for rougher conditions, and performance under a rating rule that penalizes excessive sail area. Of course, such boats often carry large crews whose weight is used to flatten the boat. This alone can extend the range of a headsail by 3 or 4 knots.

Many racing sailors do not have the luxury of either unlimited sails,

---

[3]The International Offshore Rule (IOR) has sail limitations, but these are often waived, particularly in the United States. Some classes, like Maxis, also don't enforce sail limitations.

precision crew work, or even sufficient crew to affect stability, but these factors change their requirements in detail only. For example, they may have one sail to go up to 16 or 20 knots, with the next smaller sail able to perform satisfactorily from, perhaps, 18 to 30 knots. This gives a reasonably good performance overlap and saves many sail changes when the wind is rising and falling within the overlap band. Subsequent steps in reduction of sail area may then be closer to 25 to 30 percent than to the aforementioned 15 to 25 percent.

Although cruisers may not worry as much about performance in very light air, they will be very concerned with the feel and motion of the boat. Sufficient pressure on the rig will settle and stabilize the boat. Insufficient power will permit a sailboat to bob and gyrate uncomfortably at the will of the waves. Many crews have learned that even in 45 knots of wind, it is possible to have too little sail up for comfort.

Sail area alone doesn't solve all the problems, however. The distribution of the area—for example, its aspect ratio—is important, too.

ASPECT RATIO

The measure of the configuration of a sail is called its aspect ratio. A simple way to compute aspect ratio is to divide the luff length by overlap, or LP (see Figure 9.2).[4] Up to some theoretically improbable point, taller and thinner configurations—or high-aspect-ratio sails—give better upwind performance for the same area than shorter and wider airfoils—or low-aspect-ratio sails. As discussed, a high-aspect-ratio sail has less head area and foot area (in proportion to the rest of the sail) for the flow to escape, thereby reducing induced drag and helping the lift-to-drag ratio.

When Dacron was the only choice for racing sails, heavy-weather headsails had aspect ratios of close to 1:1, with short hoists and overlaps. This was primarily the result of trying to keep the center of effort low, to minimize heeling, and the inability of Dacron to assume an efficient, high-aspect-ratio shape. Because the material is so stretchy, the middle of the sail sags off to leeward, increasing vertical curvature. These days, high-performance fabrics

[4]An aerodynamicist computes aspect ratio with this formula:

$$AR = \frac{\text{Luff Length}^2}{\text{Sail Area}}$$

The formula for sail area is given on the opposite page.

and growing sophistication with their use have allowed full-hoist nonoverlapping (Number 3) jibs for masthead boats with an aspect ratio of 3.5, or even 3.75. As noted, Number 3 jibs now have the highest aspect ratio of any sail on a boat and are often the most highly loaded.

Due to the desirability of the high-aspect-ratio headsail when sailing upwind, the aspect ratio of the foretriangle has climbed upward as well. The aspect ratio of the foretriangle, or the rig, is determined by the formula I/J, where I is the height of the foretriangle, roughly from the deck to the forestay attachment, and J is the foretriangle base from the mast to the forestay (see Figure 9.3). Typical foretriangles in the late 1960s has ratios of between 3

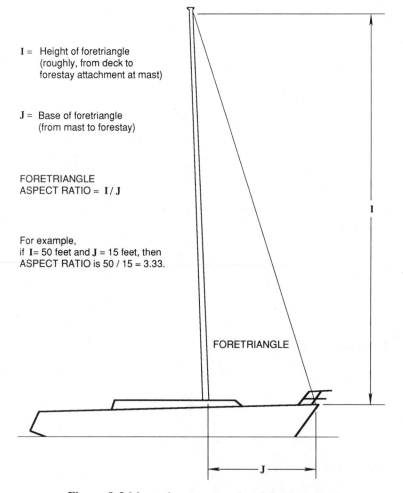

I = Height of foretriangle
(roughly, from deck to
forestay attachment at mast)

J = Base of foretriangle
(from mast to forestay)

FORETRIANGLE
ASPECT RATIO = I / J

For example,
if I = 50 feet and J = 15 feet, then
ASPECT RATIO is 50 / 15 = 3.33.

FORETRIANGLE

I

J

Figure 9.3 Measuring aspect ratio of the foretriangle

and 3.1. Since then, there has been a steady evolution to higher and higher ratios, through 3.3 to 3.5, and even higher today. Although the racing rules look harshly at this increase in aspect ratio, these changes have come about because there has been enough of a gain in performance to offset rating penalties. The aspect ratio of rigs on cruising boats has likewise climbed, but not as precipitately as on racing boats.

As the boat falls off the wind and the angle of the apparent wind broadens, the desirability of high-aspect-ratio headsails rapidly diminishes, being replaced by overall sail area. With the apparent wind 90 to 110 degrees—and more— aspect ratios of less than 2:1 have proven to be very successful on modern boats, since at such angles induced drag starts to be beneficial. For the same reason (drag changing from a liability to a benefit), older designs reached effectively with even shorter rigs.[5] This partially explains the continued success of some very old designs, such as the Concordia yawl, in the Bermuda Race, which is typically a reaching contest. It also helps to explain the success of the ketch rig in the 1989–90 Whitbread Round the World Race, which with the new course was 85 percent off the wind.

This raises an interesting point: As most headsails are designed for upwind sailing—that is, show a high aspect ratio—they lose a great deal of their effectiveness as soon as the boat turns off the wind by a few degrees. To make the best of a bad situation, many racers and cruisers will move the sheet leads outboard, when the sheets are eased. (This is discussed later in the chapter.) A better solution for the cruiser, who makes extended passages, and the racer, who has an extensive inventory, is the lower-aspect-ratio reacher or the jib-top sail.

CONTROLLING THE SHAPE OF A HEADSAIL

A sail-trimmer has a fairly extensive ''tool kit'' to control the shape of a headsail. The primary tools are backstay tension, lead position, halyard tension, and sheet tension. Backstay tension affects headstay sag, and headstay sag, as noted in Chapter 7, increases at higher wind velocities. The direct effect of more sag is to make the headsail fuller, which is the opposite of what is desired at such times (see Figure 7.6, page 139). The three corners of this sail are fixed relative to each other, so as the headstay sags, it pushes material into the front of the sail.

Rig tension is a function of the power of the backstay adjuster as well

---

[5]Changing drag from a liability to a benefit is one important reason why a reach is the fastest point of sail.

as the rigidity of the rig. For the sake of performance, it is essential that when the wind increases, the rig be tensioned as much as possible to minimize headstay sag. Up to a certain point, mechanical adjusters, such as split backstays, multiple purchases, or even levers on the backstay, work well, but eventually hydraulics are the only answer to headstay sag. Turnbuckles and similar systems provide neither the speed nor the power necessary to be competitive on the race course. That said, their reliability is attractive to a number of long-distance offshore cruisers.

Some headstay sag is inevitable, however, and sails are cut with this taken into account. Ultimately, the greater the sag, the narrower the performance band of a sail. This is true for all headsails on all types of boats. Incidentally, there are special circumstances in which increased sag is helpful, such as when sailing in leftover seas (more seas than wind), or when trying to make a flat sail work in winds below its range.

SHEET TENSION

Trimming the sheet flattens the shape of the sail. You can think of sheet tension as a coarse, or crude, adjustment up to the last foot or so, at which point its effect becomes increasingly important. When truly close-hauled, the last 2 or 3 inches can make a measurable difference in performance even on quite large boats; smaller fractions can be most significant in many dinghies. From Chapter 6, you might recall that the maximum lift-drag point and maximum lift point are close together. Figure 6.9 (page 106) shows that when the lift-to-drag ratio is at its highest, the windward telltale is just fluttering. When lift is at its highest—although at the expense of drag—both telltales are streaming. Experienced sailors know that the difference between these two points is a matter of inches of sheet tension or a few degrees of heading.

LEAD POSITION

The lead position of headsails is adjustable on most boats. Although this is a very effective tool—or perhaps because it is such an effective tool—it is sometimes misused. If used correctly, however, adjustable leads will offer a number of options for trimming sails in different conditions. The flexibility becomes even more important as headsails age and change shape. Since cruising sailors keep their sails longer than their racing counterparts, and their sails are typically made of stretchier material, understanding lead position is as important to the cruiser as to the racer.

The position of the headsail lead is important to racing and cruising sailors alike. Here Dennis Conner and crew aboard the 12-Meter Liberty *check the headsail. Moving the lead fore or aft affects the shape of the headsail; moving the lead inboard or out affects its angle of attack.* (Courtesy of North Sails, Inc.)

Fore-and-aft adjustment mainly determines the shape of the sail, whereas athwartships adjustment—that is, inboard or outboard—affects the angle of attack (see Figure 6.7, page 104). To easily determine where the fore-and-aft lead should be, extend a line from about midluff, through the clew, to the deck (see Figure 9.4). From this point, you can start making fine adjustments.

The headsail will provide most of the clues you need to optimize trim. Good sail-trimmers concentrate on a number of factors, but all start by trying to get the luff of the sail to break uniformly along its entire length as the boat slowly rounds into the wind. If the top breaks first, moving the lead forward (angling the sheet more steeply so that an extension of its line aims higher in the sail) will simultaneously trim the head and free the foot.

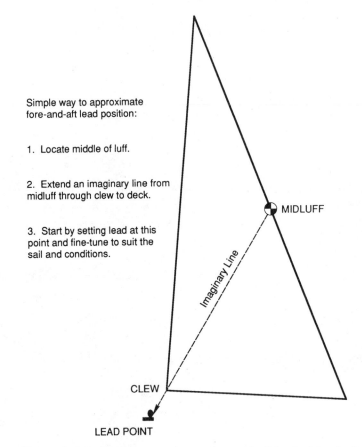

Simple way to approximate
fore-and-aft lead position:

1. Locate middle of luff.

2. Extend an imaginary line from
midluff through clew to deck.

3. Start by setting lead at this
point and fine-tune to suit the
sail and conditions.

MIDLUFF

Imaginary Line

CLEW

LEAD POINT

Figure 9.4 A simple way to locate fore-and-aft lead of headsail

Conversely, if the bottom breaks first, moving the lead aft (angling the sheet less acutely so that the pull is more along the foot of the sail) will move the clew farther from the lower luff and flatten the lower sections. At the same time, the top of the sail will rise and twist open, causing the head of the sail to luff earlier.

The preceding can be distilled to this simple rule: If the bottom telltales lift, move lead back. Or even more simply: Bottom, Back.

Once the fore-and-aft angle is determined, there are additional checks for verifying that all is well. The depth of the foot is one, and this is easy to see from anywhere on the boat. If the foot is sagging on the lifelines, the sheet may be eased too much or the lead could be too far forward. First try a little more trim. (Of course, before trimming the sail, go down to leeward and take a look at it to be sure it is not touching the spreaders. Putting a spreader through a sail is never fast.) A more subtle case for not overtrimming the headsail is that this keeps a sailboat from accelerating. If trim doesn't help correct the loose foot, try moving the lead back slightly, and then trim the sheet harder.

When adjusting fore-and-aft trim, lean toward the side of the lead back. This gives the headsail a little extra twist, effectively increasing its "sweet spot." This is the flip side to the more forgiving draft-forward sail discussed at the beginning of the chapter. A little extra leech twist ensures that at least some of the sail is working at its optimum when steering isn't precise, or when the seas are lumpy or the wind is shifting. This means most of the time, except in unusually steady winds and smooth water. You might recall from Chapter 6 that airplane wings are likewise twisted. Thus, if the wing stalls, separation is less likely to occur over the entire wing, which can keep the plane in the sky.

If, however, the foot of the headsail is drawn unusually tight, it could be due to too much sheet tension, incorrect lead location, or—a popular mistake, especially after rounding the leeward mark in a race—insufficient halyard tension. A slightly less apparent but more accurate reference for optimum fore-and-aft trim is the distance of the leech of the headsail off the spreaders.

Before leaving this subject, a caution is necessary. Changes in mast rake change the sheet lead. The only truly fixed point on a headsail is the tack, and as the head of the sail leans forward or back, the rest of the sail rotates about the tack. So raking the mast aft will require that the lead be moved forward, thus lowering the clew; moving the top of the mast forward will require that the lead be moved aft, thus raising the clew (see Figure 9.5).

ATHWARTSHIPS TRIM

Athwartships trim affects the angle of attack of the headsail. In theory, narrower angles permit the boat to sail closer to the wind, but in practice the proper lead location for different boats and sails will vary, based on such considerations as hull shape and weight, keel efficiency, rig design, and deck layout. However, before we discuss the exceptions, let's focus on the typical examples and see how they affect an "average" yacht.

Typically, the largest Number 1 genoa (150 percent overlap) will sheet at 8 to 10 degrees off the centerline (see Figure 9.6). Smaller Number 2 genoas (130 to 145 percent) sheet at about 9 to 11 degrees; and smaller-still Number 3 jibs (nonoverlapping) also sheet at 9 to 11 degrees. However, if you are sailing in flat, sheltered waters, and the Number 3 is still relatively new and

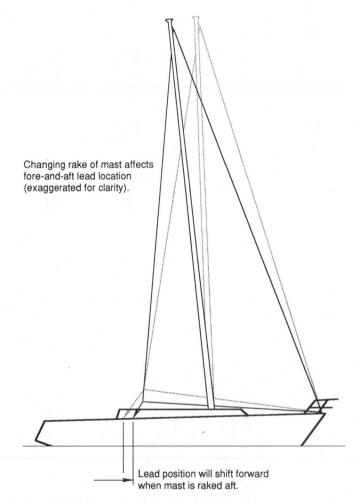

Changing rake of mast affects fore-and-aft lead location (exaggerated for clarity).

Lead position will shift forward when mast is raked aft.

Figure 9.5 Effects of mast rake on lead location

shows a straight back, angles of 9 or even 8 degrees—for some One Design boats—are feasible.

A number of popular designs have standard lead locations for the Number 1 genoa as wide as 11 or 12 degrees. For them to point as high as boats with narrower leads, the genoa has to have a finer entry for the same amount of draft in order to achieve a comparable angle of attack. Alternately, the sail must be flatter and/or more draft-aft, resulting in less power.

The width of the shroud base also affects sheeting angle. In order to sheet overlapping headsails for optimum upwind performance, the width of the

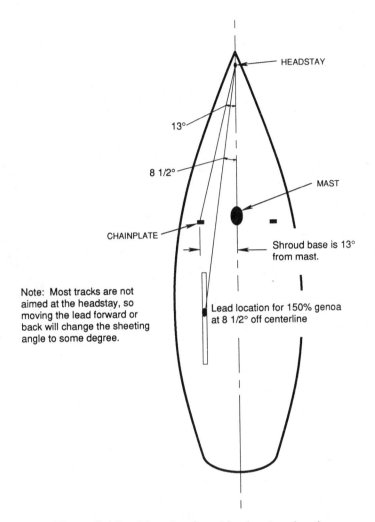

HEADSTAY

13°

8 1/2°

MAST

CHAINPLATE

Shroud base is 13° from mast.

Note: Most tracks are not aimed at the headstay, so moving the lead forward or back will change the sheeting angle to some degree.

Lead location for 150% genoa at 8 1/2° off centerline

Figure 9.6 Lead location for a Number 1 and optimum width for shroud base on a racing boat

shroud base has to be less than 14 degrees. (This angle is determined by drawing a line from the headstay to the mast and a second line to the chainplate or where the shroud passes through the deck.) Angles of 13 to 13½ degrees are good (see Figure 9.6). A few boats have rigs with a shroud base as narrow as 12½ degrees, but other limitations such as keel efficiency and the amount of heel rarely, if ever, make it possible to trim headsails hard enough to take advantage of these narrow shroud angles.

The desirability of a narrow shroud base should be put in perspective, however. The combination of higher-aspect-ratio foretriangles, narrower sheeting angles, and shorter spreaders has sorely tested the spar-maker's ingenuity and skill. The spar-maker has responded with thicker and more precisely engineered mast walls and lower-stretch rigging. This has resulted in much greater hull loading and more catastrophic results in the event of failure.

For cruisers, these sheet and shroud-base angles are likely to be too narrow. Suited as they are to upwind sailing, they presume that the crew has the ability and the inclination to make quick adjustments to broader leads for reaching and more relaxed beating. Sheeting the Number 1 headsail between 10 and 14 degrees is more comfortable and quite satisfactory for many cruisers, as they rarely, if ever, have the need to sail so close to the wind. Not only are broader sheeting angles faster when not sailing hard on the wind, but they place fewer demands on the mast, sails, boat, and crew. The latest crop of boats designed for the Whitbread Round the World Race have shroud bases as wide as 15 degrees since they are optimized for reaching and running.

Since many boats differ from the "average" yacht for one reason or another, a sail designer must know the characteristics of the boat for which he or she is building sails. For example, hull shape and hull weight (displacement) affect lead position. Heavy sailboats with full bows need plenty of power to accelerate and to muscle their way through waves. Power is limited by a yacht's stability—if not by a racing rule—so such yachts may not have sufficient sail area to accelerate to full speed. Thus they must sail with, in effect, cracked sheets, or a wider sheeting angle, to maintain speed.

The efficiency of a keel is another determinant of where sheets should lead. Some keels work a lot better than others. If a keel requires a lower angle to maintain efficiency, you might as well put the headsail leads out and go fast. Incidentally, some very good but small keels work well, but only if they have a lot of flow over them, so again sailing a few degrees off the wind at a faster speed turns out to be most effective. (Polar diagrams, sold by USYRU or private sources, discussed in Chapter 6, are helpful in determining sailing angle and thus sheet lead.)

But finally, such concerns as spreader width, chainplate base, and deck layout are other limits to where leads can be placed. Only the most dedicated racer would change spreader width or the location of the chainplates to optimize a lead. Similarly, if the deck comes from the factory with a window where a lead should be or a winch that will only accept a lead from one direction, the majority of sailors will opt not to perform reconstructive surgery on their boats.

Where it is easy to make changes, they may be worth doing, but more often, they require major structural reworking and, sometimes, for one reason or another, will actually diminish performance. For example, relocating chain-plates can require reengineering almost the entire hull, as well as rebuilding the interior; even then, the mast and rigging may be unable to handle the increased loads. In this circumstance, most people are happier to continue sailing with what they have. Moving genoa tracks is somewhat less complicated and definitely worth doing. But keep in mind that wide coachroofs, molded headliners, cored decks, and bad leads to available winches can cause head-aches that often cannot be anticipated.

When reaching and running, wider sheeting angles are necessary. This is usually not a problem for the racer, who typically has an outboard track, but it can be a problem for the cruiser, whose boats aren't always so equipped. If the stanchions are reinforced, they may be strong enough to anchor an outboard lead. If not, it might be worth adding a separate well-engineered pad-eye for such times. While on this subject, the cruising sailor in particular should also be certain that there is a place to sheet the Number 3, or the headsail that is reefed to a Number 3, for sailing upwind. This lead should be well forward and inside the shrouds at about 13 degrees or even less. Clawing off a lee shore in Number 3 conditions, where every inch of weatherliness is important, is no time to discover that there is no place to sheet the Number 3. Also, if you use a staysail or a storm jib in heavy air, as discussed earlier, be certain you have a proper lead for it, too. The proper position for that staysail stay is 40 percent of the J. Then, its lead for upwind sailing should be at about 14 degrees, slightly farther out in more severe weather. Remember that when you fall off the wind, the sheet lead for the Number 3 should be led outboard of the shrouds.

A caution is necessary when trimming the high-aspect-ratio Number 3. Because the sheet angle on this sail is almost vertical, sheet tension is especially critical. Since almost all of the trim affects the leech, it takes very little overzealousness to overtrim, or close off, the leech to the detriment of both speed and pointing. Unfortunately, overzealousness is hard to quantify. It is a trial-and-error activity almost every time the Number 3 goes up.

It is obvious from the above that determining the optimum lead angle is not an exact science, due to the number of variables and subtle distinctions. The starting point in such a test is to confirm the key references: determine the track's actual angle and the angle of the shroud base. If you are fortunate enough to have an accurate deck plan of your boat, a protractor will give ready answers. If not, you can measure your boat and make your own scale drawing for later measurement by protractor, or work out the numbers with a calculator. Remember that the angles are measured from a line drawn from the headstay to the mast.

Whenever possible, the starting point for experimentation should be the reference points, about 8½ degrees for the track of the Number 1 and 13 degrees for the shroud base (see Figure 9.6). From there, performance at broader and narrower angles has to be carefully recorded and compared to determine optimum lead angle. In an America's Cup program, where two-boat testing is common, we have spent weeks determining this.

The location of the tracks need not be the sole determinant of athwartships adjustments, however. The lead angle of the genoa sheet is readily adjusted by crosshauls and Barberhauls. A crosshaul connects to the sheet or clew and pulls the lead inboard. It can be a small block and tackle, the tail of a sheet or halyard led to a convenient winch, or a special line kept handy for that purpose. A Barberhauler (named after the ingenious Barber brothers, of San Diego, who first used it) pulls the lead outboard. It, too, can be a small block and tackle, but most decks offer the convenience of an outboard track or pad-eye through which a second sheet or short sheet can be rigged.

Crosshauling is better than nothing when the tracks are misplaced, and better than a multiplicity of fixed hardware options for occasional adjustments. One disadvantage of this setup quickly manifests itself if you forget to remove a hauler before tacking, but a more subtle disadvantage is that repeating fast settings is a lot tougher. Also, if the lead doesn't pull directly athwartships, it may introduce an adverse fore-and-aft component. Fore-and-aft components are, and should be, the domain of the sheet lead. Due to a likely introduction of this fore-and-aft factor, trimming back on the weather sheet rarely works.

Once the lead position is determined, there will often be a small improvement in pointing in very flat water if the lead is moved in toward the centerline a half to a full degree. This gives the headsail a narrower angle of attack (relative to the keel), which can be fast in flat water where the need to reaccelerate is less important. In big seas, when pointing is secondary to keeping the boat moving, an outboard lead combined with slightly eased sheet will be better than simply easing the sheet. Bearing away farther, it becomes absolutely essential to move the lead outboard to keep the top and the bottom of the sail in balance. At such times, an outboard lead or Barberhauler can, in fact, make as much as a knot's difference in speed.

HALYARD TENSION

Increasing halyard tension increases the luff tension of the sail, which pulls the draft forward and reduces total draft to some degree. Easing the halyard allows the draft to move aft and increases it. In stretchier Dacron sails, the range of halyard adjustment is as much as 3 percent of luff length. Because the material along the luff is usually oriented on the bias (off the thread line), this amount of stretch temporarily alters the geometry of the weave (rather than yielding individual fibers), so it can be done repeatedly without permanently distorting the sail. On the other hand, laminated sails, like those made of Kevlar/Mylar and polyester/Mylar, are much less forgiving of such treatment, as too much halyard tension permanently deforms the isotropic film. The low stretch of high-tech materials in all directions means that a halyard adjustment of .5 percent (of luff length) is usually sufficient. When a Kevlar/Mylar or polyester/Mylar sail requires more than 1 percent halyard adjustment, it is usually a sign of aging or poor design. Unlike Dacron, many laminated sails set correctly without all the horizontal wrinkles removed from the luff.

Changes in halyard tension have some secondary effects, too. The leech of a sail is a fixed length of low-stretch fabric, and raising and lowering the head of the sail, which the halyard does, will change the clew height. This necessitates a reevaluation of sheet tension and fore-and-aft lead position. Even if nothing has changed, it is necessary from time to time to readjust the halyard tension as all halyards have some degree of stretch, caused by changes in wind velocity or simply by the passage of time.

LEECHLINES

The significance of leechlines is that they are not designed for, nor are they capable of, adjusting sail shape per se. Sails with back sections that approach a straight line are preferable to those with rounder backs but are tougher to get completely smooth. In different loadings and over time, more leeches get loose than tight. The leechline is there to keep the loose leech from shaking, or motorboating, as it is sometimes called because of the sound it makes. The shaking may not affect speed in a measurable way, but eventually it can fatigue the sail. In Kevlar/Mylar, it can be a matter of hours or even less before the leech completely falls off; in Dacron and most polyester/Mylar, it will take longer, but it isn't wise to see just how much longer.

The effect of pulling the leechline is to cup the leech to weather. Except in the most radical instances, this is not what is referred to as a round-backed or tight-leeched sail and is not enough to slow the boat. However, it is always a good practice to check leechline tension frequently by easing it until the leech flutters, then taking up just enough to still the motion. Finally, check tension again when there are changes in sail trim or wind velocity.

Let's look at some basic rules of headsail trim.

Headsail Trim

1. Be sure there are telltales on the luff of the headsail. A good placement is to divide the luff into quarters and put a set at one quarter, one half, and three quarters up. They should be between 12 and 24 inches back from the luff—the bigger the boat, the farther aft —to keep them away from the confusing local turbulence, or form drag, of the headstay (see Figure 9.7).

2. Check the lead position. This means setting the lead angle and setting the fore-and-aft adjustment by drawing an imaginary line from midluff, through the clew, to the deck. Then fine-tune the lead position by slowly rounding into the wind. All the weather telltales should flip up at once, indicating that the top and bottom of the sail are trimmed equally. If the top luffs first, move the lead forward; if the bottom luffs first, move the lead back. Remember the rule, Bottom, Back.

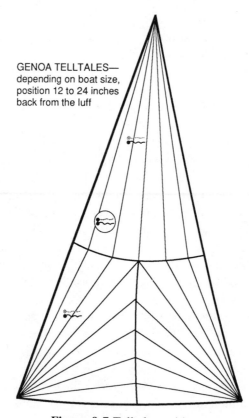

GENOA TELLTALES—
depending on boat size,
position 12 to 24 inches
back from the luff

Figure 9.7 Telltale position

Keep in mind that it is best to err on the side of too far back. This increases twist and gives the sail a larger "sweet spot."

3. Trim the sail close to, but not touching, the spreaders. (Trimming the sail against the rig hurts performance.) You may find that the optimum trim puts the leech slightly in or out from this setting, with some variation according to sea and wind conditions.

4. Use halyard tension to pull the draft forward, but do not tension the halyard so much that you get a vertical wrinkle behind the headstay.

5. Adjust the sail to suit the conditions: In flat water and medium air, trim harder and move the lead angle inboard to flatten the sail and narrow the angle of attack (see the table below). Tighten the backstay to reduce headstay sag and flatten the entry.

GENOA LEAD ANGLES

SAIL	LEAD ANGLE (Degrees)	
	Smooth	Waves
Light #1	8	10
Medium #1	7.5–8	9.5
Heavy #1	7.5	9.5
#2	9	11
#3	9	11
#4	11	12

Use these numbers as guidelines only. The optimum lead position will vary from boat to boat. If you can't easily move your leads inboard or outboard, choose a lead angle that will work best over a range of wind and sea conditions.

In waves, ease the sheet, move the lead outboard, and sail lower angles to maintain speed. Ease the halyard slightly and ease the backstay if the rig doesn't move around too much.

For heavy air, again move the lead outboard, but keep the sheet and halyard in hard to keep the sail flat. Move the lead aft to free the upper leech and flatten the head—tolerate a slightly earlier luff in the top of the sail if necessary.

For very light winds, move the lead outboard, ease the sheet, and move the lead forward enough to maintain an even break along the luff. Use light backstay and halyard tension, and sail with the leeward telltale on the verge of stalling.

Sometimes the wind at the top of the mast is at a different angle from the wind at water level. This condition, known as wind shear, should not be confused with the natural vertical twist of the wind. Wind shear is more dramatic. This might occur in light to moderate air and especially when the air is much warmer than the water. In this instance, the fore-and-aft jib leads will be correspondingly different on each tack.

6. If the main is fluttering, or backwinding, excessively, and all other settings are correct, move the headsail lead outboard or change to a flatter or smaller headsail.

7. Use the correct size sail for the conditions. Sail size, of course, is determined by wind strength and the stability of your boat. The table below shows the sail that is right for various conditions, as well as target depths and drafts. This should be used as a guide only. Experience in different conditions will show what works and what doesn't and will show the exact crossover points for your boat and sails. Indications that the boat is overpowered include excessive heel (more than 25 or 30 degrees in most boats), difficult and heavy steering, excessive leeway, and speed drop-off, in spite of stronger winds.

Conversely, indications that the boat is underpowered include

GENOA WIND RANGES

SAIL	APPARENT WIND (Knots)	
	Range	Maximum
Light #1	2–12	12
All-purpose #1	6–20	20
Heavy #1	15–23	23
#2	21–27	27
#3	24–34	34
#4	31–45	45

Use this table as a guide. The displacement and stability of your boat will affect upper and lower limits. Ask your sailmaker for specific wind ranges for each of your sails. Be sure to write these limits on each sail.

standing too straight (a simple inclinometer will quantify heel angle) and listless feel, both on the helm and in the way the boat reacts to waves, or slow speed. At such times try a more powerful setup (i.e., make the headsail deeper by easing halyard, easing the sheet, going to an outboard lead, etc.), and if this doesn't work, change to a fuller headsail.

8. Use the size and depth of the headsail to help balance the helm. A heavy helm will be relieved by putting up a smaller, flatter headsail.

9. When bearing away, move the lead outboard to broaden the angle of attack of the headsail without compromising shape control.

10. To determine whether sail trim is correct, watch the boats around you. Use them as a rough gauge for speed and pointing. Remember, however, that they may not be sailed as well or aggressively as your boat; they may be sailing in different wind and current; or they may have different strengths and weaknesses than your boat, or be much smaller or larger, so that such comparisons are meaningless. When you are doing particularly well, note the conditions and adjustments on the Genoa Trim Card. A sample as well as a form that can be copied follow.

GENOA TRIM CARD SAMPLE

GENOA: *MEDIUM # 1 (North)*	LOW END	MIDRANGE	HIGH END
Wind Range (knots apparent)	6-11	11-15	15-20
Maximum Apparent Wind Speed (from sailmaker)			20
Lead Angle (degrees)	9°	9°	10°
Lead Position (hole number)	4	3	2
Distance to Upper Spreader	8"	6"	6"
Distance to Chainplates	4"	1"	touching
Depth (% at midstripe)	18%	17%	16%
Draft Position (% at mid)	48%	46%	45%
Backstay Tension (% of max)	60%	80%	Max
Halyard Tension	6	3	Two-blocked

GENOA TRIM CARD

GENOA:	LOW END	MIDRANGE	HIGH END
Wind Range (knots apparent)			
Maximum Apparent Wind Speed (from sailmaker)			
Lead Angle (degrees)			
Lead Position (hole number)			
Distance to Upper Spreader			
Distance to Chainplates			
Depth (% at midstripe)			
Draft Position (% at mid)			
Backstay Tension (% of max)			
Halyard Tension			

CHAPTER 10

MAINSAILS

★   In the days of working sail, the mainsail was truly the "main" sail on the sloops, yawls, and ketches that evolved into modern yachts. Rating rules, materials, rigging, and sail-handling techniques have changed over the years, but the importance of the main has diminished only slightly. In addition to helping the jib and providing lift in its own right, the main is the key to balancing the helm, that is, steering the boat. Due to its important and often overlooked steering role, the mainsail can be thought of as an adjunct to the rudder. The main also must perform with efficiency and equanimity in everything from calm winds to near gale and from beating to reaching to running. No other single sail is asked to do so much through so much.

AERODYNAMIC REVIEW

As we learned in Chapter 5, the headsail occupies a favored position, a place of honor if you will, in a sail plan. The situation is less rosy for the main, however. A reason for this is that each sail has its own circulation flow, and the circulation of the headsail slows that of the mainsail where they meet in the slot (see Figure 5.15, page 89). It is easy to discern from the illustration that the airflow is moving slowly here, and, thus, this is a high-pressure region. The result is that the headsail causes the main to sail in less wind. The position of the genoa is analogous in sailboat racing to a favorable, or safe, leeward position; it benefits from upwash (a lifting wind) and increased wind speeds, and its Kutta-condition requirement is satisfied not at free-stream conditions but at a higher speed. The position of the main is comparable to the weather boat being squeezed off; it is hurt by downwash (a heading wind) and decreased wind speeds (see Figure 5.18, page 93).

The main gains one thing by living in the shadow, so to speak, of the jib. Because there is a reduction in velocity on the lee side of the main, there is a less dramatic shift from low pressure (high speed) at its forward lee side to high pressure (low speed) at the leech and thus less likelihood of the flow stalling. This means that the mainsail can operate efficiently at a higher angle of attack—more mainsheet trim or higher traveler angle—since there is less danger of stalling.

Now that we know the mainsail's realities, let's see what can be done by sailmakers and sailors to maximize its performance.

DRAFT

Draft in mains is traditionally measured in the same fashion as it is in headsails. The amount of depth, or draft, in the sail is defined as a percentage of the horizontal span of the sail at a given point; so, for example, a 1-foot depth in a 10-foot span is described as a 10 percent depth (see Figure 2.2, page 17). The amount of draft and its fore-and-aft location (see Figure 7.1, page 129) are very important in mains, and as with headsails, these factors will vary according to wind velocity, sea conditions, the boat's stability, and so forth. Almost all the same generalizations apply for both sails: making either sail fuller gives more power for acceleration; making them flatter permits higher-speed flow with less separation and drag. You might want to read again the applicable sections in the previous chapter to refresh your memory.

What follows are some representative numbers for mainsail draft. These depths are for the span, or section, halfway up the sail. The target numbers are generalizations, and as we go along, we will refine them further. A complete table is presented later in the chapter.

MAINSAIL DRAFT

Apparent Wind	Main Depth
3–6	15–16%
6–12	14–15%
12–18	12–13%
18–24	11%
24 +	10%

VERTICAL DISTRIBUTION OF DEPTH

Mains, like headsails, are fuller in the head than in the foot, and basically for the same reasons. Such a shape is more elliptical, and as explained in Chapter 6, it reduces induced drag. Also, as discussed previously, the angle where the wind meets the sail varies from bottom to top. This has been labeled the vertical shift in the wind (see Figure 6.14, page 116). In the case of the main, the direction of the air is changed (a heading shift), and its velocity is slowed by the headsail. Further, the wind that reaches the main is also profoundly affected by the mast and rigging. This is form drag.

A combination of these factors makes it necessary for the vertical differences in draft distribution to be even more pronounced in mainsails than in genoas. Quantitatively, the ideal differential from the middle quarter to the top is generally about 5 percent in quite light air, 10 to 15 percent for winds from roughly 6 to 18 knots, and then back to almost no change in stronger winds. The bottom quarter should be approximately 20 percent flatter than the middle in medium conditions and perhaps 10 percent flatter in both light and strong winds.

In most cases, it is best if the sail continues to flatten, at the same rate or greater, all the way down to the foot, but such generalities can be misleading (and, in fact, dead wrong in some cases). It is important that the crew do some experimentation (with outhaul tension and lower mast bend, for example) to determine the optimum vertical distribution of draft. This includes but is not limited to One Design boats, which can show fairly idiosyncratic design or rigging. Some of the popular One Design boats are quite old—eighty years, for example, in the case of the Star—and changes sanctioned by class authorities happen slowly, if at all, so as not to obsolete the older boats. Measured change is an important principle in many One Design classes.

FORE-AND-AFT DRAFT LOCATION

The proper fore-and-aft location of the draft is much easier to determine. If the maximum draft of a mainsail is at 48 to 50 percent aft, it will never be far from the optimum. The maximum variation is no more than 3 to 5 percent in either direction from this point, and the consequences of being slightly off are less critical in mains than in genoas.

In reality, where the draft falls is a result of satisfying other, more important aspects of the sectional shape. For example, consider the mainsail leech. In light air, a fuller, or curved, leech works like the flaps on an airplane wing, increasing low-speed lift and making the helm more responsive by providing a degree of "feedback" in the form of weather helm. In heavy air, however, curvature in the leech should be decreased; otherwise, considerable separation and induced drag may result. This drag is typically manifested as heel.

By making the leech straighter and flatter for heavy-air sailing, the whole back end of the sail will be flattened, and the draft pushed forward, as much as 5 percent. In rounding the leech to increase lift in lighter air, the draft will move aft—as far as 55 percent is sometimes acceptable. The front third or half of the main has special requirements of its own, namely to be full enough so as to sag to leeward where the flow is less disturbed by the turbulence caused by the mast, yet flat enough to work at a very narrow angle of attack.

VERTICAL CURVATURE

As noted in the previous chapter, the major loads in sails run from the head to clew, or vertically. In response to this load, the natural tendency of a sail is to sag to leeward, in the same manner gravity causes a rope hung between two trees to sag. This is vertical curvature, and as with headsails, the less vertical curvature the main shows, the better. The reason is the same, too— namely to minimize induced drag. As noted, vertical curvature introduces a bulge in a sail. If the air is asked to negotiate this curve, too, some of it will go up and some of it will go down, increasing induced drag. The main has a hard enough job to do without introducing another challenge.

So sailmakers work hard to eliminate vertical curvature. One way this is done is through the use of modern materials, polyester/Mylar and Kevlar/ Mylar, which better resist stretching and thus vertical curvature. To use the analogy above, a Kevlar/Mylar rope hung between two trees will sag less than a comparable Dacron rope will when hung between the same trees.

Mainsails are a major beneficiary of this sailcloth technology, as they are the most highly loaded sails on a boat (with, as noted, the possible and oc- casional exception of blade, or Number 3, jibs). The main is highly loaded because of size, aspect ratio, the huge wind range in which the sail is used, its roach—the extra sail area beyond the straight line drawn from clew to head—and the battens that are required to support this roach. Roach adds sail area and helps to make a mainsail less like a triangle and more like an ellipse,

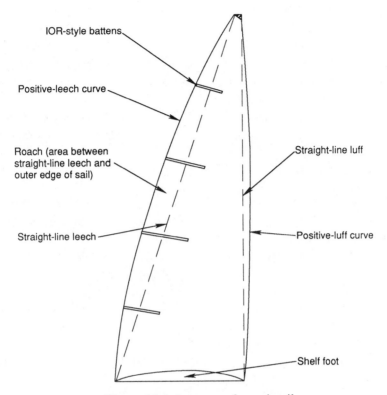

IOR-style battens

Positive-leech curve

Roach (area between straight-line leech and outer edge of sail)

Straight-line luff

Straight-line leech

Positive-luff curve

Shelf foot

Figure 10.1 Anatomy of a mainsail

a better aerodynamic shape, as discussed in Chapter 6. Battens are used to support this extra sail area and, while supporting a load, also add load to a mainsail in their own right. (Figure 10.1 shows a typical mainsail.)

ASPECT RATIO

In headsails, the aspect ratio has to be considered every time you purchase a sail. The aspect ratio of a mainsail, on the other hand, is primarily the responsibility of the yacht designer, since the size and configuration of the sail will largely be prescribed by the spars on which it is set. Still, drawing meaningful comparisons between mainsails is impossible unless we have at least a cursory knowledge of aspect ratio.

For upwind sailing, the optimum theoretical aspect ratio of a main is, as is the case with headsails, the highest that can be built.[1] This is because steady-state lift, as noted in Chapter 5, is more quickly achieved with this planform, or profile, and this shape provides the best lift-to-drag ratio through the minimization of induced drag. This helps to explain why *Stars & Stripes '88*, a catamaran, performed so well in very little wind with a relatively small but very-high-aspect-ratio sail plan.

Physical limits to the high-aspect-ratio mainsail include cloth stretch, mast strength and weight, hull deformation, the need to minimize weight aloft, and, most important, the imperfect aerodynamics of a sail that has to set in the disturbed wind off the mast and rigging. Before the high-aspect-ratio rig became a reality on sailboats—and a commonplace one at that—it had to await specifically the development of low-stretch, lightweight polyester/Mylar or, better yet, Kevlar/Mylar sails; high-strength, low-weight, aerodynamically clean aluminum or carbon fiber masts; low-stretch rod rigging; and a hull that, through the use of modern materials such as carbon fiber and Kevlar and leading-edge engineering, can handle the stresses without bending.

The value of the high-aspect-ratio rig diminishes quickly when turning off the wind. A purely downwind main can be much shorter on the luff and wider at the foot. This low-aspect shape is easier on the rig, the sailcloth, and, in fact, all sail-handling equipment. Cruisers often compromise in this direction, because they are not keen on sailing with all that potential energy just waiting to be released. But finally every sailboat has to have some windward ability.

The result is that most modern racing mains have evolved to an aspect ratio of from 2.9 to 3.5 (luff/foot). The spread in popular cruising configurations is a little lower, with typical ratios ranging from 2.7 to 3.5. If the closeness of these numbers is surprising, it should be pointed out that racing boats are limited by rules that take a discouraging—indeed punishing—view of high

---

[1] A sailmaker determines aspect ratio by this simple formula: $\dfrac{P \text{ (Luff)}}{E \text{ (Foot)}}$

When computing aspect ratio, many aerodynamicists prefer the formula $\dfrac{Luff^2}{SA^2}$

Sail area is determined from this formula: $\dfrac{E \times P}{2} = $ Sail Area

aspect ratios. Also, what seemed risky engineering ten years ago is standard practice today, so the rigs of cruising sailboats are catching up to those on racing boats. Finally, for the cruising sailor, the ability to claw upwind is like money in the bank. The cruiser may never need it, but it's nice to know it's there.

Racing mains are a compromise: They are optimized toward a high-aspect-ratio shape—as windward sailing is typically emphasized in competition—but, again, always with an eye toward the harsh penalty meted out by the racing rules. Indeed, in the absence of racing rules, racing boats might have mainsails with an aspect ratio of 4.5:1.

At some point, however, an additional compromise must be addressed. Although a high aspect ratio is good for upwind work, this doesn't necessarily mean that a very high aspect ratio is better. Ultimately, one has to factor in the rig's turbulence, or form drag. No matter how small and aerodynamically clean the mast section, part of the main close behind it will show very low efficiency. What happens is the airflow starts to follow the curve around the mast, but rather than following it precisely, at some point it lifts off, or separates. It takes some distance for the separated flow to reattach itself to the mainsail. The taller and thinner the main (the greater its aspect ratio), the greater the vertical area that will be adversely affected—and this turbulence can offset the theoretical aerodynamic advantage of low drag. To paint this in bold strokes for reasons of illustration: A sail that is 50 feet on the luff and 4 feet on the foot isn't going to be too effective when the bubble of disturbed, or separated, air extends 3 feet back into the sail. It is for this reason that some people say, only half facetiously, that the job of the front part of the mainsail is to connect the back part to the mast.

CONTROLLING MAINSAIL SHAPE

Ultimately, most racing boats will change from a headsail of one size, weight, and aspect ratio to one of a different size, weight, and aspect ratio to accommodate changing conditions, but this is not the case with the mainsail, which instead must be constantly reshaped and reconfigured to stay in harmony with the conditions. That this can be done—and done very efficiently and effectively—attests to the sophistication of modern mainsail control systems, as well as the sophistication of the sail itself. So before we turn to principles of trimming the mainsail, we will address the tools of the trade.

MAST BEND

When the mast bends, the middle moves forward relative to the top and bottom, pulling the luff of the mainsail with it. The sail functions as a large membrane, held stable and fairly taut by various loads, so pulling one edge increases the tension in that direction and flattens the overall shape. More mast bend flattens the sail, especially the leading edge, and straightens the leech; less bend forces in more shape (see Figure 10.2).

The biggest difference between trimming a headsail and trimming a main is that a mainsail does not have to contend with the undesirable and complex effects of luff sag. This is because nearly all boats are equipped with spars that can be held straight or, better yet, bent in a controlled fashion. We can characterize the amount of mast bend as ''little or none'' (.25 percent or less, equal to about 1½ inches in 40 feet of luff length); ''moderate to bendy'' (.75 to 1 percent, or 4 to 5 inches); and ''extreme'' (up to 2 percent, or 10 inches).

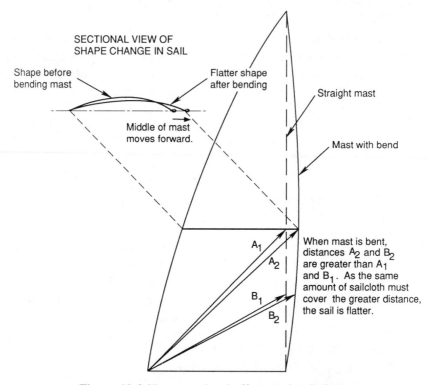

Figure 10.2 How mast bend affects mainsail shape

Bendable and Nonbendable Spars There are, as is apparent from the above, two classifications of masts: bendable and nonbendable. The former category can further be divided into moderately bendy and extremely bendy. The cruising sailor typically has a mast that either doesn't bend or bends moderately (up to 5 inches of mast bend on a sail in the preceding example with a 40-foot luff); the racing sailor is likely to have a mast that shows bend characteristics that are moderate or extreme (4 to 10 inches on the same-sized sail).

Nonbendable masts derive stiffness from large-diameter sections with fairly thin walls to keep weight down. Usually, they have some of the lower shrouds triangulated, that is, aft lowers with chainplates behind the spar and either forward lowers with a chainplate ahead of the mast or provision for a substantial and often permanent intermediate forestay. The triangle is a particularly rigid shape, and this triangulation prevents the middle of the mast from bowing forward, and since the bottom is fixed at the step and the top is held fast by the headstay, there will be little or no bend. On the other hand, this sort of rig is particularly rugged, safe, and simple and is highly recommended for shorthanded sailing and offshore cruising.

Bendable masts are built and supported in different ways. When masts —aluminum tubes—bend under load, the wall on the outside of the curve stretches, and the inside wall compresses. Bendable masts have walls thick enough to tolerate this abuse without failing. The standing rigging of bendable masts consists of the usual headstay, backstay, and shrouds, which, differing from nonbendable masts, are not triangulated, or triangulated as much, but are located more or less in line with the spar. When bending is induced, the middle of the mast moves forward, and the mast curves.

The shape of a main is sensitive to mast bend of as little as .1 percent of luff length (less than ½ inch on a main with a 40-foot luff). This means that positive control of mast bend is absolutely essential and also that it is imperative that the sail be built with mast bend taken into account. For example, a mainsail for a nonbendable mast will have little or no luff curve, and it will be relatively flat. If you have a flat sail, and it gets too windy, that's acceptable. If, on the other hand, you have a full sail for light air, and it gets windy, the sail is hopeless. A sail cut for a bendy mast, however, will have more luff curve and more overall shape because shape can be removed or added by bending or straightening the mast, respectively. This is, of course, a bendable mast's reason for being.

Before addressing how masts are bent, it should be pointed out that since mainsails are three-dimensional objects, the sideways bend of a mast is at least as critical to sail shape (and to keeping the rig upright) as its fore-and-aft bend.

An irregular sideways bend, of the same .1 percent magnitude, can undo practically everything that is done in the fore-and-aft plane.

There are exceptions, most notably in conditions featuring sudden, over-powering puffs, where a mast that bends off to leeward in a controlled fashion and so depowers the main can outperform sail trim that relies on human reaction time. Thus a small amount of lateral bend is sometimes tuned into the rigs of small One Designs, but less often on small fractionally rigged offshore boats. When a puff hits, the tip of such a spar bends off and the middle bows to weather. This has the effect of opening, or twisting, the leech, reducing heeling and weather helm, but if done incorrectly, it can topple a mast and/or, indeed, cause injury.

Why this lateral bend is sometimes found on small boats and less often on large ones involves material touched upon in Chapter 5. The small boats are more responsive due to the short chords of their sails. Thus it takes small boats less time to reach steady-state lift, the point where lift plateaus. So when a puff hits, lift builds quickly on a small sailboat. This is exacerbated by the fact that on small boats there are only so many hands to react to excessive wind. Thus lateral bend, when done correctly, can work as an instantaneous and automatic adjustment. Bigger boats typically have more time to react and more free hands to drop the traveler in puffs.

Bending the Mast   Mast bend is a powerful tool for shaping the main. It is, also, the least obvious and least understood mechanism for shaping the main. Get it right, and sailors have tremendous control of the mainsail. Get it wrong, however, and bad sail shape can be the least of your problems. Some of the more advanced methods of mast bending simply aren't tolerant of mistakes, crew inattentiveness, or mechanical failure. In some cases, the mast can fall. Thus, because of the propensity of mast bend for good as well as "evil," we linger on the subject over the next few pages.

There are a number of ways to bend a mast. No matter how it is done, the goal is to do it precisely where and as much as is desired. Most boats use more than one of the following techniques to bend their masts (some use all of them).

Deck Blocking   Some masts, called keel-stepped masts, mount on the keel, and others, called deck-stepped masts, mount on the deck. The former method provides extra support to the mast; the latter is more generous with space below decks since the mast doesn't penetrate the decks and for this reason eliminates a major source of leaking. On boats with keel-stepped masts, the spar is fixed at the masthead by the forestay and backstay, and where it penetrates the deck by the partners and at its butt end, or bottom, by the step.

The middle of the mast can be levered forward by moving any or all of these points relative to each other. For example, you can wedge the mast forward by putting blocks behind it at the deck; you can move the top aft by letting off the headstay and taking up the backstay; or you can pull aft the step, the fitting that takes the heel of the mast. The first method (blocking at the deck) is the most convenient (see Figure 10.3), since changing rake, which happens when the headstay is lengthened, calls for a number of secondary adjustments, and pulling the mast step aft requires very strong coercion, even after all the shrouds are let off. The only boats that cannot do some degree of deck blocking, or wedging, are those with deck-stepped masts.

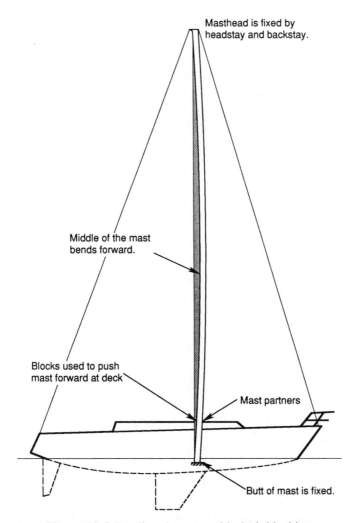

Figure 10.3 Bending the mast with deck blocking

An advantage of deck blocking is that once it is done, it doesn't require, or in most cases allow, further adjustment when sailing. You can set it and forget it. Others, however, consider the lack of flexibility a disadvantage. Another disadvantage is that the bend is low. As most of the shape in a mainsail is in the top half, low bend can miss the mark, so to speak.

Adjustable Babystay   Another method of bending the mast is using a jackstay, intermediate forestay, or babystay (see Figure 10.4). This represents the direct method, in that the stay simply pulls the middle of the mast forward.

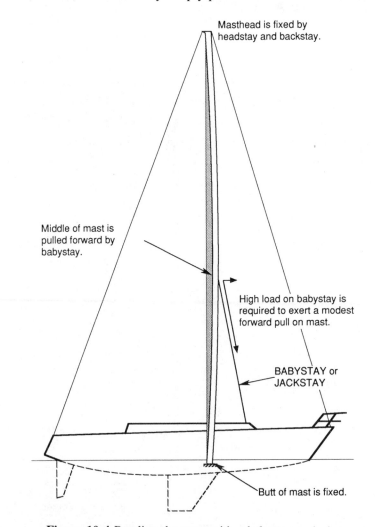

Masthead is fixed by
headstay and backstay.

Middle of mast is
pulled forward by
babystay.

High load on babystay is
required to exert a modest
forward pull on mast.

BABYSTAY or
JACKSTAY

Butt of mast is fixed.

Figure 10.4 Bending the mast with a babystay or jackstay

It is best to bring such stays down to the deck as close to the mast as possible—to keep the foretriangle open to facilitate tacking. At such small angles, however, there is little leverage, and thus the tensioning devices need to be very powerful to have much effect.

Hydraulic adjusters are the most effective way to tension such stays and can have the added advantage of being operated back aft, where the main is trimmed. An underdeck unit is preferable because it keeps the vulnerable hydraulic hoses away from flying sheets and bodies. A fore-and-aft traveler car, pulled forward by a strong purchase or winch, works well for boats up to 35 or 40 feet and can, likewise, be adjusted from the cockpit, near to the other mainsail controls. For ultimate reliability and simplicity—qualities so attractive to the cruiser—the familiar turnbuckle remains the best choice, however.

The primary advantage of the adjustable babystay is in its simplicity. Also such stays help to stabilize the mast in seas. A disadvantage of this setup is that you have to remember to disconnect the stay when jibing the spinnaker—assuming you use a spinnaker and, further, that your spinnaker requires a pole. This speaks for a quick-disconnect arrangement for the jackstay. Another disadvantage is that with a stay in the way, tacking is more difficult. The biggest mistake made with babystays and the like is underestimating the loads involved. This can result in installing an adjuster that is too weak, or installing one that is sufficiently strong, but not reinforcing the deck to which it is mounted. On the most competitive modern boats, babystays are redundant. The majority use considerable prebend (compression bending) and running-backstay tension to change the orientation of the mast. These methods will be discussed shortly.

Wedging the Mast Butt   All masts, but especially those that are deck-stepped, can be made to bend by shaving the forward edge of the bottom of the mast or, conversely, by slightly blocking up the back. Under compression, the bottom, or mast butt, wants to sit flat, and if shimmed correctly, the lower part of the mast is thrown forward (see Figure 10.5). Note that some masts, or steps, are shimmed incorrectly with the butt angled the wrong way, and the masts will defy all efforts to control them until they are reworked or properly shimmed. That is the major disadvantage with this technique; there is little margin for error.

Leveraged Bending   Boats with fractional rigs can bend the mast with backstay tension alone (see Figure 10.6). The headstay serves as a fulcrum, and as the backstay pulls the top of the mast aft, a horizontal force is exerted,

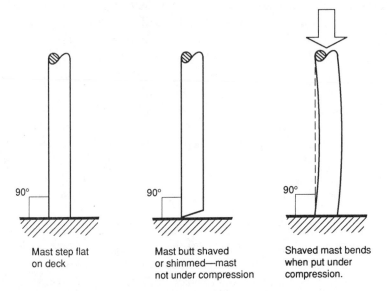

90°   90°   90°

Mast step flat   Mast butt shaved   Shaved mast bends
on deck   or shimmed—mast   when put under
                     not under compression compression.

Figure 10.5 Mast bend induced by shaving or wedging mast base

and the section below the headstay is arced forward. It does not take much vertical separation between headstay and backstay to achieve some results, as evidenced by mast bend on boats with $^{15}/_{16}$ rigs and even on some masthead boats with extremely tapered topmasts and unusually long backstay cranes.[2] A problem is that the bend resulting from this rig or the $^{15}/_{16}$ rig is at the very top of the mast, not the optimum place. At the other extreme, many authentic fractionally rigged boats (those with $^{7}/_{8}$ and $^{3}/_{4}$ rigs) use relatively little backstay tension to induce bending, as the mainsheet is sufficiently powerful to do this.

Compression Bending   The most sophisticated and adjustable method of bending the mast is compression bending. In this application, an inordinate amount of downward, or vertical, load is placed on the rig through the shrouds, backstay, and sails, pushing the masthead down toward the deck. Masts that can handle this are quite strong in compression, and the easiest way for them to relieve the load is to bend out of column. This means that the middle of the mast bulges one way or another. The shrouds keep the spar from moving

---

[2]The backstay crane, the extension at the top of the mast to which the backstay runs, increases separation between the backstay and the mainsail roach. As the position of the backstay is a finite limit to the roach, a backstay crane allows extra sail area.

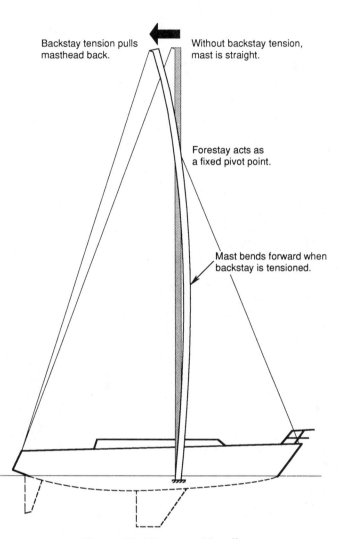

Backstay tension pulls
masthead back.

Without backstay tension,
mast is straight.

Forestay acts as
a fixed pivot point.

Mast bends forward when
backstay is tensioned.

Figure 10.6 Leveraged bending

sideways and make sure it goes forward rather than back by prebending the mast, which is accomplished by blocking it forward at the deck (see Figure 10.7).

Once bent, the mast becomes quite stable and predictable. The load on the masthead finds an equilibrium with the resistance of the mast tube to bending; it can be bent more or less by simply varying the load, which is most easily accomplished with a hydraulic backstay adjuster. To make the mast more stable, excessive force is applied so that it tries to bend even more, and

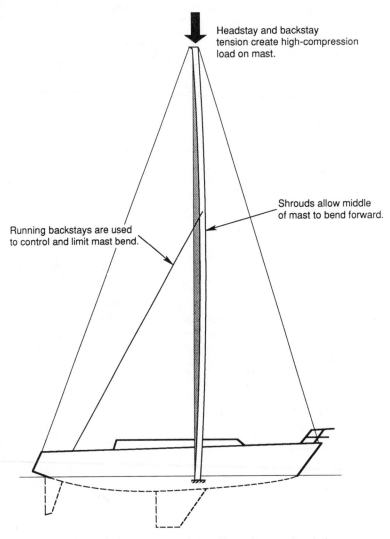

Headstay and backstay tension create high-compression load on mast.

Shrouds allow middle of mast to bend forward.

Running backstays are used to control and limit mast bend.

Figure 10.7 Compression bending of a masthead rig

then the running backstays are used to pull it back to the desired degree of bend. The mast is thus quite solidly locked in place.

Compression bending has a lot of advantages over other techniques for racing boats. For one, small mast sections are going to want to bend anyway under the high rig loads needed to control headstay sag, so existing loads are merely channeled to a useful purpose. As we will see, this bending method also offers several means for regulating the nature, or distribution, of the mast curve. Additionally, this setup doesn't require a babystay for any but the most severe offshore conditions, so tacking through a clear foretriangle is easier. It even works on fractional rigs—those with sufficiently powerful running backstays. On the other hand, this method does not show much tolerance toward crew inattentiveness or mechanical failure.

Regulating Mast Bend   Control over the degree and nature of mast bending can be divided into what is done by the rig designer and what is done by the sailors. The designer's tools include the amount of taper at the mast's top, local reinforcing, prebend, and spreader angle. Addressing taper first, a tapered tip will obviously be bendier up high. Local reinforcing refers to the technique where specific parts of the mast are stiffened by the addition of extra metal. Typically, this is done at the deck and gooseneck, where very high local loads occur. As noted, many masts are prebent; this ensures that the mast bends in the intended direction, but the right amount is dictated by how stiff the mast is down low and mainly by what sort of bend is best for the mainsail.

The angle of the spreaders also regulates mast bend (see Figure 10.8). When a mast bends, the spreaders have to move with it, which forces the highly tensioned shrouds out of line. Angling the top spreaders forward makes them push harder against the shrouds, which reduces mast bend at the top of the mast. On the other hand, spreaders angled aft increase mast bend. This means that on bendy rigs, the spreaders and their attachments must be very carefully designed and engineered, or they can fail.

Once the boat is in use, the responsibility for mast bend and mainsail control shifts to the sailors. Use of running backstays is the most direct way to control mast bend. Originally, these were temporary stays that could be set up to support the middle of the mast and be removed to let out the boom, but more recently these "runners" have evolved into essential tools for mast bend and mainsail shaping.

Backstay tension is also critical, but in a different way. The runners control or check the midmast movement, which is largely caused by the compression load of the backstay. More backstay tension means more compression and more bend. At the same time, increasing backstay tension has some secondary effects. As the mast is loaded and the middle bows forward, the tip moves closer to the deck; this, together with headstay stretch (all metal stretches to some degree), lets the mast rake aft, increasing its effective prebend. Also, if the babystay has been set up to control pumping, the effect is the same as tightening the backstay.

Since trimming the backstay to match the main to the conditions also

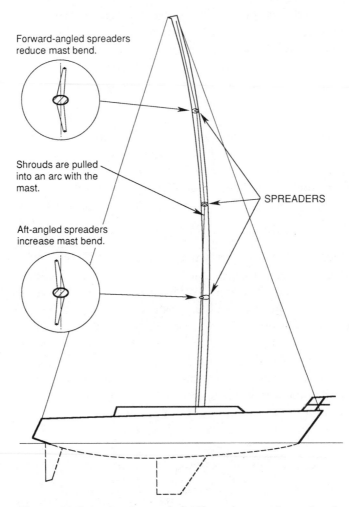

Forward-angled spreaders
reduce mast bend.

Shrouds are pulled
into an arc with the
mast.

Aft-angled spreaders
increase mast bend.

SPREADERS

Figure 10.8 Angle of spreaders affects degree of mast bend.

tightens the forestay, you have to be sure that mast tension suits the headsail
as well. So you adjust prebend and all the other elements of mast control to
work with the headsail, and vice versa. This is particularly important in some
One Design classes such as the Etchells 22, where mainsheet tension, for
example, strongly influences mast bend and headstay tension, and the main
and jib must cover a very wide range of conditions.

A mast—and its mainsail—can be overbent. Overbend can be subtle,
but a diagonal wrinkle, running from the clew to the middle of the mast, is

an unequivocal indicator that the limits have been exceeded. The degree to which different sails tolerate bend is determined not only by the degree of luff curve—how much mast bend they are designed for—but also by the material, finish, and construction of the sail. A very firmly finished material, such as yarn-tempered Dacron, used in some One Design sails, or a sail of radial construction with panels running from clew to luff will exhibit a very prominent ridge or wrinkle the moment the limit of mast bend is exceeded. A soft-finished fabric with a stretchy bias, found on many cruising sails, will accept many times that amount of bend without distorting.

We have spent considerable time on mast bend. At the same time, there are a number of other very important mainsail controls. They include the mainsheet, outhaul, flattening reef, vang, Cunningham, halyard, battens, and the traveler.

MAINSHEET

The mainsheet controls both sail shape and angle of attack (see Figure 6.7, page 104). Let's consider sail shape first since angle of attack will be addressed when discussing the function of the traveler. When the mainsheet is eased, the boom rises, the clew of the sail moves closer to its head, and the midleech spills to leeward. This leeward sag of the leech is twist (which has been more formally defined as the change in the angle of the chord lines of a sail to the centerline of the boat at various heights up a sail). A primary effect of increased twist is that sail depth is diminished.

When the mainsheet is tensioned, the opposite happens: twist is removed, the sail becomes fuller, and, at the same time, the draft moves aft. This particularly affects the depth and draft position of the upper half of the sail.

More mainsheet trim tightens the leech, but at some point an interesting phenomenon occurs. The geometry of the sail stops changing, and the cloth starts stretching. Even the lowest-stretch Dacron has a certain amount of stretch in the fill direction—perhaps .5 percent to as high as 2 percent in normal use. A Dacron sail with a 40-foot luff will have a 42-foot leech, so even the .5 percent stretch will amount to 2.5 inches over the length of the sail, and twice that is more likely. Suffice it to say that this much stretch will more than negate all the seam shaping built into the leech of the sail. The remainder of the sail is being tensioned at the same time, but loads are lower, so the middle and front stretch less than the leech does. This means that the leech is becoming very straight vertically; it also becomes freer, or twists off (reversing the earlier trend), and the sail overall becomes flatter, and the draft moves forward.

If the design and materials take this into account, the feature is very useful as it automatically adjusts the sail when the wind increases. For example: The leech becomes straighter and freer, the sail becomes flatter, and the draft moves forward, which is exactly what is desired at such times. Kevlar/Mylar stretches, too, but it is approximately eight times less stretchy than a comparable Dacron sail (see Figure 4.5, page 62), so such sails typically don't allow this automatic adjustment.

OUTHAUL

The outhaul moves the clew in the one direction in which the sheet has little ability to affect change: toward or away from the mast. It is equivalent to the fore-and-aft lead location of the headsail (see previous chapter). Increasing outhaul tension moves the clew back and so flattens the sail; decreasing tension gives the sail a fuller shape.

When the sail is trimmed in quite hard with the mainsheet and the outhaul eased, the result is a straight and tight leech. However, today's complex sail shapes are products of seam shaping, luff curve, mast tune, cloth stretch, and wind pressure, and in most conditions these factors nullify the effects of the outhaul in the top half of the sail. Practically speaking, then, the outhaul is mainly useful for controlling total depth in the foot and lower sections of the mainsail.

Still, this makes the outhaul a simple mechanism for dramatic, if local, depth changes, which is exactly what is needed by racers at mark roundings

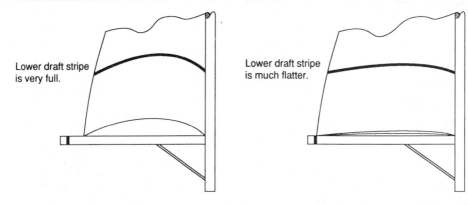

Lower draft stripe is very full.

Lower draft stripe is much flatter.

A. Outhaul eased. Shelf or lens foot is fully open.   B. Outhaul tightened to band. Shelf foot is closed.

Figure 10.9 Function of outhaul and shelf foot

when time is of the essence and the crew is fully engaged, and by cruisers who typically have rigs that feature fewer devices for shape control. Optimum upwind mainsail shape calls for a very flat foot in moderate air and relatively flat seas, and a full foot (20 to 25 percent) for off-the-wind sailing and upwind in very light air or in big seas. The outhaul works even better if the mainsail is equipped with a shelf (or lens) foot (see Figure 10.9). This is an extra panel of cloth sewn into the foot. It folds up when the outhaul is pulled all the way out, but opens when it is eased to let the bottom of the sail move smoothly away from the boom.

The shelf foot should be made of cloth that is strong enough (from the perspective of tear strength) to survive the repeated folding and unfolding and perhaps should be a little stretchy to open and close easily and smoothly. It is typically made of Dacron or polyester/Mylar. It can be made of Kevlar/ Mylar, but the relative expense of this material makes it an unlikely choice. Practically all racing mains come with a shelf foot, as do many, but not all, cruising mains. Cruisers who opt not to go with a shelf foot do so primarily for reasons of simplicity and/or cost.

FLATTENING REEF

The flattening reef is just a glorified outhaul and usually is unnecessary if the outhaul is properly designed and readily adjustable. However, it does do a few things the outhaul can't do. Because the mainsail sets on a boom, the foot wants to be straight, and it takes some special effort to introduce shape there, which, as discussed already, is desirable when sailing off the wind or upwind in very light air or in conditions where the seas are bigger than the wind. In addition to the shelf foot, extra broadseaming can be built into the bottom seam or two to provide some shape. Unlike the shelf, this shaping does not fold up neatly when the outhaul is tightened, so control comes from the flattening reef.

The flattening reef is positioned 1 or 2 feet up the leech, and when the line is snugged down to the boom, most or all of the extra sail area folds away. An ancillary benefit is that often the foot is pulled out even farther, flattening the sail more. Be aware, however, that both the flattening reef and the outhaul pull the clew away from the mast. Too much tension, and the sail can become distorted and, in fact, show an "overbend" wrinkle (from the clew to midmast). This may indicate that mast bend has to be reduced, but it can also indicate that the foot of the sail is too flat, and the flattening reef should be eased.

A less obvious function of the flattening reef is to lift the boom. This is a useful safety precaution when tacking or jibing in heavy air, particularly if the boom tends to sweep low over the deck. Lifting the boom can also help to keep it out of the waves, which can be a problem when sailing off the wind with eased sheets at a good angle of heel. Obviously, a boom dragging in the water on a heavy-air reach is not the recommended way to steer a sailboat.

VANG

The vang is a purely vertical adjustment for the boom. Although the vang may seem to duplicate the vertical adjustment of the mainsheet, it can accomplish this throughout the sweep of the boom, which the mainsheet cannot do. Vangs have to be attached close to the inboard end of the boom. This results in a less than optimum angle for good leverage, and thus vangs have to be very powerful to achieve the same effect as the mainsheet, which pulls vertically at or near to the aft end of the boom, where leverage is far greater. The vang typically attaches to a fixed point immediately behind the mast. An alternative setup—utilized by many racing boats and nearly all 12-Meters—is a circular track on the deck, which despite its appetite for deck space gives a more direct pull and saves compression on the gooseneck, boom, and lower mast.

The vang can, alternately, be led to the rail. In this case it might technically be described as a "preventer," since the boom will be prevented from swinging across the deck until the vang is released. At the point when the direction of pull is almost entirely horizontal—when, for example, it is led well forward—it is, of course, acting solely as a preventer.

For tensioning, vangs can employ hydraulics, a block and tackle, levers, or a rope led to a winch. Some vangs feature a solid tube that holds the boom up when the main is lowered completely, or reefed. Others incorporate a pneumatic device or spring return that actually lifts the boom when vang tension is released. Preventing the boom from dropping when lowering the sail or reefing is obviously a desirable safety feature.

The ability to release the vang quickly is also most desirable even—or especially—under maximum load. On many boats, the boom is low enough to hit the water when it is well eased and the boat is heeling, and the pressure of rushing water will hold the boom—even trim it. In marginal conditions, this can make the boat round up—even broach. The only escape is to hastily, if not instantly, release the vang. (See also pages 285–286.)

CUNNINGHAM/HALYARD TENSION

Luff tension on mainsails is at least as important as it is on headsails, and likewise, it is used to move the draft forward and flatten the sail. (This is the exact opposite of mainsheet tension, which primarily trims the leech of the sail. Then, the draft moves aft, and the sail becomes fuller.)

Many headsails have Cunninghams, but it is more common to increase halyard tension during a tack when the headsail is relatively unloaded. On mainsails, the Cunningham is much more useful. Racers have bands painted on their spars, which define the maximum hoist of the main. The main should be built large enough to go to the top band without stretching in the lightest air. Subsequent luff tensioning is achieved by pulling down on the Cunningham. In fact, tensioning the luff with the halyard would almost necessarily mean that the main is above the black band—a violation of the racing rules.

Most cruisers and some cruiser/racers don't have bands painted on the spars, but the principle is the same. There is a maximum hoist location where the sail will set without putting the shackle of the halyard into the sheave or catching the headboard of the sail on the backstay. Until reefing becomes necessary, it is important that a mainsail shows the maximum hoist, as this means the largest possible area is being projected, helping the boat to perform at its best. Further luff tensioning with the halyard could bring the main into this danger zone. Therefore, once the main is hoisted to the maximum point, any luff tensioning should be accomplished with a downward pull on the Cunningham. The primary reasons are that it is safer, easier, and quicker, and requires less muscle, or mechanical advantage, to pull down with the Cunningham rather than up with the halyard. If necessary, a small block and tackle can provide some additional power.

BATTENS

Battens influence the shape of the main, almost always for the better. Their reason for being is to support extra cloth out from the sail. Without battens, the extra cloth beyond the straight-line measure from head to clew has a tendency to fold over itself. This extra material, called roach, can be supported without battens by precisely balancing the shaping in the back of the sail. It is, however, an extremely delicate balance. Normal changes in trim, tensions, pressures, wind velocity, and especially cloth stretch will throw it off. The more the roach, the more delicate the balance. This is why mains for the ubiquitous Stoway Mast and the like, which don't allow vertical battens, typically have a leech with a negative curve, termed leech hollow.

Battens support the roach by cantilevering the extra area. Although battens don't obviate the need for balanced shaping, they make the sail much more forgiving. How effective battens are depends on their length relative to the girth of the sail and the amount of roach (or positive curve) the battens are called upon to support. For many years, batten length on racing and cruising boats alike followed the limits established by various offshore rating rules, most recently the International Offshore Rule (IOR), and the lengths were quite restrictive.

In the days when Dacron was the only choice for triangular sails, the stretchiness of the material and rule-legislated batten length limited how much roach could be supported. So direct was the connection between batten length and roach that batten length was the girth limit (a horizontal measure of the mainsail from luff to leech) under the old Cruising Club of America (CCA) rule and the IOR. In fact, roach on a sail was described by sailmakers as a percentage of batten length (the upper-middle batten, usually).

The use of Kevlar/Mylar and extremely bendy masts changed the shape of the main in the early 1980s. Such masts allowed more area to be put in the front of the main, in the form of luff curve. Turning to the back of the sail, lower-stretch Kevlar/Mylar made it technically possible to greatly increase roach, despite the limits of batten length. With luff and roach increases, rule-makers instituted girth measurements to control mainsail size. A few years later, they realized that girth measurements lessened the value of batten lengths as a rating control and allowed longer battens but not yet full-size battens. In this case, rating rules caused racing boats to lag behind the trend to full-size battens that was sweeping the rest of the sport.

Full-size battens are not a new idea, however. Long ago they were used on junks of the Far East. More recently catamaran sailors, iceboaters, and boardsailors have employed them in the interests of increased speed. Full-size battens allow a longer roach and thus more sail area—that is, horsepower — and since they make the sail more elliptical, they reduce drag. With improved speed came an unsuspected benefit—namely, full battens contribute to mainsail durability. For example, mainsails typically break down around the batten pockets. One reason for this is that under the constraints of racing rules, such as the IOR, the short battens end in a part of the sail that is highly loaded. When the sail flogs, the sailcloth threads bend around the batten end and can break. Full battens, however, end at the luff, a low-load area. Recently, full-battened sails have become popular on cruising sailboats as well as on boats

A full-battened main is seen on the catamaran Stars & Stripes '88—*the one with the soft rig rather than the wing (see photograph on page 124). While go-fast catamaran sailors and then boardsailors were the first recreational sailors to use full-battened mainsails, Chinese junks have had them for at least a century. They are now popular on cruising boats and some racers.* (Courtesy of North Sails, Inc.)

that race under rules other than the IOR, such as the International Measurement System (IMS), Performance Handicap Racing Fleet (PHRF), and Midget Ocean Racing Club (MORC). It seems likely that the IOR will someday allow their use.

Mainsails are now built with two basic families of battens: full-length (see Figure 7.2, page 130) and short. The latter are most commonly designated as "IOR-type" battens (see Figure 10.1). Each has advantages and disadvantages, which are noted briefly.

Advantages of Full-Length Battens
1. Improved sail durability because of reduced flogging.
2. Quieter because of reduced flogging.
3. Easier to flake on boom.

4. Very smooth shape.
5. Able to hold shape well, even in light air and chop.
6. Structural rigidity allows projection of more area.
7. Allows a sail that doesn't need as much vang tension for appearance's sake as well as performance.

Disadvantages of Full-Length Battens
1. Added weight.
2. Slides jam due to inward pressure of battens, leaving the sail partway up or down.
3. Require special, often expensive, batten-pocket ends and luff hardware.
4. Chafe against the shrouds when running or broad reaching.
5. Handling of the sail more difficult when off the boom, including shipping and storage.
6. Not legal under IOR; penalized under other rules, including IMS.

Advantages of IOR-Type Battens
1. Smooth shape.
2. Mainsail needs no special luff hardware or treatment to facilitate hoisting and lowering.
3. Legal under all rating rules.
4. When used with LazyMate or other mainsail-handling systems, manageability is almost comparable to full-length battens.
5. Easy handling when off the boom.
6. Minimal chafe problem.

Disadvantages of IOR-Type Battens
1. Not as quiet or smooth as full battens.
2. Will not hold mainsail shape or projected area as well as full battens, especially in light air and off the wind.
3. Somewhat more critical to trim, especially vang tension.
4. Not as durable.

Sails with full-length battens tend to cost more because of the extra luff hardware and detailing necessary to make them go up and down reliably. However, this added cost is somewhat offset by using relatively inexpensive untapered and uncored fiberglass battens. Surprisingly, this type of batten is often the best choice because sail shape is not compromised, and the batten material is all but unbreakable. These battens weigh more, but whether the extra weight is a problem or not depends upon the use and the user. To date, even those who race 80-foot multihulls have been happy using fairly heavy untapered stock battens, but a gunkholer who has to raise and lower the sail frequently might find the extra weight unacceptable.

In racing sails with IOR-length battens, the flex characteristics and weight of the battens are given greater emphasis. The most important consideration is the inboard end, which in the upper battens falls at or near where the sail shows the maximum curvature. A batten with insufficient tip flex (a result of too little taper) will cause a pronounced bump. Lower in the sail, the batten may be located entirely in a section of the sail that is sufficiently flat to allow the use of untapered battens.

The effects of different batten characteristics on sail shape are not complicated. Stiffer battens will make the leech straighter, flatter, and more open; softer (bendier) battens do the opposite. By regulating the rate or location of taper, battens can be made to flatten one part of the sail, usually the leech, while allowing more curve at their inboard ends.

Full-length battens react the same way. Although they tend to assume the shape of the sail underneath them, the stiffer they are, the flatter the section. In offshore boats, full-length battens are usually put into the pockets with little pretensioning. However, when put in under considerable tension, they will force more draft into the sail. The trade-off is that this can accelerate chafe on the batten pockets, and thus if more draft is desired, it is usually better to get it via softer battens so as to avoid chafe.

A major source of chafe for the mainsail is the topping lift of the boom. Now that solid vangs, which also support the boom when the sail isn't hoisted, are becoming more and more popular, a major source of this problem is being eliminated.

TRAVELER

We have looked at the diverse ways of controlling mainsail shape, all the while ignoring the angle of attack of the sail. (The angle of attack is the angle between the apparent-wind direction and the chord line of the sail. For a given heading, wind speed, and boat speed, the angle of attack will increase as the sail is trimmed.) It is the job of the traveler to control angle of attack.

Having only one device to control angle of attack is obviously more convenient than having to deal with several devices and the secondary effects of each. Suppose we want to decrease angle of attack in order to prevent, for example, the mainsail from stalling. If there were no traveler to control angle of attack, it would be necessary to ease the sheet to let out the boom, but this would permit the boom to rise at the same time (forget the vang for a moment) and alter the carefully adjusted shape. If the vang were set, then easing the main would allow changes in angle of attack without changes in shape, but shape adjustments would be delegated to the vang. This will be slower and more cumbersome than a well-designed sheeting system.

In the preceding examples, we are assuming that there is sufficient wind to cause the boom to rise. In reality, this is often not the case. Furthermore, the correct boom location when going to windward is, more often than not, at or close to the centerline. (This is an optimum angle of attack most of the time because locating the boom above the centerline, though sometimes tempting in light air to make the boat more responsive to the helm, will likely stall the main. Positioning the boom below the centerline will likely cause the main to "backwind.") No matter how much tension is applied, neither a vang nor a centerline-mounted mainsheet can set the boom on the centerline, but the traveler pulled slightly to weather can accomplish this easily. That said, if you rarely go upwind, there is less of a need for a traveler as the mainsheet and/ or vang can do an adequate job of adjusting angle of attack.

The greatest value of a traveler comes when reaching in big winds and waves. At such times, the mainsail plays a major role in balancing the boat, and being able to trim and ease the main rapidly might make the difference between the helmsman maintaining control or losing it and broaching. Although other devices, such as the mainsheet and vang, can do the same job, the traveler can do it quicker, and at such times speed counts. The mainsheet, by comparison, typically works on the principle of multiple purchase to provide a mechanical advantage, and thus adjustments, while requiring less muscle, are comparatively slow. With the mainsheet, the trade-off is more inches of line for less work, and when a broach is imminent, this can be an unacceptable trade-off. This is true for the vang as well.

The traveler, to be most effective, has to be free-running, with adequate purchase on the adjustment lines. Then, it is worked in close coordination with the needs of the steerer—that is, eased rapidly to keep the boat under control and trimmed again when power is required.

MAINSAIL AND HELM BALANCE

As discussed, when the center of effort of the sail plan is over the center of lateral resistance of the hull, the boat is balanced (see Figure 6.4, page 100). Balancing a sailboat is important from the perspective of safety and enjoyment. An unbalanced boat does not want to go in a straight line, and the rudder may have to be pulled, for example, well beyond the desirable 3 to 5 degrees off centerline (see Figure 6.5, page 101) to keep the boat on course. Obviously, the resultant drag is highly counterproductive, and the work considerable, be the steerer a person or a machine. Additionally, a properly balanced boat will help the helmsman to steer well. It will constantly try to work itself to weather, but won't fight when steered off to leeward. Steering a sailboat should be a pleasurable experience, and the more well-mannered and responsive the boat, the greater the pleasure.

Mainsail trim is one of the most important elements in properly balancing a sailboat.[3] This is true because the sail has considerable leverage and because it can be adjusted in so many ways that cause the boat to turn more or less in one direction or the other. It works this way: Trim the main and, if you want to get fancy, ease the jib, and the bow will turn toward the wind. Ease the main and trim the jib, and the bow will turn away from the wind. Such an effective steering system are sails that boats that have lost rudders have steered across oceans using only sail trim.

As noted, when sailing upwind, the ideal balance point for the helm is about 3 to 5 degrees of rudder angle—weather helm. (Seven degrees can be acceptable, but once you approach 10 degrees there is usually something wrong.) This rudder angle enhances the hydrodynamic lift of the hull and helps the boat to work its way to weather. Off the wind, little or no rudder angle is best.

The effects of the mainsail on helm balance should be considered in terms of sail shape and angle of attack. Angle of attack is the most obvious, since in this respect, the main acts in the same way as a rudder. There is no appreciable turning effect when the mainsail is luffing; this is analogous to the rudder on the centerline. As the main is trimmed, it deflects the wind more strongly, pushing the stern to leeward and making the bow turn into the wind. At a certain point, the sail stalls completely, and its influence on steering and power drops off abruptly but only when the sail is at a considerable angle of attack to the wind. Rudders, when pulled too much or too abruptly, stall like this, too.

The shape of the sail is a little less obvious but works in the same way. That is, the more air it turns, the more it turns the boat. If in light air you want to increase the turning force—make the boat more responsive to the helm—power up the sail, that is, make it deeper. If in heavy air you wish to

---

[3]Other elements include the hull shape (keel size and location, hull lines, and the fore-and-aft location of rig) as well as such time-dependent factors as heel (which puts the rig out to one side and makes the hull asymmetrical in the water), weight distribution on the longitudinal axis, and waves slapping the bow or stern. However, only the rudder, the main, and to a much lesser degree the headsail are readily adjustable, so obviously they are the most important.

decrease the turning force, change sail shape by decreasing camber and increasing twist, and so on, and ultimately change the angle of attack of the main by dropping the boom to leeward.

The turning effect from the sails is increased, interestingly enough, by heel. This becomes clearer if the boat is returned to the upright position. An upright boat has a symmetrical hull, which tracks straight as the flow around either side is equal. When it heels, however, its underwater profile is asymmetrical, and the water flowing past the asymmetrical hull creates more lift on one side than the other. For example, a boat heeling to starboard will turn to port. No sailboat is immune to this undesirable turning motion, but some hulls are more susceptible to this than others. Beamy pinched-end boats, the typical IOR shape, are the worst offenders; narrow boats with full ends, a typical cruising boat shape, are close to neutral. This is one reason why cruising boats are often easier to steer than their IOR brethren.

As important as it is to find the best possible compromise between lift and drag, it is absolutely imperative that the boat steers well and is well behaved. One reason for this is that water is twenty-five times as dense as air, and drag and turbulence in water are that much worse. The best solution is to use the mainsail to fine-tune an already well-balanced boat and rig.

MAINSAIL TRIM

Now that we are familiar with the sail-control systems, let's look at some basic rules of trim, beginning with upwind trim.

Upwind Trim

1. Set sheet tension and traveler position so that the boom is roughly on the centerline. This is a good all-around position until you start to get overpowered; then let the boom fall to leeward to reduce weather helm.
2. Trim the mainsheet so the upper batten is parallel to the boom. (This presupposes that the main has the correct vertical curvature, draft distribution, and sectional shape.) When the upper batten is parallel to the boom, all the elements of the mainsail—twist, camber, angle of attack, etc.—should fall into place. As a practical matter, to determine the angle between the top batten and boom, crouch under the boom and sight upward, lining up the two reference points.
3. When the main is trimmed correctly, the telltale on the top batten

should be streaming aft most of the time and stalling (curling behind the main) once in a while. This is at or close to the optimum lift-drag point. In ideal pointing conditions—flat water and medium air—trim the mainsheet harder so that the top telltale is stalled most of the time and the top batten pokes slightly to windward.

4. Use leech tension to control helm and pointing. The tighter the leech, the more helm and the higher the boat will point. Remember, however, that you must have speed before shifting into the pointing mode.

5. Use the traveler as the accelerator. When you need more speed, "step on the gas" by dropping the traveler to leeward and footing off. On the other hand, pull the traveler toward the centerline to slow down and point.

6. The position of maximum draft in the main should be roughly 48 to 50 percent aft from the luff. Move the draft forward when you need power to accelerate or to punch through seas.

7. The Cunningham adjusts draft position. Pull it just tight enough to remove most of the wrinkles along the luff. Older sails need more luff tension to keep draft forward. Newer sails are usually fastest with a few of these wrinkles showing.

8. Make the main fuller for light air and waves. Make it flatter for heavy air and smooth water. This can be done by bending the mast with the backstay and/or mainsheet. Remember that these controls also make the headstay straighter, which is likewise desirable in these conditions. The mainsheet, however, doesn't have much effect on the headstay for boats bigger than 25 feet, particularly when the wind is above 8 or 10 knots. In smaller boats, however, the mainsheet, which is so easily controlled, is an excellent way to shift gears quickly when a puff hits.

9. Sometimes you may start to see long "overbend" wrinkles in the main, extending from the lower-middle part of the mast toward the clew. These indicate that the main has reached maximum flatness through mast bend and outhaul and is starting to turn inside out. If you're overpowered, it's good to see a hint of these wrinkles, but if underpowered, they mean that the sail is too flat. Reduce mast bend by tightening runners/checkstay and easing backstay, in that order. In small boats, ease the vang and mainsheet to straighten the mast. Overbend wrinkles are less of a problem for cruisers due to the softer, stretchier cloth and the nonbending masts they prefer, but if such wrinkles do occur, easing the outhaul should alleviate this condition.

A warning is necessary. If the cruising sailor sees overbend wrinkles and doesn't have a bendable mast, a quick check of deck blocking, headstay length, headstay integrity, shroud tension, and the like, is in order. These wrinkles can also be caused by side bend, so a mast that is not straight sideways (caused by turnbuckle working loose or chainplate failure) could give this reading. Something may be broken or is starting to unscrew. The rig might be in danger.

Target depths and draft positions for the mainsail for upwind sailing are provided in the table below.

MAINSAIL: TARGET DEPTHS AND DRAFT POSITIONS

Apparent Wind (Knots)	Lower Stripe Depth	Lower Stripe Position	Middle Stripe Depth	Middle Stripe Position	Upper Stripe Depth	Upper Stripe Position
3–6	14–15%	45%	15–16%	45%	16–17%	45%
5–12	12%	50%	14–15%	50%	15–16%	50%
10–18	10%	50%	12–13%	50%	13–14%	50%
16–26	8–9%	50%	11%	50%	11%	50%
24–30	9%	50%	10%	50%	10%	50%

These numbers are general targets only. Even with the best sail-measuring tools (e.g., Sailscope), it is typical to have errors of plus/minus 1 to 2 percent for depth and plus/minus 2 to 3 percent for draft position.

Downwind Trim

1. Ease the mainsheet until you just start to see "backwind" along the luff. This trim position maximizes both projected area and forward driving force. Play the main to keep it on the edge of luffing.
2. Ease the outhaul and Cunningham to make the sail fuller when turning away from the wind. If the luff of the sail is tight, you may also have to ease the halyard to get rid of the vertical wrinkle along the luff. Too much halyard tension is often seen when racers round the weather mark or cruisers exit a channel after sailing upwind and reach off.
3. On an overpowered reach, leave the outhaul tight to minimize windward helm. Make sure the vang is played to keep the end of the boom out of the water. When the boat heels too much, dump the

mainsheet. At such times, the cruising sailor should keep the sail flat and the boom out of the water. If the boom dragging in the water becomes more than just a very occasional problem, it should be corrected by reefing. The danger is that if the boom drags in the water, it can cause a broach and/or break.

4. Adjust the mainsheet and vang so the upper batten is parallel to the boom. This is a good all-around setting for downwind sailing, as well as upwind. On reaches (where flow is attached to the main), set the leech so the upper-batten telltale streams aft most of the time. It is preferable to twist the main when sailing off the wind. This minimizes backwind from the lower leech of the genoa or spinnaker. Also, overtrimming slightly has been known to work.

5. Be careful not to overdo the vang in light and medium air. In these conditions, the weight of the boom itself is usually enough to get sufficient leech tension. On heavy-air runs, however, be sure to use a good bit of vang. Otherwise the twisted upper leech will make the boat want to roll. To dampen rolling, overtrim the mainsail. Overtrimming also reduces chafe between sail and shrouds, a typical problem when running.

6. If racing in light air, have a crew member hold the main out so the boom won't swing into the middle of the boat. This is particularly necessary when heeling the boat to windward on a run. Be sure that the boom is held out, not down; any downward pressure on the boom will make the leech too tight.

7. The mainsail trimmer should follow the spinnaker trimmer's lead. The spinnaker is a more sensitive sail and will usually be affected by wind changes first. If you're trimming the chute, be sure to tell the helmsman (or mainsail trimmer) whenever you make a significant trim change. The first sail takes priority when jib-reaching as well. Trim the headsail first. If you trim the main first, you'll have to redo it after genoa trim is changed. This is important to the cruising sailor in particular because jib-reaching—which is fast, comfortable, and a relatively uncomplicated point of sail—is a favorite option when day-sailing without a destination.

8. If you get out of control on a windy run, overtrim the main slightly and head up a little.

As with genoa trim in the previous chapter, use the following mainsail trim card to record settings that have produced optimum performance. Again there is a sample form and one suitable for copying (see page 234).

MAINSAIL TRIM CARD SAMPLE

MAINSAIL: *North K/m 88*	LIGHT AIR	MEDIUM	HEAVY AIR
Wind Range (knots apparent)	0 - 12	12 - 20	20 +
Top Batten (angle to boom)	parallel	parallel	slightly open
Outhaul (inches from band)	2"	max	max
Cunningham	none	little	hard
Depth (% at midstripe)	15 %	13 %	11 %
Draft Position (% at mid)	50%	50%	50%
Backstay Tension (% of max)	50%	75%	95%
Boom Position	centerline	centerline	traveler eased
Battens	soft top 2	soft top 1	stiff
Rudder Angle (degrees)	3°	4°	5°

MAINSAIL TRIM CARD

MAINSAIL:	LIGHT AIR	MEDIUM	HEAVY AIR
Wind Range (knots apparent)			
Top Batten (angle to boom)			
Outhaul (inches from band)			
Cunningham			
Depth (% at midstripe)			
Draft Position (% at mid)			
Backstay Tension (% of max)			
Boom Position			
Battens			
Rudder Angle (degrees)			

MAIN–JIB INTERACTION

A major theme of this book is that the jib and main have an interactive relationship, and a change in one affects the other. Good sail-trimmers can trim the main and jib; the gifted few can trim the two pieces together so the whole is greater than the sum of its parts. That, indeed, is how the wind "sees" a sail plan: as one long foil, not two separate ones.

The best way to ensure the relationship between these two sails is complementary is to focus on the slot, the area where the two sails come together. It is the width of the slot that is important, and this dimension is controlled by traveler position, mainsail depth, sideways mast bend, genoa-lead angle, genoa sheet tension, and mainsheet tension. Adjusting these controls fine-tunes the interaction between mainsail and headsail.

In medium and heavy air, it is most desirable if the forward section of the main flutters, or shows "backwind" evenly from boom to headboard. Further, this should occur at the same time as the windward telltales of the genoa lift. Let off the traveler to induce this fluttering in the mainsail, then readjust the mainsheet. If the top flutters before the bottom, the mainsail is twisted too much. So trim the mainsheet. If the bottom flutters first, ease the mainsheet to induce more twist.

Another indication of the relationship between the two sails is the amount of backwind, or fluttering. Too much means that the slot is too narrow. The size of the slot can be increased by 1) easing the genoa sheet a little bit; 2) trimming the main; 3) flattening the main; 4) changing to a headsail with a smaller LP; 5) moving the genoa lead outboard or back; and/or 6) making sure the mast doesn't sag to leeward in the middle.

REEFING

Mainsails are meant to stay up through thick and thin, as the expression has it, but if they are large enough for good light-air performance, they are going to be too large for very strong winds. Offshore boats have to be able to reduce mainsail area in heavy winds or a storm, and various types of reefing systems have been developed to do just that.

Jiffy—or slab—reefing is probably the oldest method of reefing. Although its origins apparently predate the clipper ship era of the previous century, it is still the most popular way to shorten sail, likely due to its reliability, flexibility, and low cost. It requires one or more reef rows—basically an

Most sail-trimmers focus on the front of the headsail and the back of the main. The best then turn their attention to the slot, where the two sails overlap. There they trim the back of the jib and the front of the main—the area partially in shadow in this photograph. The width of the slot ensures that the relationship between the two sails is complementary. (Michael Levitt photo)

alternative tack and clew—to be built into the main above and roughly parallel to the boom. But before getting into the specifics of the use of this and other popular reefing methods, let's consider when a reef is appropriate.

Trimming to Reduce Heel   Most boats sail fastest with a maximum heel angle somewhere between 20 and 30 degrees, after which the keel becomes too horizontal for maximum efficiency, and the hull is no longer sitting on its fastest lines. But speed isn't the only consideration, and many cruisers prefer less aggressive, or less uncomfortable, heel angles.

Once the limit of heel has been reached, the first thing to do is make sure that the sails are trimmed so as to minimize heeling—that is, the sails flattened as much as possible, the drafts moved forward, and the leads moved to outboard settings. Not only does proper sail trim reduce heeling, but it improves speed and makes the motion and handling of the boat much more pleasant.

Shortening Sail Usually Begins with the Headsail   Eventually, though, it will be necessary to reduce sail area. Now the question becomes, Should the main be reefed or the headsail reduced? Usually, the correct answer is to reduce headsail area. The first consideration is balance. A reefed mainsail not only reduces mainsail area, but it moves sail area forward. Moving the sail's center of effort forward can upset the balance of the sail plan to the point where the wind is able to blow the bow to leeward. In an extreme case, it might be impossible to sail to weather.

There are aerodynamic considerations as well. The main is a fairly high-aspect foil on modern boats, whereas overlapping genoas (Number 1s and 2s) show a considerably lower aspect ratio. As has been discussed, a higher-aspect foil will generate less induced drag and less heeling moment for the same area and show a superior lift-to-drag ratio. Changing the low-aspect genoa to a smaller jib (typically one with a higher aspect ratio due to its long luff and reduced overlap) contributes to a better lift-to-drag ratio for the whole rig.

You might further recall that when compared with the headsail, the mainsail has a tougher job to do. Not only does it have to contend with the adverse circulation of the genoa, but the jib places the main in a header. Then, too, the main works in an area of disturbed flow behind the mast and rigging. Most important, however, the mainsail and jib have an interactive relationship, and mainsail trim has an important effect on the performance of the headsail as well as on the latter's angle of attack. From this discussion, it follows that reefing the main rather than changing to a smaller headsail means that the main will have less chance—and thus be even less effective—at doing its job. Also, due to the interactive relationship, the reefed mainsail can make the headsail less effective at doing its job.

Reduction of sail area is a consideration, too. In a modern, high-aspect masthead rig, the foretriangle alone will be roughly 10 to 30 percent larger than the main. With a 150 percent genoa set, the main will constitute about 35 percent of the total sail area. One reef, typically about 20 percent of mainsail area, will reduce total sail by 7 percent, whereas changing from a 150 percent to a full-hoist 130 percent genoa gives almost a 9 percent area reduction, along with all the other benefits described above. (There is one exception to these rules: A larger headsail/reefed-main combination can work when the apparent wind is at least 60 degrees aft, because by then steering and balance are usually coming under control, and the lift-to-drag ratio is less important.)

These should be convincing arguments for deferring mainsail reefing, but sooner or later it has to be done. Exactly when that is will vary from boat to boat and from crew to crew, and for safety reasons, it is better to err on the side of reefing too early than too late. With that qualification firmly in mind, we offer some general guidelines.

When to Reef the Main
1. The headsail in use has its clew at or forward of the mast, and the aspect ratio of the headsail is as high as or higher than the main.
2. The boat wants to heel more than 20 or 30 degrees (whatever its maximum heel angle is from the perspective of speed or comfort), even with the main flattened and the traveler eased so that the front half of the main is "backwinding" but not flogging.
3. The helm has become heavy—overpoweringly so—and the boat is trying to round up even at an acceptable angle of heel. This is a clear indication that the overall balance of the sail plan will be hurt by a further reduction in headsail size.

The Number of Reefs   Determining the correct number of reefs in a main setup for jiffy reefing is surprisingly not a simple matter. Too many are almost as bad as too few. This is because sails are patched at reef points and patches are bulky and heavy, and it is made even worse by the fact that the weight and bulk of the aft reef points fall in the leech area, where wind loading is at its maximum, as is structural loading from the weight of the battens. In lighter air, weight there means that the sail wants to fold in on itself or, in waves, to flag back and forth. Even for cruisers—for whom optimum performance may not be as important—the extra weight and thickness can dramatically increase handling problems when the sail is down.

Thus, it can be concluded that one wants the fewest number of reefs to meet expected conditions, but how many are right is determined ultimately by the specific boat and its intended use. Here are some recommendations that should be applied very loosely due to the number of variables involved:

One Designs and Day Sailors: No reefs.
Day Cruisers that go more than two hours from the nearest port:
Under 30 feet: 1 reef that reduces mainsail area about 20 to 30 percent.
Over 30 feet: 2 reefs, each of which reduces area about 15 to 25 percent.
Day Racer/Cruisers:
Under 30 feet: 1 reef with 20 percent reduction.
Over 30 feet: 2 reefs with 15 percent reduction each.
Overnight Cruisers: 2 reefs, each of which reduces area 15 to 25 percent.
Offshore Cruiser/Racers (i.e., short races): 2 reefs with 15 to 20 percent area reduction each.
Grand Prix Racers: 2 mains, an "inshore" main (no reefs) and an "offshore" (basically the same design and material, but with 2 or 3 reefs with 15 to 25 percent area reduction).

Certainly the ultimate form of reefed main is no main. And too often one sees boats sailing in heavy winds with small jibs and no mains. Although, at times, this setup can be comfortable and requires a relative lack of work, it is *not* recommended, as the mainsail serves an important and often overlooked function of helping to support the mast. From the perspective of rig integrity, if you are going to fly only one sail, a reefed main or, in severe conditions, a storm trysail (discussed at the end of this chapter) is a better choice. If you need to sail closer to the wind than the fully reefed main or the storm trysail will allow, a small jib is sometimes added, but is not flown in lieu of a reefed main or trysail. A small staysail can substitute for the storm jib.

Reaching Reefs   Most reef rows are parallel to the foot of the sail, or on boats with low booms they may be tipped up slightly at the outboard end to provide a little more headroom. In any case, they are meant to reduce sail area for the sake of stability and control.

The reaching reef is a diagonal reef, from the tack to a point somewhat up the leech, and the purpose of this angle is to lift the end of the boom out of the water. As discussed, it comes into use in very rough offshore conditions on a boat with some combination of a long and low boom and low freeboard, or on any boat where the heel and roll regularly put the boom in the waves.

Jiffy-Reefing Procedures   As noted, jiffy reefing, or slab reefing, is the most common method for reducing sail. Used by cruisers and racers alike, it works well with any batten configuration. There is an essential sequence to this maneuver that can make the process as easy as tacking, but if not followed exactly can lead to trouble, even to major disaster. Jiffy reefing should go like this.

1. Make sure all reef lines are free, and that every step is assigned to somebody who can reasonably get to it in time. Not only do things like reef lines start to tangle when the sail luffs for too long, but battens can break or fly out, the sail material (especially Kevlar/Mylar) fatigues, and the halyard can jump the masthead sheave and jam. If the boat doesn't have a solid vang—to lift or support the boom when the halyard is eased—*make sure the topping lift is snug*. This is vital for the safety of all concerned. If there is a leeward-running backstay, make sure it is free enough so the sail will not beat against it. Be certain the vang is released as well.

2. Ease the mainsheet and almost simultaneously lower the halyard to the predetermined correct height, which should be marked on the halyard. In all the shouting, flapping, and confusion of reefing, having an accurate ''reef'' mark on the halyard is invaluable. The correct height allows the luff-reef ring to be slipped over the tack hook, or positions the tack high enough above the boom for a block and tackle to provide some adjustment.

3. If the new tack is fixed (not adjustable), then the halyard has to be very strongly retensioned. In a Dacron sail, the luff should be pulled into a large wrinkle, and even a laminated sail (such as polyester/Mylar or Kevlar/Mylar) can be stretched more than might seem appropriate. This is because as soon as the sail is sheeted again, the halyard will stretch, and the loads will work around the sail, leaving the adjustment just about right. But if the halyard is not tensioned enough, eventually the sheet will have to be eased again, and the halyard retensioned.

4. Ideally, the reef tack is adjustable via a block and tackle or whatever other system is used for the Cunningham. This means precise tension can be applied after the sail is trimmed, saving a few seconds, and that luff tension can be regulated without resorting to the halyard. This system also obviates the need for the aforementioned overtensioning of the halyard, and the potentially harmful effects if it is done too much or for too long.

5. While the luff is being adjusted, the clew-reef line—the outhaul, in effect—can be slowly tensioned, enough to reduce flogging and keep the lines from wrapping around themselves, but not enough to pull the reef tack away from whoever is trying to fasten it.

As soon as the tack is secured, trim the clew-reef line, once again pulling harder than seems normal and somewhat overstretching the foot of the sail.

Clew-reef lines are usually rope and therefore likely to stretch even more than halyards, which are wire. If it seems too hard to trim the clew-reef line, make sure the rope isn't sucking a part of the sail into the outhaul block, and check again that the vang and sheet are well eased. A ripped sail can result from these problems.

6. As soon as the clew is fixed, trim the mainsheet. You have a sail again, helm balance is restored, and the boat will start to charge ahead once more. Now there is time for most of the crew to relax while one or two see to the remaining tasks.

7. Check luff and foot tensions. A reefed main should be very flat all over, at the most 8 percent deep. If after reefing, the main is too full, the boat will be slower and show more heel and weather helm than a boat with a flat but unreefed mainsail. If the sail is too full, ease the sheet and readjust luff or foot tensions.

8. Check mast bend from the perspective of sail shape as well as the structural integrity of the mast. The amount of mast bend that was correct before reefing is often too much after reefing. This can be because the sail has been lowered to a part of the mast with a different degree of bend or because the reef-line tension is different from the clew tension.

After reefing, glance up the mast and make sure that the bend is still regular and the spar stable. The leech load of the sail, which previously was offset by headstay tension (in a masthead rig), is now pulling the mast back in an unsupported section and could cause a sudden inversion (reverse bend). In very heavy seas, it may be necessary to set up an intermediate headstay and to ease the backstay tension slightly to reduce mast compression.

9. General housekeeping should be done last, after making sure the sail is set correctly and the mast is going to stay up. This means cleaning up loose lines and if necessary readjusting the topping lift or vang. Also, the reefed part of the sail should be tied neatly on the boom. Modern reef systems place all the actual load on the two reef cringles, at the front and back of the sail. The small reef points across the sail are not patched or reinforced, and are only there to keep the sail up and out of the way. The sail can rip if these points are subjected to too much strain. To make sure none of the sail ties are forgotten when unreefing—which can easily rip a sail—it is best if the ties are of a contrasting color to the sail.

Reefing downwind is only slightly different from reefing upwind, as discussed, owing to the pressure of the sail against the rig. Rather than easing the sail with the mainsheet, it may be necessary to trim it almost to the centerline and take a fair amount of tension on the clew lines before lowering the halyard.

Other Types of Reefing   The popular Stoway Mast, discussed in Chapter 7, "The Shapes of Cruising and Racing Sails," and others like it make quick and easy work of reefing. To reef such sails, the mainsheet is eased, allowing the sail to luff but not flog violently. The roller-furling rod is then operated, and the outhaul is eased at the same time. The only tricks are to keep slight tension on the outhaul so the sail furls under tension and to roll the sail in such a direction that the wind keeps it pressurized. This means on starboard tack roll counterclockwise, and on port tack roll clockwise. The electric Stoway emits an audio warning when it senses improper furling and will shut itself down before minor trouble becomes a major problem. The simplicity of this process, when compared with jiffy reefing, provides eloquent testimony on why such devices are popular with cruising sailors, in particular those who sail shorthanded and/or on large boats with big mainsails.

This mast, which had some reliability problems in the early days due primarily to the mast slot being too narrow and the sail cavity being too small, is reasonably foolproof today. In fact, the major trade-off is the lack of horizontal battens and a compromised sail shape, as discussed in Chapter 7. As with jiffy reefing, one can reef the mainsail when sailing off the wind. This, in particular, is desirable, as an unnecessary turn into the wind when the going gets tough is not fun, or worse.

Roller-reefing systems, where the sail is rolled around the boom, have come and gone in recent years. Some ingenious mechanisms were developed but a number of problems were never solved, including but not limited to getting enough tension along the foot and attaching a proper, powerful vang to the boom.

The popularity of full-battened mainsails, however, has seen a new twist on this old idea, which works on these mains and mains with IOR-type battens. In its newest manifestation, the mainsail rolls around a rod inside the boom, rather than rolling around the boom. It is the boom version of the Stoway Mast, and Hood is one of the companies that offers such a product, under the name Stoboom. Sailtainer is another version.

With the sail furled inside the boom, a normal vang is possible. To work, some compromises in sail shape are necessary, but they are small compromises. For example, in the Stoboom system the angle between the foot and the luff (at the mainsail's tack) should be 86 degrees, rather than the usual 90 degrees, or more. This 86-degree angle causes the furl to "walk" aft, and forward again, helping to maintain proper foot tension. Because of this requirement, such booms don't allow much luff curve, making them inappropriate for boats, be they cruisers or racers, that use a lot of mast bending for sail shape. With such systems, reefing works best when heading directly into the wind, not the most comfortable direction, to be sure, but it will work within 30 degrees of the wind. It is also helpful if the sail is made of stiff materials, yarn-tempered Dacron or polyester/Mylar, as wrinkles make furling more difficult. Full battens, however, help to alleviate wrinkles in any event. That said, with the Stoboom, the bottom batten cannot be full length; however, two-thirds length is recommended.

STORM TRYSAIL

The storm trysail is neither a reef nor a mainsail, but a hybrid. Most sailors will never be in conditions that would warrant using one, but a trysail is an excellent sail for its purposes, which are to provide balance, control, crew safety, and some degree of windward ability in otherwise impossible offshore conditions.

The trysail sets on the mast like the main, though ideally it has its own track beginning at the deck, and is attached by slides so it can be bent on while still in the bag (and kept there) in anticipation of use. (If it sets on the same track or groove as the main, it can't be bent on until the main has been completely lowered and removed from the groove, which is undesirable.) The storm trysail specifically does not sheet to the boom, but to the rail well aft. This means that if the boom is broken, the trysail is still perfectly effective, but more important, the boom can be snugged down and immobilized so it isn't a hazard to the crew.

The storm trysail should not be confused with a performance sail, but alone or in combination with a storm jib or small staysail, it will balance the helm and can provide enough steerageway to work a boat to windward and away from danger. As with the main it replaces, balance is a key part of the duties of a storm trysail. With a jib alone—which is not recommended, as discussed earlier—the bow will be constantly blown off to leeward, and bringing it back up may be impossible.

Virtually all rating rules call for a storm trysail with maximum triangular area of .175 × P (mainsail luff) × E (mainsail foot). Since the sail is battenless, with a hollow leech, its area is effectively about 25 to 30 percent that of the main. A reef row exactly halfway up the main will accomplish the same reduction in area, but trysails do not have to be sheeted to the boom, do not have battens that can break and even rip a sail, and are designed for the strain and violent fatiguing caused by gale-force winds.

SPLIT RIGS

Spreading the sail area on two or more masts offers some benefits that make this approach attractive in certain applications, despite its diminished popularity in recent years.

In some respects, the split rig represents a continuation of the cutter-rig concept, in that it allows the sail plan to be broken into smaller units, each of which is then easier to set, reef, and furl. The variety of sails offers good performance via a progression of headsail shapes and sizes. Individual spar sizes and rigging loads are also reduced.

The three most common split rigs are yawl, ketch, and schooner. The yawl and ketch feature a mizzenmast that is shorter than the main mast. The old distinction, from the days of long overhangs and the rudder attached to the keel, has the mizzen behind the rudder post on a yawl. On the ketch it is in front. Practically speaking, the difference is that the yawl mizzen is a small balancing sail, whereas the ketch mizzen may be almost as large and important as the main.

The schooner rig is quite a bit different in that the forward mast is the shorter of the two. The mizzen is, in effect, the mainsail, and the foresail is often a hybrid form of staysail/headsail, setting either on the foremast without a boom or on a wire between the masts.

The main advantages of a split rig are reaching performance and versatility. The configuration is not very good for going to weather, and in fact at such times most ketches and yawls are faster with the mizzen down and furled, but for offwind (50 to 130 degrees apparent) angles, the additional drag is not a liability and the option of setting impressive amounts of sail between the masts offers a dimension not found in sloops. (If the mizzen is used to go to weather, it has to be very flat, since it has to set behind the main and headsail with a very narrow angle of attack. It also has to be strongly made, since a primary function is to act as a storm sail.)

The versatility of the split rig allows it to cover a broad range of conditions by varying the combination of sails. In light to medium air, every normal sail can be set; as the wind builds through 20 knots apparent, the genoa can be dropped or rolled up, and the boat can carry on with staysail and main, performing much like a fractionally rigged sloop. Finally, the main can be dropped and the boat will balance and handle nicely with staysail and mizzen. This can be appropriate in as little as 20 to 25 knots of wind. (This is not as risky to the mast as is sailing with only a headsail, since a staysail has less leverage.)

On the other hand, there are reasons why the split rig is not in great favor today. It is more complex, two masts are more expensive than one, and the necessary standing and running rigging can consume a fair amount of deck space. These characteristics are especially undesirable on smaller boats, where the value of splitting the sail area into smaller units has been negated by modern sail-handling systems such as roller-furlers. Moreover, though considerable work has been done to improve windward performance, the only arena where split rigs can compete evenly or with an advantage is in long-distance offshore racing.

For offwind sailing, almost any staysail configuration seems to add to performance. Small sails cause the least interference with the main and are certainly better at angles closer to the wind. They can be as simple as a tall, thin staysail that works like a blade jib in front of the mizzen. The larger staysails work better when sailing broader angles and can be beneficial even when blanketing the lower part of the main. Generally made of light nylon, they can tack near the main mast and sheet to the end of the mizzen boom. The only caution is that they can also restrict or completely block forward vision and are thus inappropriate in crowded waters.

★

CHAPTER 11

DOWNWIND SAILS

★   For the racer, sailing upwind has the tactical complexity of a chess match with a grand master. It is a sublime mental challenge and when the wind blows can be an ultimate physical challenge for the crew and boat. For the cruising sailor, the ability to claw upwind off a lee shore can be lifesaving. However, for sheer fun—at times sheer speed and often ultimate comfort—nothing beats sailing with the wind aft of the beam.

Offwind sailing is often the most joyful maneuver of the sport. A spinnaker is a billowing, unrestrained device that blows this way and that into a thousand shapes. This is the adult version of kite flying, and it is not surprising that a spinnaker is often called a kite. When you think of it this way, it is fitting that the act and action almost invariably involve bright colors, and this is not just because of the unequaled ability of nylon to be dyed. Colorful off-the-wind spinnaker photographs, seen on magazine covers, posters, and even color TVs, speak a universal language of beauty, joy, speed, and freedom.

A LINGUISTIC HISTORY OF SPINNAKERS

The spinnaker is such a magnificent object that any number of people have been eager to claim its invention and naming. Who was first to use the sail and who was first to use the word *spinnaker*, or *spinniker*, as it was first spelled, has been a subject of considerable debate, particularly when the sail approached what was thought to be its 100th birthday in 1966. This linguistic history reveals much about the importance and use of this sail.

The spinnaker has been a part of sailing at least since 1866. The *Oxford*

English Dictionary (OED) says without much certainty that the word *spinnaker* is "said to have been a fanciful formation on spinx, mispronunciation of *Sphinx*, the name of the first yacht which commonly carried the sail." It finds the first use of the word in print in a yachting magazine in 1866: "The *Sphinx* [set] a 'spinnaker,' a kind of large balloon jib. . . ."

Indeed, most versions about who was first to use the sail revolve around the English yachts *Sphinx* and *Niobe*. Apparently, William Gordon, owner of *Niobe*, used such a sail on a large racing yacht in a match race off the Isle of Wight in England on June 5, 1865—some fourteen years after the schooner *America* raced in the waters of the same English yachting center and won a trophy that came to be called the America's Cup. Gordon, who ran a small sailmaking business in Southampton, later sold a similar sail to Herbert Maudslay, the owner of *Sphinx*, who used it the following year.

Another version, espoused in the book *Tom Diaper's Diary*, written in 1939 and published in 1950, refutes the "fanciful formation" or "mispronunciation" of *Sphinx*. Tom Diaper was a noted British racing sailor whose father and grandfather skippered *Niobe*. According to his grandfather, when the sail was first hoisted, a professional crew member commented, "That ought to make her spin"—that is, go fast. A gentleman aboard the boat supposedly shortened that to "spin-maker," then soon enough to spinnaker.

The earliest spinnakers were made of lightweight cotton and were asymmetrical in shape. Poling out a headsail when sailing downwind had been a common practice of seamen, and so the early spinnakers had more in common with headsails than with the more or less symmetrical sails we think of today as spinnakers. They were also much smaller than today's sails; in fact, they were typically flown inside the headstay.

Hunt's Yachting Magazine writes in its June 1869 issue, "*Rosebud*'s crew especially deserves great credit for their smartness in handling their troublesome customer, i.e., the spinnaker." Although some think little has changed with this "troublesome customer" in the ensuing 120 years or so, spinnaker design has never been better. The spinnakers of today are easier to fly, more forgiving, and more close-winded, which inevitably means they are faster over a broader range of wind and sea conditions. They are faster because the newest designs do not need constant trimming to keep them filled; the sheet may be eased liberally, which gets the spinnaker away from the boat. A sudden and total collapse is a rare occurrence today and a symptom of a sail that is too full—as most were until several years ago—or too flat. As important, devices like take-down lines, spinnaker socks, and even poleless spinnakers for cruisers have removed much of the fear of flying this free-spirited sail.

A SHORT HISTORY OF SPINNAKER DESIGN

There have been only three or four seminal designs in the 125 or so years of the spinnaker (see Figure 11.1). The rest have been variations on these themes. The first revolutionary spinnaker was created by Ratsey & Lapthorn on City Island, New York. A giant step beyond the asymmetrical sails of *Niobe* and *Sphinx*, this was the first symmetrical spinnaker. It consisted of cloth cut to form a series of upside-down Vs with a common seam running down the middle.

The cross-cut spinnaker followed, created by Ted Hood in the early 1950s.

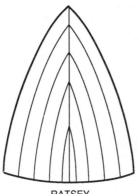

RATSEY

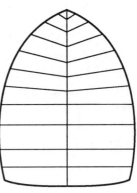

HOOD CROSS-CUT

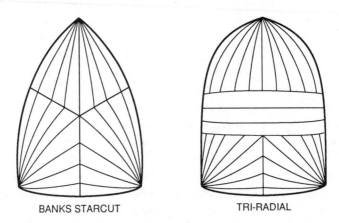

BANKS STARCUT

TRI-RADIAL

Figure 11.1 The Spinnaker Hall of Fame

Recognizing that the mains and jibs of the day were horizontally cut, Hood reasoned that this horizontal, or cross-cut, orientation might work well for spinnakers. He decided to test this theory. In making a spinnaker for a 210 (a Ray Hunt design), Hood tried orienting the panels at every possible angle from vertical to horizontal. He flew the sails on a test pole outside his Marblehead loft. The clews of the sail were kept at the same height, and Hood put a stick across to measure which panel orientation had the greatest projected area. Since a downwind spinnaker is primarily a wind-blocking device—with little or no attached flow—Hood reasoned that projected area could be key. As Hood predicted, the sail with the greatest projected area proved to be cross-cut. Where the outline of the Ratsey spinnaker resembled an upside-down V, the Hood spinnaker was shaped like an upside-down U. When considered this way, a U obviously projects more area than a V. Hood's cross-cut spinnaker proved to be significantly faster.

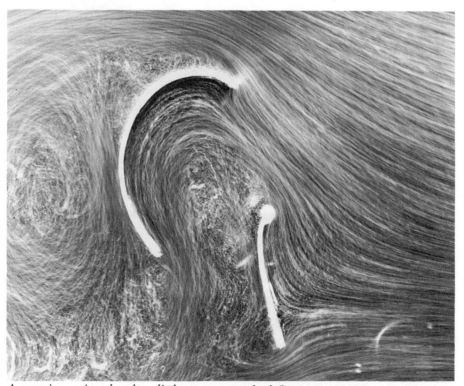

A running spinnaker has little or no attached flow, as is evident in this photograph taken in a water channel. (Arvel Gentry photo)

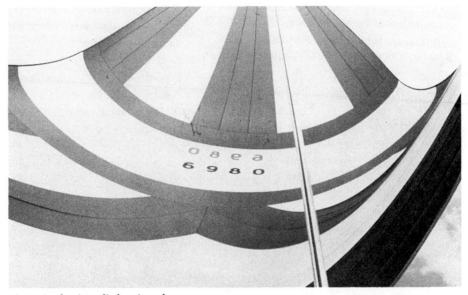

A typical tri-radial spinnaker. *(Courtesy of North Sails, Inc.)*

The Hood sail, like the Ratsey, had a miter—a seam running down its center. Due to excessive stretch on the miter seam, particularly in the heads of larger sails, the radial spinnaker was conceived in the late 1960s and early 1970s. This was perhaps the single most creative step in spinnaker design. Three sailmakers were responsible for this: First in 1969, Bruce Banks offered a Starcut, a specialized close-reaching sail. Then Hard Sails developed a radial-head spinnaker. Shortly thereafter, North produced the tri-radial. The tri-radial spinnaker resulted from combining the assets of the radial-head spinnakers with radial-clew corners. This oriented the load in each corner toward the thread line. Because this matching of strength to load greatly inhibits stretch, the sail more tenaciously holds its designed shape over a wide range of wind speeds and wind directions.

THE SPINNAKER OF TODAY

After fifteen years, the tri-radial spinnaker is a mature product. In terms of boat speed, there may well be little to distinguish among the tri-radial spinnakers made by top sailmakers in the world. This has had some amusing consequences. As noted elsewhere, I rode a successful spinnaker made for *Freedom* to the top of the America's Cup. Spinnakers have opened doors for me, ranging from America's Cup yachts to Maxi boats. I can remember, for example, sailing aboard *Condor*, Bob Bell's Ron Holland–designed Maxi, in 1981. An owner of Sobstad then, I was on one watch, and Lowell North, who then owned North Sails and was one of the world's most visible sailmakers and successful sailors, was on the other. It was a long downwind race, and I would come up for my watch, relieving North, and cast a withering eye on the spinnaker with the North logo. With all the cheekiness of youth, I'd comment to the crew, "That sail looks awful! Let's change to the Sobstad." North would come up for his watch and say the same thing about the Sobstad sail. The truth is that no one could tell which sail was faster. Fortunately, the crew was amused by our considerable professional vanities.

With the maturity of the tri-radial spinnaker, most designers are concentrating on small changes that improve its various parts. One such small improvement that nevertheless had a large effect on the newfound "user-friendliness" as well as the speed of the sail is flattening the head. It was determined that head angles too large for the aspect ratio of a sail created a spinnaker with too full a head. The extra fullness had to go somewhere, and it went straight into the middle of the sail. This produced a head that was overly U-shaped with leeches that curved in toward each other (see Figure 11.2).

Making the top half flatter accomplishes two things: It gets the spinnaker away from the sail plan so it does not disturb the main. When the flow off the spinnaker disturbs the mainsail, it requires that the main be overtrimmed. This can cause excessive heeling. More significantly, this spinnaker shape projects the most area. The flat shape is achieved by cutting each head gore with a nearly straight line in its upper half. A gore is any radial panel, whether in the head or clew (see Figure 11.3). When all the gores are sewn together, the result is a relatively flat plane that pushes out the leeches of the sail, resulting in greater projection.

Full spinnakers with large head angles will be very stable dead before the wind due to their great overall depth. But as soon as the wind starts to go forward, the closed leeches that are a trademark of such designs will cause the boat to heel excessively, causing more leeway and less headway. Needless to say, this can be a slow way to get where one wants to go.

The shape of the horizontal panels also determines the cross-sectional shape of the center of the spinnaker, as is true in mains and headsails. Recently these shapes have been designed with uniform curvature. Spinnakers designed to be reachers have horizontal shapes very much like an arc (see Figure 11.4). All-purpose spinnakers, designed for both reaching and running, are only slightly more elliptical than the reachers, and spinnakers designed to be pure runners are even slightly more elliptical than the all-purpose sails.

The clews of most spinnakers extend about 25 percent up the luff. This

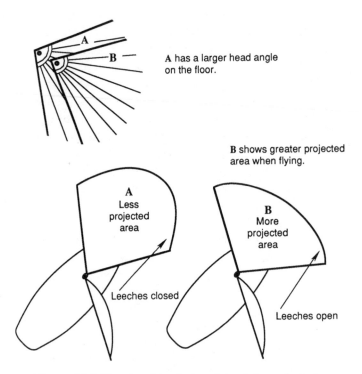

A has a larger head angle on the floor.

B shows greater projected area when flying.

Figure 11.2 How head angle translates into projected area

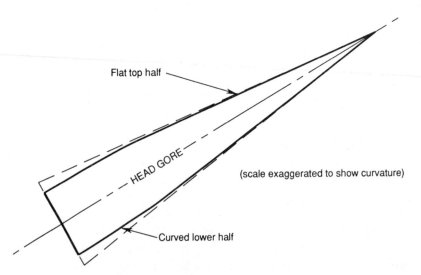

Figure 11.3 Shape of the head gore

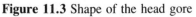

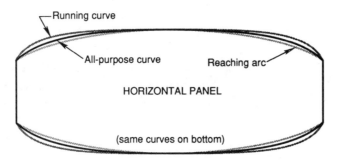

Each curve is slightly more elliptical than the previous curve.

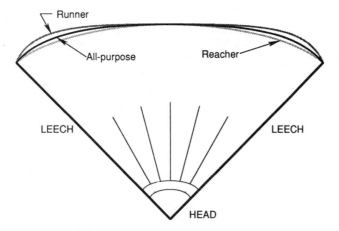

View of same curves from head of spinnaker when flying

Figure 11.4 How horizontals shape the three types of symmetrical spinnakers

is high enough to spread the clew loads sufficiently before they reach the horizontal panels and create distortion. Unlike the head gores, which have a definite curvature in the lower halves (see Figure 11.3), the clew gores are nearly straight-edged triangles with very little, if any, shape cut into them.

To ensure a nice continuous centerline profile, the center miter curve is created by adding or removing cloth where the two clew gores are joined, thus influencing the angle at which the foot comes into the boat. A reaching spinnaker does not need as much curvature in the center miter section due to the extra sheet tension and narrow sheeting base, which naturally brings the centerline curve into the boat. A running spinnaker, on the other hand, does not have as much load on it and therefore requires more built-in curvature.

THE COMPUTER IN SPINNAKER DESIGN

The computer has been helpful in perfecting spinnaker design. The advantage of a design system based on three-dimensional computer modeling becomes apparent when one considers that the spinnaker is the most complex set of curves in sailmaking.

Three-dimensional computer modeling offers other benefits, to be sure. For example, it creates a spinnaker that is much fairer in curvature from top to bottom than one that can be achieved via a computer program that works in two dimensions or by working on the loft floor. A 3-D program sees the

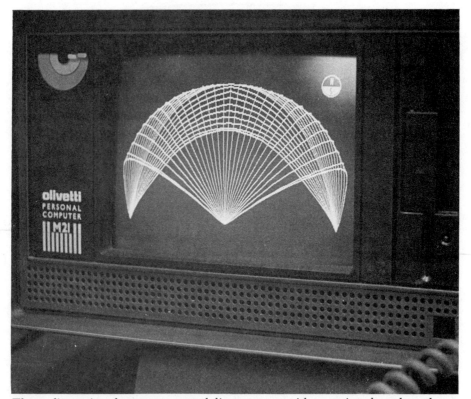

Three-dimensional computer modeling can provide a spinnaker that shows fairer curvature. It also neatly handles scaling problems. Furthermore, it allows a spinnaker that is reproducible, and reproducibility is so fundamental to design progress. (Courtesy of North Sails, Inc.)

sail as a continuous flying shape and shapes every seam horizontally and vertically so that each section is perfectly matched to the next. A more elementary 2-D program uses a flat on-the-floor description and relies on large "hits" of horizontal broadseaming at a relatively small number of seams to build shape into the middle and lower parts of the sail. The result is that the profile of the sail has "corners" at the junctions. This is very hard to detect from aboard the boat when flying the sail but is readily apparent if you look at such a spinnaker from another boat.

Another advantage of computer modeling is that it can be combined with a computer-controlled plotter/cutter. The CAD-CAM link means a fast design can be repeated ad infinitum, and as stated so often in this book, repeatability is a first principle of modern sail design. With repeatability, design progress follows a comparatively straight path; without it, progress is hit and miss.

The three-dimensional computer-design program works this way: The designer starts by laying out the basic framework, or skeleton, of the sail. The sailmaker describes the flying shape of the miter (the center seam) and leeches. The foot section completes the boundary, or edge conditions, of the sail. Then, the cross-sectional shapes are described at several sections up the sail. The program then develops a faired surface over this skeleton.

In the case of a main or genoa, a designer can get a reasonably accurate idea of what all of these curves look like from on the boat due to the relatively small amount of total curvature involved. This isn't true with a spinnaker, however. From on the boat, you can get a good idea of the cross-sectional shape and overall stability by just flying the spinnaker. But because the total curvature is so substantial, one really needs to see the sail from off the boat and from different vantage points in order to get a complete picture of the flying shape.

In observing a spinnaker from off the boat, there are two primary positions from which to view. One is the profile view, in which you line up the leeches and evaluate the thickness and/or variation of thickness of the curves as you go up the sail, that is, the relative positions of miter and leeches. The other is perpendicular to the foot chord (an imaginary line connecting the two clews). From here you can evaluate the projected area, or spread, of the sail. These same orientations are used by the designer when working with the computer program. The graphics capabilities of the program allow the sail to be rotated on the computer screen in order to check the molded shape.

While the technology is wonderful, not everyone needs a sophisticated computer program to design sails. If one were designing spinnakers for a handful of One Design classes, a drafting pencil and a little trial-and-error testing would most likely suffice. However, if you build spinnakers of many different sizes and different aspect ratios and for vastly different-sized boats, a three-dimensional design program offers several advantages.

First, the computer automatically handles the scaling problem of modifying the broadseam distribution to account for the change in proportions of the sail. For example, suppose the sail designer has a successful .5-ounce design, which was developed for One Tonners, and wants to blow it up to be used on a Maxi ultra-light displacement boat (ULDB). In the absence of a good computer-design program, this is an extremely complex nonlinear problem to handle by the seat of the pants. However, with the three-dimensional computer program, all the sail designer has to do is type in the new dimensions with the same flying shape, stand back, and there it is.

Then, too, there is the problem of creating a wholly new design, for example, a specialized Gennaker for a 12-Meter or a catamaran. Any two-dimensional broadseaming or trial-and-error formula would be useless in this situation because this sail is significantly different in curvature both vertically and cross-sectionally. With a three-dimensional program, the designer is able to manipulate the design, using the visual display to mold the desired shape. In several hours of work on the computer, he or she can create a shape that otherwise would have taken several weeks to achieve and perhaps would have involved several experimental sails that did not work as hoped.

This situation isn't hypothetical, but actually occurred during the 1986–87 America's Cup in Perth, Western Australia. Tom Schnackenberg, the sail designer for Alan Bond's syndicate, had secretly developed an inventory of reaching Gennakers, which the Bond group had hoped to spring on the foreign challenger in the America's Cup races. This was a breakthrough design in view of the fact that the size and shape of a 12-Meter spinnaker are strictly controlled by the rules—that is, the sail must be symmetrical. A genoa, however, isn't so strictly regulated. There is, for example, no limit on luff length, only on foot length. So what Schnackenberg did was design a "genoa" with very long luff, maximum girth, and very powerful asymmetrical sections, then flew it like a spinnaker. Whether it was an oversized asymmetrical spinnaker or a genoa was open to debate; what wasn't was that the sail was fast, particularly when the wind was from 80 to 105 degrees apparent.

Not surprisingly, this new spinnaker caught the attention of our *Stars & Stripes* syndicate. We had a videotape of this defender's race in which *Australia IV* put up their Gennaker and blew past *Kookaburra III* on a reach. It was obvious that Schnackenberg had hit on something. We had to design a sail like this and get a couple built in a hurry. This was right at the end of the challenger's elimination series, so there was little time for development. Our first designs had to be good. We called in Mike Schreiber who works for North Sails in San Diego. Mike, John Marshall, our design director, and I ran and reran the videotape, getting a good mental image of what the sail looked like from different angles and relating these to the curves in the North program.

Fortunately for us, the taping was done from a helicopter, and as luck would further have it, the camera angles corresponded to the design perspectives used by the computer program. After a few hours of manipulation to duplicate the image of the Gennaker on the computer screen, we were ready to cut a sail. The result was a very similar sail to what we had seen on the tape. We ended up making one more sail with some small modifications, which was successful.

But copying and optimizing are not all that this sophisticated computer-design system can do: It can lead as well as follow. With this computer system and its CAD-CAM link, the sail designer can, for the first time, compare the molded shape to the flying shape. But it is more basic than that: For the first time, the computer can accurately describe the flying shape of a spinnaker. This has been so difficult because the spinnaker is such an active sail—it is made of such light cloth and is under so little restraint—that it doesn't stay still long enough to allow one to conceptualize it.

To get around this problem, a particular spinnaker in use is photographed hundreds of times in a process called photogrammetry. This is done using several cameras that are linked so they shoot at the same instant. All of these on-the-water photographs are then digitized, fed into the computer, and averaged by the computer to produce an average flying shape. The significance of this computer averaging is that, for the first time, the flying spinnaker stands still—it is frozen in time. Next the designer compares the flying shape to the molded shape produced from the Mold program (see Figure 8.1, page 156), which was used to design and build the sail. Then the designer uses the Flow and Membrane programs to search for a pressure distribution that makes the molded spinnaker in the computer fly like the digitized version of the real sail on a boat. (The pressure distribution is a function of such environmental forces as wind and wave loadings, cloth stretch, and pole height.) This links the three pieces: the molded shape, the environmental forces, and the flying shape.

One result of this technology is a new tri-radial spinnaker (see photograph on next page). This sail, called the Tru-Radial, has fewer shaping seams than the three or more in the typical tri-radial. No longer are there hard spots where the vertical and horizontal panels meet, or unfair changes in curvature. The thinking is that wind will flow over this smooth sail the way water flows over

The new True-Radial spinnaker, a child of computer modeling, has eliminated all horizontal panels. There is only one horizontal joining seam on 41500. The result is a sail with a fairer curve from top to bottom. It is interesting to compare this photo with the spinnaker shown in the photograph on page 250. (Courtesy of North Sails, Inc.)

a fair hull. One interesting manifestation of this sail is that it luffs evenly from top to bottom—the entire luff shows the same orientation to the wind. The top is not, for example, overtrimmed, nor is the bottom undertrimmed (this is further discussed later in the chapter).

DESIGNS FOR DIFFERENT WIND SPEEDS AND ANGLES

The spinnaker of today has become the most specialized sail on a boat. For example, spinnakers come in various weights of cloth, various sizes (full-girth and reduced-girth), various aspect ratios, and different types (all-purpose, runners, and reachers). To the casual observer, the differences in design may seem unnoticeable, fussy, or, worse still, opportunistic on the part of the sailmaker. It has been found that subtle alterations in the geometry or construction of a sail can dramatically alter its effective range, stability, and overall performance.

CLOTH

Spinnakers have been built out of nylon for nearly forty years. Although nylon spinnaker cloth has not undergone the drastic changes that working sails have through the refinement of Kevlar/Mylar and polyester/Mylar, significant developments have occurred nonetheless. In 1979, warp-oriented nylon cloth was introduced, which is specially woven with the tri-radial configuration in mind. The number of warp yarns was increased to further minimize distortion caused by stretch. The result has been that designed shapes can now be maintained in greater wind velocities, or to put it another way, the sail has a greater range. A second advancement occurred in the early 1980s, when the finish on cloth became more substantial. Although this does not have the same impact as adding extra threads in the weaving process, a heavier finish further inhibits stretch, particularly in the bias (diagonal) direction.

That said, nylon fabrics are not as tightly woven as Dacron fabrics, nor are they heat-set as much to consolidate them into a very dense weave. Therefore, despite the improvement in finishing, nylon fabric is often subject to very high stretch on the bias. Sailmakers must take this bias stretch into account when designing sails made from nylon. Large spinnakers are made from a large number of narrow pie-shaped panels radiating from the corners of the sail to mitigate such stretch. With this type of construction, there is almost no bias load on the cloth. By using several small panels, the load is matched to the strong threads.

Spinnakers typically come in four or five weights of cloth. The most common weights are .5, .75, 1.5, and 2.2 ounces per sailmaker's yard. The actual finished cloth weighs about .25 ounce more than these designations due to the process whereby the finish (melamine, urethane, and/or silicone) is impregnated after the weave is heat-set.

Different yarn diameters as well as the amount and type of finish cause the difference in weight and strength between the cloths. This difference is expressed in denier, the weight of the fiber in grams per 9,000 meters. The table shows how the cloths compare.

Over the past several years, there has been a growing interest in the use of Mylar laminates in spinnakers. Many applications have been tried. Some have been successful, others not. To date, only the reaching spinnaker, which has a significant amount of attached flow and is thus more susceptible to stretch than is the running spinnaker, has benefited from this low-stretch fabric. In most cases .25-mil (.00025-inch) or .5-mil (.0005-inch) Mylar is laminated to substrates of nylon, polyester, and even Kevlar scrims. This process tends to make the finished product heavier than its nylon counterpart, but when used in a reaching spinnaker, the extra weight is offset by the lack of stretch, providing enhanced performance. A disadvantage of the Mylar laminate is that the sail becomes inherently less stable, and this instability must be addressed in the design with rounder leech sections, which increase stability. The material also has less tear strength.

COMPARISON OF NYLON SPINNAKER CLOTH

Cloth	Actual Weight in Oz. per Sailmaker's Yard	Denier Warp	Fill
.5	.82	30	30
.5	.75	20	30*
.75	1.06	30	30
1.5	1.81	70	70
2.2	2.18	140	140

*There are two weights of .5-ounce spinnaker cloth. What distinguishes them is a different number of warp threads, which in the chart is reflected in weight. This second .5-ounce cloth is stretchier since it is lighter and less warp-oriented. Some sailmakers use this lighter cloth in less heavily loaded areas of spinnakers—to make the overall sail lighter—or for .5-ounce spinnakers where light weight is the critical variable.

SAIL SIZE

The size of a spinnaker is determined by the size of the boat's foretriangle, that is, the I and J measurements (the height and base of the foretriangle, respectively). Whether racer or not, offshore boats follow, in most cases, the International Offshore Rule (IOR) limits for spinnaker luff length (SL) and spinnaker maximum width (SMW) (these dimensions are shown in Figure 11.5). The maximum size of spinnakers is then determined using the formulas

$$\text{Spinnaker Luff Length (SL)} = .95\sqrt{I^2 + J^2}$$
$$\text{Spinnaker Maximum Width (SMW)} = 1.8 \times J$$

These numbers represent maximum-size spinnakers. Obviously, racing rules as well as design considerations allow a spinnaker to be smaller than the maximum. Spinnakers follow the same rules as genoas: The size decreases and weight of cloth increases as the target wind range increases.

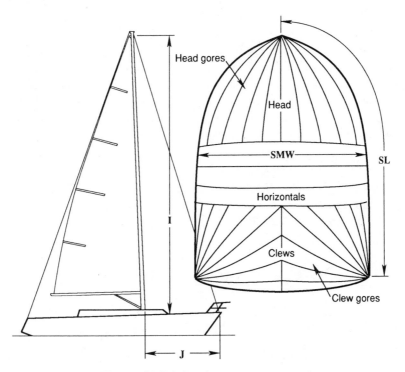

Figure 11.5 Spinnaker measurements

If a boat is not a racer—of if the racer or the yacht designer thinks the speed increase is worth the penalty assessed under the rules (this will be addressed shortly)—spinnakers can be larger. However, oversized spinnakers are the exception rather than the rule. Most boats aren't stable enough to benefit from oversized spinnakers.

ASPECT RATIO

The aspect ratio of a spinnaker is most important. From a design standpoint, the aspect ratio of the spinnaker equals the SL (spinnaker luff length) divided by the SMW (spinnaker maximum width). During the last decade, the aspect ratio of the spinnaker has climbed steadily, along with the aspect ratio of the rig. In the late 1970s, production boats had spinnaker aspect ratios of about 1.75, while racing boats were about 1.8. In contrast, production boats of today have aspect ratios of about 1.83 and racing boats are about 1.9.

How does this increased aspect ratio affect a spinnaker? The taller and thinner spinnaker tends to be a better reacher and inferior runner. When reaching, the narrower sail does not overlap the mainsail as much as the shorter and wider sail. There is greater separation between the trailing edges of these two sails and thus less disturbed flow. This obviates the need to overtrim the main, and the boat heels less and sails faster. However, when running with the high-aspect-ratio spinnaker, it is not possible to get as much sail area out from behind the mainsail, and the boat is slower.

As aspect ratios climbed—as spinnakers became taller and narrower—so, too, did the use of so-called penalty poles.[1] Many sailors and/or designers concluded that with spinnakers becoming narrower, they were giving away too much speed downwind. Penalty poles are common on sails with aspect ratios nearing 1.95 to 2. Sometimes a yacht designer will incorporate a penalty pole in the original design, but more often, it will be added after sea trials to correct a deficiency in downwind speed.

OTHER DESIGN CONSIDERATIONS

Aspect ratio is the most important calculation in determining the design of the spinnaker, because from it, the designer determines the optimum maximum chord depth—the depth of the spinnaker at its deepest point. (Much time has

---

[1]The IOR applies a penalty to boats with poles that exceed the J measurement. This is the derivation of the expression *penalty pole*. For measurement purposes, the J measurement then becomes corrected to the

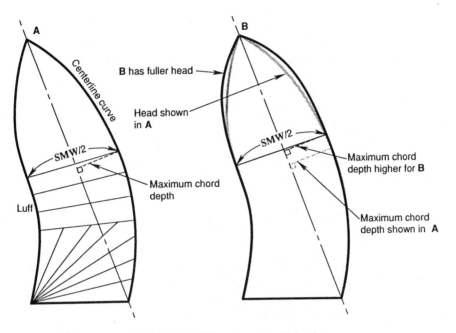

Figure 11.6 Spinnaker chord depth

been devoted to computer—or 3-D—design. The following concentrates on traditional 2-D design because this is the most common way to design spinnakers, and the principles are easier to see and therefore understand.)

To determine chord depth, a spinnaker is typically folded in half along its centerline (see Figure 11.6). Then a line is drawn from the head to the centerline at the foot. Next, a second line, perpendicular to this line, is drawn to the widest, or deepest, point on the centerline curve. This line represents the maximum chord depth. In the same manner as a genoa or mainsail, if the chord depth is short, the sail is flat, whereas if the chord depth is long, the sail is full.

Once the aspect ratio and chord depth have been determined, many other variables can be narrowed down. Among them is the location of the SMW, which will affect the fullness of the head: the higher the SMW in the sail, or the higher the maximum width falls, the fuller the head, and vice versa.

The point of reference for the location of the SMW is the spinnaker midgirth (SMG). This is the measurement at 50 percent of luff length. In the

---

new pole length. For example, if the J is 20 feet and the new pole is 24 feet, then the new J measurement—or JC, which stands for J-corrected—is 24.

case of the .75-ounce "all-purpose" spinnaker, the SMW, or maximum width, coincides with or is placed very near to the middle of the sail (see Figure 7.10, page 148). This allows good projected area—desirable when running—but, at the same time, presents a head that is not so deep that when reaching, the airflow has difficulty staying attached to the curved sections. If, on the other hand, the maximum width of the spinnaker is above the middle of the sail, the sail gets its area higher in the sail. This makes for a sail with good projected area, and the sail is likely to be a good runner. Finally, if the maximum width is below the midgirth measurement, the sail grows fuller beneath the center of the sail, or SMG. It is thus flatter overall and is likely to be a good reacher.

SPINNAKER TYPES

Cloth weight, sail size, aspect ratio, and location of maximum width aren't all that account for the number of spinnakers in the sail locker of a race boat. Wind angle, too, is important. This has resulted in, as discussed, at least three general types of spinnakers: all-purpose, reacher, and runner. Also, the specialized needs of some cruising sailors have given rise to a fourth type, the asymmetrical cruising spinnaker, which can be further divided into genoalike cruising spinnakers and spinnakerlike sails.

The All-purpose Spinnaker   The all-purpose spinnaker is the most popular sail by far, favored by racers and many cruisers alike. The design is most effective for wind directions of 90 to 150 degrees off the bow. Since these are the most commonly sailed angles, for reasons of comfort and speed, there is a great demand for this design.[2]

No matter what the wind speed, the all-purpose design almost always shows a maximum-size SL, SMG, and SMW. What enables this design to be most effective over these wind angles is its balanced profile from head to foot. The head is not overly full, as is the runner, or overly flat, as in a reacher (see Figure 7.10). The chord depth is such that it evenly distributes the amount of curve in the head with that below the head.

Some minor adjustments can be made in the three cloth weight categories of the all-purpose spinnaker. Since the .5-ounce spinnaker is designed for use

---

[2]When heading to the bottom mark or on a course that takes one dead downwind, most boats would rather jibe from reach to reach to increase their apparent wind. Not only is this orientation more comfortable, but it often optimizes VMG, or speed to the mark. Downwind VMG is determined by the formula $VMG = Vs \times Cos\ \theta$, where Vs is boat speed and θ is the angle away from a dead run. A cruising sailor can also use this principle to save time on a long downwind passage.

in conditions where the sheet and guy are not heavily loaded (0 to 10 knots apparent wind), chop and/or confused seas can dramatically affect the stability of the spinnaker. To offset this, the .5-ounce spinnaker is generally designed slightly fuller than the .75 ounce and 1.5 ounce. With this increased fullness, the .5 ounce remains more stable through the ranges of light wind and is easier to trim and fly.

As noted, the .75-ounce all-purpose spinnaker is slightly flatter than the .5 ounce. This design is intended for use in wind speeds of 8 to 15 knots apparent, and since it is easy to fill the sail, stability is no longer a concern. A general rule is that a spinnaker is fastest when it is as flat as possible and remains easy to fly. This, as described earlier, is due to the fact that the flatness translates into greater projected area and more open leeches.

The 1.5-ounce all-purpose spinnaker is the flattest of the three. It is intended to be used in wind speeds over 15 knots apparent. Like the .75-ounce all-purpose, stability is even less of a consideration. The three weight sails—.5, .75, and 1.5—grow progressively flatter by about the same amount. The difference is only inches from one chord depth to the next. In all three sails, a nice uniform profile curve is maintained from head to foot, even with the changes in chord depth. Most racers with boats under 50 feet don't carry a full-size all-purpose 1.5-ounce spinnaker. This is due primarily to the sail limitation rule, but also to the fact that most of the smaller boats are not stiff enough to carry a full-size 1.5-ounce when sailing at closer wind angles. For boats under 50 feet, a reduced-girth 1.5-ounce reacher is more common.

The Reaching Spinnaker   Reaching spinnakers are designed to be used when the wind direction is between 65 and 120 degrees apparent. There are full-size (max SMW) and reduced-girth (less than max SMW) reaching spinnakers. How to determine what size your boat needs depends on the aspect ratio of the rig, the stiffness/stability of the boat, the wind speed in which you intend to use the spinnaker (this also determines cloth weight), and finally, the wind angle(s) for which you want the sail optimized.

Unfortunately, there is no perfect size or chord depth for all reduced-girth reaching spinnakers. Generally, the smaller the SMG (the girth measurement at 50 percent luff length), the flatter the chord depth, and the closer to the wind one can reach in heavier and heavier wind. If only one reacher is carried, it will usually be between 90 and 95 percent SMG. The theory behind the design of a reduced-girth reacher is simple. Just as a Number 3 genoa is smaller and flatter than a Number 2 and Number 1, a heavy-air 1.5-ounce reacher is smaller and flatter than sails used in lighter winds or at lower angles.

The fact that the foot is the widest part of the most popular reduced-girth reacher should not be overlooked. This means that when sighting up the leech of the spinnakers, there is not much roach. This will keep the head very open, thus minimizing sudden breaks in the spinnaker and reducing excessive heeling.

The shape of the horizontal panels of a reaching spinnaker is a very gradual arc as compared with the slightly elliptical horizontal shape of the all-purpose and running spinnakers. The degree of shape in the horizontal panels determines the chord depth (see Figure 11.7). Note that C-A has more shape than B-A.

In the top illustration in Figure 11.8, the horizontals from Figure 11.7 are joined and two spinnakers are built. (All other variables are the same.) In the bottom illustration, the two sails are folded in half to determine chord depth. When there is less shape in the horizontal panels (B-A), chord depth is smaller (shorter), and the sail is flatter. With more shape in the horizontal panels (C-A), chord depth is larger (longer), and the sail is fuller.

With a very gradual curve (the flatter sail in the illustration), the wind can flow freely over, and stay attached to, the surface of the spinnaker without separation. Attached flow, as stated, is very important in a reaching spinnaker. In preparation for the 1980 America's Cup, we spent many hours and built countless reaching spinnakers of varying shapes in order to understand the importance of attached flow. We affixed telltales across the entire spinnaker, and in the most ideal situations found that we only had attached flow over 60 percent of the sail. But such sails proved to be fast. The photograph on page 268 depicts attached flow around a reaching spinnaker. It is helpful to compare this water-channel photograph with the photograph on page 249, which shows the lack of attached flow around a running spinnaker.

Before leaving the subject of the reduced-girth reaching spinnaker, contrast the difference between this sail with the all-purpose spinnaker discussed in the previous section. Figure 11.9 shows that, as stated, subtle alterations

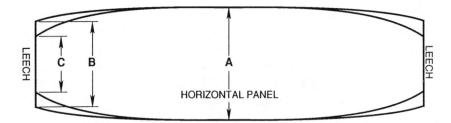

Figure 11.7 How the degree of shape in the horizontal panels determines the chord depth

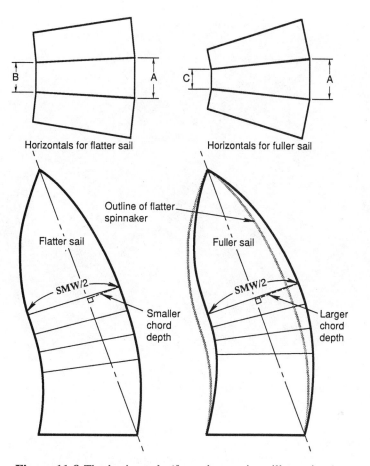

Figure 11.8 The horizontals (from the previous illustrations) are joined and two spinnakers are built and then contrasted.

in the geometry or construction of a sail can dramatically alter the sail's focus and overall performance.

Full-size (100 percent SMG) reaching spinnakers are a development of the past ten years. Prior to this, if one wanted a reacher, the sails were smaller and flatter. The full-size reacher of today is a far more versatile sail. It has the size to be fast at broader wind angles, and with its smaller head angle and narrower top, it can be flown at up to 70 to 80 degrees apparent with little difficulty. Currently, One Ton–sized racing boats are permitted to carry four spinnakers. A full-size .75-ounce reacher fits very nicely into the inventory of a boat of this size.

As this photograph taken in a water channel shows, a reaching spinnaker has a significant amount of attached flow. (Arvel Gentry photo)

From a design point of view, what makes a 100 percent SMG spinnaker a reacher as opposed to an all-purpose spinnaker is the length of the head gores and the location of the maximum chord depth. By lengthening the head gores, lowering the chord depth location, and flattening the chord depth, one can build a spinnaker that has a very flat head and very open leeches. The result is a sail that can close-reach quite effectively (without collapsing suddenly or causing the boat to heel excessively) but an undistinguished runner. The all-purpose spinnaker represents a better compromise.

Unlike the reduced-girth reacher, which is almost always made of 1.5-ounce cloth or heavier, the full-size reacher can be built out of any weight of cloth. As has been pointed out, the apparent-wind speed is still the deciding factor in determining the proper weight sail to be used. Several of the Maxis have .5-ounce, .75-ounce, 1.5-ounce, and 2.2-ounce full-size reachers *and* all-purpose spinnakers of the same weights in their inventories. Having all four weights in both designs covers almost every conceivable wind angle and wind speed.

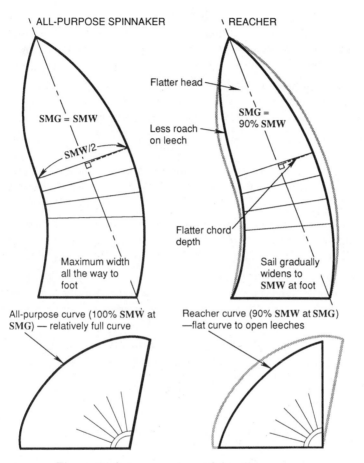

Figure 11.9 A comparison of the all-purpose spinnaker and the reduced-girth reacher

Runners Running spinnakers are used for wind angles ranging from 130 to 180 degrees. As noted earlier, projected area is key, and for a long time, designers thought the larger the head angle, the more projected area and the faster the sail. Nice in theory but less so when the sail meets the wind. What happens is that the extra fullness has to go somewhere, usually straight into the middle of the sail. This produces a head that when set is overly U-shaped with closed leeches—a hard sail to fly (see Figure 11.2). In summary, a sail that collapses all the time—even one that shows the greatest projected area when it is flying—isn't likely to be showing the greatest projected area over time. It is analogous to a world-class sprinter trying to win a big-time marathon. Although such a thing can and has happened, it is less likely to happen if the sprinter falls down every two or three minutes. With spinnakers, it is an all-or-nothing situation, and those times when the spinnaker is collapsed aren't contributing anything to the total amount of projected area or speed downwind.

The runner of today can better be described as showing the most projected area while still being easy to fly. This requires a compromise between projected area, or flatness, for speed, and fullness, for stability. This fundamental change has made all the difference between the good and bad running spinnaker.

A runner is particularly difficult to design because when sailing directly downwind, a boat is most vulnerable to waves and chop. When running, the sails are not usually under much load, and the boat is therefore quite unstable when compared with sailing upwind or reaching. This fact alone speaks for a full sail, but not for the fullest sail that can be built. By increasing fullness, the running spinnaker will not collapse as easily as the boat rolls from side to side. One exception to this, however, is that in smooth water—when sail stability is less of a problem—a fairly flat spinnaker can be fast, due to its greater projected area.

The horizontals of the runner are similar to those of the all-purpose design, the difference being that the runner has the most elliptical shape of any of the designs (see Figure 11.4). This makes the edges of the spinnaker slightly rounder, adding stability.

Cruising Spinnakers   As the demand for performance-oriented cruising sails has grown dramatically over the past decade, sailmakers have responded with many innovations to allow cruising sailors to sail faster and with less fuss and muss. Among these innovations is the cruising spinnaker. This has come to describe a wide variety of sails that are built out of nylon, usually of .75-ounce cloth, to be used when sailing off the wind. These sails can be divided into two basic categories: those that are more genoalike in physical appearance and those that are more spinnakerlike. Both types of cruising spinnakers are asymmetrical, with a defined luff, leech, and foot.

The genoalike category consists of sails that have a radial head and can be cross-cut, vertically cut, or tri-radial in configuration (see Figure 11.10). Depending on the type of headstay or headstay device, the luff of these sails can be hanked on the headstay, fed into a grooved headstay, tacked down right behind the headstay, or allowed to fly entirely free of the headstay. Having all of these luff options, and the fact that such sails are closer to a genoa in

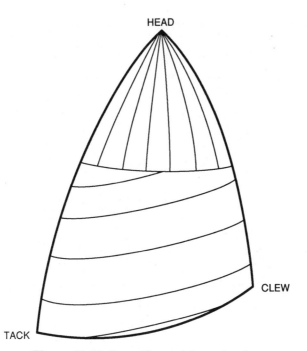

Figure 11.10 Genoalike cruising spinnaker

size as well as "disposition," makes handling the sail much easier than the spinnakerlike sails. In most cases, one crew member can go forward and pull the sail down the headstay, and usually do so without it falling overboard.

These sails are typically adjustable at the tack to help change the draft location depending on the wind angle. Because the sails are high-clewed, the helmsman can clearly see under the sail, allowing good visibility forward. As a rule, the overlap is as large as can be easily sheeted on board. This typically results in a sail with about a 170 percent overlap (see Figure 7.4, page 137). Such sails are not intended to be sheeted hard or used when sailing particularly close-reaching angles. That said, the less wind there is, the closer one can sail to the wind with these sails, but this is not their primary reason for being. One sheet attached at the clew is all the extra equipment that is needed. However, as the wind goes farther aft, the clew can sag under the weight of the sheet. A whisker pole can alleviate this problem but is not mandatory.

The spinnakerlike sails are much larger and fuller in the head than the genoalike sails. These sails look much more like spinnakers with long radial-head gores and only a few cross-cut horizontals. The foot sections are sometimes modified with vertical panels or even a radial tack and/or clew (see Figure 11.11). These sails fly unattached at the luff and away from the headstay. Usually, they have the tack clipped onto the headstay with a downhaul running aft to the cockpit so that the draft can be adjusted depending on the point of sail. The tack does not attach to the deck but is at a height only a little lower than if it was flown from a spinnaker pole.

Although the head is fuller and the sail will project more area aloft, the overlap is very similar to that of the genoalike sails. Since these sails are not attached along the luff, they are more difficult to handle when setting and taking down. As with the genoalike sails, one sheet is all the extra equipment needed except for the downhaul. A whisker pole is unnecessary due to the fuller head, which helps keep the sail projecting as the boat sails downwind.

From a design point of view, the spinnakerlike sails are not only fuller in the head but in the midsection. This is necessary to support the head. The shapes that are cut into the sails are very similar to those of reduced-girth

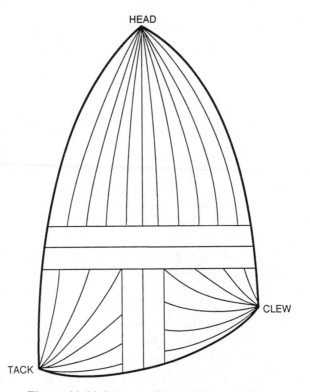

Figure 11.11 Spinnakerlike cruising spinnaker

reaching spinnakers. These sails have a definite luff, leech, and foot, and they are asymmetrical in shape from luff to leech, unlike normal spinnakers. Their maximum draft is forward of the center. This is not the case with the genoalike sails, which have their draft farther forward.

A sail sock or some similar device can be attached to the head of this spinnaker—in fact, most spinnakers—to mitigate the launching and retrieving difficulties that can occur at any time but particularly when sailing shorthanded, a common situation for the cruising sailor. These devices are made of a light-weight fabric with several hoops spaced evenly along the length of the device (see Figure 11.12). Lines run down the inside in such a way that, when pulled, the sock slides up the sail, allowing it to open and the sail to set. When the sail is in use, the sock sits at the top of the sail, out of harm's way. When the sail must come down, a line attached to a hoop at the bottom of the sock is pulled. As the sock comes down, the sail disappears, and at the same time, the air is pushed out. The sail and its sock can then be easily lowered to the deck. (The use of these devices is discussed in more detail later in this chapter.)

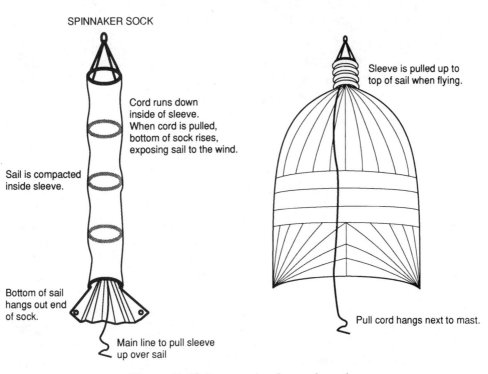

SPINNAKER SOCK

Cord runs down inside of sleeve. When cord is pulled, bottom of sock rises, exposing sail to the wind.

Sail is compacted inside sleeve.

Bottom of sail hangs out end of sock.

Main line to pull sleeve up over sail

Sleeve is pulled up to top of sail when flying.

Pull cord hangs next to mast.

Figure 11.12 How a spinnaker sock works

A spinnaker sock facilitates raising and lowering a spinnaker. The devices are particularly popular with cruising sailors. (*Courtesy of North Sails, Inc.*)

SPINNAKER INVENTORY

For the cruising sailor, one cruising spinnaker or one all-purpose spinnaker will usually suffice. If the boat is under 50 feet, most likely it would be built out of .75-ounce nylon. Racing, however, is a far different game, and those who play this game know that there is safety in numbers. To put it another way, the more spinnakers, the merrier. That said, racing handicap rules typically limit the number of sails. This is an attempt to keep costs down, and usually there are two responses to such rules: the boat's owner either buys the number of spinnakers allowed or buys more but only carries the number allowed during a race. If the latter, the owner will then select the spinnakers to be carried on board for that day's racing, depending on the weather conditions and the race course.

As noted, if only one spinnaker is to be carried when racing, it will typically be a .75-ounce all-purpose design. This gives the broadest range of coverage. A two-spinnaker inventory would consist of a .75-ounce all-purpose and .5-ounce all-purpose design. Adding the .5 ounce enables one to be relatively fast in very low winds where the .75 ounce would have difficulty projecting. If, on the other hand, one sails in consistently windy conditions, the second spinnaker might better be a 1.5-ounce all-purpose.

A three-spinnaker inventory might consist of a .5-ounce all-purpose, a .75-ounce all-purpose, and a 1.5-ounce 90 to 93 percent SMG reacher, depending on the aspect ratio. This is a very popular combination for Performance Handicap Racing Fleet (PHRF) and club racers. It nicely covers the spectrum of wind ranges. After the three-spinnaker inventory, one starts to get into some specialty sails—spinnakers that are designed for very specific wind angles and wind speeds.

A four-spinnaker inventory might consist of a .5-ounce all-purpose, a .75-ounce all-purpose, a .75-ounce reacher, and a 1.5-ounce 90 to 93 percent SMG reacher. The .75-ounce reacher is full-size with the chord depth flattened, and the maximum girth falls lower for optimum reaching. This inventory is geared toward sailing in conditions where medium wind speeds are likely, and the .75-ounce spinnaker is the workhorse.

A five-spinnaker inventory might consist of a .5-ounce all-purpose, a .75-ounce all-purpose, a .75-ounce reacher, a 1.5-ounce 95 to 97 percent SMG reacher, and a 2.2-ounce 85 to 87 percent SMG reacher. The specific width of the 1.5- and 2.2-ounce reduced-girth spinnakers would be determined by how stiff the boat is, how big it is, and the aspect ratio of the rig. Generally, the larger the boat, the larger the spinnaker it can carry. With this inventory, the 85 to 87 percent SMG spinnaker is used for very close reaching or when sailing downwind in very extreme conditions.

A six-spinnaker inventory would be the same as the five, with the addition of a full-size 1.5-ounce or full-size .5-ounce reacher. Whether the boat most often sails in light or heavy winds would be the determining factor. If the 1.5-ounce 100 percent SMG spinnaker is the sixth choice, it would be best if the other 1.5- and 2.2-ounce spinnakers were 95 and 85 percent, respectively. This would better cover the gaps and the spectrum of conditions.

After the six-spinnaker inventory, it is difficult to be too specific because the inventory has to be customized to a boat's characteristics. Also, at that point, the boat is in the 65 to 80 foot range, and what works for one is not necessarily best for another. The 80-foot Maxi typically has a complete inventory of sails, with a .5-ounce reacher and all-purpose, a .75-ounce reacher and all-purpose, a 1.5-ounce reacher and all-purpose, and a 2.2-ounce reacher and all-purpose. All of these are full-size. These boats are so stiff that they can typically carry maximum-size sails in almost all conditions. They usually have one or two reduced-girth 1.5- or 2.2-ounce spinnakers as well. These are saved for conditions that border on the dangerous.

To summarize, an inventory of spinnakers for race boats from 20 to 65 feet might consist of the following:

SPINNAKER INVENTORY FOR THE RACE BOAT

Boat Size	.5 Oz.	.75 Oz.	1.5 Oz.	2.2 Oz.
20–24		AP 100%		
25–28		AP 100%		
29–35	AP 100%	AP 100%	90–92% SMG	
36–41	AP 100%	AP 100%/REA 100%	100/92% SMG	
42–47	AP 100%	AP 100%/REA 100%	100/92% SMG	
48–54	AP 100%	AP 100%/REA 100%	95/100% SMG	85% SMG
55–65	AP 100%	AP 100%/REA 100%	95/100% SMG	100/85% SMG

Note: AP stands for all-purpose; REA stands for reaching spinnaker; SMG (spinnaker mid girth) designation almost always means reaching spinnaker.

SPINNAKER TRIM

A mainsail has a mast, boom, sheet, and halyard to keep it under control; a headsail has a headstay, sheet, and halyard. Then consider the spinnaker: First of all, it is typically bigger—at 180 percent overlap significantly bigger—than a mainsail or jib. Then, too, it has no control device(s) running the length of any of its sides; rather, it has but two fixed points: the halyard and the end of the pole. Such things account for the lack of control over this sail as well as the possibility for dramatic shape changes.

It is easy to be confused by a spinnaker because of its relative size and lack of control, but a spinnaker is little different from any other sail. There are only four things sailors can do to affect spinnaker shape.

1. Raise and lower the pole to change the depth, particularly at the top of the sail.
2. Similarly, raise and lower the pole to change where the depth or draft falls.
3. Trim the pole back and forth to change the angle of attack.
4. Trim or ease the sheet or change the lead to control the power of the sail and angle of attack, as well as the depth of the spinnaker at the bottom.

Amount of Draft　First, let's consider overall depth. The rule of thumb is this: The closer the leeches are to each other, the deeper the sail (see Figure 11.13). When you lower the outboard end of the pole, the two leeches get tighter, moving them closer. This results in the sail becoming deeper. This, by the way, is contrary to popular wisdom. On the other hand, raise the pole and the leeches get looser—they move farther apart—and the sail gets flatter.

This can be distilled to these simple rules:

Pole Down, Sail Gets Fuller.
Pole Up, Sail Gets Flatter.

Draft Position　Pole height also affects where the draft falls. In discussing spinnaker trim, it is sometimes helpful to focus on related controls in the mainsail and headsail. Perhaps it is best to think of pole height as a Cunningham in a mainsail. For example, lower the pole—tighten the Cunningham—and draft moves forward. Raise the pole—loosen the Cunningham—and draft moves aft.

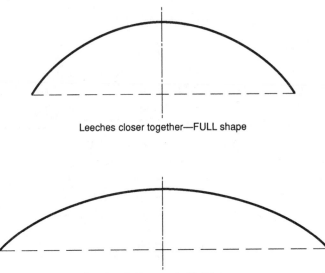

Leeches closer together—FULL shape

Leeches farther apart—FLAT shape

Figure 11.13 Spinnaker depth as a function of pole height

When discussing where the draft falls, we are really talking about the shape of the sail's leading edge, or luff. You may recall from Chapter 9, "Headsails," that the lead of the genoa is brought forward or back so that the entire leading edge luffs, or breaks, at the same time. An even break is most desirable in a spinnaker, too. Where the draft falls—a function of pole height—determines whether the sail luffs, or breaks, evenly or not.

Pole height and angle of attack, which will be addressed shortly, are critical to proper spinnaker trim and should be adjusted as conditions warrant. The main concern is to have just the right amount of luff curve. Having the pole too low will put too much fullness in the luff, stalling it in that area. If the pole is set too high, the luff will become unstable, and the sail will need to be overtrimmed to keep it from collapsing.

Although the correct pole position is desirable while running, it is even more critical while reaching. This is particularly true with specialty reaching chutes where the general rule is, The flatter the sail, the lower the pole. On a reach—where the airflow is still attached—telltales on a spinnaker can indicate proper pole height. The top and bottom telltales (see Figure 11.14) should look the same. If not, raise or lower the pole accordingly. If the pole is too high when reaching, the bottom telltale flutters first, and the sail breaks at the bottom first. If the pole is too low, the top telltale flutters first, and the break starts at the top. Judging pole height by telltales not only provides an earlier warning of improper sail trim than does easing the sail to a curl but also is better from the perspective of boat speed. Easing a sail to the curl—the traditional method—actually reduces sail area.

Telltales aren't particularly helpful when running, however, because the flow is stalled. So when running, ease the sail until the luff curls, but remember not to overdo this since a curl diminishes area. As when reaching, the goal of this exercise is to make the spinnaker luff, or break, evenly up and down its leading edge. The relationships are the same, too. If, for example, the pole is too high, the lower luff will curl before the upper. If the pole is too low, the upper luff curls first.

Rather than relying solely on ad hoc techniques, as described above, the key to sailing fast is to experiment with your boat and determine which settings are fast in various wind speeds and at various wind angles. These settings should be repeated whenever conditions are the same. This doesn't mean that fine-tuning shouldn't be done—or the settings be reworked entirely if you are suddenly slow—but excessive fussing with spinnaker trim can be slow, too.

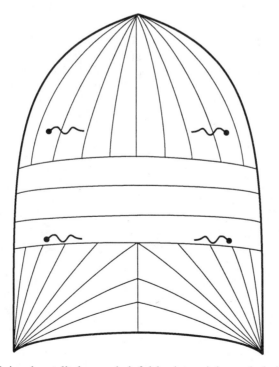

Figure 11.14 Spinnaker telltales are helpful in determining pole height on a reach.

Angle of Attack   As noted, angle of attack is controlled by easing or trimming the pole. When the wind is aft of 120 degrees, the pole should generally be squared, at a right angle, to the apparent wind (see Figure 11.15). This right-angle rule provides maximum separation between the spinnaker and the mainsail, which is desirable.[3] With the wind ahead of 120 degrees, the pole should be oversquared—or closer than 90 degrees to the wind (see Figure 11.16). Oversquaring the pole keeps the sail from getting too full and, thus, too inefficient to be fast on a reach.

Of course, oversquaring and squaring the pole can also affect draft. When the pole is oversquared, the sheet requires more tension to keep the spinnaker full, making the foot flatter. When the pole is squared, the sheet can be eased further, making the sail fuller.

The height of the inboard end of the pole is easier to address. Generally, it should be the same height as the outboard end. This keeps the spinnaker as far from the mainsail as possible. This separation means that the mainsail doesn't have to be overtrimmed, contributing to excessive heel.

Sheet   The spinnaker sheet is analogous to the genoa sheet; in conjunction with the spinnaker pole, it controls angle of attack. Less understood

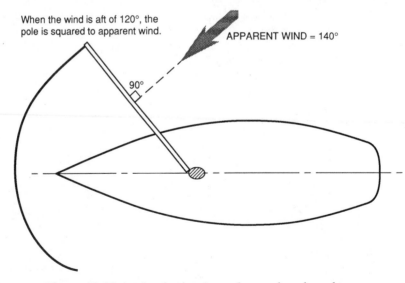

When the wind is aft of 120°, the pole is squared to apparent wind.

APPARENT WIND = 140°

90°

Figure 11.15 Angle of spinnaker pole on a broad reach or run

[3]Due to its light weight and large size, the spinnaker is the most important sail on a reach or run. Therefore, never sacrifice spinnaker trim for mainsail trim. If the trim of one has to be sacrificed, let it be the mainsail.

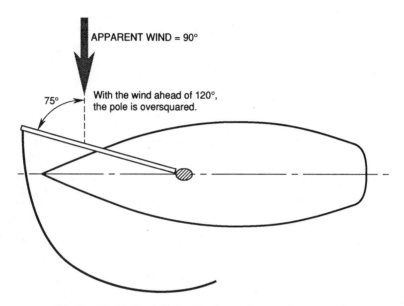

Figure 11.16 Angle of spinnaker pole on a beam reach

is that the sheet also controls power in the sail by controlling leech twist. Although most people just run the spinnaker sheet to the back of the boat and forget about it, where the sheet leads should be determined by wind angle and wind speed. Simply considered, the theme of this exercise is to maximize the power of the sail without overwhelming the stability of the boat. Even when reaching, a boat doesn't like to heel much beyond 25 or 28 degrees.

When reaching in light air, the sheet lead should be moved forward, minimizing twist and adding power. When reaching in medium air, the lead should be moved back to free the leech, keeping the airflow from stalling. When reaching in heavy air, run the sheet to the back of the boat. This keeps the powerful bottom sections of the spinnaker quite flat and the upper leech area very open and twisted.

When running in light air, the lead of the sheet should be just under the boom. This tightens the leeches and gives the sail more curvature and therefore more stability. (The only time you might want to move the lead forward of that position is if the wind is still light but the seas are particularly confused.) The sheet lead is, again, under the boom when running in medium air. This is because you want the sail to lift as high as it can without the leeches twisting off. In heavy-air running, make sure that the sheet leads forward of the boom to prevent chafe on the sheet and to choke the spinnaker to keep it from oscillating. This helps to keep the boat under control.

An alternative to changing the spinnaker lead is a Barberhauler, which is typically a line running through a block that can be attached anywhere on the rail. Then, the sheet can be left at the back of the boat, and the lead change is affected by moving the Barberhauler. As it is a far simpler matter to move a Barberhauler than a sheet lead, it is much easier to experiment with the lead position in order to determine optimum settings for your boat.

STAYSAILS

A staysail can add two-tenths of a knot to a 30 footer on a reach. Although such a number is very significant to a racer, the trouble of flying another sail, particularly such a complex one despite its small size and innocent appearance, might not be worth it to the cruiser. Then, too, the staysail needs attached flow to work. This means that its effective working life is limited to winds from 75 to 120 degrees and then only if conditions are favorable: moderate to fresh winds and fairly smooth water. Even then, these numbers aren't carved in stone; a more important number is the one on the boat's knotmeter. Thus, check boat speed a minute before hoisting the staysail and two minutes after. If it doesn't appear to be working, take it down.

There are three basic types of staysails. The Dazy staysail is full-hoist and has an LP from 80 to 85 percent. It has a high clew that can sheet through the end of the boom or to a wide portion of the boat. The sail is made of lightweight Mylar and is usually cut quite full. It can do double duty as a wind seeker or drifter. The SLS (special little staysail) is the equivalent of a Dazy staysail, except it is designed for the smaller foretriangles of fractionally rigged boats and can be as small as 70 percent. Last, there is the less common tall spinnaker staysail. It is a full-hoist sail with an overlap from 90 to 110 percent. It is designed to be flown in heavier winds than is the Dazy and thus is made of heavier material. The sail is also cut medium-full to provide power on broader reaches without becoming too full in fresh winds when close-reaching. The clew is high to permit boom-end sheeting. Due to the higher aspect ratios of today's rigs, this big staysail is used less often.

A staysail can be tacked on the centerline or to weather. Additionally, the tack can be moved forward or back, depending on how much exposure is desired.[4] Increased exposure, however, is generally at the expense of the spinnaker, so when trading one for the other, again keep an eye on the knotmeter. At the risk of belaboring the obvious, the theme of this exercise is to

---

[4]Also racing rules often control how far aft such a sail can be tacked.

maximize boat speed, not to have a perfectly flying staysail. Generally, when wind is on the beam or forward of it, the staysail is tacked on the centerline. When you free up a bit and the spinnaker pole is brought aft, the staysail tack can be moved to the weather side. In ideal conditions (close reach, fresh air, smooth water), the staysail can be tacked well forward. In lighter winds, it is tacked aft to give the spinnaker more breathing room.

When the mainsail boom is within the lifelines, the staysail is typically trimmed to the leeward rail. When the boom is eased beyond the lifelines, the staysail is usually sheeted at the boom end to widen the sheeting base. If, however, this boom-end sheeting moves the lead too far aft—causing excessive twist and insufficient foot depth—raise the tack off the deck on a pennant or move the lead to the deck forward.

Similar to a headsail and spinnaker, this sail should have telltales on its luff, and the telltales should break evenly. That said, err on the side of luffing the top of the staysail—that is, the lead should be slightly more aft than is optimum. If, on the other hand, the lead is too far forward and the upper staysail leech is closed, the staysail directs disturbed air into the head of the spinnaker, which should be avoided. The effect of the staysail on the spinnaker is so direct and so considerable that often when the spinnaker collapses, the staysail has to be luffed—even dumped entirely—before the spinnaker will refill. If this occurs often, take the staysail down.

BLOOPERS

The racer has one more sail in his or her grab bag of tricks: the blooper. These days spinnakers are huge—by far the largest sail on a masthead boat—and when the wind blows, a sail is often needed to balance the spinnaker. The blooper—a triangular sail flown to leeward of the spinnaker and with its loose halyard to leeward of the mainsail—can balance the sail plan and even dampen rolling.

Without a blooper, a large spinnaker flown in moderate to heavy air imparts a windward roll. This, in turn, causes the boat to steer to leeward, which in short order can cause an accidental jibe. A blooper can mitigate this rolling.

Although a blooper can stabilize the boat in medium and fresh air, it can make a real mess if the wind is over 25 knots or so. At such times, more sail area is definitely not the solution to one's problems.

In fresh winds, the halyard of the blooper can be raised a bit to keep the foot clear of the waves, which is most desirable. If it drags in the waves, the

A blooper can help to dampen rolling in moderate and fresh air. In heavier winds, however, more sail area is not recommended. (Michael Levitt photo)

sail can be run over by the boat. The sheet is typically trimmed through a block at the end of the boom. This helps prevent chafe on the main.

A working jib, or a staysail, tacked on the centerline (see Figure 11.17) can also help minimize rolling, as can vanging the main hard enough to remove twist. Sail twist is generally an ally when sailing upwind in heavy air, but in heavy off-the-wind conditions, mainsail twist further depowers the sail. This allows the spinnaker to be even more dominant. Speaking of mainsail twist—and more specifically of the vang that controls it—it is, as will be apparent, most important that the vang be equipped with a quick-release device. Then, when a blast of wind hits, the vang can be released along with the mainsheet. Releasing the vang luffs the upper half of the mainsail and allows the boom to be eased even farther without it dragging in the water. A boom dragging in the water can in short order steer a boat into a broach.

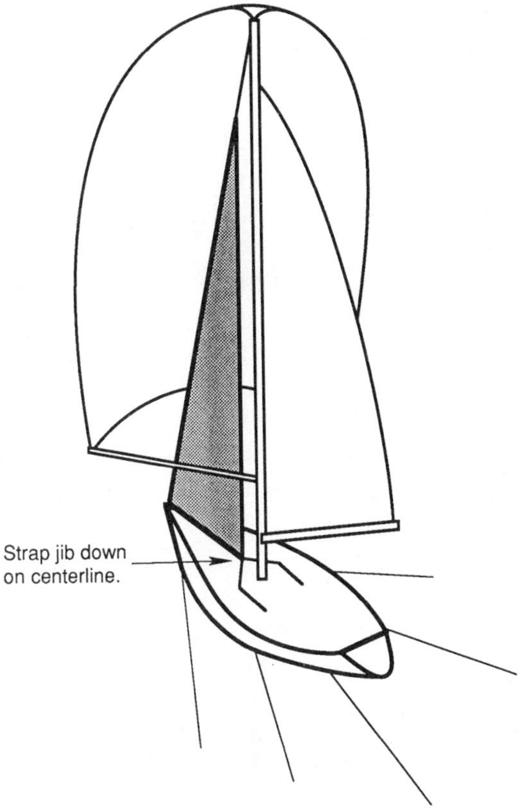

Figure 11.17 A working jib, or staysail, tacked on the centerline, can reduce rolling.

BROACHING

The rudder is, of course, the normal device to steer a sailboat, but as discussed, sails can also steer a boat. There are times—particularly when spinnaker reaching in heavy winds—when the sails take over. The result, as many sailors know, can be the dreaded broach—where the boats spins wildly out of control to weather. The effects of a broach range from inconvenient and embarrassing, to costly in terms of equipment, to even deadly. That said, a crew's coordinated series of actions can help to prevent a broach or at least minimize its effects. The crew should be acquainted with these preventative measures before using them becomes necessary. When a boat is about to broach, there isn't sufficient time to learn the proper release sequence. Typically, there is barely sufficient time to duck one's head and hold on. These two actions, in fact, should be instinctive. The key to avoiding a broach is to release the sails from the back of the boat to the front. When a broach is imminent, do the following.

1. Ease the mainsheet.
2. Ease the boom vang.
3. Ease the staysail sheet, if flying one.
4. Quickly and dramatically ease the spinnaker sheet to ventilate the chute and unload the rudder.
5. If all else fails and a broach can't be avoided, steer into the broach to collapse the chute.

Minimizing the Effects of a Broach If, however, despite your best actions, a broach is unavoidable, there are things that can be done to minimize its effects. In general, boat speed is an asset during a broach, because the slower you go, the more the apparent wind moves aft, further heeling the boat. On the other hand, rudder drag and heel are liabilities. The following actions can minimize the effects of a broach.

1. As the boat starts to broach, the rudder is likely to be hard over and stalled. If this is the case, quickly straighten the helm to reattach flow.
2. Collapse the sails as described above from back to front. When the boat straightens up, you should still have most of your speed.
3. With the sails still luffing, bear off sharply to a broad reach. You must do this to avoid a second broach, which commonly occurs when the spinnaker refills. A second broach is even more difficult to recover from because you are going so slow.
4. Once you have borne off to a broad reach, trim the sails—this time from front to back. Then build speed back before trying to sail close to the wind again.

THE ACCIDENTAL JIBE

Although flying a spinnaker in light and medium air can be a sublime athletic experience, in fresh to heavy air, it is not for the timid. If trouble lurks upwind where a broach awaits, so, too, does it lurk downwind where the boat can accidentally jibe. Then, too often, an accidental jibe is followed by a broach as the boat continues its out-of-control swing to weather. For the racer, heavy-weather spinnaker flying is an act that continually requires the weighing of discretion, valor, the skill of the crew, and the stability of the boat. For the cruiser, heavy-weather spinnaker flying is an act probably best avoided.

THE PREVENTER: TO USE OR NOT TO USE

A preventer, as its name indicates, is a line that prevents the boom from swinging uncontrollably to the other side during an accidental jibe. Whereas a preventer—or a vang tackle used as a preventer—is usually a good idea in light and moderate air, whether to use a preventer or not on a heavy-air run is a more complicated call. If there is no preventer when the boat jibes accidentally, the main will just jibe over to the new board and not force the boat to lay over. The helmsman then is often able to regain control of the boat on the new board and keep going. Once control is reestablished, either the mainsail or the spinnaker is jibed—whichever is appropriate. The danger of not sailing with a preventer, however, is obvious and can, in fact, be deadly. In an accidental jibe, someone might get hit by an uncontrolled boom as it makes its terrifying arc across the boat. So serious is this that it caused a fatality in the Southern Ocean Racing Conference (SORC) in 1979.

There are no clear-cut answers to some situations. Setting a preventer has its drawbacks, too, some of which can be serious. If a preventer is set when a broach occurs, the main will back and fill on the wrong side. This can pin the boat down, even if the spinnaker is let go. A similar problem can happen on a boat with a fractional rig; following an accidental jibe, the running backstays can trap the boom and thus hold the mainsail even if a preventer is not rigged. Running backstays make it especially difficult to right this wrong because the boom must be walked through them one at a time.

If you opt to use a preventer, it should be led aft to a winch, so, when necessary, it can be released under control. It is most important that the preventer—or the vang if it is being used that way—has sufficient line so it doesn't need to be disconnected from the winch when the boom is swung to the opposite side. This way the boom can be controlled when released. The babystay as well should be rigged in heavy-air running conditions to minimize mast stress.

CRUISING SPINNAKER SAIL-HANDLING

Genoalike cruising spinnakers handle much like normal headsails. The major concern is that they not be blown into the water when being raised or doused. When such sails are not attached at the luff or when using a spinnakerlike cruising sail, which is not attached at the luff, a less casual routine is necessary when raising, jibing, and dousing the sail. A spinnaker sock is highly recommended for use at such times, and the following sail-handling tips are based specifically on the use of the Snuffer, the product distributed by North Sails. Obviously, similar products from other sailmakers will require different techniques to varying degrees.

Rigging   Differing from a normal spinnaker, which has an interchangeable luff and leech, the cruising chute has a defined and unvarying luff and leech, or front and back. Typically, the leech is shorter than its luff. For this reason, a 5- to 8-foot rope pennant should be attached to the clew. Among other things, this line makes it easier to find the clew when the chute is stuffed inside the spinnaker sock. Tie a bowline at the end of the pennant to attach the sheet. As an alternative, the cruising-spinnaker sheet can remain attached to the cruising spinnaker, eliminating the need for a pennant.

Setting   1. Before hoisting, be sure there are no twists in the sail. To ensure this, use a system called noodling. The cruising spinnaker is pulled first from the head so that the leech and luff are straight and come together. Then, they are run back into the bag starting from the foot. The tack, head, and clew should be left out of the sock to make them easy to find and to facilitate their hooking up.

Secure the tack fitting of the cruising spinnaker, which keeps the spinnaker under control, to the headstay. Typically, different types of headstays require different types of tack-fitting devices. Secure the tack-pennant line, which governs the height of the sail, in the same manner as a spinnaker pole, to the bow cleat. A better, although more elaborate setup would be to run the tack pennant through a block at the bow, then lead the control line into the cockpit. This precludes the need to go forward to adjust the height of the tack when under sail. The cruising-spinnaker sheet should be led aft to a snatch block on the boat's quarter, passing outboard of all rigging and stanchions. Nothing spoils a good spinnaker set like a sheet led under the lifelines.

2. Hoist the cruising spinnaker, making sure the external control line and exit hole at the head of the spinnaker sock face aft. A key point here is that the less sag there is in the sail and sock, the easier the hoop will slide up and down when the sail is let out of the bag or snuffed. Minimizing sag is important, but it is also important to have sufficient space at the masthead for the gathered sleeve and hoops.

3. Bear off on a broad reach.[5]

4. When ready to set, pull down on the sock's control line (see Figure

---

[5]If you don't use a spinnaker sock, bearing off on a broad reach will ensure that the sail is partially blanketed by the mainsail. Then the halyard should go up smoothly and quickly. Avoid trimming the sheet until the sail is completely hoisted or it can fill prematurely.

11.12). This raises the external hoop, exposing the cruising spinnaker to the wind. If the hoop catches on the clew patch, carefully raise the hoop by hand above the patch before using the control line.

5. Gently sheet in the cruising spinnaker as the hoop is raised. The exposed portion of the sail will fill and help push the hoop to the masthead. Continue pulling down on the control line until the spinnaker sock is fully raised. Because the control line is external, the crew can walk aft while setting the cruising spinnaker and secure the control line to the mast when fully set.

6. Troubleshooting: If the sock fouls on the set, make sure the control line faces aft and is not twisted around the outside of the device. If the line is wrapped around the outside, unsnap the control line from the snap attached to the hoop, untwist the line, and reattach the control line to the snap. This is the only time the control line should be unfastened from the snap.

If the spinnaker sock still persists in fouling, take the cruising spinnaker down and double-check to make sure that the internal part of the control line is not wrapped around the head pennant. (This is also a good precaution when first packing your cruising spinnaker as this can easily happen in the process.) If it is fouled on the pennant, just reach in from the top, unattach the pennant from the cruising-spinnaker head swivel, and free the control line from around it. That should solve the problem.

Trimming the Cruising Spinnaker When close-reaching, the tack pennant should be adjusted so that the tack is level with the bow pulpit. The sheet should be eased until a slight curl develops at the luff. This is important since the air flows across the cruising spinnaker from luff to leech, and thus the sail is subject to stalling if overtrimmed. Overtrimming this sail also makes the boat cranky and difficult to steer. Telltales may be added to the luff of the sail to avoid overtrimming at wind angles from 50 to 80 degrees. The telltales should consist of yarn or ribbon placed about 10 inches in from the luff tape and halfway down from the head. Use the leeward telltales as you would with a genoa on a reach. Ease the sail until the leeward telltales begin to stream. At this point, you will begin to see a slight curl at the luff indicating that the sail is trimmed properly. (When broad reaching, the telltales aren't useful since the flow is stalled.)

When beam reaching, the tack should be allowed to rise to about the level of the gooseneck of the boom. This increases the projected area of the cruising spinnaker and makes it easier to fly. As when close-reaching, the sheet should be eased so that the luff curls slowly but persistently. As the wind moves aft, the tack pennant is eased to allow the sail to fly high and away from the mainsail. When sailing on a broach reach, the optimum tack position is generally between the gooseneck and the first reef position.

Sailing dead downwind in a light breeze with the cruising spinnaker can sometimes be faster and easier if the mainsail is partially reefed or even dropped entirely. The cruising spinnaker is so much larger and lighter than the main that the extra efficiency gained by doing this more than offsets the loss in mainsail area. In stronger breezes, however, it is prudent to keep the mainsail fully hoisted. Then, in the event that the cruising spinnaker needs to be doused quickly, the mainsail can provide a wind shadow, allowing the sail to be dropped with greater control. When there is no danger of an accidental jibe or broach, keep the mainsail vanged or use a preventer. Be careful not to bear away too far lest the cruising spinnaker collapse in the lee of the mainsail and wrap around the headstay.

Jibing the Cruising Spinnaker　The cruising spinnaker can be jibed easily by sailing onto a run and letting out the sheet so the sail blows out ahead of the boat. The sheet is then walked out around the bow as the boat turns slowly away from the wind. The idea is to control the sail with the rate of the turn. The sheet is then re-led to the stern quarter and trimmed. The cruising spinnaker should never be tacked.

Dousing　**1.** Ease the sheet to collapse the cruising spinnaker.
2. Pull the control line down until the cruising spinnaker is fully snuffed. Again, remember that the less sag in the luff of the sail, the easier this maneuver will be.[6] Lower the spinnaker in the sock.

RACING SPINNAKER SAIL-HANDLING

The setting, jibing, and dousing of the racing spinnaker is typically, but not always, a team sport. It usually involves several people with clearly defined duties. Perhaps the best way to summarize these relatively complex tasks is through time-and-motion studies—showing who does what, and when. Although not every boat has the luxury of a bowman, pitman, mastman, and other crew, the tasks don't change—what changes is the number of jobs each crew member is called upon to do.

---

[6]If you don't use a spinnaker sock, a crew member should go forward to gather in the luff and body of the sail as the sheet is eased completely. The halyard is then dropped with control, but the halyard should have a wrap or two on the halyard winch in the event the sail fills unexpectedly, and the halyard needs to be quickly snubbed. In a breeze, be sure to bear away onto a broad reach so the cruising spinnaker may be more easily controlled in the lee of the mainsail.

LAY-AWAY SPINNAKER SET

	15 Lengths to Mark	2–3 Lengths	At the Mark	After the Mark
HELM	Call distance and time to mark.	Call for pole to be raised.	Call "Hoist." Ease mainsheet.	Steer fast.
COCKPIT #1	Load guy on winch.	Pull clew to end of pole.	Trim guy.	Adjust guy.
COCKPIT #2	Load sheet.	Take up slack in spinnaker sheet.	Trim sheet when guy is back and halyard up.	Trim sheet.
COCKPIT #3		Ease mainsheet.	Grind guy.	Grind sheet.
PITMAN	Prep jib halyard, topping lift as necessary.	Raise topping lift. Load spinnaker halyard.	Tail spinnaker halyard. Cleat foreguy at mark.	Adjust.
MASTMAN	Attach inboard end genoa. Adjust Cunningham/outhaul.	Jump topping lift of pole.	Jump spinnaker halyard.	Help gather jib.
FOREDECK	Attach spinnaker gear. Attach topping lift.	Push up outboard end of pole.	Feed chute out of bag.	"Jib down." Gather jib.

KEY POINTS

1. Spinnaker bag attached to lifelines about halfway between mast and pulpit. Be careful spinnaker doesn't creep out of bag before you hoist it.
2. As boat turns around mark, jib should only be eased enough (roughly to the lifeline) to bear off; otherwise it will get in the way of spinnaker.
3. Make sure spinnaker halyard is up and guy pulled back before filling chute.
4. Square pole quickly to fill spinnaker from bottom up and avoid wraps.

JIBING

	Before	During	After
HELM	"Prepare to jibe."	"Trip."	Look for target speed.
COCKPIT #1	Load new guy.	Ease foreguy. Tail both afterguys.	Trim new guy. Adjust foreguy.
COCKPIT #2	Load new sheet.	Tail both sheets.	Trim new sheet.
COCKPIT #3		Pull main over when helm yells "Trip."	Grind new sheet or guy.
PITMAN	Prep topping lift.	Release topping lift.	Adjust topping lift.
MASTMAN	Raise inboard pole end.	Trip pole. Swing pole to bow.	Jump topping lift. Re-set inboard pole end.
FOREDECK	Pull slack in new after-guy. Check halyards—attach to tack horn.	Place guy in pole end. Yell "Made."	Move halyards back.

KEY POINTS

1. Skipper must steer boat under spinnaker; this may require an S course.
2. For heavy-air jibes, use "choker blocks" (snatch blocks at chainplates) affixed to sheet to decrease power of sail.
3. With end-to-end jibe, mastman should help bowman with pole.
4. Before jibe, square pole all the way back, then call for the "Trip."
5. With a dip-pole jibe and single gear, bowman should put a sail tie around new guy and take this forward to help handle new guy.

SPINNAKER TAKEDOWN

	10 Lengths from Mark	2–5 Lengths	At the Mark
HELM	Specify type of drop. "Raise genoa."	Call for drop.	Concentrate on good rounding.
COCKPIT #1	Retension backstay.	Put genoa sheet on winch. Begin to trim slowly.	Trim genoa.
COCKPIT #2	Trim spinnaker sheet.	Release spinnaker sheet. Help gather chute.	Grind genoa sheet.
COCKPIT #3	Grind spinnaker sheet. Pre-set traveler and running backstay.	Release guy when half of spinnaker is aboard. Begin trimming main.	Trim main.
PITMAN	Prep spinnaker halyard. Prep top lift. Tail genoa halyard.	Release chute halyard before guy.	Release topping lift for bowman.
MASTMAN	Jump genoa halyard. Check outhaul/Cunningham.	Gather chute.	Store chute.
FOREDECK	Jib sheets over pole? Attach jib halyard. Feed jib up foil.	Gather chute.	Store pole. Hail "Clear to tack."

KEY POINTS

1. Be sure spinnaker halyard is released first. Release guy when chute is controlled.
2. Windward takedown: Pole off and packed at 5 boat lengths. Release sheet next and halyard last. Beware of jib hanks tearing chute and jib sheets under pole.
3. String takedown: Gatherer pulls string from below in forward hatch (boats longer than 32 feet). Works best when spinnaker collapses before halyard is released. Never release halyard when chute is flying on centerline of boat. Ease guy first.

★

C H A P T E R   1 2

INVENTORY

★ As should be apparent by this point in the book, there are a host of decisions that have to be made when selecting an inventory for your boat. They include the type of cloth, nylon, Dacron, polyester/Mylar, Kevlar/Mylar, Spectra/Mylar, and any number of combinations thereof; the weight of the cloth, from .5-ounce nylon spinnaker cloth to two-ply 18-ounce "bulletproof" Dacron; and the design of the sail, from aspect ratio, to panel layout, to the number of reef points. If we are talking about a medium-size racing boat, multiply these considerations and several others by at least three headsails, perhaps two mains, three spinnakers, and sundry staysails, and the decisions of what sails to buy can seem overwhelming. However, if the task is viewed broadly, a limited number of solutions are possible.

To avoid losing sight of the forest for the trees, there are three overriding factors that should govern sail selection: 1) the type of sailing you do; 2) the type of boat you sail; and 3) a firm commitment to keep it simple.

TYPE OF SAILING

The most important consideration is the type of sailing, or how the boat is typically used. Implicit in this is where most of your sailing is done, and the strength of the predominant winds. Broadly considered, people use their boats in five different ways: 1) Grand Prix racing, 2) One Design racing, 3) racing/cruising, 4) offshore cruising, 5) inshore cruising.

The Grand Prix racer's driving principle is performance. These are competitors at the top end of the sport, and they include those who race One Tonners, Maxis, Admiral's Cuppers, and the like. For them, price, longevity, and, to a degree, ease of handling are secondary considerations. (For the purposes of this chapter, longevity should be defined as a sail's useful, or effective, life in racing, cruising, or whatever activity, not just when the sail finally falls apart.)

Some One Design racers, such as those who sail Olympic boats, J-24s, and the like, have the same concerns as the Grand Prix racer—that is, performance comes first. However, inventories for such boats are typically controlled by class rules in the interest of keeping the boats equal in speed and/ or of keeping costs in check. Other One Design sailors opt to sail in less competitive boats and in less competitive events. This latter group has many of the same concerns as the racer/cruiser addressed below.

The racer/cruiser's boat is by definition a dual-purpose boat, but the distinction actually goes deeper still. Compared with the pure racer, the racer/ cruiser's interest in performance is tempered to a greater extent by concern for price and value. This means an emphasis on how long a sail will be fast, and whether it will cover a broad enough range to eliminate another sail in the inventory.

The offshore cruiser is the cruising equivalent of the Grand Prix racer. Although simplicity is a concern for such sailors, the sea demands that they have the right sails for all conditions. Performance is important, but reliability is essential.

The inshore cruiser opts to sail in relatively protected waters. There is obviously a vast difference between the requirements of people who day-sail within sight of land and those who venture offshore into whatever the ocean may bring. The former can usually head for a safe harbor when conditions get rigorous; for the most part, the latter must put up the right sails and then grin and bear it. The inshore cruiser can be comfortable with a simple, limited, inexpensive inventory.

TYPE OF BOAT

The most important factor about type of boat is size. This typically determines the number of sails—therefore, their type, specification, and weight. A number of other characteristics implicit in boat type can have an effect on inventory. They include rig type, displacement, stability, and sail-handling gear.

KEEP IT SIMPLE

Whether racing or cruising, sailing big boats or small, it is best to go with the simplest sail inventory that will fulfill all your requirements. This means the minimum number of sails to do the job, which in turn means sails—typically headsails—with the widest range. If you don't have simplicity as a guiding principle, almost invariably you will wind up with the opposite: an overly complicated inventory.

INVENTORY FOR RACERS

The unequivocal theme of sails for full-race boats is maximum performance. Speed differences in sailboats are often quite small, so those who play this rarefied game search for every advantage possible. This leads directly to sails, the engine, or power plant, of a boat.

A sail for a race boat is judged—in order of importance—by its shape; by its ability to hold that shape in a wide range of conditions; and last, by its weight. Sail shape, the most important criterion of such sails, is a function of cloth stretch, and typically low-stretch cloth allows a more precise execution of design. The ability to hold that shape is also a function of cloth stretch. For example, a stretchy sail used in winds below its designed range is too flat and lacks power; used in winds above its designed range, it is too full and inefficient. An ancillary benefit of low stretch is an increase in a sail's effective wind range.

This brings us to weight. Obviously, lightweight sails are important to the Grand Prix racer. In light winds, a lightweight sail assumes a more efficient shape since less wind is needed to pressurize it into its designed shape. In addition, light cloth means less weight aloft, which reduces a boat's pitching and heeling. Not to be minimized is the fact that light sails also significantly reduce the total sailing weight of the boat. For example, the typical sail inventory on a One Tonner weighs about 200 pounds when the main and genoas are made of Kevlar/Mylar as opposed to 350 pounds when they are made of Dacron. Light weight also allows the crew to handle the sails more efficiently. However, light weight generally isn't as important as shape control, so it is usually a mistake to compromise shape in the name of light weight.

As far as sailcloth goes, racing boats fall into two categories: offshore and One Design. For the offshore racer, sail selection is rarely controlled by class rules; for the One Design racer, as noted, it generally is. Offshore racers have been searching for sails with reduced stretch since racing began. Weight for weight, Kevlar/Mylar laminates are at present the best answer to reducing stretch. The reasons why are apparent in Figure 4.5 (see page 62).

Kevlar/Mylar   Sailmakers keep experimenting with the weight of Kevlar/Mylar racing sails, but this is no easy task, as an underbuilt Kevlar/Mylar sail usually looks acceptable at first but quickly loses its shape and becomes fragile. If the shape of such a sail is well supported vertically (up and down the leech), then the cross-sail and diagonal loadings can usually be addressed quite easily with a closely woven Kevlar and polyester weave laminated to Mylar. However, take some of the vertical stretch control away from this part of the sail—by making it out of lighter-weight cloth, for example—and more stress will be felt in the horizontal and diagonal directions of the cloth. As sailmakers are less able to control horizontal and diagonal loadings in most low-stretch fabrics, like Kevlar/Mylar, the result could be an overloaded sail, then loss of shape, and finally sail failure.

Kevlar/Mylar sails offer many advantages, but they are expensive. A well-built Kevlar/Mylar sail can cost from 30 to 100 percent more than the equivalent polyester/Mylar sail. Another consideration about price is that at the present time, it is not possible to make a Kevlar/Mylar sail last as long as one made of Dacron or polyester/Mylar—so the cost must be amortized over less time, if you care to think about it this way. Kevlar/Mylar sails generally lose their shape after a season or two due to flogging, wrinkling (when they are folded), overloading, and rough handling. (The care and handling of sails are addressed in Chapter 14.)

Polyester/Mylar   For those on more limited budgets or for those who sail in less competitive waters, polyester/Mylar offers many of the advantages of Kevlar/Mylar at a far less daunting price. Smaller sails for smaller boats, lighter sails for many boats, and staysails for nearly all boats typically don't require the amount of stretch control provided by Kevlar/Mylar and can effectively—and cost-effectively—be made of polyester/Mylar.

Polyester/Mylar materials tend to be stronger in the warp direction than in the fill direction, because in processing, the warp yarns are pulled straight, removing any crimp (see Chapter 3, "Characteristics of Sailcloth"). When sail layout takes advantage of this warp-oriented characteristic, the sails stretch less and outperform polyester/Mylar sails having fill-oriented construction. For this reason and to take advantage of the added support provided by the multidirectional panel orientation, radial sails are the rule in sails made of oriented high-tech materials, like polyester/Mylar.

CLOTH WEIGHT FOR RADIALLY CONSTRUCTED
POLYESTER/MYLAR SAILS

Boat Size, LOA	20′	25′	30′
Masthead Main	5.0 (see *Note*)	5.5	6.5
Fractional Main	4.5	5.0	6.0
Light #1 Genoa	2.0	2.5	2.5
Medium #1	—	—	3.5
Heavy #1	3.0	3.5	4.0
#3	5.0	6.0	7.0
Staysails:			
Tall Spin	2.5	2.5	3.0
Dazy	1.0	1.0	1.5

Boat Size, LOA	35′	40′	45′
Masthead Main	7.0	8.0	9.0
Fractional Main	6.5	7.5	8.5
Light #1 Genoa	3.0	3.8	3.8
Medium #1	4.0	4.5	5.5
Heavy #1	4.5	5.5	6.5
#3	8.0	9.0	—
Staysails:			
Tall Spin	3.0	3.5	3.5
Dazy	1.5	1.5	1.5

Note: Measurements are in ounces per sailmaker's yard. The chart goes only to 45 feet because polyester/Mylar sails are not commonly used on boats above this size.

Spinnakers for Race Boats Spinnakers have different requirements than headsails and mains. The most important quality is weight; they must be as light as possible in order to fly properly in light winds. This requirement typically means nylon. The other important properties of nylon spinnakers, as noted in Chapter 3, are tensile strength, tear strength, stretch resistance, and low porosity.

The standard weight for the all-purpose spinnaker is designated as .75 ounce. This is the likely choice if only one spinnaker is carried. Such cloth is produced by a number of suppliers with slightly different finishes. Some are coated with urethane to eliminate most porosity and reduce stretch; others are resin-finished for significantly lower stretch and almost no porosity. There seems to be no clear winner between the two styles of finish. The finishes bring the actual weight of this material up about .25 ounce to 1 or 1.1 ounce.

OFFSHORE RACING BOATS' MASTHEAD INVENTORIES

Race	22–27'	28–32'	33–38'	39–45'	46–55'	Comments (see *Note*)
Main	X	X	X	X	X	Kevlar mains, maximum-length battens.
Light #1		X	X	X	X	In 1- and 2-genoa inventories, shape and sailcloth are compromised in favor of simplicity.
Medium #1	X	X	X	X	X	
Heavy #1				X	X	A third full-size genoa allows more specialization in the other headsails.
#2	X	X	X	X	X	In boats up to 38', a good #2 makes it easier to do without a heavy #1.
#3	X	X	X	X	X	Kevlar blade—the biggest sail that will fit in foretriangle.
#4				X	X	The assumption here is that larger boats will compete in less protected waters.
Dazy Staysail	X	X	X	X	X	Size and material vary according to taste.
Light Spinnaker	X	X	X	X	X	.5-oz. nylon
Medium Spinnaker		X	X	X	X	.75-oz. nylon
Heavy Spinnaker				X	X	1.5-oz. nylon
Reacher	X	X	X	X	X	This is a flat, low-stretch, specialized reaching sail.
Total:	7	9	9	12	12	Smaller boats can use the .5 oz. in higher winds and eliminate the .75 oz.

Note: For a Grand Prix racer, these are fairly minimal inventories. Additional sails would include spares, more spinnaker and staysail options, and other specialty sails. (Spinnaker inventory was discussed in more detail in the previous chapter.)

For light-air sails, .5-ounce nylon cloth is the typical choice. (Depending on the number of warp threads, the actual weight of this material is .75 to .82 ounce; see Chapter 11, "Downwind Sails.") This material is remarkably tough but is not suitable as the only sail for any but the smallest boats. Heavier spinnaker cloths are available in 1.5- and 2.2-ounce weights for heavy-air sails. A variety of other materials are being tested for spinnakers. Polyester/Mylar has proven effective in some cases, especially in reaching spinnakers where the low stretch of the material prevents the draft from migrating aft, thus allowing the sail to overpower the boat.

INVENTORY FOR ONE DESIGN RACERS

A wide range of boats fall into the One Design racing classification. These boats are often limited by class rules to sails built from woven polyester (Dacron) cloth. The best sails for such boats are optimized around how the rigs work and how the crews sail the boats. Sometimes, this means low-stretch cloth and—surprisingly—sometimes not. For example, single-handed dinghies like the Finn and Laser have unstayed bendy masts. For a bendy mast to work most effectively in puffy or heavy air, stretchy cloth is often chosen to permit the sailor to depower the sail.

Similarly, consider the Soling. This three-person Olympic boat has no running backstay to tighten the forestay. Therefore, to tighten the forestay so that the jib sets properly, the mainsail is typically sheeted in hard—harder than optimum sail trim might otherwise dictate. A mainsail for this boat should have some stretch on the leech so that it can be overtrimmed without the leech becoming too tight. Contrast this with the J-24 and Star, which have completely adjustable rigs. Such boats usually are faster with sails made of very low-stretch cloth—in the same manner as offshore racing boats.

As Kevlar/Mylar and polyester/Mylar are verboten for most of these One Design boats, low-stretch Dacron is the choice. This Dacron is almost always heavily coated with resin and is called Yarn-Tempered, Duroperm, or HTP, depending on the supplier. All such heavily coated sails should be carefully handled by sailors—for example, rolled rather than folded—since the resins break down when the sails are creased. The tear strength of these materials is quite low to begin with, so protecting the sails from untaped cotter pins and other sharp instruments of destruction is also recommended.

As discussed in Chapter 4, resin coatings can be applied to any woven sailcloth. The coating masks the basic stretch characteristics of the untreated cloth, but the stretch characteristics reemerge as the finish breaks down. This can be mitigated by properly matching the base cloth to the needs of the sail.

The makeup of the One Design racer's inventory is usually specified by the class association. Common inventories for a variety of One Design boats are listed in the following chart:

ONE DESIGN INVENTORY

Boat	Main	Jib	Comments
Star	4.5 coated	4.5 coated	Very light sails; limited life
Soling	5.0 soft	4.5 coated	Mainsheet used to tension headstay
	5.0 coated		Light-air sail
J-24	6.0 coated	6.0 coated	Mylar genoa allowed in 1988
Etchells 22	5.5 coated	5.5 coated	
Finn	3.8 soft	—	Bendy, unstayed mast
Lightning	3.8 coated	3.8 coated	
Laser	3.8 soft	—	See Finn
Snipe	3.3 soft	3.3 soft	
FD	4.5 coated	4.5 coated	Big overlap on jib
Hobie 16	5.3 soft	5.3 soft	Production sails dictated by rules

INVENTORY FOR CRUISER/RACERS

Many sailors race occasionally—in local club events, informal midweek competitions, or occasional race weeks. Other than this, their sailing involves cruising or day sailing. For them, good performance is desirable, but sails with ease of handling, durability, and toughness are mandatory. (The distinction between durability and toughness is important. Durability means a sail doesn't make wholesale changes over time; toughness means a sail can absorb abuse without breaking.) Because of rapid changes in the world of sailcloth, these sails are usually made of the materials that only a few years ago were considered high-tech and seen only on full-race boats.

While new cloths have emerged, the development of Dacron, which has been used in sailmaking for almost four decades, hasn't stood still. Much thought and experimentation have gone into finding weaves and finishes that optimize the performance of Dacron sails, which are still popular on cruiser/

CRUISER/RACER INVENTORY

	22–27'	28–32'	33–38'	39–45'	46–55'	Comments (see *Note*)
Main	X	X	X	X	X	Most of these could be Dacron, for longevity, especially if rating rule allows full battens.
Light #1			X	X	X	Compared with the race inventory, wide-range sails are even
Medium #1	X	X	X	X	X	more important.
Heavy #1					X	
#2		X	X	X	X	In boats up to 38', the #2 helps fill the Heavy #1 gap.
#3	X	X	X	X	X	Kevlar blade—the biggest sail that will fit in foretriangle.

#4

					X	Presumes less ambitious offshore agenda than full-race boats.
Dazy Staysail	X	X				
Light Spinnaker		X	X	X	X	.5-oz. nylon
Medium Spinnaker		X	X	X	X	.75-oz. nylon, reaching oriented in smaller boats
Heavy Spinnaker				X	X	1.5 nylon, or 1.7 Mylar. Reaching oriented.
Total:	5	7	8	9	11	

Note: Typically these boats have fewer sails than do Grand Prix racers for reasons of cost and simplicity (i.e., fewer sail changes and less complex sail selection decisions). Surprisingly, some cruiser/racers have more sails than racers, in the form of a second inventory that reserves the racing sails for that purpose and allows the cruising sails to be matched to that activity. The spinnakers specified above are racing, or symmetrical, spinnakers. Many such boats augment the racing-spinnaker inventory with asymmetrical cruising spinnakers.

racer boats. For example, mains made for masthead rigs—where the rig is adjustable and where the aspect ratio of the sail (luff divided by foot) is over 3:1—work best if the cloth shows a very-low-fill stretch and a medium-soft bias. This combination of properties in woven cloth is provided by weaving big fill yarns with small warp yarns. This allows the leech of these sails to open the proper amount in puffs, but also allows the mainsail trimmer to have good control of the leech.

Spectra/Mylar is a recent addition to the racer/cruiser's grab bag. Spectra/Mylar, like Kevlar/Mylar, shows low stretch, but unlike Kevlar/Mylar, it doesn't lose its strength through flogging. Unfortunately, to date the material shows some propensity toward creep—unrecoverable stretch under load over time. This compromises sail performance somewhat, but due to a significant savings in weight, Spectra/Mylar is a viable option for jibs and mains on large cruiser/racers.

INVENTORY FOR OFFSHORE CRUISERS

In terms of cloth, offshore cruising sails require a different trade-off than racing sails. These sails must be strong, durable, and easy to handle. They should stand up to flogging and moderate overloading and should last for many seasons. Performance is important in such sails, but the ability to hold shape is more important. This quality makes the sails easier to use and makes passages safer, faster, and more enjoyable. Such sails should also look good. By any measure, baggy and wrinkled sails don't enhance the lines of a classic cruiser.

Tightly woven Dacron with a moderately soft finish is generally the material of choice for such sails. A tight weave is necessary so that the sail will continue to look good and perform well even after the finish has broken down.

A number of laminated cloths designed for cruising sails have recently been developed. One is a cloth/Mylar/cloth sandwich with polyester cloth on both sides and Mylar in the middle (see photograph on page 61). This combination provides the low stretch and warp orientation of polyester/Mylar (making the material so appropriate for radial sails), as well as the toughness and durability of Dacron. Modern bonding techniques have largely solved the problems of delamination, so with reasonable care, these sails should last a long time. An ancillary benefit of this sandwich construction is the material's remarkable flexibility, or "soft hand," as a sailmaker might put it. This makes it an easily handled material.

Another option in high-tech cruising cloth is a laminated combination of

SAILCLOTH WEIGHTS (IN OUNCES PER SAILMAKER'S YARD) FOR CRUISING SAILS

Boat Length, LOA	20'	25'	30'	35'	40'	50'	60'	70'
Main	4.5	5.0	6.5	7.0	8.0	10.0	12.0	16.0
All-Purpose Genoa	3.8	3.8	4.5	5.5	7.0	8.0	9.0	10.0
Working Jib	5.0	5.5	7.0	7.5	8.5	10.0	12.0	18.0

a light, open polyester cloth with Tedlar—a film produced by Du Pont—on both sides. This film has excellent UV resistance but much less strength than polyester/Mylar. To control shape effectively, the material requires weights similar to Dacron, however. As light weight is usually a high-tech sail's principal reason for being, this requirement casts serious doubts on the effectiveness of this material at this time. (The complete inventory is on pages 306–307.)

INVENTORY FOR INSHORE CRUISERS

Many sails are only used for casual day sailing. Since typically little is asked of such sails, price may be their most important consideration. In terms of cloth, the most economical choice is usually a moderately tightly woven fabric of polyester with a little extra resin to overcome the material's weak bias. Such sails do not perform as well as good-quality cruising sails but will definitely be less expensive. (The complete inventory is on page 308.)

OFFSHORE CRUISING INVENTORY

	22–27'	28–32'	33–38'	39–45'	46–55'	
Main	X	X	X	X	X	Probably fully battened or long battens.
Storm Trysail				X	X	Remains a sensible and effective sail in difficult offshore conditions.
RF #1 (see *Note*)	X	X	X	X	X	Full size, for horsepower in fair weather. Too light to be partially furled on larger, heavier boats.
RF #2			X	X	X	All-purpose, slightly re-duced LP, possibly with Yankee-like high clew. Partially reefable.
RF #3/#4	X	X	X	X	X	Genuine heavy-weather workhorse.
Storm Jib		X	X	X	X	If possible, this should set on an inner forestay. The best solution is a cutter-

type forestaysail that can work with a high-clewed #2 or the #3 or #4 set on the headstay. Choosing between a cruising spinnaker of either type and an all-purpose spinnaker is often a matter of style, but against the cruising spinnaker's relative ease of handling and reaching performance is the symmetrical spinnaker's stability and speed on long, broad, tradewind passages.

	4	6	7	8	8
Cruising Spinnaker and	X	X	X	X	X
Medium Spinnaker		X	X	X	X
Total:	4	6	7	8	8

Note: RF stands for roller-furling. These inventories must be adequate to cover any conceivable conditions encountered offshore. Storm trysails, for example, should have their own mast track where they can be bent on and are ready to hoist well before they are needed. These inventories also include performance-oriented sails, such as full-size Number 1s and spinnakers, since part of the fun and exhilaration of a long passage in fair weather is making the boat sail at peak performance.

INSHORE CRUISING INVENTORY

	22–27'	28–32'	33–38'	39–45'	46–55'	Comments
Main	X	X	X	X	X	Probably fully battened.
RF #1 (see *Note*)	X	X	X	X	X	LP between 130% and 150%, depending on boat, local conditions, etc. This sail must be capable of being used when partially furled.
RF #3/#4	X	X	X	X	X	May sheet inside or outside the shrouds; partial furling is optional.
Cruising Spinnaker	X	X	X	X	X	A cruising spinnaker is a matter of personal preference, but if you have one, you should have a sail-sock device.
Total:	4	4	4	4	4	

Note: RF stands for roller furling. Since these boats tend to stay in well-defined areas, it is possible to tailor sail sizes, weights, and options to local conditions. Sailors in this category are best able to take advantage of the many innovative new sail-handling devices.

CHAPTER 13

BOARDSAILS

★ Windsurfing, or boardsailing as it is more properly called, has had a profound impact on the sport of sailing in the last decade. Not only has it brought a new generation of people into the sport of sailing, but in its short history, boardsailing has been welcomed to the Olympic fold and has set the sailing-speed record.[1] A sailboard, piloted in 1990 by a Frenchman, Pascal Maka, was officially clocked at 42.9 knots (49 mph), making it the fastest sail-powered vessel in the world. Before boardsailors took aim at this record, it belonged for many years to the 60-foot proa *Crossbow*, which sailed at 36 knots. The first boardsailor to break this record was the same Pascal Maka, who in 1986 sailed 38.6 knots (44 mph).

To put Maka's 49-mph speed into perspective, one could get arrested driving a car that fast in a residential neighborhood, and the speed is legal on limited-access highways. To reach such speeds, there can't be a weak link in the power train, and sails—the high-tech, hybrid engines for these diminutive rocket ships—have helped lead the charge into the record books.

A look into the sport's history takes us to 1967 when Hoyle Schweitzer, a surfer, and Jim Drake, a sailor and aerodynamicist, combined their sports and invented the Windsurfer. The radical idea of mounting a sail on a surfboard and requiring the rig to be held up by a standing sailor was—according to legend at least—conceptualized at a cocktail party. Although it is unlikely that the principals had any idea then about the ramifications of what they were creating, the sport they dreamed up was an ultimate synergy—far greater than the sum of its parts.

---

[1] Boardsailing made its debut as a full medal sport in the 1984 Olympics. That was a mere seventeen years after its invention. No sport has received the Olympic designation as quickly. In the 1992 Olympics, there will be a second sailboard class, this one for women.

THE WINDSURFER SAIL

The original sail designs were very simple—primitive by today's standards. They were horizontally cut with a sleeve to fit over the bendy, vaulting pole–like mast. A novel boom arrangement accommodated the standing sailor by raising the gooseneck off the deck by four feet. The boom comprised two pieces of heavy teak bent into a wishbone affair, allowing the sailor to manipulate the free-sail mechanism on both sides, or tacks. The sail was mounted on a universal joint, which required the sailor to hold up the rig, which, in turn, supported the sailor. There is no rudder on a sailboard. Rather, the board is steered by manipulating the rig: Move the rig forward and the sail's center of effort moves ahead of the board's center of lateral resistance, and the board turns off the wind; move the rig aft, and the board moves toward the wind (see Figure 6.4, page 100). The idea was sufficiently inventive that the principals were awarded a patent in 1970 in this and several other countries on the universal joint and wishbone rig.

The early sails were made of 3.9-ounce semifirm Dacron, or polyester as it is more properly called, and were, to put it kindly, extremely full in shape—bordering on being baggy. In the early days of the sport, control was not a major consideration, as the sail needed to be full and powerful for sailing in the light winds of Southern California where the sport was invented. If control was not a consideration, expense—or lack thereof—was. Equipment had to be inexpensive because, like surfing, the sport was aimed at those who neither wanted nor could afford the finer things in life. Simplicity was the watchword of windsurfing in the early days. Today sailboard sails are among the most sophisticated and, square foot per square foot, the most expensive sails in the whole sport of sailing. Against this background, the naivete of those barefoot days seems astounding.

It wasn't until the mid-1970s—when the Europeans embraced the sport with an enthusiasm formerly reserved for skiing—that higher-performance sail designs were developed. Heavier wind conditions in the North Sea and the Canary Islands, two popular sailing sites, required smaller, flatter, more controllable sails.

The giant step from the light winds of Southern California to the heavy winds of a few favorite sailing sites of Europeans and Hawaiians precipitated a revolution in the sport of boardsailing, in fact, in the entire sport of sailing. In big winds, the sailboard began to show its true colors. At such times, a sailboard's free-sail system is raked to weather, generating upward lift. In those same conditions, a traditional sailboat heels away from the wind, making the rig more and more overburdened and inefficient. In effect, when the wind blows, a sailboard gets lighter and shows less wetted surface; the traditional sailboat, due to the downward push, gets heavier and has more wetted surface. The amount of board in the water at 42 knots is the equivalent of a size-12 pair of sneakers. The fact that a sailboard has no rudder—only a small skeg for lateral resistance—further contributes to a sailboard's lack of wetted surface and, thus, speed. These differences are some of the secrets of the headlong dash of the sailboard.

HAWAIIAN INFLUENCE

In Hawaii in the early 1980s more progressive developments in the sport of boardsailing and in the evolution of sail design were taking place. Hawaiians harnessed the trade winds on undersize, custom-shaped fiberglass boards, which were closer to surfboards in length and shape than to the early sailboards. Not only were their boards homemade; so were their sails. Sailing year-round in heavy winds, the Hawaiians had special requirements when it came to gear. The most obvious was that everything had to be beefed up—heavily reinforced. The sport they were redefining—in fact, inventing almost daily—was neither sailing nor surfing but some strange, if magnificent, hybrid.

RAF SAILS

For increased structural rigidity, and therefore control, sailboard sailmakers borrowed ideas from hang gliding and high-performance catamarans by incorporating full battens in the sails. The full-batten design offered superb control of the sail, but still the leading edge of the sail was not aerodynamically clean. This was exacerbated by the fact that the full battens were not well integrated into the sail, and they tended to migrate aft of the mast's wind shadow, making the front part even more inefficient. In 1983 sail designers concluded that if the sleeve of the sail was tailored to match the curve of the mast and shape was added there, the full battens would protrude forward of the sleeve line and stay there, allowing for a more efficient leading-edge shape. This, in essence, overrotated the leeward edge (see Figure 13.1), which reduced the wind shadow on that side. The result was a dramatic increase in aerodynamic efficiency. This concept was dubbed the rotating-asymmetrical foil, or RAF, and was—and still is—embraced by nearly all of the major sailmakers in the field.

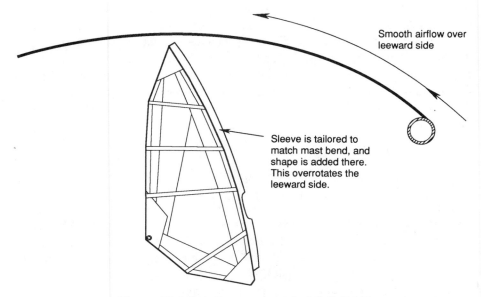

Figure 13.1 Rotating-asymmetrical foil (RAF)

CAMBER-INDUCED SAILS

However, within a year another significant advance took place. It was reasoned that if the leeward-edge treatment on the RAF provided such a dramatic leap in efficiency, imagine what would happen if the entire leading edge of the sail was "double-surfaced"—that is, given a three-dimensional airplane wing–like leading edge. The camber-induced sail, designed with a semiwide sleeve supported by molded plastic inducers, was the result. These inducers are, in essence, rigid extensions of the full battens, and they wrap around the mast. This locks in the draft (as we will see shortly, draft stability is very important to such sails), and it cleans up both the leeward and the windward sides of the sail's leading edge, improving the sailor's control of the rig (see Figure 13.2). On the negative side, camber inducers are harder to rig, add a bit more weight to the sail, and generally require an oversized luff sleeve, which can fill with water, making the sail somewhat harder to uphaul, or waterstart. Most notably, inducers significantly increase the cost of boardsails. Nevertheless, they offer the sailor improved speed and comfort, and this design, like the RAF, has become standard. In the ensuing years, sailmakers have devised many different camber systems to support the enlarged sleeve and to facilitate

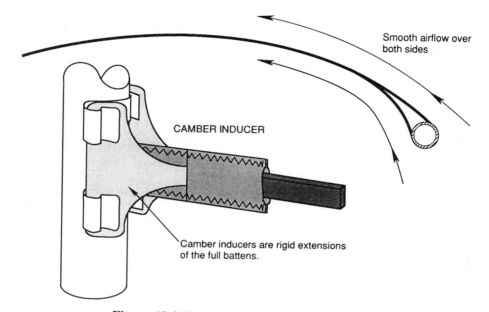

Smooth airflow over
both sides

CAMBER INDUCER

Camber inducers are rigid extensions
of the full battens.

Figure 13.2 The principle of the camber-induced
sail and an example of a camber inducer

rigging. One popular solution is to use only one camber just above the boom
and leave the other battens RAF-style.

BATTENS

Battens perform a vital function in locating and stabilizing the draft in these
sails. Full battens support the designed-in shape of the sail much as a skeleton
supports the body. Boardsail battens should be tapered to create an optimum
foil shape as well as to minimize weight. Generally, the stiffer the batten, the
more rigid the framework, and the faster the sail; the softer the batten, the
more the sail is able to "breathe," or shift more smoothly from full power to
less power. Therefore, stiffer battens are utilized in speed and slalom designs,
where speed is paramount; softer battens are used in wave sails where feathering
or depowering the sail during maneuvers on the waves is essential.

Today the boardsailing market has evolved in many directions, for example, wave riding, slalom racing, speed sailing, and course racing, and sails
of very different designs are available for each of these disciplines and for

wind ranges within these categories. Wind range is so important. Whereas a mainsail on a traditional sailboat must cover a range from a near gale to a zephyr, a boardsail is designed to do nothing of the sort. Slalom sails, for example, might cover a range of from 3.2 square meters (35 square feet) to 9 square meters (97 square feet), or more, and increase at ½-square-meter intervals. This means that ten sails cover the same range that one mainsail does. The diversity provides sailmakers with tremendous design freedom to optimize sail size as well as shape, but confronts customers with some very tough choices about sail size and type.

A look at the design considerations for each type of sail is instructive.

WAVE SAILS

Wave sails show a high aspect ratio and high clew height. The high clew allows the rig to fit better into the critical wave section and makes the sail a smaller target for waves (see Figure 13.3). The trade-off, however, is that a high-aspect-ratio sail is more likely to stall from oversheeting and thus tends to be slower than a low-aspect-ratio sail.[2] For increased control, the wave sail is relatively flat and its draft location is, of the four types of sails, the farthest forward—approximately 35 percent of the chord. Fewer battens than other types minimizes weight and improves its balance, or handling; these characteristics are further enhanced by the fact that the sails typically employ a combination of long (full) and short battens, or convertible battens, which can be used as either long or short battens at the sailor's discretion.

Windows in these sails are oversized and are positioned higher than in the other types to allow the sailor to judge better the waves. RAF designs make ideal wave foils as they are lighter, handier, and more versatile. Having a smaller luff sleeve than a camber-induced sail, they are easier and quicker to waterstart, which can prove very important after falling in breaking surf. For reasons of durability, such sails are designed to be flown on epoxy masts.

SLALOM SAILS

Slalom courses are oriented downwind. As lower-aspect-ratio sails work better off the wind, slalom sails show a lower aspect ratio than the wave sail (see Figure 13.4). In addition to a longer foot, slalom sails typically have a lower

---

[2]A lower-aspect-ratio sail, for example, a slalom sail, has its Achilles' heel as well: while being faster, it is harder to turn. In general, a high-aspect-ratio sail, like a wave or speed sail, as we will see, is quicker to react in gusts but it dies in lulls. A low-aspect sail is slower to react to gusts but better through the lulls. This is consonant with the time discussion (see Figure 5.14, page 87).

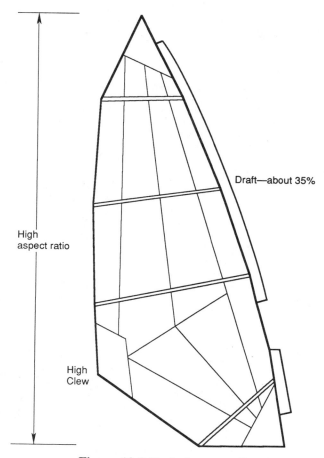

High
aspect ratio

Draft—about 35%

High
Clew

Figure 13.3 Typical wave sail

clew. This profile responds well to pumping for acceleration after rounding marks, for example, and improves power through the lulls. The low clew height also allows the foot to maintain close contact with the top of the board, minimizing induced drag. This will be discussed shortly.

Since speed and acceleration are more important in these sails than light weight, handiness, and control—the desirable characteristics of a wave sail—slalom sails typically show more full battens for support. A combination of heavier but more efficient camber inducers and lighter RAF battens is utilized.

Compared with a wave sail, maximum draft is designed aft (approximately 40 to 45 percent of the chord). The draft-aft shape allows for increased flow attachment. Reduced luff curve and increased roach make for more twist in

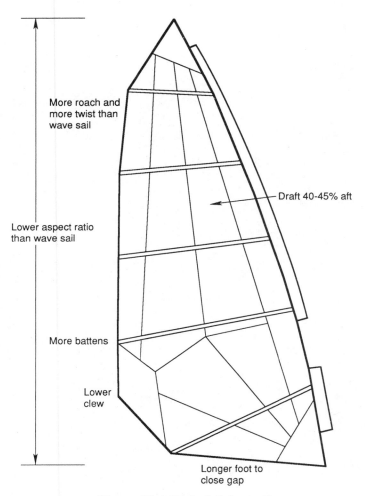

Figure 13.4 Typical slalom sail

the leech section, and this increased twist expands the wind range of a sail. Increased twist further contributes to higher reaching speeds. There is additional material at the foot of the sail, and this "roachy foot" closes the gap between the sail and the board, thus maximizing straightaway speed.[3] To close the gap,

---

[3]This is the boardsailing equivalent of the end-plate effect, which significantly reduces induced drag (see Chapter 6, "From Aerodynamic Theory to Practice"). Closing the gap and, indeed, overall sail efficiency are also improved by the fact that a sailboard's mast base can be adjusted fore and aft. This permits very specific tuning of the sail's center of effort with the board's center of lateral resistance (see Figure 6.4,

Frenchman Pascal Maka was the first boardsailor to break Crossbow's *record. In 1986, Maka sailed at 38.6 knots, or 44 mph. Maka's new record is 42.91 knots, or 49.41 mph, set on February 27, 1990. (Courtesy of Fanatic A.R.T.)*

the sail's rake angle, or swept-back angle, is lowered to accommodate the foot profile. This, too, accounts for the speed of sailboards.

SPEED SAILS

In 1986, when Pascal Maka's record-breaking speed of 38.6 knots galvanized the sport, the 40-knot barrier seemed a distinct possibility. The quest to break the barrier was as compelling to boardsailing as the sub–4-minute mile was to track or the sound barrier was to aviation. There was no dearth of boardsailors

---

page 100). Thus, even at speed, or especially at speed, sailboards require a minimum of steering. And, as sailors know, steering—whether done with a rudder, the rig, or foot pressure—is slow. On a sailboard, drag is further reduced by the total lack of standing rigging. In fact, the sailor's body—an inherently inefficient aerodynamic shape, as downhill skiers and bicycle racers know—may prove to be the major impediment to breaking the 50-knot barrier.

hoping to prove to the world that they had the "right stuff." In November 1988, the 40-knot barrier was broken by Erik Beale, who sailed 40.3 knots. As noted, Maka regained his record with a speed of 42.9 knots. Maka's achievement was sailing at the outer reaches, and because of this and because of the sheer heart-stopping fun of sailing at freeway speeds, speed sailing is becoming a more important part of the sport.

Speed sails, designed to be used on a broad reach and in overpowered conditions, are flatter than slalom sails—particularly at their leading edge—to favor high-end straightaway speed (see Figure 13.5). As discussed in Chapter

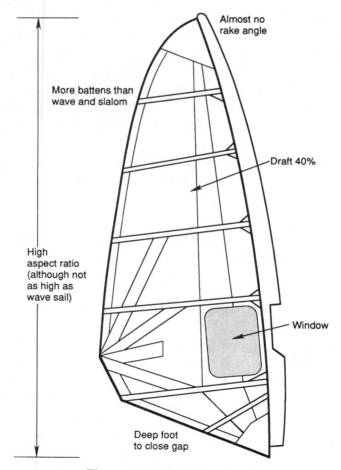

Figure 13.5 Typical speed sail

6, this flat shape shows increased flow attachment when the wind blows. Due to the wind orientation of the courses, these sails show a lower aspect ratio than the wave sail, for example. Speed sails are also characterized by an almost excessive use of full battens—both RAF and camber-induced—that provide a rigid winglike structure. This batten treatment locks in both shape and the sail's center of effort.[4]

Such sails are also designed to be flown on very stiff masts with a slightly more flexible top section. Double- or partially double-surfaced sails have shown increased efficiencies in some applications (see Figure 13.6). The windows of speed sails are typically constructed from extruded clear Mylar, called Monofilm. Monofilm is made of 4- or 5-mil Mylar. This material is clear because there is no fabric substrate. The size of the window is reduced to a minimum as the courses are typically controlled by organizers, and thus the need to see other boards, boats, or swimmers is less important.

Wing-mast sections have in some cases been employed to clean up the leading-edge entry. Typically, these sails have almost no rake angle, as an upright sail is faster. The gap between the sail and board is closed through a deep foot. The flatter foil section calls for a draft-forward position (approximately 40 percent of chord).

COURSE-RACING SAILS

Sails used in closed-course racing, as in the Olympics, are very similar to slalom sails, particularly in aspect ratio, depth, and draft. A foot profile that allows the gap to be closed is preferable, but ease of handling when tacking and jibing is most important for tight racing situations. In the Olympics, the sails, rigs, and boards are determined by a selection process, making boardsailing in this competition a One Design event. This selection process, done before the summer Olympic Games, typically determines the style of course-racing sails.

Other than the Olympics, the majority of closed-class racing is One Design. Thus, sail parameters are often controlled by board manufacturers or class associations.

---

[4]Draft migration—never desirable—is particularly troublesome for boardsailors because of the transmission of pressure through the sailor's arms. In the interest of speed, the power should go directly from the rig through the sailor's body to the board. If a sail is changing shape—the draft migrating fore and aft—power is lost.

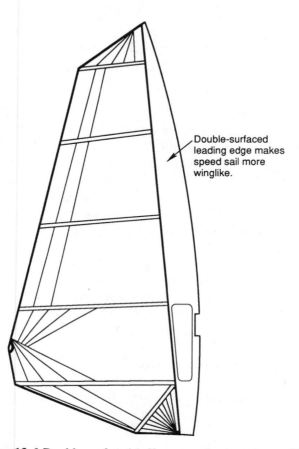

Double-surfaced leading edge makes speed sail more winglike.

Figure 13.6 Double-surfaced luffs are used on some speed sails.

MATERIALS

Sailcloth technology, discussed in detail in Chapters 3 and 4, has made quantum leaps in recent years. Today's custom and production boardsails take full advantage of this sailcloth revolution. Boardsails are made of polyester/Mylar, Dacron, Kevlar/Mylar, Spectra/Mylar, and a dizzying combination thereof. For example, Dacron is typically used in luff areas for its ability to absorb shock; Mylar, married to any number of other substances, might be used in the body for its low-stretch capabilities, light weight, and durability; and Kevlar/Mylar and Spectra/Mylar might be used in areas that need reinforcing.

Figure 13.7 is a good illustration of the complexity of cloth designed for the boardsail. Note that in this knit construction, discussed in Chapter 4, the warp and fill yarns lay on top of each other, but do not interweave. This gives the cloth low crimp and thus low stretch in both the warp and fill directions, although some crimp is imparted by the light knitting yarns that lock the warp and fill threads. Such knits allow a lightweight cloth while still using heavy yarns, which provide good tear strength and good seam strength. Mylar film covers both sides of the fabric, further protecting the sail. Durability is also improved by the spaces in the fabric where the two Mylar films meet. There is also a ripstop thread to stop a hole from spreading. Such protection is important because such sails spend much of the time on rocky or sandy beaches, or else splashing into the water at highway speeds.

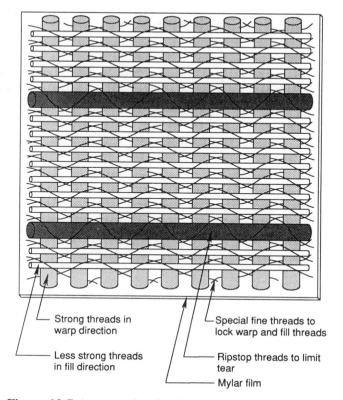

Figure 13.7 An example of polyester/Mylar boardsail cloth

MONOFILM

For a complete discussion on sailcloth, turn to Chapters 3 and 4. However, one material is unique to boardsails—at least at this time—and this is Monofilm, made of 4- or 5-mil Mylar. As there is no fabric substrate, the material is transparent. Monofilm was first used for windows of speed sails, but it is now being used for entire sails, in particular for speed and slalom sails. The material has a distinctive, almost glowing, high-tech look, is lighter and smoother than traditional sailcloth, and is less stretchy than other fabrics. Although monofilm shows some initial resistance to tearing, once started, sail failure is typically complete and final. That said, some advocates swear by the use of clear packing tape to repair torn sails. Nevertheless, the lack of durability could prove the fatal flaw of this material.

WINDOWS

As a boardsailor's vision is almost always blocked by the sail, windows are important for safety as well as to allow the sailor to judge the wind and waves. Boardsailing without windows would be like skiing through a mogul field while blindfolded. Windows in boardsails are most commonly made of PVC. This material, more formally known as polyvinyl chloride, permits good visibility and maintains this desirable quality for an extended, but not indefinite, period. It is also highly resistant to scratching and punctures. However, the high stretch of PVC means that it causes the sail to deform in gusty winds. This makes the draft move aft, which, as noted, is undesirable. The material is also extremely heavy—it weighs more than the combined weight of all the other panels in a sail—and tends to fog over time, particularly if the sail is stored when wet.

SAILCLOTH APPLICATIONS

As a general guideline for the application of sailcloth to boardsails, warp-oriented laminates are utilized in longitudinally (unidirectionally) loaded panels like the leech and foot. Balanced laminates work well in the body of the sail where loads are more multidirectional. Stretchy materials, like Dacron, are utilized in the luff where the shock-loading effects of pumping are primarily felt and where the downhaul exerts a powerful force. To be more specific:

Wave Sails
Body: polyester/Mylar—the Mylar is typically on one side
Luff: 5-ounce Dacron to absorb shock loading, mast pumping, wave impact, etc.
Sleeve: 7-ounce Dacron

Slalom Sails
Body: polyester/Mylar. The Mylar can be a scrim. Monofilm also used
Luff: Dacron or polyester/Mylar—single-sided
Sleeve: Dacron

Speed Sails
Body: Dacron or Kevlar/Mylar in the form of a scrim. Monofilm or Spectra/Mylar also used
Luff: polyester/Mylar—single-sided
Sleeve: Dacron or polyester/Mylar—single-sided

Race Sails
Body: Dacron or polyester/Mylar—single-sided
Luff: Dacron or polyester/Mylar—single-sided
Sleeve: Dacron

PANEL ORIENTATION

The optimum panel orientation of a boardsail is an extremely controversial subject. There are many factors that must be considered before choosing a panel orientation, for example, type of sailcloth, intended use of the sail, and intended wind range, as well as fashion. Some sailmakers prefer the radial layout (see Figure 13.8), while others opt for vertical panels. However one lays out the cloth, the key to design is a panel layout that allows the sailmaker to pinpoint the draft, stabilize it, and minimize stress loading. Additionally, the sail must be flawlessly executed, fast, easy to handle, and durable enough to last several seasons. Also, the sailmaker must design a product that utilizes a roll of cloth efficiently and is easy to produce in numbers. Last but by no means least, the boardsailing market is extremely fashion-oriented, so the sailmaker must make a sail that looks different and is, at the same time, aesthetically pleasing. For such a small sail, this is a tall order, and designers specializing in such sails must be extremely creative.

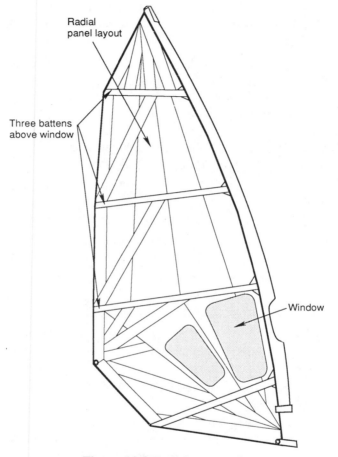

Radial
panel layout

Three battens
above window

Window

Figure 13.8 Radial wave sail

SAIL WEIGHT

The smart sailmaker uses the minimum weight of cloth to accomplish the job in each panel. Anything else is wasteful in terms of resources and is unacceptably heavy for the sailor who has to hold up the rig. Composite manufacturing is utilized to optimize cloth efficiency and minimize weight. Therefore, the sail is designed so that high-stress locations are reinforced as necessary but are built light in the skin areas, like the body of the sail. Lightweight Mylar laminates typically cover these skin areas. The use of high-tech materials with high strength-to-weight ratios also helps to keep sails light yet low-stretch.

While low weight is an absolute requirement, where the weight falls in the sail—high or low—is of considerable importance, too. How the rig feels in the hand is sometimes described as handiness, which is a function of rig weight, draft location, draft stability, and the location of the center of effort. The center of effort (the sum of all lifting forces exerted on the sail surface) must be designed to fall low in a boardsail. If the center of effort is high, the sailor will feel power aloft and won't have sufficient leverage to control the sail, particularly in gusty conditions. With a low center of effort—say, at shoulder level—the power band of the sail is directly in front of the sailor and thus more manageable.

Battens are a major part of the overall weight of a sail, and therefore, not only is the total number of battens important, but how many of them are above the window and their length can have a profound influence on the swing weight, or handiness, of the sail. For this reason, wave sails, which show a high aspect ratio to begin with and for which handiness is so important, normally have only three battens above the window (see Figure 13.8). Alternatively, slalom (see Figure 13.4) and speed sails (see Figure 13.5), which show a lower aspect ratio and require draft stability and leading-edge integrity above all else, normally have four or five battens above the window—often camber-induced—and up to two foot battens.

TWIST

Leech twist is a hot topic in boardsailing circles, and the subject of considerable debate. As it does on big boats, twist serves three purposes: 1) it matches the change in apparent-wind angle and wind speed from the bottom of the mast to the top; 2) it is a good way to match sail shape to wind angle (specifically, a twisty leech is fast when reaching, while less twist is fast when beating); 3) since twist reduces a sail's angle of attack and therefore lift, it can be used to extend the range of an overpowered sail, which is especially helpful when the wind is gusty. A boardsailor needs this flexibility because changing, shortening, or reshaping sails when underway is not practical. And, of course, the job of holding up the sail belongs to the standing sailor, not to the standing rigging.

On a big boat, the combination of traveler, mainsheet, and Cunningham allows sail-trimmers to directly control mainsail twist. With a boardsail, the sailor must rely primarily on the stiffness of the mast, the cut of the sail, and rig tuning (outhaul, downhaul, twist-control strap—if so outfitted—and batten tension) for control of twist, or leech tension.

For example, given two identical sails with equal downhaul tension, the sail rigged on a stiffer spar will exhibit less twist in any given wind velocity. Leech twist is further influenced by the amount of offset, or roach (see Figure 13.9), where the roach falls, and the spacing between batten stations. The batten offset is increased for additional twist at that section of the leech. For a symmetrical twist down the leech, the leech profile is designed as an arc. For twist focused at the head, the head offset is maximized while the lower leech is straight between battens.

Where the roach falls, high or low, is important. A cursory look at the different sail designs on the market illustrates this point. Some sails show maximum roach toward the bottom of the sail (see the pinhead sail in Figure 13.10); others show maximum roach toward the top (the fathead sail). The more roach up high, the twistier the sail will be. A pinhead-type design will be much less twisty given equal amounts of luff curve and mast stiffness.

The total number of battens and the space between battens also characterize the twist profile of the leech. Obviously, the more battens there are—or the less space between the battens—the less the sail is able to twist. Also, some sailmakers cut away a part of the leech to facilitate twist (see Figure 13.11). This type of sail is less popular these days.

Luff curve is also important to twist. The more curve, the more the mast is expected to bend. As in archery, the more bend to the bow, the more tension on the bowstring. In this case, the bow is the mast and the leech and foot

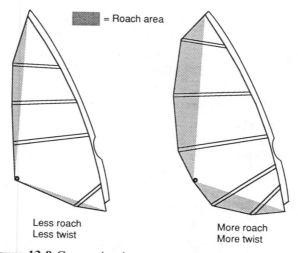

= Roach area

Less roach
Less twist

More roach
More twist

Figure 13.9 Connection between amount of roach and twist

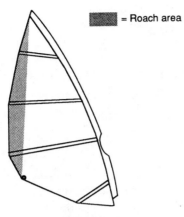

= Roach area

Pinhead—Roach area is
low in sail. Less twist.

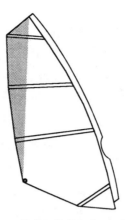

Fathead—Roach area is
high in sail. More twist.

Figure 13.10 Where
roach falls—low or
high—determines
twist, also.

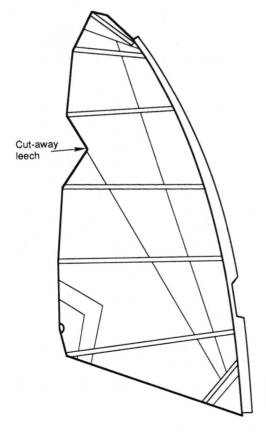

Cut-away
leech

Figure 13.11 Cutting away a section
of the leech is another way to increase
sail twist.

panels are the string. Luff curve, then, determines the tension on the leech. Therefore, given two identical leech profiles, the sail with more luff curve will exhibit less twist at any given wind velocity. Finally, there are the tuning devices: downhaul, outhaul, batten tension, and twist-control strap. The use of these sailor-manipulated mechanisms, which affect draft, location, leech profile, and twist, is addressed on pages 330–337.

MASTS AND BOOMS

As is evident from the preceding section, the mast has a profound effect on sail performance. Fortunately, the boardsailing market is of sufficient size (an estimated 10 million boardsailors worldwide) to demand the attention of many high-technology manufacturers. Their diverse products are good. The materials most often used in mast construction are epoxy (resin/glass), aluminum, and carbon fiber.

The main advantage of epoxy masts is their durability under all wind and sea conditions. The epoxy spar is extremely versatile and relatively inexpensive to produce. For a time, it appeared that epoxy masts would obsolete those made of aluminum, but this has not turned out to be the case. Aluminum mast-makers have been as aggressive about technical advances as have the composite people. Aluminum is a superb material in this application because of its inherent tensile strength to weight. Rolled aluminum can be custom-produced to taper according to the sailmaker's requirements. The current trend in performance-mast design is a stiff lower to middle-upper section with a softer tip (Mast C in Figure 13.12). This taper allows for good draft control low in the sail, with the softer tip providing more twist. Most racing masts are constructed of aluminum. Disadvantages are that without proper anodizing, aluminum can corrode and fatigue. Also, once kinked or dented, the aluminum spar is fragile.

Today new weaves, such as carbon fiber, are available. This material makes for a light, stiff mast that allows for increased sailing performance. Strength to weight is the primary advantage of such masts. Disadvantages of carbon fiber masts are additional expense and lack of durability, particularly in the waves. Nevertheless, carbon fiber masts and, in fact, carbon fiber booms may well represent the future of boardsailing.

In terms of sail control, second in importance to the mast is the boom. When a boom bends in gusts, it is the same as easing the outhaul. This is unacceptable since a boardsailor is interested in the direct transmission of the power in the sail through the body to the board.

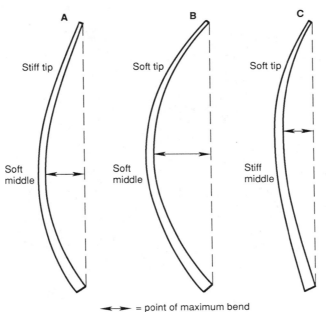

Figure 13.12 Comparison of mast-bend characteristics

Early booms were very narrow because sails, prior to the RAF and camber-induced, were flatter. It was also thought that a narrow bend would allow for greater control. Then the rage swung to extrawide booms that allowed the sailor to hike while keeping the sail upright. During this trend, boom front ends, which determine the overall bend profile of booms, increased to 100 degrees or more. Today, boom widths are available in two configurations: wave and slalom bend (see Figure 13.13). The wave bend is narrower, about 65 to 75 degrees wide at the front, providing greater control as the sailor is able to position his or her body over the board while maneuvering on the waves. The maximum bend is forward to correspond to the draft-forward shape of these sails.

The slalom bend is wider, 80 to 90 degrees, allowing the sailor to hike while keeping the sail over the board and upright. Slalom sails are cut fuller, so the added width is required to accommodate the increased draft of the sail. To match the draft-aft shape of the slalom design, the slalom boom reaches a maximum bend farther aft, at approximately 40 to 45 percent. In either case, boom stiffness is very important. If the boom flexes, the sail gets deeper, which, as noted, is unacceptable.

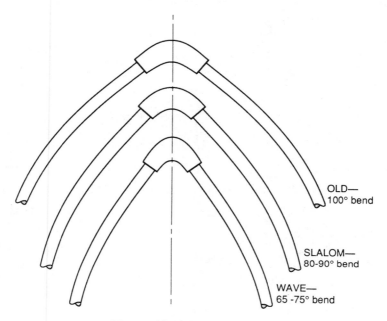

OLD—
100° bend

SLALOM—
80-90° bend

WAVE—
65 -75° bend

Figure 13.13 Boom angles

SHAPING THE SAILBOARD SAIL

Much of the appeal of boardsailing comes from its ease of rigging. Yet as simple and as quick as it is to rig a windsurfer sail, most sails spend their entire active life incorrectly tuned. Tuning boardsails involves adjustments of the following: downhaul, outhaul, twist-control strap (if so equipped), and batten tension.

The first three all involve bending the mast. What follows are two examples that show the effects of mast bending on a sail. For the sake of simplicity, we'll assume that the sample sail has no shape built into the seams. In rigging the first example, the mast is bent to a curve less than the built-in luff curve of the sail. The result is a fold of extra cloth running down the luff. This extra cloth makes for a full sail. This is analogous to straightening the mast on a conventional sailboat to give the sail more shape for light winds or for sailing off the wind.

In example two, the same sail is rigged, but this time we have tuned the sail so that the mast is bent exactly to the luff curve of the sail. The result is a flat sail. The salient point is that the more the mast is bent, the flatter the sail.

Downhaul and Outhaul   The downhaul and outhaul are used to bend the mast. To invoke the analogy of a bow and arrow again, tensioning either of these devices can be considered stringing the bow. As the string is tensioned, the two ends of the bow move toward each other, causing the bow to assume its characteristic, tensioned curve.

However, which string is pulled determines twist. Since downhauling bends the mast, effectively bringing the two ends closer together, it follows that more downhaul tension will cause the leech and foot to become looser. This affects sail twist. To summarize this: Increasing downhaul tension reduces leech tension, which increases the amount of twist in the leech.

The reverse is true when it comes to outhauling: The more the sail is outhauled, the less tension along the luff and the more tension along the leech, causing less leech twist.

Based on the above, we can make the following observations.

1. Downhauling bends the mast (and flattens the sail) by vertically tensioning the luff.
2. Increasing the downhaul reduces the tension along the leech, increasing twist.
3. Outhauling bends the mast (and flattens the sail) by tensioning the leech and the foot.
4. Increasing the outhaul tensions the leech, reducing twist.

Before we proceed, one point needs clarification. In Chapter 10, "Mainsails," it was explained that increasing the downhaul moves the draft forward. This is only partially true on an unstayed sailboard rig. As a sailboard sail is downhauled, the draft does indeed move forward, but once the downhaul begins to flatten the luff, the draft will start to move farther back in the sail. This is because there is no extra cloth left to form the draft in the front of the sail.

If we combine our understanding of outhaul and downhaul with a simple understanding of preferred aerodynamic shapes for sailing, we are able to rig our sail properly for any given wind strength. As far as shapes go, we need only know that in high winds a flatter sail is desirable, while in lighter winds a fuller sail is desirable. (The aerodynamic basis for this can be found in Chapter 6.)

Fine-tuning   Let's assume that we are rigging for high wind. To flatten the sail, we need to bend the mast. We know this can be achieved by pulling on the outhaul and the downhaul. Begin by tensioning the outhaul. How much do we pull on it and, more complicated, how much do we pull on the downhaul?

A sail with insufficient downhaul tension shows horizontal wrinkles along the luff.
(Eric Aeder photo)

These are fundamental and, as is probably apparent by now, related questions.

The amount of downhaul is the hardest to gauge. To understand where the correct downhaul setting should be, we'll describe what sails with incorrect downhaul settings look like. A sail with insufficient downhaul will show horizontal wrinkles up the luff (see above photograph). On the other hand, a sail with too much downhaul tension could have one, two, or all three of the following symptoms: loose upper leech, loose foot, and/or too much flatness along the luff.

Initial adjustments are done with the sail on the ground, but the sail should be held up and flown in the wind to determine the correct downhaul tension. This is because pressurizing the cloth with the wind is an important component of sail tuning. Then, readjust the downhaul until the sail shows no signs of incorrect downhaul tension. If after adjusting the downhaul perfectly, the sail is too flat or too full, the downhaul will have to be adjusted again.

As noted, the outhaul and downhaul have an interactive relationship. If the sail appears to have insufficient downhaul, it could actually mean that it has too much outhaul; if the sail appears to be downhauled too much, it may need more outhaul. The best way to fine-tune the sail is to use the downhaul indicators while watching for the preferred depth, or draft, at the boom area. The preferred depth will vary from one manufacturer to the next, between different types of sails, and for the different requirements of sailing in light winds versus strong winds.

For light-wind sail adjustment, go through exactly the same steps as outlined above, except set the sail fuller.

Twist-Control Strap Now let's turn to the third adjustment device: the twist-control strap, which is found on many, but not all, boardsails. It consists of a strap attached to the foot of the sail at the tack (see Figure 13.14). The twist-control strap, like the outhaul and downhaul, bends the mast and changes the shape in the sail. When tensioned, the strap pulls the foot in toward the mast while increasing the tension on the leech, reducing twist. The effect on the leech is similar to that produced by a boom vang on a traditional sail (see Chapter 10). The clew is lowered, the leech is tensioned, the mast bends more, and the upper section of the sail is flattened. To increase leech twist, the twist-control strap is loosened. When used in conjunction with the downhaul and outhaul, the twist-control strap enhances a boardsail's ability to be tuned.

How Characteristics of the Mast Affect Tuning Masts with different bend characteristics will require different tensions on the outhaul, downhaul, and twist-control strap. When we rig two identical sails, but rig one on a stiff mast (Mast C in Figure 13.12) and the other on a soft (less stiff) mast (Mast B), we apply more tension to the stiffer one because it is harder to bend. As noted, this increase in rig tension—specifically the increase in outhaul tension—will result in more tension on the leech and the foot. More tension on the leech means less twist at the leech. It follows then that a softer mast allows more leech twist. As described, the stiffer mast could be downhauled

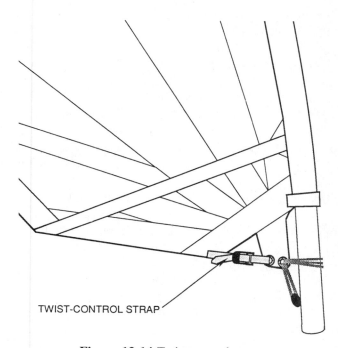

TWIST-CONTROL STRAP

Figure 13.14 Twist-control strap

more to further leech the twist, but this excess luff tension would cause the sail to be too flat along the luff.

Batten Tension   Correct batten tension also affects sail shape. Ideally, the curve of the batten should be exactly the same as the built-in profile of the sail. The profile of the batten is crafted during construction as the manufacturer tapers the batten at its luff end according to the specifications of the sail designer. The batten must be tensioned in the sail in order for it to assume its designed shape. If undertensioned, the batten does not prove to be very effective (see opposite page, above). The battens should be tensioned so that all wrinkles running through the batten pockets are eliminated (see opposite page, below). If the batten assumes an S profile on the leading edge, and wrinkles still run through the batten pockets, then the batten is too flexible and has been poorly matched to that particular sail. The batten should be replaced. The sail in the photograph on page 336 is perfectly tuned.

What follows are some additional rigging tips and reminders.

Vertical wrinkles, or scallops, along luff indicate insufficient batten tension.
(Eric Aeder photo)

Correct batten tension. *(Eric Aeder photo)*

This sail is correctly tuned. Notice that although a boardsail is adjusted while lying on the ground, it is tested before sailing by holding it up into the wind and then trimming it. This allows the wind to pressurize the sail.
(Eric Aeder photo)

Rigging

1. To avoid overstretching the luff and possibly damaging the sail, always outhaul before downhauling.

2. Don't let your sail flutter in the wind without the boom fully secured in front and back. Fluttering, as will be discussed in the following chapter, breaks down sailcloth.

3. The boom should be affixed to the mast between chest and eye level.
4. Battens should be tensioned so that all wrinkles at the batten pockets are eliminated.
5. Always adjust the height of the mast base so that the tack of the sail is no more than 4 to 6 inches above the deck of the board. This effectively closes the gap between the foot of the sail and the board, which is so important, particularly in slalom and speed sails.
6. Always hold up the sail and trim it before entering the water to be certain that the sail is correctly rigged for the particular wind strength.

Derigging
1. To avoid overstretching the luff and possibly damaging the sail, always release the downhaul before releasing the outhaul.
2. Release batten tension.
3. Roll rather than fold polyester/Mylar sails. Any crease put in polyester/Mylar will be permanent.
4. Store sail in the bag in a cool, dry place.

TROUBLESHOOTING

Symptom	Solution
Horizontal wrinkles are along luff.	Apply more downhaul and/or reduce outhaul.
Luff is too flat and sail does not rotate well.	Reduce downhaul and/or outhaul.
Leech and foot are too loose.	Reduce downhaul and/or increase outhaul.
Sail has a twitchy/jerky feeling.	Increase downhaul to provide more twist.
Sail does not point to weather.	Reduce downhaul to decrease twist. Increase tension on twist-control strap.
Sail is unmanageable/overpowered.	Flatten sail by increasing outhaul and downhaul. Change to smaller sail.

★

C H A P T E R   1 4

CARE AND REPAIR OF SAILS

★ The question most often asked of a sailmaker is, How long will my new sail last? If it is a cruising sail, the answer will address the sail's ultimate life, but for racing sails, a more important measure is its performance life—that is, how long will it be fast? Ultimate life and performance life depend greatly on the sail's nature and nurture. Nature can be thought of as lineage or pedigree. From the choice of cloth, to design, to panel layout, to construction details, nature is the small and large things the sailmaker does to a sail before it leaves the loft. Nature has been the focus of this book. Nurture, on the other hand, can be thought of as a sail's care and handling after it leaves the loft. This is primarily the sailor's job and is the focus of this last chapter.

With the advent of high-tech materials used in both racing and cruising sails, it's more important than ever to handle sails with extra care. The carefree days of stuffing a Dacron racing genoa into a bag barely large enough to hold it or of haphazardly flaking or roller-stuffing a mainsail on the boom and forgetting about it until tomorrow, next month, or next season are long gone.

This out-of-sight, out-of-mind attitude does not work anymore, if, in fact, it ever did. With a modicum of care, modern sails, in particular those made of polyester/Mylar, will last as long as Dacron sails. Kevlar/Mylar racing sails and heavily resinated Dacron sails used in some One Design classes demand greater care so as to maximize their effective life, but greater care should not be confused with intensive care.

Longevity is not all of it, however. Another reason for taking care of sails is that they simply look better. Most would agree that it is most incongruous to see a well-maintained sailboat sporting misshapen, threadbare, wrinkled, or stained sails.

WHAT RUINS SAILS

Deterioration of sails is generally caused by one or more of the following: flogging, chafe, improper handling, moisture, sunlight. Although it is difficult to avoid a "thou shalt not" tone in the following discussion, most sailors believe in the maxim that thou shalt not spend unnecessary money.

Flogging It is unfortunate that Kevlar/Mylar, which for its weight possesses such otherworldly resistance to stretch, is so easily damaged. For years, it was assumed that Kevlar/Mylar was more sensitive to the sun's damaging rays than Dacron and polyester/Mylar. The truth is that Kevlar/Mylar is particularly sensitive to flogging, which can be defined as the uncontrolled flagging of a sail in the wind.

In the 1986–87 America's Cup held in the rollicking winds of Western Australia, it became abundantly clear how sensitive Kevlar/Mylar is to flogging. With all the luffing, tacking, stalling, and starting that are the theme of match racing, the useful life of a Kevlar/Mylar sail was shortened enormously. A Number 4 or 5 jib on a 12-Meter could have an effective match-racing life as short as five races. Although this seems incredible—particularly in view of the $15,000 price tag of such 12-Meter sails—with four weather legs and the aggressive prestart maneuvering, boats might tack as many as 100 times, even more. For example, when our *Stars & Stripes* sailed against *Kiwi Magic* in the third race of the challengers' finals, we tacked about 140 times. This is the equivalent of a full season of fleet racing at the Performance Handicap Racing Fleet (PHRF) and International Offshore Rule (IOR) level.

Flogging is anathema to any sails but in particular to those made of Kevlar/Mylar. With proper care, however, the life of a Kevlar/Mylar sail can be increased by as much as a full season. To prevent flogging, avoid motoring to the start of a race with the Kevlar/Mylar main up. In light winds, in particular, the battens tend to wave back and forth, hinging at the front of the batten pockets and damaging the Kevlar/Mylar material. Similarly, when raising the sail, don't motor into the wind at full throttle. Also, in heavy air, reduce sail to avoid prolonged flogging of the main. Always keep the leechline tight enough so the leech isn't fluttering. Further, take the Kevlar/Mylar mainsail off the boom after each race or at least cover it with a sail cover. Remember to remove the battens and roll the sail (rather than fold it) before carefully putting it away in its bag. Likewise, Spectra/Mylar sails should be rolled rather than folded or merely stuffed into a bag since creasing shrinks the sail (see Chapter 4, "The Making and Application of Modern Sailcloth").

The flogging of a genoa is less avoidable, and thus it is important to use a Kevlar/Mylar genoa only when racing. Don't motor to the start of a race with a Kevlar/Mylar headsail—indeed any headsail—up. When reaching, try to keep the lead position of the genoa in the right location. A proper lead will prevent the upper portion of the genoa's leech from flogging. Also, when tacking, make sure the jib is cast off early enough and the tailor doesn't overtrim the sail on the other side. At the finish of a race, take the headsail down and motor in.

Although tests show polyester/Mylar sails to be as sensitive as Kevlar/Mylar to flogging, experience shows polyester/Mylar genoas to have a longer ultimate life. A two-year-old, heavily used polyester/Mylar sail may have lost some shape, but it is less likely to break or tear than is a similarly aged Kevlar/Mylar sail.

Dacron is less sensitive to flogging—but less sensitive is not the same as invulnerable. The finishing process when manufacturing Dacron stabilizes the weave and gives it a certain firmness, which prevents the sail from stretching in all directions. When this finish is gone, the sail becomes more elastic. The flogging of a Dacron mainsail destroys the temper in the cloth, thus weakening the fabric, but more important is that it destroys the shape-holding ability of the sail. Consequently, all the above cautions are also appropriate to Dacron sails.

Chafe   Flogging is not the sole "gift" of tacking to a headsail. Tacking also causes chafe and abrasion. The chafe that occurs when a sail rolls around the shrouds, spreaders, and mast, getting poked here and there by the stanchions and babystay, takes a considerable toll on a genoa. A good sailmaker knows where the sail is likely to be damaged and reinforces these critical areas with patches. Therefore, spreader and stanchion patches on all headsails, be they Kevlar/Mylar, or polyester/Mylar, or Dacron, should be a requirement.

That, of course, is the sailmaker's job. The crew's job is to make sure that all pins and protruding items on the boat are well covered or taped to prevent the sail from tearing or distorting. Take the time to go over the boat with a roll of duct tape and cover every exposed cotter or ring pin. Make sure that the turnbuckles, not just their pins, are covered completely. Be certain that the ends of the spreaders do not protrude much beyond the shrouds, and that all the cotter pins connecting the spreaders to the mast are covered with silicon or are taped.

Additionally, chafe protection should be applied to the seams of all sails. The stitching and seams are among a sail's more vulnerable areas as they are raised on the surface and thus more susceptible to abrasion. For this reason, avoid dragging an unbagged sail over nonskid decks or along a dock or parking lot.

One of the best ways to prevent seam chafe is to apply a coating of Tuff-Seam—a protective coating—or a similar product, to vulnerable areas. The leech of the mainsail also benefits from such treatment as it is often chafed by the topping lift or running backstays. Seams that rest against the shrouds when the mainsail is eased out on a run should be similarly protected, as should any part of the mainsail that comes in contact with the spreaders. Batten pockets that rest against the shrouds when the sail is eased out on a run are other prime areas for treatment. A caution about applying this coating: The chemical smell can be overpowering. If you must do this work yourself, take appropriate precautions as spelled out by the manufacturer.

Full-batten mainsails are easily chafed when they come in contact with a shroud or lazy jacks. One precaution that is particularly helpful on such sails is for the sailmaker to sew nylon webbing on the outside of the batten pockets. It has a shiny finish and wears well.

Improper Handling Genoas should leave a sail loft with a maximum wind-speed number stamped on the clew (see Figure 3.8, page 42). This warning has nothing to do with the sail's effective range; rather, it anticipates the sail's yield point. This number is determined by calculating the maximum upwind loads with the sail trimmed hard. Then a safety factor of 30 percent is subtracted for safe working load. Using a sail above its recommended wind range is a ready-made formula for an unplanned visit to your sailmaker. Such improper handling will stretch the cloth to a point where it will not recover its original shape. In fact, the sail can break. If your racing headsail does not have this number stamped on the clew, return it to your sailmaker and insist that its maximum wind range be determined. The sail should be marked accordingly.

If the sailmaker has done his or her job properly, marginal materials were not used when constructing a sail for a given wind range. A substantial "fudge factor" is important. Once this number is known, racing sailors should change sails or reef when appropriate; successful racing often depends on this. Those who opt for Spectra/Mylar sails should pay particular attention to this rule considering the material will creep—stretch permanently—when loaded to 30 percent of breaking strength. Cruising sails should be reefed when appropriate so they will not be permanently stretched.

As noted, Kevlar/Mylar sails and Spectra/Mylar sails should be rolled rather than folded. In truth, this is the best treatment for all triangular sails. Rolling is common operating procedure with One Design sails where a Yarn-

Tempered or heavily resinated Dacron fabric is commonly used. If rolling is impractical on an offshore boat, it is best to fold the sails and store them in long sausage bags. It is also advisable to crease the sails in different places each time. Repeated creasing of a sail in the same places, particularly with Kevlar/Mylar, will likely cause it to fail in these spots. It is akin to bending a wire over and over in the same place; within a short time, the strength is gone, and the wire breaks easily.

The luff of Kevlar/Mylar and polyester/Mylar sails should not be over-stretched. Therefore, tension the halyard and Cunningham only enough to remove horizontal wrinkles from the luff. It is also helpful to put a mark on the genoa halyard so the sail isn't overtensioned when coming around the leeward mark.

Polyester/Mylar is particularly sensitive to heat. Don't let such sails bake in the summer sun in a car or in the car trunk. Further, don't let such sails come in contact with any part of the boat's engine or exhaust or even rest against a cabin light for too long.

Moisture   Drying sails and then stowing them in a dry place will protect them from mildew. The sailcloth material itself isn't particularly susceptible to mildew, but dirt and grease stains seem to attract it. That old standby Tilex—used in kitchens and bathrooms—works well on mildew spots. For those who sail on salt water, it is advisable to rinse salt from the sails with fresh water and let them dry before putting them away. Salt not only damages the cloth, but also promotes the deterioration and corrosion of any fittings sewn to sails. Similarly, any foreign objects, such as screws and the like, that sometimes stick to wet sails and find their way into sail bags should be removed. As the metal rusts, it can rust through several layers of cloth.

It is best to dry sails on a clean and well-kept lawn and never when the wind is anything but gentle. Drying sails by hoisting them should be done cautiously, if done at all. Flogging is often the result even in the calmest winds, and flogging is, as is now clear, a sail's public enemy number one.

Nylon sails are most sensitive to moisture. In tests, wet nylon sails actually change dimensions. Depending on the weight of the cloth, a nylon sail can expand by as much as 2 percent. What is most surprising is that this material loses about 15 percent of its strength when damp and becomes three times stretchier. This explains why a wet spinnaker or blooper is more likely to blow out. Interestingly enough, nylon regains its strength when dry. So when discussing the care and handling of nylon sails, the best rule is, if possible, keep them away from water. Wash the salt off and dry them thoroughly before putting them away. Another reason for drying such sails is that if they are not completely dry, dark colors will sometimes bleed into lighter ones.

As the lightest-weight sails in a boat's inventory, nylon sails require special care when set or doused. An untaped cotter pin or a nasty meat hook on a halyard can completely destroy a spinnaker or cruising chute in seconds. It is a good idea to survey your boat often for such hazards and either tape them or correct them.

Sunlight   Sunlight was thought to be the worst problem for Kevlar/Mylar sails. (The reader may recall Ted Hood's attempt to treat a Kevlar/Mylar sail with carbon black to protect it from the sun.) Recent tests, however, have shown that after three months in the Florida sun, the four common cloths used in mains and jibs—Kevlar/Mylar, polyester/Mylar, Spectra/Mylar, and Dacron—show the same reduction in strength: about 40 percent. While tests indicate that polyester/Mylar sails are as sensitive as Kevlar/Mylar sails to sunlight, experience shows that polyester/Mylar sails have a longer ultimate life.

Nylon, used in spinnakers and bloopers, is particularly sensitive to sunlight. In the aforementioned test of the sun's effect on sailcloth, nylon lost 40 percent of its strength in a *one*-month period when exposed to direct sunlight. Offshore passages or races of long duration where a single spinnaker is up for days on end can do enormous damage to such sails. Little can be done to protect nylon from the deleterious effects of prolonged UV exposure. (Protecting the roller-reefing main and jib, which have the greatest exposure to sunlight, is discussed in the next section.)

CARE OF ROLLER-REEFING SAILS

Prior to the advent of the roller-reefing headsail, the mainsail was considered the "sail for all seasons," that is, it was up almost all the time. Now that headsails can be reefed effectively, cruising sailors are demanding an equally broad range from headsails. An all-purpose roller-reefing headsail should be designed to accommodate the lightest and heaviest winds, not an easy compromise to be sure. Also, the reefing process, which puts inordinate strains on the sail, requires that the sailmaker do several things to extend its life. For example, extra reinforcement must be used on the foot and leech as these areas are subjected to the greatest strains when the sail is roller-reefed. AeroLuff or some sort of carefully shaped foam (see photograph on page 179) should be used on the luff of such sails to flatten them properly when reefed.

The shape of the reefed sail is governed by such leading-edge treatments. AeroLuff, for example, uses a sleeve that is sewn to the front of a genoa, which, in turn, zips around the headstay. Inside the sleeve is a bolt rope that fits in the headstay groove. The top and bottom of this rope have been removed so the bolt rope comprises about half the length of the headstay. When you haul on the reef line, the front of the genoa starts to roll at the location of the bolt rope—in the middle only. This removes depth from the center of the sail first; the top and bottom lag behind. Without AeroLuff or another carefully shaped foam treatment at the luff, the reefed headsail ends up being full-bellied—the opposite of what is desired when the wind blows.

One disadvantage of foam, however, is that when the sail rolls up completely, you are left with a large-diameter furl around the foam on the headstay. In extreme cases, this can cause some windage problems when sailing, as well as at the dock or at anchor. In the worst cases, it also can do damage to the forestay and furler itself.

Obviously, the reefable headsail is an extraordinary labor-saving device. It has reduced the work of a half-dozen crew to half that many, even fewer. Less work, however, does not mean no work. For example, it is important that sailors move the genoa-lead blocks to accommodate the different reef positions (see Chapter 9, "Headsails"). If this is not done, the top of the sail can twist away from the boat and flog until the leech of the sail is destroyed. This is even more important when you realize that all of this flogging typically happens out of sight of the helmsman.

Also, although the headsail size can be reduced in very small increments, it is best if the reefable headsail is treated as, for example, a Number 1, Number 2, and Number 3, and marked accordingly at the foot. This allows the corresponding lead positions to be clearly marked on deck. When a reef is necessary, you furl the headsail to the mark at the foot and move the turning block to its respective mark. Then you don't have to worry about the proper lead position when the going gets rough.

When finished sailing, it is also a good idea with these sails to release halyard tension. Under constant halyard tension, the luff of the sail can actually stretch 5 or 6 inches, ruining the sail.

As roller-furling sails are almost always up, they are particularly vulnerable to ultraviolet degradation. Thus, various materials are used to protect the leech and foot of a roller-reefing genoa—the areas that remain exposed when the sail is rolled up. The most common is Acrylan, which is used on the foot and leech panels. This material shows the best resistance to ultraviolet rays, but is heavy and does not add strength to the sail. Because of Acrylan's weight and deleterious effect on shape, special UV-protected Dacron is becoming more popular. Some high-tech cruising sails are made by marrying Dacron (polyester) to Tedlar, a film produced by Du Pont. This material is lighter than Acrylan and shows excellent UV resistance. However, it is not as strong as polyester/Mylar, and to control shape, it requires similar weights to Dacron.

There is, however, a liability to the UV-treated Dacron. The treatment wears off in time. Acrylan panels likewise wear out, but it is obvious when Acrylan panels wear out and are about to fail. With UV-treated Dacron, the loss of the coating and then the failure of the sail are much harder to detect —indeed, failure typically comes as a complete surprise. And it is the rare cruising sailor who enjoys complete surprises that involve gear failure.

DETERMINING THE CONDITION OF SAILS

For most of us, the sailing life is not an endless summer, so the winter hiatus is a fact of life. This can be an ideal time to get your sailmaker's undivided attention, as it is traditionally a slow time of year. It is the best time to bring your inventory in for a status report, to have repairs and alterations done and the sails cleaned, and to replace any sails. A sailmaker who does not take advantage of the winter break to perform these services for his or her customers is probably undeserving of your business.

What follows is a list of items for you or your sailmaker to check to determine the condition of sails. It is also a good checklist for those buying a used boat. With a sail inventory representing up to 20 percent of the price of a boat, the condition of the sails can make or break a deal. Ignoring sails before buying a used boat would be analogous to buying a used car without checking under the hood.

Mainsails

1. Check luff and foot slides and their attachments for wear and tear. Similarly, check the luff and foot rope for chafe. Headboard rivets or fastenings can prove to be vulnerable, and their condition should be noted and repairs made if necessary. Headboard slides (these are generally under the greatest load) quite often break. Also note that certain slides on the luff and foot of the sail take more load than others. This varies from boat to boat; however, most commonly, the first slide in from each corner and the slides near reef points are the most heavily loaded. Make sure that the slides aren't broken or elongated. If one breaks, it increases the load on the next one, and so on.

2. Look for seam chafe, seam elongation, and worn threads. Stitch holes that have stretched mean the seam is weakened. Visible daylight through seams is a telltale sign of impending trouble. Look for daylight above clew patches, and for chafe in the way of reef lines. Check sail attachment rings for deterioration (oxidation and cracks). Check the plastic cleats on leechlines for wear. On larger mainsails, go over the straps attached to the corners to determine whether the stitching is still in good shape.

3. Go over the general condition of the cloth. A good sailmaker can determine the condition of cloth by evaluating its "hand," or feel. Cloth most commonly breaks down in front of batten pockets where the sail goes through hinging action. These days, most mains are heavily reinforced in this area, not only to prevent breakdown but also to spread the loads of the batten tips more uniformly. With the growing popularity of longer—or full-length—battens, this type of wear has been reduced. However, it is still common with boats that use shorter IOR-style battens.

4. When running, as has been noted, the well-eased mainsail can chafe against the shrouds. This is particularly hard on seams. If wear is apparent, the seams should not only be restiched but be protected. Tuff-Seam is good at preventing or minimizing this type of chafe. Incidentally, the particular vulnerability of seams speaks against sewing them with white thread. With white thread, it's particularly difficult to see areas of chafe and broken threads. If you have a sail sewn with white or light-colored thread, mention to your sailmaker that a thorough inspection should be done.

5. If your racing or cruising boat has running backstays or a topping lift that rubs against the leech of the mainsail, check the area for wear. If wear is apparent, it is often a good idea to put added chafe protection, such as leather around the edges, in the critical areas. In fact, mains for fractional-rigged boats are particularly vulnerable to such chafe and typically benefit the most from preventative measures.

Genoas

1. Ascertain the condition of the hanks or the luff tapes on all genoas. If the hanks are sewn on, inspect the whipping. If the hanks are pressed on, make sure the hank itself hasn't twisted and is still securely attached. As with the main, go over the seams thoroughly, especially where they are likely to chafe: at areas in contact with the shrouds, spreaders, and stanchions. Likewise, check the sail attachment points—the rings and webbings—for deterioration, and the plastic leech- and foot-cord cleats for damage. It is also a good idea to check spreader and reinforcement patches, particularly at the borders. Sails tend to hinge here and, more often than not, will end up breaking in such spots. A solution to this problem is to have your sailmaker stagger the reinforcement on either side of the sail.

2. If your roller-reefing genoa is a few seasons old, it might be a good

idea to have the Acrylan or sun-shield material replaced. Depending on the amount of ultraviolet exposure and heat, this material has a limited life. Also, rings at the tack and head of roller-furling genoas take a lot of abuse and should be thoroughly inspected, particularly if they are pressed directly into the sail.

Downwind Sails

1. Because the nylon used in spinnakers, cruising chutes, and bloopers is so much lighter than Dacron and even Kevlar/Mylar, you or your sailmaker should pay special attention to such sails. For example, light-air spinnakers and cruising spinnakers often have pressed aluminum rings in the corners. These sail attachment points should be checked for deterioration and cleaned if necessary. Elongated stitch holes along seams are a telltale sign of a nylon sail whose strength has been reduced. Often you can see daylight through these seams when the sail is flying. Reinforcement of the areas adjacent to the corner patches is also a good idea.

2. The next time you have a repair done where your sailmaker cuts out a portion of the spinnaker, have him or her test the nylon cloth for tear resistance in both directions. How the cloth fares in this test provides a good indication of the sail's overall strength and condition.

LAUNDERING SAILS

For aesthetic reasons alone, dirty, grease-stained sails are unacceptable to most of us. For those who aren't up to large, messy, difficult jobs, take your sails to a sailmaker who has access to a commercial sail-washing facility. Such facilities typically employ special chemicals and have the knowledge to use them correctly. For example, for removing adhesive, like duct tape, from a sail, professional sail cleaners might use methyl ethyl ketone (MEK), a dry-cleaning chemical, either diluted or not, depending on the condition of the sails. This chemical also takes dirt and soot off a sail rather well. It works on polyester/Mylar sails, too. MEK is, however, extremely toxic and working with it is not for the do-it-yourselfer.

If you choose to launder sails yourself, the most important advice is to use a mild soap, like dish-washing soap. Never use abrasive cleaners. Spot removers, like K2r, work effectively on spots on Dacron sails without doing any damage.

WINTER STORAGE

Before storing sails away for a significant length of time, they should be washed and dried thoroughly. Racing genoas built from high-tech materials such as polyester/Mylar and Kevlar/Mylar should never be stored in overheated areas and should never be left folded with hard creases. They should be rolled.

As mentioned earlier, nylon loses a great deal of its strength when wet and thus should never be stored wet—no sail should—or in a damp environment. Unheated basements or attics are unsuitable places for storing sails. Also, before such sails are packed away for the winter, be sure that no foreign materials, such as metal objects, are stowed inside the sail, because, as noted, oxidation from aluminum or rust from stainless steel can wear a hole through several layers of nylon fabric. For the same reason, staysails with wire pennants should be folded so that the wire is exposed and kept outside the bag.

In some ways, storing sails properly is like aging good wine. If you don't have the time, the place, the inclination, and the patience to do the job correctly, don't waste your time or money. The results are likely to be disappointing. Many sailmakers offer this service.

SAIL-REPAIR KIT

Little in this world lasts forever—despite the best nature and nurture—and sails sometimes break or fail at sea. Therefore, for those who venture any distance from shore, a sail-repair kit is necessary for emergency repairs. These are just three sample lists of some of the items that you might want to include in this kit.

Tools	Hardware	Materials
Scissors	Stainless steel O-rings	Sq. yd. of each sail-cloth
Palm	Seizing wire	Nylon webbing
Needles of different sizes	Spare hanks	Duct tape
Awl, pick, or spike	Spare slides	2″ Dacron tape (3 oz.)
pins (tacks)	Grommets	2 yds. Dacron insignia cloth
Pliers	Pins	¼″ or ½″ double-sided seam tape
Hot knife		
Hammer		

Tools
Seam ripper
Razor knife
Grommet set
Pen or marker
Punch
Screwdriver
Cable cutter (optional)

Materials
Light thread
Heavy thread
Waxed twine
Beeswax

One tool that should be highlighted is the battery-operated hot knife. A DC-operated hot knife is an invaluable tool on a sailboat not only for sail repairs but for cutting and finishing lines and for soldering items. Because thread and most sail fabrics melt—just as Dacron or nylon lines do—a hot knife is an ideal way to seal an edge or a piece of thread. Kevlar/Mylar cloth, however, won't melt with a hot knife.

BASIC SAIL REPAIR HINTS

Before providing a step-by-step description of the most common sail repairs, these tips might prove helpful.

- Do your best to dry thoroughly the area to be repaired.
- Lay the sail flat—use pins to help do this—before putting on adhesive cloth or cutting the sail for repair.
- When putting nylon straps on corner rings, always pretension the straps so they will pick up and distribute the load; otherwise the ring and sailcloth will likely separate.
- Always be sure to use the proper-size needle when sewing the cloth as big holes in light cloth weaken the area.
- Buy a good heavy-duty palm, which is used for passing a needle through cloth. Imagine the force needed to push a needle through bulletproof Kevlar cloth, and you will realize that cheap palms can, in fact, be dangerous.
- Remove any broken or loose thread from a seam or tear before applying adhesive tape or cloth.
- For small tears in light cloth, adhesive tape—rather than sewing—is often all that is necessary. Use good judgment; don't overdo repairs, for in some cases overdoing a repair is as bad as not doing enough.

- Do not rely on duct tape for long-term repairs. Use it only for small temporary fixes. Not the least of reasons is that the adhesive in this tape attracts dirt and is very hard to remove without using extremely caustic chemicals (see section on laundering sails).

- Keep your sail-repair kit handy. Don't bury it under a bunk or provisions.

SAIL REPAIR TECHNIQUES

Although many associate sail repair with trying to work on the motor of a car, there are many instances where a little common sense, a basic understanding of sail engineering, the previously mentioned tools and supplies, and—most of all—patience will enable you to repair your sail at home or at sea. While replacing a broken slide or patching a small tear is within the mechanical competence of most of us, some of the other repairs discussed, such as a blown-out clew ring, are more challenging. They are described here to help those who want to do the repairs or for those who have to. That said, by no means is this a complete course in sail repair; it only presents the basics. Those who desire more information should consult other sources.

DEMYSTIFYING SAIL REPAIR

Unless you have access to a heavy-duty sewing machine, most of your repairs will involve hand stitching. The usual home sewing machine is capable of sewing spinnakers and two or three layers of 6-ounce Dacron or polyester/Mylar, but will never be able to handle the buildup of material that occurs in the corners of a sail. To machine-sew a sail, you need a spool of V-69 Dacron thread and need to know how to adjust the thread tension on the sewing machine. If you use a home machine, you need to change to a bigger-diameter needle than you would normally use for home sewing. Because there are too many variables to discuss here, the best advice is trial and error on some scrap cloth (which you can usually get for free from your sailmaker).

By far, the most important skill you need to repair is not a skill but good common sense. When you fix a part of the sail, check another similar part to see how the sailmaker did it the first time and use this as a guide to repair the damage.

Small Holes and Tears   If a sail is well engineered and constructed—its nature, as mentioned in the beginning of this chapter—and you nurture the sail through its life, you should expect to avoid most catastrophic sail damage. However, small holes and tears do occur despite careful handling of sails. Defining a "small" hole or tear can be perplexing, but, in general, if the hole is less than 2 inches in diameter or if the tear is less than 8 inches long, it's small. With prompt attention, you can cover any small hole or tear so that the hole will not enlarge, and the sail will not tear further.

The best way to look for small holes in a sail is to position the boat so the sail is blocking the sun from your eyes and carefully look over the entire surface, paying particular attention to parts of the sail that come in contact with the boat or rig. Sunlight will pour through any holes; note the position of these holes so that you can repair them. It is usually a good idea to take down the sail sooner than later because a small hole or tear can quickly enlarge.

To repair a small hole or tear, you need scissors and insignia cloth. Make sure the area to repair is dry and free of salt. For holes, cut two circles from the insignia cloth with a diameter roughly four times that of the hole. For tears, cut strips of insignia cloth 8 inches longer than the tear and 4 to 5 inches wide. Lay the sail, with the hole or tear exposed, on a flat surface (table, floor, cockpit sole), and apply one of the insignia patches over the hole. Turn the sail over and apply the second patch on the opposite side. Use hand pressure to make sure the patches are on firmly.

Broken Hank   The bronze hanks a sailmaker installs on the luff of headsails normally need only to be rinsed with fresh water now and then and sprayed with a lubricant (WD-40 or equivalent) once or twice a season. When this is not done, the most common problem is the piston plunger corroding and rendering the hank unusable. Before replacing it, try the lubricant. If this doesn't free up the hank, you will have to replace it.

There are two types of hanks in use today. The most common is the pressed-on style, where the ear of the hank is fitted through a grommet and bent to close the opening. To remove this type, you need a large screwdriver to pry open the ear (if you have large cable cutters, you can cut the ear off). Avoid positioning the screwdriver so as to damage the sail or yourself. When the hank is removed, check to make sure the grommet is not pulling away from the sail. If it is, you need to reinforce the grommet with a webbing strap (see the section on partial corner ring failure, page 354). When the grommet is ready for the new hank, push the ear through the grommet, making sure you install the hank with the plunger on the same side of the sail as the rest of the hanks. With the sail on a firm surface, hammer the ear closed.

The other style of hank differs from the pressed-on style by virtue of its lack of an ear. Instead, it is laced (hand-sewn) onto the luff. To remove this hank, cut the hand stitching with scissors. Tie one end of a 3-foot length of heavy waxed twine onto either one of the lacing holes in the hanks with two half hitches, and proceed to reeve the twine back and forth between the two holes, tying off the twine after every fifth loop with two half hitches. Continue until the holes do not allow more twine to be threaded through and tie off the last pass with two more half hitches. Cut off any remaining twine.

Broken Mainsail Slide Like the genoa hanks, mainsail slides need minimal maintenance. A freshwater rinse now and then and periodic lubrication with a dry lube such as the spray-on Teflons should suffice. Avoid using grease or oil to lube slides. Grease easily gets all over the sail and can weaken the plastic compound in the slide. Ultraviolet damage is the biggest culprit in slide failure. To spot it before the slide breaks, look for discoloration in the slide or brittleness in the webbing that attaches the slide. If your inspection of luff and foot slides reveals a damaged slide, replacement is relatively easy.

There are two methods of attaching slides: shackling and webbing. To replace a shackled-on slide, remove the screw or bolt on the shackle and take off the slide. With the slide removed, make sure the grommet is not pulling away from the sail. If it is, you need to reinforce the grommet with a webbing strap (see the section on partial corner ring failure, page 354). When the grommet is ready for the new slide, put the shackle through the new slide and refasten it to the sail.

The webbed-on slide is obviously more difficult to change. You need scissors, palm, heavy needle, pliers, awl, waxed twine, 10 inches of nylon webbing (whose width is less than the opening of slide), and a hot knife.

Cut off the old slide and remove all traces of the old webbing. Insert 1½ inches of the new webbing through the new slide, and with one hand gently press this short section of webbing against longer piece. With your other hand, slide the tip of the hot knife between both pieces for one-half second. This melts a small part of the webbing onto itself. If you prefer, you can stitch the webbing together. The pliers, palm, beeswax, and awl are used to help the needle pass through the material.

With the webbing now attached to the new slide, you can begin to reeve the webbing through the grommet and the slide. Remember to keep the slide the same distance from the edge of the sail as the other slides. After you have four to five layers of webbing (two or three on each side), load a needle with 2 feet of waxed twine, put on your palm, and stitch it together. If you can, stitch between slide and sail. Finish the stitching off with two half hitches, and cut and seal both the twine and any excess webbing with the hot knife.

Seam Repair When the stitching in a seam breaks, it's important to repair the seam before it fails or the sail tears near the seam. You now know that stitching fails because of chafe or UV damage, so regularly inspect the parts of the sail that are subject to these hazards. If you discover broken stitching, you can sew the seam back together either with a sewing machine or by hand stitching.

You need scissors, a seam ripper, double-sided tape, pins, light needle, thread, and 2-inch insignia tape.

Mark the area to be stitched with a pen, marker, or piece of tape. Dry the area to be repaired and find a flat working surface. Remove all traces of broken stitching with seam ripper and gently peel apart the two pieces of the seam. Apply double-sided tape to one side of the seam, using the pins to tension the seam enough to remove any wrinkles. Remove the paper backing from the tape and lightly pat the seam with your hand as you peel away the backing. When the seam is restored, apply firm pressure over the section with your hand to secure the seam. Remove the pins and stitch the sail back together with a zigzag stitch with a sewing machine or by hand. Start and finish the stitching at least 2 inches beyond the broken area.

When the stitching is complete, apply the 2-inch insignia tape over this portion of the seam on both sides of the sail. The main purposes of the tape are to prevent chafe and help lock the stitching together.

Torn Sail Nothing is more disheartening to the sailor than watching a sail tear apart. Whether it is the head of a spinnaker pulling away from the rest of the sail or a genoa or mainsail tearing from luff to leech, it's one of those things that is so discouraging. Before further damage occurs, carefully retrieve the sail and its pieces.

Then you need the following from your sail-repair kit: scissors, 2-inch insignia tape, double-sided tape, thread, needle, pins, palm, hot knife, waxed twine, and enough of the same type cloth to repair the tear.

Before diving into the repair, let's discuss the goal. It should be to get the sail back together so that you can finish your cruise or race, not to restore the sail to perfect condition. Think of the tear as a series of straight lines. What is needed is to apply a cloth strip, using double-sided tape, to both sides of the sail and sew the sail back together. Tears that run in more than one direction should be treated as separate straight-line repairs. The most difficult repair is when a piece of the sail is missing. In that case you sew in a piece the approximate size of the missing portion, then proceed to repair the sail. Read the preceding section on repairing broken seams, as we will be using the same technique here.

First dry the sail and find a flat surface into which you can push pins. For spinnakers and other lightweight sails, you will be using 2-inch-wide insignia tape; for mainsails and genoas, you need to cut 2- to 3-inch-wide strips from similar cloth and use a hot knife to seal the edges. Apply double-sided tape to both edges of the patches. Pin the sail so that there are no wrinkles around the tear and both edges of the tear are butted against each other. This is the most important step; take your time and redo it if necessary.

With the sail pinned out, you can start applying the strips, peeling away the paper backing and using firm hand pressure to stick the cloth to the sail. You will most likely have to join two or more strips together to cover the length of the tear. At the joints of the cloth patches, allow at least ½ inch of overlap to sew them together. If after the sail is taped back together, you have enough insignia tape and cloth to put a patch on the opposite side, flip the sail over, pin out the tear, and apply the second set of strips. Remember to line up both sides of the strips so that each row of stitching sews both of them.

Now comes the time-consuming part: the stitching. Put in two rows of zigzag stitching (one row for spinnakers) on either side of the tear. Distance apart is not critical, nor is appearance. Remember to sew any joints in the strips used to patch the sail.

Corner-Ring Failure   Due to the extreme loads radiating into the corners of a sail, any fitting in a corner is subject to the highest load of the entire sail. This is especially true in the clew of all genoas, the clew and reef cringles on mainsails, and all corners of spinnakers. If a sail is constantly used above its wind speed range, it's likely that these corners will start to pull away from the rest of the sail (partial failure) or entirely pull out from the sail (complete failure). Pressed rings are the biggest offenders in this category, but this failure is easy to see. Look at the area of the ring opposite the direction of the pull of the jib sheet, halyard, or reef line. If you start to see the sail pulling away from the ring (partial failure), you can usually add a nylon strap or two to the ring and prevent further damage.

To fix partial ring failure, you need double-sided tape, 14 inches of 1-inch nylon webbing, palm, heavy needle, waxed twine, awl, and pliers. Start by applying the doubled-sided tape to the 1-inch webbing. Peel away the paper backing and stick 7 inches of the webbing on the sail opposite to the direction of maximum load. Bring the other half of the webbing through the ring and onto the opposite side of the sail in the same direction so that you will be able to sew both halves of the strap at the same time. Again, the pliers, palm, beeswax, and awl are used to help pass the needle through the sailcloth. As you stick the second side down, make sure the strap is under tension. Without tension, the strap will do little or nothing to help keep the ring in place. Finish the repair with two rows of straight stitching. Start with 3 to 4 feet of thread.

Begin the stitch at the end of the strap and work your way toward the ring, keeping stitch spacing to ½ inch or so. The closer the spacing, the better. To end the stitch, go back to the previous hole and tie off the thread.

To fix complete ring failure, you need pen or marker, scissors, two or three pieces of 14-inch-long 1-inch nylon webbing, palm, heavy needle, waxed twine, awl, pliers, double-sided tape, and stainless steel O-ring. Start by tracing on the sail the position of the new ring. With scissors, remove any part of the sail that will interfere with the ring. Next, apply the 1-inch webbing straps in the same fashion as when repairing partial ring failure, remembering to tension the straps. Because the ring is being replaced, more than one strap is needed to spread the load over the surface of the sail. Arrange the straps in such a way that they fan out from the ring opposite to the directions of the loads. In a genoa clew, this means one strap up the leech, one strap toward the middle of the luff, and one strap toward the direction of the tack. For the head of a genoa, use two straps—one aimed toward the leech and one aimed toward the luff. Use the same stitching technique as above. If pushing the needle through the sail becomes too difficult, use an awl to punch holes for the needle.

Although all of these repairs, if done correctly, will make your sail usable again, you should bring the sail to your sailmaker when time permits so that he or she can inspect it and, if necessary, bring the repair up to professional standards. This obviously applies more to a sail that has been torn or a sail with a seam that has been restitched than to a slide or hank that has been replaced.

★

BIBLIOGRAPHY

BOOKS

Conner, Dennis, with Stannard, Bruce. *Comeback*. New York: St. Martin's Press, 1987.

Dellenbaugh, David, ed., *The North U. Fast Course*, 2d ed. Milford, Connecticut: North Sails, 1988.

Donaldson, Sven. *A Sailor's Guide to Sails*. New York: Dodd, Mead & Co., 1984.

Hopkins, Robert, and Marshall, John., eds. *The North U. Fast Course*, 1st ed. Milford, Connecticut: North Sails, 1980.

Howard-Williams, Jeremy. *Sails*, 5th ed. Clinton Corners, New York: John de Graff, 1983.

Jobson, Gary, and Toppa, Mike. *Speed Sailing*. New York: Hearst Marine Books, 1985.

Kenny, Dick. *Looking at Sails*, 2d ed. Camden, Maine: International Marine Publishing Co., 1988.

Kinney, Francis S. *Skene's Elements of Yacht Design*, 8th ed. New York: Dodd, Mead & Co., 1981.

Langewiesche, Wolfgang. *Stick and Rudder*. New York: McGraw-Hill, 1944.

Marchaj, C. A. *Aero-Hydrodynamics of Sailing*. New York: Dodd, Mead, 1980.

Marchaj, C. A. *Sailing Theory and Practice*. New York: Dodd, Mead, 1964.

Ross, Wallace, with Chapman, Carl. *Sail Power*, 2d ed. New York: Alfred A. Knopf, 1984.

Sail magazine. *The Best of Sail Trim*. Charlestown, Massachusetts: Sail Publications, 1975.

357

ARTICLES

Barthold, Charles. "Special Report: Cruising Sails." *Yachting* (September 1987), p. 80.

Gentry, Arvel. *Sail* magazine series (monthly from April to December 1973) and published scholarly papers.

Sylvester, Steve. "Bay Area Sailmaker's Search for the Perfect Foil." *California Boardsailor* (Summer, 1987), p. 12

Wheeler, Peter. "State of the Art: Spinnaker Design." *Yacht Racing/Cruising* (renamed *Sailing World*; September 1982), pp. 67–70.

INDEX

★

Italic page numbers refer to photographs or figures.